Praise for *When Nothing Else Matters*

"The nexus at which the decline in Jordan's physical prowess and public image converge is deftly and devastatingly captured in Michael Leahy's *When Nothing Else Matters*. The staff writer for *The Washington Post* goes beyond the easy recounting of the familiar into a depth that is thought-provoking and engaging."

—Steven J. Lyons, *Chicago Sun-Times*

"Incisive . . . Michael Leahy reveals a great deal about Michael Jordan's inglorious stint with the Washington Wizards, but he reveals even more about the back-scratching culture of sports journalism, which allows flawed figures like Jordan to balloon into false idols."

—Scott Tobias, *The Onion A.V. Club*

"*When Nothing Else Matters* is a close-up portrait of an aging star's vanity, a cold-blooded case study in organizational politics . . . a scathing media criticism."

—Tom Scocca, *New York Observer*

"At its best, *When Nothing Else Matters* is the fourth act of a Shakespeare play. . . . Jordan is Macbeth in high tops. . . . *When Nothing Else Matters* tells the gripping tale of an aging superstar moving reluctantly from the one place where he was in complete control to a world where the rules weren't as clear cut."

—Allen St. John, *The Washington Post*

"[An] exceptional book. It says much about the cozy relationship enjoyed by elite athletes and the journalists who routinely cover them that it took a nonsports writer to produce the most telling insight into this twentieth-century icon."

—Dave Hannigan, *The Sunday Times* (London)

"Leahy is that most unwelcome of characters around a pro sports team: a truth-teller. Where others were intimidated by Michael Jordan, or just plain blinded by his star power, Leahy stood his ground and assembled a tough-minded, fair and gripping account that reveals something far more interesting than Michael Jordan the icon—he gives us Jordan, the man."

—Michael Sokolove, author of *The Ticket Out*

"Michael Leahy may be the first author to overcome his awe of Michael Jordan and let us see another Jordan, the legend in the autumn of his career. In this book we don't just meet a myth streaking across the sky—we meet a very human being finally returning to earth. *When Nothing Else Matters* transcends its subject, for as we watch Jordan descend, we also somehow see ourselves."

—Glenn Stout, series editor of *The Best American Sports Writing*

WHEN NOTHING ELSE MATTERS

Michael Jordan's Last Comeback

Michael Leahy

Simon & Schuster Paperbacks
NEW YORK LONDON TORONTO SYDNEY

SIMON & SCHUSTER PAPERBACKS
Rockefeller Center
1230 Avenue of the Americas
New York, NY 10020

First Simon & Schuster paperback edition 2005

For information about special discounts for bulk purchases,
please contact Simon & Schuster Special Sales:
1-800-456-6798 or business@simonandschuster.com.

Designed by Paul Dippolito

Manufactured in the United States of America

10   9   8   7   6   5   4

The Library of Congress has cataloged the hardcover edition as follows:

Leahy, Michael, date.
   When nothing else matters : Michael Jordan's last comeback / Michael
Leahy.
      p.   cm.
   1. Jordan, Michael, date. 2. Basketball players—United States—Bio-
graphy. I. Title.
GV884.J67L43 2004
796.323'092—dc22
[B]   2004059041

ISBN-13: 978-0-7432-5426-7
ISBN-10:   0-7432-5426-0
ISBN-13: 978-0-7432-5427-4 (Pbk)
ISBN-10:   0-7432-5427-9 (Pbk)

For Jane and Cameron

"The very fact . . . of not being conscious of being in despair, is itself a form of despair."

—SØREN KIERKEGAARD,
THE SICKNESS UNTO DEATH, 1849

"Playin' it, bein' it, makin' the shots, . . . it's huge, it's a whole difference . . . Nothin' compares to that . . ."

—MICHAEL JORDAN, BASKETBALL EXECUTIVE
AND OWNER, 2000

Contents

WHEN NOTHING
ELSE MATTERS

Introduction

IT BEGAN DERAILING AFTER SEASON ONE. HIS WORLD WAS FUBAR by then. A promising young teammate, Richard Hamilton, had dared to stand up to him in a mutual searing of egos, and found himself traded. The mounting dissension on the team called to mind a word that Michael Jordan and some of his old Chicago Bulls associates exchanged during the Bulls' glory days to describe something or someone gone bad indefinitely. It was a code word, an acronym. FUBAR: Fucked Up Beyond All Recognition. By his last season, the Washington Wizards were hopelessly FUBAR.

Michael Jordan's three years in Washington—about a year and nine months as an official executive and two seasons as a player—were troubled from the start. Before his comeback began, *The Washington Post* dispatched me to watch him for an entire season, and much of a second. I valued the experience, even the awfulness, which I hesitate admitting because I realize it sounds peculiar and a little perverse. But if you wanted to know what forces—money and a sense of entitlement, most of all—coarsened professional sports in the last gasps of the 20th century and the beginning of the new millennium, it behooved you to have been witness to the Wizards and the Michael Show.

Not everybody around me thought so. The Wizards coach, Doug Collins, called me a "stalker." Someone at my own paper, a sportswriter friend of Jordan, let it be known that he wouldn't talk to me, wouldn't read me. The coolest, savviest person was always Michael Jordan. Looking for a solution to the problem my presence caused, unable to banish me like an irksome teammate, he quietly turned toward his people for a solution, leading one of his publicists to advise me that I would perhaps enjoy more cooperation from Jordan if I could assure her that I would not be writing a book. Besides orchestrating deals and advancing fables, the protectors of a sports god have only a few essential duties: to shelter Him from taxable income and any unseemly truths, not always in that order—and to keep people like me away. Seduction is part of the game, and writers are often easy prey, anxious to have the cachet that accompanies being regarded as a Jordan favorite.

"He's Jordan's guy," someone would say of a journalist who made it known he was a Jordan friend. You never heard such an admission, or description, outside of sports journalism. No one ever refers to a top political columnist in this country as, say, "Bush's guy" or "Clinton's guy" or "Kerry's guy," because for a political columnist to be regarded as anybody's guy would be the ultimate insult. By contrast, the sports industry is filled with athletes' buddies and mouthpieces.

Michael Jordan offered them the celebrity's form of friendship: small morsels of self-serving information in exchange for the tacit understanding that they'd never write or say anything critical about him. So you didn't read much, say, about how he called a teammate a "faggot."

Understand this: Truth, or complete truth, is a deferred commodity in sports when it comes to idols. It isn't only some of the media that stay quiet. No one is more responsible for hiding truths than a team's management and ownership. The big truths are placed in a lockbox as long as the god makes the franchise a lot of money. And Michael Jordan made a lot of money for a lot of people.

But ownership at least saw a tangible benefit. For the media, the rewards were scant. Jordan sometimes would tell his media favorites about a teammate or club official he'd lost confidence in, or a trade he wanted to see happen. In special cases, he'd invite them to parties. He wouldn't give them much, but they'd be grateful just the same.

The consequence? The consequence is that sometimes sportswriting is a fairy tale, and that you're reading this because you hope it's not.

Now that it is over, I can tell you this: You can have all the money and power in this world, and while it might protect you against all sorts of intrusions, it doesn't insulate you from somebody like me. I am not gleeful about that. It just is. I am the paid voyeur with a press pass following you from city to city, and staring at you in locker rooms and other public settings, and glimpsing too many of your quasi-private moments in hallways, and asking you questions in Wilmington, Washington, Detroit, Cleveland, Chicago, Indianapolis, New Jersey, Houston, Milwaukee, Miami, Phoenix, Minneapolis, Salt Lake City, Boston, Atlanta, San Antonio, Philadelphia, L.A., New York, Dallas, Everywhere, and who has nothing to lose if my omnipresence has come to make you uncomfortable.

Nothing to lose is the key. A subject can't possess a hold over you, can't be allowed to block you from writing what you know by hinting that he'll never talk to you again if you cross him. There can't be anything the celebrated athlete can take away from you—notably special access to him. I had nothing special, and so nothing to lose. It freed me. How did it work each night? people ask me, and I never know how to answer that, because I never really abided by any of the norms—the protocol, the emphasis on limiting the number of questions that weren't about the game that evening, the silly deference to officials dissembling, the interest in numbing questions about that "turning point" in the second half, the discretion not to ask anything the subject didn't want posed, the nodding of a head to some babble being spouted by a self-serving coach, the complicity of some of the media in what was seldom more than a public relations exercise by that coach, that star, the Washington Wizards executives and NBA officials.

It was that babble that so offended, and that babble that triggered the urge to know what was really happening.

1

The Purge, May 2003

FROM HIS START IN WIZARDS MANAGEMENT, MICHAEL JORDAN courted danger. He liked to signal that he did not have many equals and certainly not any superiors. He referred to the team's principal owner, Abe Pollin, who had bought the team before Jordan entered kindergarten and hired Jordan as club president, as nothing more than a "partner." He spoke about him in a kind of modified conditional tense, couching explanations of his possible future moves by saying once that he would be consulting "my guys . . ." and "Abe, if he's still a part of the situation." His lieutenants dropped hints that Pollin blocked trades and acquisitions; that Michael couldn't wait for the tightfisted elderly owner to sell the team, so he could be replaced by a younger, bigger-spending visionary—someone who would be a suitable match for Michael's style and ambition. They sent signals that Michael wanted to dump or demote the owner's right-hand woman, Susan O'Malley, who was as close as a daughter to Pollin.

During Jordan's comeback, the Wizards' top brass silently endured his presumption. The new revenue sparked by Jordan's return, and the franchise's hunt for national respect, accounted entirely for ownership's meekness. Pollin, a septuagenarian builder and philanthropist who wanted his life story known and who had never found anyone to publish a book about him, had won basketball's version of the Lotto. Everyone suddenly wanted time with him. His arena became a salon for rappers and Cabinet members, foreign titans and Hollywood's royalty. His luxury boxes swelled with new tenants. Jordan's presence on the court turned the Wizards into the league's biggest home draw and made Abe Pollin's floundering franchise profitable, by better than $10 million during each of his two playing seasons in Washington. But the bountiful times obscured the mounting private irritation of Pollin and O'Malley, who liked the burgeoning revenue but chafed under Jordan's slights.

No one thought about it much at the time, but Pollin and O'Malley always held the only power that mattered. They treated Jordan deferentially until his last game had come and gone and the money stopped. Then they moved on him. A mere three weeks after he had taken off his uniform for the last time, Jordan exited the MCI Center alone in a Mercedes convertible with Illinois plates, banished, an out-of-work man trying to navigate his way through traffic, on his way to throwing down a few drinks that evening and flying into jock exile.

Like Babe Ruth, he saw the truth too late. The truth was this: A sporting god enjoys supreme power only as long as he plays, earns and fills seats. The moment he ceases to be a team's principal revenue stream is the moment his dominion ends. One day Jordan enjoyed nearly all of the sway in his relationship with Wizards officials; the next day, none.

He knew basketball, but not much of real life, and seemingly nothing of the lessons from his own history: it was the second time in four years that he had been blindsided and outmaneuvered. His 1999 end in Chicago—where he had been spurned for a top front-office job and a slice of ownership after his playing days ended—should have taught him something about the cost of poor relationships. But, in their delusion, Jordan and his people thought Chicago was an aberration; that his longtime foil, Bulls vice president and general manager Jerry Krause, had sabotaged him with the blessing of an ungrateful owner, Jerry Reinsdorf, and that history would record the moment as Reinsdorf's and Krause's biggest folly.

When financially struggling Charlotte and lowly Washington offered him the reins of basketball and slices of ownership during 2000, Jordan felt vindicated. He asserted his supremacy immediately in negotiations with Pollin, guaranteeing that there would be strains in their business marriage. Their relationship already had been forced to overcome the memory of a heated exchange, a year earlier, at a meeting between NBA owners and players hopeful of resolving a player lockout and negotiating a new labor contract. Jordan, who would not be retiring from the Bulls for a few weeks, had come to New York to show his solidarity with players. When Pollin complained about rising player payrolls and his losses, Jordan snapped at him: "Then sell your team."

Pollin responded icily: "Neither you, Michael, or anybody else, is going to tell me when to sell my team."

Their marriage was fraught with risks, complicated by Pollin's desperate need to rekindle fans' interest in his terrible team, and Jordan's belief that he deserved privileges unprecedented among executives of NBA teams. Jordan demanded the freedom to work merely part-time in Washington, leaving plenty of days for his business endorsements, television commercials, golf and gambling outings. He made clear he would not be obligated to scout, working mostly out of his house in Chicago. He would attend only a handful of Wizards games, and accept only minimal marketing and promotional responsibilities. He did not sound like a man interviewing for a job, because he wasn't: He had a superstar's presumption, a conviction that the owner would, must, give in to him because the owner needed his magic.

But no longer did he have the same magic, because he was no longer a playing superstar, a reality he never fully embraced. It had hurt him in his final dealings with the Bulls, whose ownership never had confidence in his potential as an executive. Bulls officials privately questioned his work ethic off the court, viewing him as a guy who could not sit still in an office, in constant need of games and adrenaline fixes. They had treasured his sway on the court, as this translated to a box-office bonanza, but after his retirement announcement in Chicago, the Bulls no longer saw the margin in genuflecting.

The Wizards immediately sold a few hundred season tickets upon his hiring as president, but, as an executive, Jordan's allure proved short-lived, proof of what Chicago executives understood: People do not crowd into arenas to stare at executives in luxury boxes. Moreover, Jordan did his best Howard Hughes imitation, out of sight generally, watching most games, even when in Washington, alone, on a flat-screen TV in his office. His tenure as Washington's club president was undistinguished: a losing club, thousands of empty seats on most nights. He worked part-time—flying in to meet with his staff, watching a few games, good-naturedly dismissing suggestions that he scout some college kids in person, flying home. He groused in 2000 about how an executive's job couldn't compare to playing, and when, in returning to the court, he gave up the presidency and his slice of ownership—as mandated under NBA rules—he released the Wizards from any further obligations on his voided executive contract. Unshackled,

Pollin could now do with him what he wished when Jordan's playing days ended.

The sagging performance of the Wizards during his comeback—thrilling nights bracketed by many more sour ones; a falling out in his relationships with teammates; and successive seasons at 37–45 under the volatile Doug Collins, the Jordan-tapped coach with a proven record of alienating players in two other cities and now self-immolating amid a Washington team weary of his eruptions—had augured a long, cold winter ahead in the 2003–2004 season. Remarkably, even in the face of two disappointing seasons, Jordan acted like he enjoyed leverage in his upcoming negotiations to regain the club presidency. He said he had "options" if the Wizards did not give him the authority he wanted.

It was a star player's way of negotiating, the bluster of a sports god. Only he was a lesser god now, and not even a player. In his final Washington days, with the assistance of his personal staff, he took out a full-page newspaper advertisement, in which he thanked scores of little-known basketball industry figures for their contributions to his career, and conspicuously failed to mention Pollin. It was petty payback, and a kind of assisted suicide.

And now Jordan learned what Ruth did: There was a price to be paid for so flagrantly offending ownership. Ruth never could get a managerial job, doomed by his rakish appetites and long indifference toward ownership's feelings. Jordan never grasped the concept of consequences. It was not that Pollin lacked empathy for former players. The Wizards were famous for keeping underachievers on the payroll—staffers at all levels of the organization whose work reeked of complacency but who could always rely on Pollin to remain their steadfast patron. One Pollinphile, Hall of Famer Wes Unseld—whose management of the Wizards played a part in rendering the franchise one of the league's worst, but who referred to the owner at all times as "Mr. Pollin" and exuded respect—had held onto his Wizards executive job for seven years, proof that the owner would overlook even catastrophe in the case of a loyal subservient.

However, if a Wizards player crossed management, something cold awaited, past the 79-year-old owner's grandfatherly smiles and parting gifts. In Pollin, Jordan finally met a man whose zest for merciless payback matched his own. Pollin did not request, and would not wait, for NBA officials to intervene and orchestrate a face-saving Jordan exit. There would be no face-saving allowed. Damning stories about Michael Jordan's work habits and relationships leaked out, and it was no secret that Pollin's people did most of the leaking. Tired of the god's disrespect, and aware that a retiring Jordan could make him no more millions, Pollin didn't wait a month before kicking Jordan out on the street. "I don't want you as a partner, Michael," he told him during their brief meeting.

By then, fewer people in Jordan's retinue had a stake any longer in staying quiet about him either. They privately mocked his heavy-handed style, his choice of Doug Collins as a coach, and his savaging of young teammates. You might call that betrayal, but I think it is human nature: When finally safe to do so, after years of self-serving servility, sycophants and even honorable men turn on the star—the boss and alpha male—for the sake of their manhood. They feel the need to tattle, if discreetly so; it is their only way of evening the score, of undoing their emasculation. They do it even if they entertain the idea of perhaps working with him someday again. They are a conflicted bunch. But they knew too much about Jordan. They knew of his abusiveness around teammates, his isolation and self-absorption. Out of some weird amalgam of fealty and fear, they had stifled it too long, until it must have felt like their deference bordered on cowardliness.

That lockbox, closed for two years, had been pried open, and truth flew out. A Wizards official talked of how Jordan had tried to hold up Pollin at the 11th hour of their negotiations in 2000 for the club presidency, insisting that he be required to work out of Washington even fewer days and attend fewer games. Another Wizards official noted, sardonically, how Jordan had gone drinking at a nightclub on his last night as a Washington resident, reduced to being just another disconsolate man who'd lost his job that day.

But if Jordan was getting trashed, so was Pollin—or Pollin the Midget, as a pair of his fiercest antagonists from the Jordan camp dubbed him—the owner accused of having decided upon Jordan's dismissal long before the end of the 2003 season, waiting just so long for Jordan to fill Pollin's seats for a season and help in the promotion of future ticket packages. The theory went that Pollin had used him; that he had flattered, marketed, bled and finally eviscerated his meal ticket. Pollin angrily denied it, suggesting that Jordan's fate had turned on fairly recent events—particularly stories of how the heavy-handedness of Collins and Jordan fomented anger and alienation among the Wizards.

Short of reading the owner's mind, it seemed impossible to know what had pushed his buttons, the why and when of things. I had a nagging sense that he had conveyed to me long before, perhaps around the start of Jordan's comeback, an uncertainty about Jordan's future with the organization. My old notes reflected this sense, but I had no useful Pollin quotes on the subject. Perhaps I'd read too much into my impression, I told myself. Maybe I extrapolated some meaning, which can happen to writers, long down the road. We dream, too—vulnerable to our delusions. I forgot about the matter and moved on.

A long time later, I stumbled on two old microcassettes in a musty corner of a drawer. They bore the scratchy voice of an elderly man. I listened to one tape, dated October 9, 2001, and heard a mumbling Abe Pollin—Abe Pollin offhandedly suggesting the uncertainty of Michael Jordan's future at the end of a conversation alone with me, during preseason training camp in the first of Jordan's seasons with the Wizards.

Having flown down to Jordan's hometown of Wilmington, North Carolina, for the team's intrasquad game at its training-camp site, an exultant Pollin already had spoken to a scrum of reporters at halftime, pointing out that Michael had four steals in the first half and scored whenever he wanted. He gloated a little, indicating that the woes of the Washington Redskins would allow the Wizards to fill the vacuum and excite sports fans. He radiated gratitude—"We are so fortunate to have the greatest player in the history of the game playing for us"—and noted that while vacationing that past summer on the Black Sea, and touring Bulgaria and Russia, he had found himself besieged by an attention he'd never known, in the form of foreigners everywhere asking him if Jordan was coming back as a player. "I mean, the whole world is waiting for him, and he's not going to disappoint them—he's fantastic," Pollin exclaimed, adding that he had a gut feeling the Wizards would be making the playoffs, beaming as members of the press corps shed their neutrality to congratulate him and Carolinian strangers shouted "Mr. Pollin, Mr. Pollin." You would have thought he might be George Steinbrenner, or Mark Cuban. Maybe he could even shop his biography now.

He'd discovered what Bulls ownership had: Celebrity attached itself to anyone close to Michael Jordan. He talked more about the flocking Russians and Bulgarians. A public relations person signaled an end to the questioning, the press scrum broke up, a smiling Pollin moved on. My recorder still running, I followed, in the way of writers pressing for more, and asked him about Jordan's health, preoccupied by what I'd learned about his hurting knees.

Pollin smiled and nodded, as if braced for the question. We were alone, alongside a wall. He was lean, in that whittled down way of elderly people, but much taller than most people imagined, a healthy 5' 10", and you realized that people regarded him as a midget only because he generally found himself photographed alongside 6' 6" and seven-foot basketball players. He was a wealthy man cursed by contrasts. He did not have as much money as most of the NBA owners, particularly the league's younger and more flamboyant titans, like the Maloof brothers in Sacramento and Dallas's Mark Cuban, and resisted shelling out what the mega-rich did on their player payrolls. He had a jiggly turkey neck, which stuck out in the company of lithe, firm athletes and younger owners, and sometimes left the mistaken impression of a man lacking vigor. Actually, he had a penchant for playing aggressively, in business and elsewhere. His involvement in political causes, particularly on behalf of Democrats and Israel, was passionately hands-on, and he helped to lead a high-profile charity in the Washington community that paid for the college tuition of many impoverished kids, with Pollin personally having picked up the tab for a long line of young graduates. He was tough, fiscally responsible when it came to his businesses, socially conscious and philanthropic, the model of what society purports to want in its titans.

But sports fans can be a cruel, monomaniacal breed. Only games and standings matter to the most rabid, which, depending upon how you want to look at it, evinces either an endearing, childlike intensity or a severe case of arrested development. In the end, their judgments are as bottom-line as a magnate's, and by the fall of 2001, many thought Pollin's effectiveness had long since passed. His team had not won a championship since 1978 and hadn't advanced deep into the NBA playoffs since Jimmy Carter was president.

The Wizards had become something very close to a joke long before Jordan's arrival, a trusty foil for every respectable team, the NBA's version of the Washington Generals to everyone else's Globetrotters. Unscientific polls of Washington sports fans generally placed Pollin near the bottom in popularity among the owners of local teams. He was viewed as cheap—loath to invest the kind of big money viewed as a prerequisite for landing the league's best players, and absolutely miserly many years earlier in having failed to provide first-class practice facilities for his players or care for their rudimentary professional needs. His acts of stinginess, as revealed in a later *Washington Post* story, had included making players pay for the laundering of their game and practice uniforms.

By the late '90s, a sizable portion of fans viewed Pollin as an effete anachronism—a sap who mistook well-behaved players for desirable players, and generally preferred morally upright losers to pricey and athletically gifted bad boys. He had traded away talented miscreants. He made no apology for this. If his players ran egregiously afoul of the law, or seemed to flout the community's norms, Pollin would not hesitate to get rid of them, swiftly, without mercy.

Such acts won him kudos from observers shocked to discover an American team owner who prized an ethic greater than winning. But the jibes over time from local sports media, and outraged calls from basketball fans to Washington radio sports shows, underscored that, in the Washington sports community, as in most of the country, ethics counted for less than victories. The derision cast an unflattering light on something puny and unacknowledged in the sports culture, on just how much American fans invest themselves in games, living vicariously through the fortunes of people they don't know and never will. *Win. I need you to win, so I can feel like a winner, too.* Increasingly, Pollin became scorned as a rich, do-gooding ninny whose piety and frugality stood in the way of Washingtonians' basketball resurgence.

But then, in early 2000, just as both the organization's and Pollin's reputations had hit bottom, Wizards minority owner Ted Leonsis and Pollin landed Jordan to serve as club president. Leonsis had offered an ownership share, and Pollin offered power. Jordan's landing became Pollin's resurrection.

About 10 months afterward—or during the season before the start of Jordan's playing comeback—I met with Pollin to discuss his good fortune. The good already had been muddied. Tensions had arisen between the owner and the Jordan group, and Pollin wanted to take the opportunity to assure me—despite whatever I might have heard from Jordan aides or Jordan himself about Pollin's reluctance to spend money or engage in trades—that he had not vetoed any of Jordan's proposed acquisitions or trades, not one. "I don't care what they say," he snapped. He looked alternately tense and agitated, stealing glances at an aide a couple of times as if to signal that the questioning should not go on much longer.

But the Pollin at the Wilmington intrasquad game was a different man, relaxed, assured, talking giddily about his new bounty. He knew that all his empty seats would be filled and that he likely would lead the league in sellouts. No one realistically expected a championship even with Jordan, but it would be nice, thought the owner, for the team to ascend into the league's top echelon by having a long playoff run. That would be possible only if Jordan stayed healthy, and Pollin understood that the season might hinge on how the star's old and aching knees held up. He admitted amiably to me that he too had worried about the toll a season might take on the body of a man approaching 39, and that Jordan assured him he wouldn't have come back if he didn't feel absolutely healthy.

That's all I needed for the time being. I thanked him and, looking for a way to end the conversation on a pleasant note, observed that it must be nice for him to know that, at the end of Jordan's playing days, the star would be rejoining Wizards officials in his executive capacity. There was a pause. Pollin said nothing. I kept babbling, momentarily ignorant as to the meaning of what was happening. Pollin stared at my tape recorder, as my handwritten notes reflect. My tape ran. I casually asked whether they had discussed Jordan's role in the organization once his playing days ended, a question offered up as a softball, an invitation for Pollin to deliver the always winning bromide about how he couldn't wait for the day when the great star rejoined the brass.

"We said we would talk about it," Pollin answered curtly.

Huh?

"So we both have an open mind," he added sharply.

I remember thinking how peculiar the moment felt—Pollin's sudden brusqueness, his grim expression, the way he licked his lips with palpable anxiety, the absence of any expression of delight over the prospect of Jordan returning to work with him. There was no, I can't wait. No, We'd be excited to have him one day leading our basketball operations again. Not even a smile laced with sly suggestiveness: Well, let's just say whoever gets him will be lucky.

I wrote it off largely to his remoteness, to the pique of a magnate who did not want to be prodded into saying he would be rehiring anybody. But even after his exact words had faded for me and I'd forgotten about the tape, his tone lingered.

To listen to that tape now is to realize Jordan was in trouble even then—that his aides' shots at Pollin from the shadows, and his own sniping at Pollin and Susan O'Malley, had left him on the outs, unless he proved his loyalty to Pollin over the next two years. In having given up the club presidency and returned to the court, he'd presented Pollin with a dream scenario: new wealth and enhanced stature, followed by the unilateral power to decide Jordan's fate. Later, Jordan would insist that Pollin had privately assured him ("I thought you were a man of your word," he supposedly said at their disastrous final meeting) that he could have the club presidency back when he stopped playing. But this is unlikely. Pollin's terse remark to me, which he had to understand might end up in print anytime, signaled his ambivalence, only nine days into the Jordan comeback.

Characteristically, Jordan's self-assurance made him blind to what was unfolding, especially as Pollin and O'Malley routinely acceded during the two seasons ahead to virtually whatever he wished, agreeing to extravagant improvements, for instance, in players' and coaches' facilities and amenities, keeping him happy as the club's coffers fattened. If he did not want club officials talking to a particular person, particularly a writer, they didn't. If Jordan wanted the team to switch hotels in Seattle—where the Wizards had previously stayed at a hotel owned by Pollin's younger brother, Harold—it happened, without any consultation of Pollin's staff, which, while malleable, became privately perturbed in the face of a lengthening series of Jordan's dictates. If he balked at the way management marketed his image, bitching privately about Susan O'Malley's aggressive ways, his wishes became fiat; his complaints about her quietly endured. There would be no feud stoked from management's end—only unremitting deference toward a demanding star.

Jordan went through his Wizards life issuing decrees, on the assumption that, even without the club presidency, he still held de facto power. It didn't matter that under NBA rules governing a player's conduct, he wasn't supposed to have any executive responsibilities; the team consulted him, as its putative leader, before any personnel move. Doug Collins referred to him as his boss, and as the man who would soon again be the official club president. In a rare display of irritation during Jordan's final season, a Pollin aide sent down word to Collins that Michael Jordan was not his boss—not even an executive at that moment, actually—but simply a player; that Collins had one and only one boss—Abe Pollin. Collins, who generally obeyed any Pollin dictate, could not help himself, routinely referring to Jordan thereafter as the future team leader. It was no wonder that Jordan felt he possessed the power that mattered most in the organization.

Since his arrival in the NBA, he had lived no other way—knew no other kind of working relationship. The money that Jordan made for a team and a league trumped rules. Only if a team's revenues were ever threatened would anyone intervene. Such slavish deference could not help but shape him. He never had superiors, only partners. He never had duties, only mutually beneficial arrangements. His only true obligation was to self-fulfillment and winning. It was the ethic, increasingly, of a generation of athletes.

Something was out of whack by the end—which is the importance of any story about Michael Jordan's last comeback and the NBA over those two seasons. All the sweet little allegories and nice lessons have been shredded—they're casualties, really—done in by the vanity and presumption of many of the league's idols, who live nowadays in a kind of bubble, coming of age as young men who know little else other than being catered to, isolated from everyone but the coteries present to service their needs. To walk through an arena hallway on special nights and see an NBA superstar's retinue, Jordan's or anyone else's— the agent, the under-agent, an attorney, the publicist, the shoe guy, the sports-drink guy, the club executive hired only because the star urged the owner to hire him, the chief security guy, the driver—was to understand the extent to which the star serves as a life-support system. He is the sun around which all the smaller bodies revolve. He is the one and only reason for the existence of all these others, who earn their keep by sheltering him, blissfully so, from the tedium and headaches lying beyond the locker rooms, parties and posses.

And therein lies the peril of the bubble: It's hard to see real life coming. It's not far from idyllic insulation to What the hell just happened to me?

The stars are typically dumbfounded and self-pitying when misfortune pierces the bubble and, as was the case for Jordan in his final Washington weeks, usually the last to see catastrophe arriving. If you are looking for explanations, it's best to begin with that bubble. It was blissful and, in the end, it was Jordan's undoing. His was an American story, and he was the irrepressible American athlete, relentlessly hardworking at his craft, as beautiful as a comet to watch, singularly focused on winning and satisfying his other prodigious appetites, full of plans and a burgeoning sense of personal entitlement that ran amuck. During those final two basketball seasons, after two aborted retirements, his self-absorption left him dumb to the hostility he incited among the Washington Wizards' top officials, not dumb as in idiotic, but dumb as a post just the same, as dumb as a pampered man can get—until he was flummoxed by his fate, furious that someone would want to hold him accountable. He was the quintessence of modern athletic greatness and the modern athlete's self-absorption.

His presumption knew no bounds in the final weeks. Even as everything was unraveling and he desperately needed to broker a reconciliation, Jordan could not conceal his disregard for an owner who, for all his shortcomings, had built something over 39 years that Jordan, seeing it as something owed, had come to take, a piece at a time. That was more than pompous; that was hallucinatory; it was hubris bordering on nuttiness. But it was also the logical extension of 20 years of pampering and deification: He could no longer distinguish between his due and delusion, and no one in his circle had ever seen the angle in warning him. He lived in a bubble for One.

But how he got there—and what business forces convinced him that he deserved deference and power—is just as important. In its promotion of Jordan and other superstars, the NBA always made narcissism just another entitlement—and that is the story the league in particular doesn't like broached—how its marketing fostered big heads and ego orgies all across the country, at a severe cost to the culture. The NBA was never alone: Shoe companies and like-minded corporations sold young Americans on the idea that to buy their products meant touching God. Lastly, professional sports enjoyed its incestuous relationship with the sporting media, which, from its 20th-century origins, had seen the profit in profiling, which is often to say mythologizing—wittingly or unwittingly—ballplayers, boxers, tennis players, decathletes, drivers and coaches; in short, in hawking romanticized heroism in order to sell their newspapers, magazines and TV shows.

There could have been no Michael Jordan without a frothing print corps and superheated television coverage. From the beginning, no professional sport could have existed or grown without sports media—which meant that the relationship between the typical newspaper sports page and an athlete always has been different from that, say, between newspapers and politicians.

From the early 20th century, the business of sports needed newspaper sports pages, and vice versa. That symbiosis necessarily means today, as it meant then, that newspapers and the rest of media must declare some athletes to be compelling figures—stars worthy of our attention—or else who will ever buy a newspaper to read a sports section? And if no one cares, who will pay money just to watch men with balls?

That has been the primary challenge of sports from the first days of American professional leagues, and not an easy one to surmount. Picture a group of well-to-do men a century ago in Eastern bars posing this seminal question to one another: How do we get people to give a damn about a mere game—and particularly a game being played by people they don't know and could care less about? There would be puzzled stares. And because there was nothing intrinsically important early in the 20th century about young men who possessed the rather quirky talent of hitting a baseball far, the hero had to be invented. A man who was otherwise quite ordinary in character and intellect—but who could swat a baseball 450 feet or make a long hook shot—was a man, by God, in need of being pumped up to God-like status. The act of throwing a fastball or making a last-second shot had to be equated with the powers of the Maker.

Sports always has had to travel the hero route, which is dicey—because if the hero is ever revealed as something less, the resulting disillusionment can be profound. Michael Jordan wasn't sports' first marketed hero, just its biggest, and when the backlash struck during his final season—following stories about his abuse of teammates, his self-pitying tirades and a civil trial pitting him against a former mistress—it was certain to be infinitely more costly to his image precisely because his publicity apparatus had spent two decades, in the great tradition of American sports, depicting him not only as a wonderful performer but as an extraordinary human being—heroic, selfless, loyal, family-oriented, stable and serene. By his end in Washington, in much of the public's view, there was the whiff of a fraud about him, an outcome for which Michael Jordan could rightly blame the marketing and mythologizing of Michael Jordan as much as himself. Except for this: He had pushed the button on the mythologizing, too.

After his dismissal by Pollin, he moved rapidly to find a way back into the game, as nothing else mattered. The expansion Charlotte franchise's owner, Robert Johnson, the founder of Black Entertainment Television, told the press he'd like to have Jordan as an executive in his new club's organization, though it was thought that any ownership share Jordan received would be modest, and that he would need to pay for it himself. Jordan declined Johnson's offer.

He had come full circle, and now found himself back at his home in the Chicago suburb of Highland Park, back where his search for own-

ership and power had begun three years earlier, when another Charlotte owner dangled a position he didn't take. He had looked then for
another place to land and found Washington, where he thought it the
natural order of things that one day he would run everything. Nothing
else mattered, or nothing else mattered for a while. But he got restless,
he missed games too much, and suddenly nothing else mattered but to
play again. He was a man pulled by impulses, and his impulses were to
be his undoing. His end in Washington was written in his beginnings,
when he sat in his office and said to me that nothing compared to playing, nothing. It was a kind of plea. It was the start of his comeback, the
first seed.

2

"Nothin' Compares to Bein' It"

THERE ARE HOLES IN MEN THAT NO ONE ELSE CAN SEE, THAT NOT
even love and laurels can fill. In the winter of late 2000, Michael Jordan
was restless, and 30 pounds overweight. He had thought he didn't need
the game any longer, which is what most sports idols believe in the
beginning. Retirement looks like a never-ending summer vacation to
the departed athlete then—golf dates, a little carpooling, a lot of casino
action if he wants it, cigars, brandy and no workouts ever again at 7:00
a.m. No psychotic teammates or stormy coaches. No baying reporters.
No need to contemplate a 10:00 a.m. shootaround on game day in
Detroit after a red-eye flight and three hours of sleep. The quiet days
were a balm, a bit of soothing compensation after two decades of being
overscheduled and always having to win, and it was very good for him,
until one day it wasn't. Sitting in his Washington office, he found it
hard to explain, in the way an estranged mate finds it hard to explain
why he needs the exasperating lover back. He just woke up one day and
felt the hole. It was the precise moment when he wanted back the
thing that, three years before, he had no longer wanted.

The feeling began gripping him sometime around this day in mid-
December 2000, a few months before he began publicly flirting with a
comeback. He had agreed to an interview with me to discuss his performance as an executive, and spent about half of the time talking
instead about what it had meant to be a player, and how much he
missed it. "Nothin' compares to bein' it," he said, so wistfully as to signal that he regretted ever having left it, that what he had in its place

was not nearly enough. The quiet of his executive life, once his dream, had become a kind of house arrest.

His cell looked like this: about 30' by 20', newly furnished and accessorized at MCI Center in Washington, with pale walls and an executive's power desk. He had a giant military-gray ashtray for his cigars and a Sony flat-screen television and a view of a distant pharmacy. There he sat at mid-afternoon, on a cold Wednesday. "I didn't want to quit," he mumbled, shrugging. "I never wanted to quit."

He looked outside. I looked outside. I found myself sitting in a chair across his desk, where, as a part owner and the president of basketball operations, he lorded over the lowly Washington Wizards—the equivalent, as jobs go, of King of the Leprechauns. The team had a game that night, and again the arena would be about half empty, no matter what the official attendance said. He absently waved a cigar. He ran a hand over his shaven pate. "I miss *bein' it*," he said. He put down the cigar and unconsciously tapped his midsection on which he could feel a roll of fat.

On the outside, it was the same Jordan—the same slightly pigeon-toed walk, the same courteous, if remote, brown-eyed stare, the same slouch of the celebrity who brought himself down into a guest's Lilliputian world to meet your gaze at eye level. But something wasn't right. He confessed to frustrations, mostly over what he regarded as the unfairness of a new wave of stars being compared to him, players whose best nights, he observed sardonically, brought them "closer in the public mind to a guy who had those accomplishments *tenfold*."

He betrayed the anxiety of a deity who worried about his legend slowly receding. "I don't want to sound bitter or old or whatever," he muttered. "I'm just saying that when Michael Jordan is not playing—" He abruptly stopped himself, only then seeing where he wanted to go with this, thinking of the buzz surrounding the Los Angeles Lakers superstar Kobe Bryant. "If a guy—for instance, the other night, Kobe Bryant scores *51 points*. Now that is a huge story. And then comparisons start to be made to Michael Jordan. But people tend to forget that Michael Jordan scored 50-plus points *three games in a row*. You understand my whole point? . . . People tend to migrate to the [current] player because two years have elapsed from seeing Michael Jordan on the basketball court."

Having become his own best booster by then, he began chronicling the old accomplishments of this athlete whom he called "Michael Jordan," speaking of himself at considerable length in the third person. It was jarring, in part because it sounded so strained, and because he had seldom lapsed into such silliness when he was the model of the serene, plainspoken idol. Third-person references were the oratorical swagger stick of the pompously insecure and the cliché-happy, and neither of those archetypes ever had described Michael Jordan. The afternoon served as a reminder about the fragility of being a deity. Jordan shook his head, his mourning palpable.

Start with his misery then—for misery, the mother of men's reinvention, gave life to his comeback. Three o'clock had arrived, and he looked out a window onto this slate-gray afternoon with freezing winter precipitation in the Washington forecast. His eyes scanned a parking lot and some street beggars. Every few minutes he drifted back to the past. "I read something about Kobe or Vince Carter and it gets the competitor in me going, you know," he said. "And you hear things that bother you. Somebody has a big game, Vince, Kobe, and people on television talk about them the way they would've talked about Michael Jordan. And that gets the competitor in me going because what they don't understand is Michael Jordan did all these things and—" He paused, checking himself. How far did he want to go with this? "I miss the insanity of being out there. The insanity, the wildness, everything on the line. I'd really love to play those guys. But I—" He fell silent.

The official birth of the comeback would not come for another nine months, but its gestation already had begun amid the frustrations of his days. Golf had proven to be no substitute; management was at best a velvet coffin. Being a Wizards executive had given him few pleasures, except on those days when he could get rid of underperforming players and their high-priced contracts. He'd convinced himself that he had allowed himself, unfairly, to be trapped by circumstance back in Chicago, when he'd retired in early 1999. "I didn't want to quit," he said. "I wouldn't have quit if Phil hadn't quit."

He changed the subject, though in a while came back to Jackson. "Does Phil have a game tonight?" he asked. By then, Jackson coached the Los Angeles Lakers, a team that already had won an NBA title under him—number seven as a coach for Jackson, on his way to number eight in a few months. "Does he?"

"I don't know," I answered.

He pursed his lips, trying to remember. It seemed to matter a great deal, to know where Phil was. "Maybe he does."

"I know you guys have a game," I added.

"No," he mumbled, "*I* don't."

His Wizards would be facing the Philadelphia 76ers and Allen Iverson in about four hours. But he was right: He had no game.

What's better, being president and an owner or being on the court?

Jordan laughed, looked out the window.

"No way this compares," he said. "Playin' it, bein' it, makin' the shot, . . . it's huge, it's a whole difference. Nothin' compares to that. But that's gone." For the moment, his position would be that his playing career was gone, irretrievable. "I didn't want it to be," he said softly, "but it is."

At his retirement press conference in 1999, he'd said he was mentally exhausted, but now he had another perception of that time. He said he'd felt just fine.

You could have played another season?

"Easy," he said.

Two seasons?

"Easy."

A third?

"Easy. My body would have told me when to stop."

A third season would have meant that he would be playing at that moment.

Now and then a passing siren bleated from the streets, and his head jerked, involuntarily, toward his window. He had a view of the panhandlers standing near a parking lot as snowflakes fell.

It was not a vista for gods. Over the previous year, he had descended from the firmament and landed hard, taking his place here in the Wizards offices on the arena's elevated second floor, which was not exactly the second circle of Hell, but, as Dante might have pointed out, you could see it from here. His playing days had left him believing he had the power to do anything; his adulthood was an exercise in absolute dominion. But then he tried to assert his will on the Wizards, which was less a team than a plague. Stars and would-be stars typically rotted in Washington; the young and swift were traditionally traded for the old and withering; malaise generally set in during training camp.

The Wizards were already dead on the vine by that December afternoon, off to the worst start in franchise history, en route to losing 63 of 82 games by season's end. Jordan could not bear to watch more than a few of the home games in person. He typically took sanctuary in his office just off the Club Concourse level of MCI, where he could glare at his flat-screen television and curse his team while surrounded by discomfited friends. There was a dime-sized splatter on the bottom of the television, where, just a week earlier, he'd fired a beer can at the image of a Wizards player who had infuriated him. *"How can you put up that fuckin' shot?"* Jordan demanded of the tiny player on the screen. *"What the fuck are you doing?"*

The image did not answer him but instead threw a pass intercepted by the opposition and turned into a layup. Jordan howled, bombarding the screen with anything he could find—the remote control, pens, more cans, balls of paper. "What the fuck are you doing? *What the fuck are you doing?"*

His friends had tried to sneak out of the room, not wanting to be caught in another of his gales. He wheeled on them, glowering at his old Bulls teammate, longtime buddy and now assistant general manager Rod Higgins, a probing look that Higgins read as, *Where the hell do you think you're going?*

Higgins sat down. Jordan glared at him, as if demanding an explanation. "How can anyone take that fuckin' shot? How . . . could . . . anyone . . . take . . . *THAT . . . FUCKIN' . . . SHOT?"*

Higgins became a little uncomfortable. "Michael, I didn't take the shot, okay?"

Jordan knew that he had fooled himself in promising fans a .500 season. No one on the TV screen seemed to understand what he wanted, part of the reason why he had contemplated putting a walkie-talkie right next to Wizards coach Leonard Hamilton, to advise him on plays, substitutions and strategies. "I could say, 'Think of doing this. Or call a fucking time-out,'" he explained. "But then I thought: I got a coach, I should let him coach. But still it'd be nice to say, 'Think of calling a fucking time-out.'"

"Fucking" came out of him with agitation. The losing was taking its toll on his moods. Just nine days earlier, he had completely lost it. As he watched from managing owner Abe Pollin's box, the Wizards lost spectacularly to the Los Angeles Clippers, against whom they had a 19-point lead in the fourth quarter before blowing up like the Hindenburg—slowly enough that you could see the immolation happening, but just fast enough that no one could stop it. In the final minutes, powerless and embarrassed, Jordan felt himself going silently berserk. Heads wheeled from lower seats to look up at him, stares that he read as demanding that he *get on the court and fix this.* Some people screamed at him to put on a uniform and come back. He stared through them, at which point he noticed TV cameras pointed his way. "I thought, Any second I'm gonna start cursing and all those cameras are gonna show it to everybody," he said.

He stayed composed, but just barely long enough. Out of the cameras' sights once the game ended, he stormed into the Wizards locker room and exploded, telling the players they had become a "disgrace to the fans"; that they were afflicted by a "losers' mentality"; that he wouldn't hesitate dealing away any of them except that no one in the room had any trade value.

The players looked back blankly at him; he saw no fire. Leonard Hamilton would resign by season's end, but the end was still a long ways off. "I can see why the fans get [ticked] off and boo," he said. "I'm angry, too. Some of [the players] don't push themselves. They take shortcuts."

He asked that fans and the media reserve judgment about his leadership of the Wizards until he could "make my team." Making the team meant unmaking it, for starters. Only when he ridded himself of underproducing stars with high-priced contracts could he have adequate money to spend on new players. That meant trying to unload the contracts of the team's three best-known and most extravagantly paid veterans—forward Juwan Howard, and guards Mitch Richmond and Rod Strickland—whose combined price tags left the Wizards knocking up against the ceiling of the NBA's salary cap. The Wizards had been a costly disaster, with Jordan's task akin to rebuilding a mismanaged Eastern European hellhole whose ineptitude and cycles of binge spending had left nothing at his disposal other than some sunny platitudes.

Merely the sight of Howard—who had a seven-year, $105 million contract through the end of the 2002–2003 season—reminded livid fans of the franchise's history of miscalculations. Playing in his seventh season in Washington, he could score 22 points on one night, then disappear in plain sight and score fewer than 10 in the next game. He worked hard, but nearly whatever he produced offensively, he gave away defensively. The fourth-highest-paid player in the NBA, Howard was neither strong enough at 6'9" and 250 pounds to match up effectively with the league's most formidable power forwards, nor quick enough usually to play on the perimeter with smaller forwards. His talents left him in limbo between positions—a tweener, as analysts said disparagingly. Fans heaped abuse on him.

But the Howard problem paled against two trades, preceding Jordan's arrival, which had stripped the Wizards of their best talent.

Three years before, the Wizards dealt away the supremely talented young forward Chris Webber to get Richmond. Webber was 25 at the time and on the cusp of stardom, by then a four-year Wizards veteran for whom the team had given up a roster player and, more critically, three first-round draft choices—essentially sacrificing the club's future for one player. Then Webber was gone, the Wizards ridding themselves of him, at least in part, because of several off-court legal problems—allegations that he smoked marijuana and was disorderly in a nightclub. In exchange, the Wizards received Richmond, who was 32 and a former All-Star entering his twilight.

Webber had become an All-Star in Sacramento, while Richmond remained a genial man who earned $10 million a year and would be jettisoned at the 2000–2001 season's end, when the club paid off his contract that ran through the end of the 2001–2002 season. The Wizards had tried unsuccessfully to deal him to other clubs, but no one much wanted a 35-year-old guard with a fat contract any more than a team wanted the 34-year-old Strickland, who would be released with his pair of bad hamstrings at the season's end, when the Wizards exercised his $5 million buyout clause. Another $10 million guard who came to Washington in 1996 with all-star credentials, Strickland arrived from the Portland Trail Blazers, in exchange for Washington's young 6'11" power forward Rasheed Wallace. By the time Jordan became team president, Wallace was an All-Star and malcontent in Portland, and Strickland, after two strong seasons in Washington, had settled into being a chronic disappointment. In December of 2000, he was suspended for a game after missing two practices and a team flight to Miami. A month later, he was arrested on a DUI charge.

Few teams in NBA history had ever paid so much for such steady trouble and incompetence. While saddled with one of the NBA's worst records, the Wizards had the league's fifth-highest payroll. Just the salaries of Strickland, Richmond and Howard—the last of whom received about $16.9 million in the 2000–2001 season—placed the Wizards over the league's salary cap, ensuring paralysis for the time being.

The frustration and gallows humor grew within the organization. "Rick Pitino told me I was crazy to take this job," Leonard Hamilton dared to say one morning in an arena hallway, referring to the then Boston Celtics coach.

Looking for tough players, Jordan dealt away center Cherokee Parks to the Clippers for powerfully built 6'6" forward Tyrone Nesby. The newcomer seemed perfectly cut from the Wizards' mold, finding himself kicked off the bench for insubordination during a game before the end of his second full month.

But in time, Jordan would get a break. In February of 2001, having known that he would need to unload Howard on an NBA team whose owners had financial pockets deep enough to take a chance on an over-paid potential bust, Jordan found his answer in the Dallas Mavericks and their young, free-spending owner, Mark Cuban. In the best move of his managerial tenure, Jordan got rid of Howard and two Wizards reserves, in exchange for five Mavericks, including the once promising Christian Laettner.

Now, with Howard's contract no longer hanging around their necks, Jordan could renew his search for promising players. But in Washington, suspicions had arisen that Jordan's personnel hopes stemmed less from study than impulse. Most days, he sat at home in Highland Park, where he lived about 20 days out of every 30, watching Wizards games alone in his basement like a general in a bunker, and doing his Wizards business via phone.

He did not work 24/7; it was not a phrase in his lexicon. His rhythms at work and play were his own. In Chicago, he sometimes drove his three children to school, telephoned General Manager Wes Unseld and other Wizards colleagues about possible trades, chatted with other teams' executives, did some Nike business, flew out of town to take in a football game, played some golf, made late-night calls and monitored the rest of his business interests.

By the time he found himself in Washington, on this December afternoon in 2000, he had been gone from Chicago for a full week. The day before, he was . . . where was he *yesterday?* He thought about it for a second and it came to him. Florida. He had flown there to complete some business that had nothing to do with basketball, receiving the National Hockey League's approval for his purchase of a slice of the Washington Capitals—which one of his Wizards partners, Ted Leonsis, agreed to sell him when Jordan became the Wizards' pres-ident of basketball operations.

The previous Saturday, while the Wizards played in Milwaukee, he and his wife, Juanita, discreetly boarded their jet and flew to the Bahamas, where they were guests at the posh opening of a Paradise Island hotel, watching a Whitney Houston concert for a while before going off to gamble—Jordan winning about a half million at the black-jack tables.

Some of those closest to Jordan openly wondered whether he was overextended. A former Bulls assistant coach, Tex Winter, the architect of the Bulls' famed triangle offense, asked whether his basketball com-mitment could endure amid all his other interests.

"I don't question his abilities," said Winter, by then an assistant under Phil Jackson with the Los Angeles Lakers. "But how many irons does he have in the fire? I do question that. Eventually he'll lose a lot of inspirational value and credibility if he doesn't spend more time [in Washington] and devote more time and attention to the players and team."

Jordan told the skeptics that it didn't matter where he worked. He had phones and beepers, and could do business anywhere. Lines like that made some NBA executives snicker. "Some [executives] smirk a little when his name comes up," said one general manager. "They'll say, 'This is the real world.' Let me tell you: There's no protection on this side of the desk. I hear of him and some of these ex-players going off, traveling places. We work fifty, sixty hours a week all year. I'll tell you one former player who's done it right is [Jerry] West [former vice president of the Los Angeles Lakers]. Jerry traveled to places like Transylvania, Kentucky, to scout. He went in an ice storm to see a player. I've never admired a player more than Michael. It's just that we're not off fishing or whatever it is. And it's just going to make it harder that he's not [in Washington] a lot."

An agent who had dealt with basketball executives for a decade said, "I'm afraid for Michael. He's going to get his teeth kicked in. He doesn't bring any of the needed skills—knowing the salary cap in and out, knowing how to negotiate with agents and GMs on that side of the table. And they can't wait to outsmart him."

Jordan defenders insisted that Jordan had no real opportunity to improve the team with major trades or acquisitions because Abe Pollin had shackled him, determined to avert a significant rise in player payroll. Pollin freely admitted that he wanted to guard against hefty contracts that would place the club over the salary cap and leave it vulnerable to luxury-tax penalties, which amounted to a one-dollar penalty for every dollar over the cap, or a million-dollar penalty for every excess million. But the owner emphatically denied having blocked any deals, an issue that swiftly became a source of tension between Pollin and his new chief executive. Jordan did not discourage the notion of their differences, saying in his office that he and the team had pulled away from deals after hearing reservations from his "partners"—his appellation, in this case, for Pollin alone. At least publicly, he simultaneously tried putting the best face on what was happening with the owner. "I'm not going to say I'm smart about every decision; I definitely have to understand, you know, the financial situation down the road," he said casually. "So, based on their observations of long-term things, we backed away from a couple of deals."

Backed away from a couple of deals: He would not back away from saying it, despite Pollin having denied that he discouraged any trade. It was the first hint of a division between the two men.

Compounding the challenge for Jordan and Pollin was that neither man had ever sought out the other to make their relationship happen. They had enjoyed no professional courtship, all the romancing of Jordan having been done by Ted Leonsis, an Internet kingpin and a short, squatty, ebullient man who admitted being so awed in Jordan's presence that he actually had paused during a meeting to call his family and let them know that he found himself with the idol. The America Online marketing executive began his wooing of Jordan over dinner in 1999, at a Chicago restaurant, and later presented him the outline of a proposed deal dependent on Pollin's willingness to grant Jordan control over the basketball operations of the Wizards.

Jordan remained carefully noncommittal. He had many potential NBA suitors at that moment, and seemed to possess leverage in negotiations with everyone. From the beginning, no matter where he went to listen to offers, Jordan wanted, at a minimum, authority over a franchise's basketball operations and a slice of ownership.

But it would be better, he reasoned at the start of 1999, to own the majority share of a club with a group of investors and have unquestioned control over a team. Ready to join the plutocrats and modern-day Gatsbys in skyboxes, he saw ownership as the last step in his evolution: player to star; star to economic power; powerhouse to owner. Jordan dreamed of forming an ownership group that would purchase a controlling interest in the Charlotte franchise, which had become an embarrassment to the NBA. Early in 1999, the league's commissioner David Stern arranged for a series of meetings between Jordan and George Shinn, the owner of the Charlotte Hornets, who had been named as a defendant in a sexual assault lawsuit. He would be eventually acquitted, but his franchise reeled from a series of misfortunes. Several of Shinn's marquee players had fled for more money elsewhere, and the owner was unable to rally support among city leaders for the construction of a new arena. Without a glittering edifice adorned by skyboxes and other NBA amenities, it looked certain that the Hornets would leave Charlotte, in search of a city likely to yield greater box-office revenues. Jordan became viewed as a potential savior who could persuade players to stay, deliver an arena, attract more fans and keep the franchise in Charlotte.

But negotiations broke off when Shinn would not agree to any joint ownership deal ceding complete control of Hornets' basketball and business decisions to Jordan. The Hornets would leave in 2002 for New Orleans.

In September 1999, Jordan listened briefly to representatives of the Vancouver Grizzlies and the Milwaukee Bucks, but neither group seemed prepared to hand over the control he wanted. Then came his meetings with Leonsis and the mogul's partners in their holding company, Lincoln Holdings. Only four months earlier, Lincoln had bought the NHL Washington Capitals from Abe Pollin, as well as 44 percent of Pollin's Washington Sports and Entertainment, which controls the Wizards, MCI Center, the Women's National Basketball Association Washington Mystics, US Airways Arena and local branches of Ticketmaster. When Pollin chose to retire and relinquish ownership, Leonsis would have the contractual right to purchase the remaining interest in the Wizards as well as to buy from Pollin the MCI Center and the Washington Mystics. Leonsis enjoyed the status of a putative successor, giving off the air of a managing partner of the Wizards during his discussions with Jordan.

Any deal struck between the two men, however, would be contingent on Pollin consenting to transfer authority over basketball operations from his general manager, Wes Unseld, to Jordan. By January 2000, Leonsis and Jordan reached agreement on the basic outline of a financial agreement: Leonsis's Lincoln Holdings group would give a roughly 10 percent stake in the Wizards to Jordan, as well as a minority stake in the Washington Capitals. Later, reports would spread from unidentified sources that Jordan had received $30 million to $50 million of Lincoln equity without paying a dime. Leonsis would coolly deny it, declining to answer whether Jordan would receive the equity simply for work he did for Lincoln and the Wizards—a pretext that would have been tantamount to free equity.

Through early 2000, Leonsis presided over the deal-making that most mattered. Leonsis, not Pollin, served as the charmer, the one who, aware that Jordan had invested in CBS SportsLine and formed a soon-to-be-foundering Internet venture with John Elway and Wayne Gretzky called MVP.com, whetted Jordan's appetite for the Internet's future by talking of his AOL experiences and sketching possible ways for Jordan to plunge into entrepreneurial opportunities in the sector.

All along, Pollin remained a third wheel, never an engaging intimate with whom to share stories over drinks, simply a possible impediment to the deal were he not to give Jordan enough authority, or at least the appearance of authority.

By then both the Wizards' and Pollin's reputations had hit bottom. The team had not sold out a game all season, its season ticket sales having dropped over the last year, according to reports, by almost 25 percent, down to about 6,400 seats. Its losing head coach, Gar Heard, was under siege. For frothing Washington fans and the media, the news that a wooed Michael Jordan might be seriously contemplating a move to their city represented Pollin's last chance to prove his commitment to winning.

The elderly owner and the idol dined together at Pollin's house in Bethesda, Maryland, and over the days ahead, reached agreement on a broad definition of Jordan's powers as the club's chief basketball official. Jordan agreed to Pollin's insistence that Wes Unseld remain as general manager, and that the other longtime Pollin favorite, Susan O'Malley, carry on as president of Washington Sports and Entertainment, with responsibilities over the marketing and business end of the franchise. That hazy division of executive responsibilities between Jordan and O'Malley invited the probability that, on occasion, O'Malley would tread on matters that Jordan believed to be his turf. This seeming likelihood was never a hurdle during negotiations, which concluded with Jordan signing a five-year contract to serve as president of basketball operations, though not before Jordan attorney Curtis Polk, late during the negotiations, irked Pollin by extracting his concession to a clause obligating Jordan to attend no more than six Wizards games each season. In the end, Jordan had everything he wanted, including an assurance from Pollin that he would have *control* over the Wizards' basketball operations.

But there existed a murky line in the Wizards' executive offices between "control" of basketball operations and *absolute* control over everything involved with basketball-related spending. In late 2000, with both Pollin and Jordan perturbed over the issue of power, the media-leery owner agreed to a private interview in his office. He did not seek to hide his irritations with the reports, leaked by the Jordan camp, that he had barred several trades and become an insurmountable obstacle to Jordan's capacity to deal with other teams.

"Incorrect," Pollin said. He shook his head disgustedly.

He laid out their business relationship: Jordan had a written agreement, signed by Pollin, that gave him "control over basketball." That kind of language seemed clear, except it wasn't so clear, indicated the owner. Pollin believed the phrase to mean control over personnel decisions, but that it stopped well short of ultimate authority over expenditures. "We also have a *handshake*," Pollin added, his way of saying their agreement went deeper than mere words on a document. Pollin maintained—never to be publicly disputed by Jordan—that both of them had orally agreed "that no deal would take place unless I agreed with it." Pollin called it his "moral right."

Pollin waved his hand back and forth through the air, the way you would erase a blackboard, as if to say that this whole discussion was beside the point anyway. He insisted that Jordan had come to him with only one proposed deal—the trade for Tyrone Nesby—and that he had given it his blessing, despite realizing that Nesby's contract meant the team's payroll would rise by another $3 million the following season.

The claims of the Jordan camp increasingly angered him. He momentarily lost his cool. *"I don't care what they said,"* he snapped. "The only deal they came to me with was [the Nesby trade], and I approved it."

He had particularly grown weary of the suggestion that the star and his underlings felt so discouraged that they had stopped approaching him with possible trade scenarios. *"'Scenarios' is just a bunch of bull.* Nesby was the trade. All the others were talk."

He was waving those arms again, trying to wipe the nastiness away. He searched for a pleasant topic, trumpeting Jordan's benefit to ticket sales and marketing, acknowledging that about 500 more season tickets, and 2,000 10-game packages, had been sold since Jordan's arrival. "Susan O'Malley is not bashful as far as asking him to do things, and Michael has really been terrific for her. He's done an awful lot. Marketing was not supposed to be part of the deal. The deal was to run the basketball team. Marketing is Susan's deal. But he has been terrific for marketing and Susan, so I'm very grateful."

But things were not terrific there either. Back in his office, Jordan had begun resisting and resenting his place in the club's marketing strategy, and in Susan O'Malley's plans in particular. He did not want to be obligated to market a *poor* team, he told people. He could have stayed in Chicago and just as well have let the Bulls market his face, if marketing was what he wanted to do.

Besides, he thought, he had done his fair share of marketing already, having consented to the use of his name and image in such Wizards ticket promotion themes as "Jordan Is Back." No one should expect more, he thought. "I've tried to give them a jump-start, you know: 'Jordan's back'; having my input, blah-blah-blah. I even told them it would be a *limited* situation, so that I don't feel like I'm gonna have to try to sell a product that's not selling itself."

Now Jordan was letting loose. His voice rose. His words came in a rush, making clear that O'Malley and her marketing strategies had lost their appeal for him. "If I go out there and do all that [promotion and marketing] and my team comes back and they're four-and-twenty, what do you think people are gonna say? They're gonna say, *The product is not selling itself.* It's not. The [Wizards] are not seventeen-and-four. They're four-and-seventeen. So what are you trying to say about, Come out and watch the Wizards. Come out and watch the Wizards *what? Lose?* If we were seventeen-and-four, then I would feel an obligation and more comfortable going out and saying, Hey, look, we've turned this thing around, they're working hard every day, blah-blah-blah. *That, that* to me."—now his voice rose another level still, loud, adamant, a touch angry—"shows a plan to me that shows how my attitude and personality have impacted the whole process. Until [that happens], I cannot even think about going outside to talk [market and promote]."

In Chicago, he never had been a traditional employee. He never had had a genuine boss before, someone like Pollin who would signal through O'Malley his expectations and hopes for a little extra work now and then. When you hired Michael Jordan, you contracted to get Michael Jordan's services, as Jordan defined them.

O'Malley got on his nerves. A blond, single fortysomething who by her own admission had little serious time for anyone or anything not related to business, she never exhibited the slightest awe around Jordan, this alone making her unlike Ted Leonsis and 99 percent of the business strangers whom Jordan met for the first time. She did not hesitate approaching Jordan and telling him that she would appreciate it if he were to perform some small marketing chore on behalf of the team, having a way of standing quite close to him, like a pint-sized politician aggressively buttonholing a somewhat reluctant colleague, a powerful woman who did not hesitate to wield power or remind others she had it. She did not take *no* easily or sometimes coolly, renowned for her persistence, which made her a success in Pollin's circle but left her often regarded as a pain in the ass in the largely male world she inhabited.

Doubtless, sexism had something to do with it, and so, too, did the stories that made their way around MCI about how she believed in a tough accountability when people did not deliver what she wanted. The latest tale was of a Wizards player complaining that he had lost an opportunity to put his family in a luxury box one evening because O'Malley had withdrawn the privilege after he failed to appear for a community event. Whether true or not, the tale had the effect of leaving people to worry more about O'Malley, which might have been the intent. Neither she nor Pollin backed down from people, which made them very much like Jordan, and therefore, given their irreconcilable agendas, virtually guaranteed their mutual antagonism.

And Jordan had problems beyond O'Malley. As the players, coaches and management were targeted for mockery in light of the Wizards' awfulness, there was no immunity even for the new club president, by then increasingly criticized in the local press for being inattentive and inaccessible. In a style of management that a recluse would have loved, Jordan traveled undercover in Washington, sometimes watching games alone in his office without the public even knowing he had sneaked into town, then flying out of the city just as stealthily. He had become something spectral, less man than apparition. Jordan liked the remove. He aspired to the privileges of other wealthy American barons—to watch games from a gilded room, undisturbed, never revealing himself unless he saw an advantage in it. "It's nice to watch comfortable in an office," he said. "People aren't staring and calling for you to go out there and play. I like to be relaxed up here. It's more comfortable."

A couple of Jordan intimates said privately that the critics failed to understand a fundamental Jordan concern: that he wouldn't permit himself to be exploited as he suspected other retired black athletes had been. He wouldn't be the Wizards' "show pony," he declared. The losing team, he declared, "doesn't represent *anything* I'm about—winning, success, work ethic."

Meanwhile, he exercised the powers of a typical NBA basketball executive. Soon after his arrival in Washington, he had fired the coach, Gar Heard, and in time found Leonard Hamilton at the University of Miami, hired him and would soon be saying good-bye to him, too. He could act decisively but, just the same, his powers and influence were limited. Despite the "president" in his title, he enjoyed less sway than ever. Worse, his team was awful, and showed no signs of improving anytime soon. Old rivals rubbed it in.

In a home game against Indiana, the Pacers' voluble star Reggie Miller, a favorite target of hecklers, started jawing with a few courtside fans while having his way with the Wizards guards, particularly Mitch

Richmond. Markedly slowing after 14 years of playing 40 minutes a night, Richmond moved on his hurting knee like an old ram stepping gingerly on a steep slope.

Jabbering to the hecklers while abusing Richmond, Miller missed a three-point shot and fell back, landing on the lap of a heckler's wife. He delivered a message for the couple and everyone around them: "Tell Michael Jordan that he better make some changes. He better do *something*." Miller gestured at Richmond. "He can't guard me. He's too old."

No amount of resolve could make up for age and a bad team's dearth of talent, thought Jack Ramsay, the coach of the Portland Trail Blazers' 1977 championship team. He had discussed the shortcomings of the Wizards with Jordan, who, half smiling, shook his head. "I got the impression that he'd thought he was going to step in and get a quick fix with these guys and didn't," recalls Ramsay. "In the old days, he could make even a journeyman good. That was over, and I think it surprised him."

As Ramsay recalled it, he said to Jordan, "This is a harder job than you imagined, isn't it?"

"It sure is," Jordan replied, that head still shaking.

In his office, I said to him that there was something incongruous about his presence there; that his job in Washington sometimes seemed so surreal as to be an act against nature—Michael Jordan signing a contract to run the Washington Wizards; Michael Jordan owning a share of the Wizards rather than the Chicago Bulls. "You being with the Wizards—it's like Babe Ruth or Mickey Mantle owning the Minnesota Twins," I blurted.

He fingered his cream tie and, adolescent-like, pressed it against his mouth, holding it there like a mischievous schoolkid muffling a laugh.

"Well, you're right," he said.

He managed to raise the subject of Chicago every few minutes. When stuck on the road for any appreciable time, he talked wistfully of Chicago. "I'm in the business world now," he said philosophically, "but I wish all my business connections were in Chicago, because that's where my home and roots are. But"—he reminded himself of the upside to his presence here—"this is a good deal for me here."

He stared back at his muted TV.

He shared a longing: He wished the owners of the Chicago Bulls had asked him a year or two earlier to be a partner and run their team, "so that I could have at least thought about their offer."

He had not so much chosen Washington as landed in it, after the Bulls declined to offer him a piece of ownership and power. Since then, a portion of the Chicago media, which gleefully excoriated Bulls owner Jerry Reinsdorf and chief basketball executive Jerry Krause for letting Jordan get away, had encouraged the impression of a god exiled. The city's Jordan detractors regarded the idol as a traitor for taking his talents elsewhere. It was not nearly that bad in either case. It was not that bad because all things and all men pass, and even owners die or sell out, and surely the day would come when Jerry Reinsdorf would be old and Michael Jordan would not.

That suggested a question: If in 5, 6, 8; 10 years from now, Jerry Reinsdorf and his partners wanted to sell the Bulls, would he rule out trying to buy the team?

The office became very quiet, and Jordan's eyes blinked, blinked, blinked, did not move off that window. The question, catching him by surprise, was freighted with potential pitfalls, and it seemed reasonable, as his silence lengthened, that he might decline to answer it altogether. "No, I don't want to rule it out," he said softly.

And if he were nearly anybody else in the world, he would carefully have left it there and said not another word. But he was a man at ease talking about possibilities, having invented himself out of fantasies. He saw them not as delusions but as prelude—visions to be realized, destiny at the end of the lane he was bursting through.

He sat in this Washington office and looked through that distant pharmacy and said again, "I really wish all my business interests were here," and meant Chicago in that moment, as if he'd never left it. Its pull on him was irresistible, and no one could logically blame him for that any more than one could rail at the lover who dreamt of going back. "I don't want to rule it out," he repeated.

Could it be the most natural thing in the world?

"It is, it is, it is," he said brightly, fiddling with his tie.

Happy now, he was also careful, noting that he had given his loyalty to Leonsis and Pollin; that only when he had "turned this situation around in the right direction" would he ever consider leaving for the Bulls.

And he could have stopped himself there, too, but by now he had a vision of it—the Bulls' phone calls, some tentative offer he'd made to buy the team, the prospect of a deal, the spurned king returning.

"If that situation is put on the table," he said slowly, "I would sit down with Ted, all my guys . . . and Abe, if he's still part of the situation, and say, 'Look, the Chicago team wants to sell. It's a great fit for me, it's my home. Washington has turned itself around and is headed in the right direction, what do you think?' And I would totally honor their input before making a decision."

He shrugged, smiling sheepishly. He looked a little relieved. There. It was out. He looked like any man who had purged himself of a fantasy.

Tired of his cigar, he waved it like a bored professor with a pointer, then dropped it in the ashtray a last time. He had a box of the Cubans in his office, and an SUV, and a driver waiting if he wanted him, and $400 million in banks and property. But no game. "It's real hard not havin' it," he said. "But that's gone."

He had tried sating his competitive appetites on golf courses and in Caribbean casinos. A man with much time on his hands, he had no idea how to fill it. The scarcity of his passions raised questions as to what he was about. What did he stand for, exactly? That he seemed not to be evolving concerned some old associates, however. A former producer of his Nike ads, a Portland public relations executive named Jim Riswold, softly warned that if he wanted his appeal to endure in retirement, Jordan now needed to stand for something beyond games, to find a cause or passion, *something.*

Riswold, whose commercials had helped to make the young Jordan a star on the order of Hollywood's leading men, believed that the idol was already being supplanted as the top endorsement star by Tiger Woods. "Tiger's more influential because he's opened a game," said Riswold. "I'd like Michael to talk about issues larger than sports now— maybe something like the role and responsibility of the athlete in an era where we're preoccupied with the glorification of the athlete. If a retired athlete has a cause outside the arena, people listen. If not, they don't."

Years earlier, when Nike faced condemnation for its low-wage sweatshops overseas, Jordan had stayed mute. When Charlotte mayor Harvey Gantt asked for his support in a North Carolina senate race against the rabidly conservative Jesse Helms, Jordan quietly declined, worried about how his involvement might affect sales of his shoes, famously confiding to friends, "Republicans buy shoes. too." His involvement in the city of Washington, overwhelmingly black and deeply impoverished in parts, had been minimal. He had carefully made himself a blank slate in all matters outside basketball.

Once he thrived precisely because of this congenial indifference to all things political and controversial. Having disarmed issues of race long before by never acknowledging them, he'd become White America's favorite TV commercial pitchman back in the '80s, an epoch tailor-made for Michael Jordan. He was, as much as anything, an invention of those times, his early years in the NBA neatly coinciding with burgeoning American businesses and appetites—the explosive growth in media and shoe companies; the country's addictive fascination with celebrities; the global ascendancy of the NBA; and, most important, the elevation of glamour to an exalted social attribute.

It was a great time to be Michael Jordan, marketed as the embodiment of Beauty and Grace, on his way to becoming worth more than $100 million in his first decade in the league. Sports in America always had practiced a kind of monotheism, and he was the god of his times. As with any deity, America quickly forgave him his idiosyncrasies and excesses, most notably his gambling forays on golf courses with shady men who lifted large sums from him. The media pounced, then retreated. Scrutiny of him eased, the press according him a deference that seemed born of the see-nothing-know-nothing '50s. By his second retirement, he ranked among the most recognizable people on the planet and, unquestionably, its most famous athlete. "I've always appreciated the respect," he said in his office. "I know there're a lot of people out there who remember."

But the world had moved on. Kobe Bryant had become the sport's newest darling, and Vince Carter the prince of air, and Michael Jordan a basketball executive who, with time for gambling weekends in the Bahamas, had largely fallen off the front pages and sports sections, taking his place on the celebrity gossip pages—the press noting his travels in small items, another aging star whose luminescence dimmed in his inert state. As Riswold predicted, the supreme young golfer Tiger Woods had eclipsed Jordan in popularity to become Madison Avenue's most popular commercial spokesman, taking in $20 million more from endorsements than the former king at his peak, with Jordan's shoe line now featuring younger athletes pushing his gear. Jordan thought it silly that so many fans and writers heralded any young athlete whose significant accomplishments spanned no longer than a couple of years: Didn't they have any idea how long *he* had dominated? he asked.

In this cold winter of 2000, looking out the window from behind his immense desk, he felt cuffed. "I didn't want to quit," he said. "I get itches to play. Then you see the fans talking about these other players and comparing them to you . . ." *Comparing them to Michael Jordan.* It was too much for him. He stopped himself, bit down on his lip.

This is not the way it was supposed to be. At some point, three years of solitude had become too much. He had turned on a television, heard the cheers for new gods and despaired that a game had moved on without him.

"I never wanted to quit," he said. "Never. . . . It's natural to feel that. It's the itches you get."

Do you ever get a case of the itches so bad that you want to come back?

"In terms of playing? *No.*" He couldn't admit it yet.

Not even sometimes?

"It's a what-if, a what-if. I have a lot of what-ifs. But these are things that you have to deal with. . . . You know that your time has come and gone. No one said you weren't going to have to deal with some things."

It did not sound like he was dealing with it particularly well.

If so, he wouldn't be the first. Great athletes, the gods especially, get restless. Their addiction to the game kicks in, and sometimes life offers no adequate substitutes. Muhammad Ali—who had resolved never to leave beaten and battered, who seemed to have succeeded when he retired after beating Leon Spinks in a rematch at age 36 and winning the heavyweight title for an unprecedented third time—came back at 38 to be pounded by Larry Holmes. One of Jordan's golfing buddies and a fellow sports-team owner, hockey legend Mario Lemieux, had fled retirement to play again for the Pittsburgh Penguins.

The itches, as Jordan knew, could get anybody. Why should anyone have been surprised? Nobody took the brushes away from Michelangelo at 37. No one would have cheered the retirement of Hemingway at 38. Why should anyone expect, let alone demand, that athletes not feel entitled to experience the same slow decline as the rest of us?

As 2001 began, many people resisted the idea of a Jordan comeback for the same reason they didn't want anyone putting another paint stroke on the *Mona Lisa:* You don't mess with perfection. They cringed at the thought of Jordan defiling the exquisiteness of his 1998 ending. The seeming final shot of his career, an 18-foot jumper over the Utah Jazz's fallen guard, Bryon Russell, had given him and the Bulls their sixth NBA championship. Only a few other professional athletes—Bill Russell, Gene Tunney and Rocky Marciano came to mind—had ever retired as champions, and no other famous American athlete ever had matched Jordan for prevailing at his end under more pressure. Why mar that? the critics asked.

But why did their perfect ending need to be his? Cal Ripken, in his own twilight at that moment, had given thought to Jordan's dilemma. And Jordan had read what Ripken, then still active as a player, said: "I can't understand how Michael Jordan could give up playing when he did—not with all he could still do, *can still do,* you know? I'm not passing judgment on Michael. . . . I'm just saying I could never do what Michael did. I just love playing too much."

Like Ripken, Jordan had come in with Reagan. He was one of those athletes whose career reminded you, against your will, of your own passages, and mortality, of the days fleeing. It could make you a little queasy. But it also explained why many people like Ripken greeted the thought of a Jordan comeback with intense interest. A comeback stops time; even turns back the clock. Ripken would not have minded the clock stopping. Many interested parties came to feel this way in time, including a melancholy Michael Jordan. He had a choice: He could reclaim the basketball court, or he could sit in this office, looking forward to watching his flat-screen and dealing with Susan O'Malley and Abe Pollin.

Even gods get the itches. A month later, he began working out. In another month, word spread that Michael Jordan was contemplating a comeback.

Before returning to the court, Jordan had two key managerial tasks to carry out. With Leonard Hamilton resigning at the end of the Wizards' 19–63 season, Jordan now needed to hire a talented coach, and use the Wizards' first pick in the NBA draft to land a potential superstar around whom to build the team for many years. It was a combination of duties that, if successfully completed, would likely make the Wizards a fixture in the playoffs in the near future. The most winning coach, and his personal favorite, was beyond his reach: Phil Jackson had a lengthy contract in Los Angeles. Jordan made a call to his former Chicago Bulls teammate John Paxson. For the moment, Paxson was part of a broadcasting team covering Bulls games, but most observers in Chicago believed that the Bulls were grooming him to help run the franchise someday. Jordan wanted him.

Jordan always had loved Paxson's savvy and reliability during their playing days. The mere mention of Paxson prompted Jordan to recall the smaller, slower man's finest moment, a long, open jumper—off a pass from Jordan, of course—which had clinched the Bulls' third championship against Phoenix. On and off the court, Paxson had thrived in the basketball profession because he subjugated his interests to the organization's and its stars. Jordan knew he could work with him. Just as importantly, the selection of Paxson would mean that Jordan wouldn't need to turn to a stranger to coach him if he came back and played, an increasingly likely prospect.

On the phone, Jordan said hi and quickly offered him the head coaching position.

Paxson said he was flattered. But he added he couldn't take the job. Private family matters made it impossible for him to leave Chicago. He thanked Jordan, wished him well, and the two old friends promised to keep in touch.

It marked the third time in a year that a potential Wizards coach had gently rebuffed him. Before hiring Leonard Hamilton, Jordan tried to land Mike Jarvis, the longtime coach of St. John's University, who said no after salary negotiations broke down. He called the University of Kansas coach Roy Williams, who had soared in stature since his days when he joked with Jordan and beat him at pool as a young assistant under Dean Smith. The two men casually talked about Jordan's daunting task in Washington. Williams said sympathetically, Looks like you have a *really* big challenge there.

So does that mean you're not going to be my coach? Jordan asked lightly.

His words sounded, said someone who knew of the conversation, like they were meant to feel out his listener, inviting Williams to take the subject of coaching the Wizards seriously or treat Jordan's line like a joke. A surprised Williams laughed, but he did not bite. He said he liked things at Kansas.

Only then had Jordan hired Leonard Hamilton, passing over one of his failed Bulls coaches, Doug Collins, a former NBA All-Star player whose two head-coaching stints had ended in disappointment. Now a year later, Jordan took another look at Collins, who had been fired after three seasons in Chicago, and dismissed midway into his third season in Detroit. Collins's pattern and that of his teams had been similar in the two cities: swift improvement, talk that his tutelage had improved the play of a key youngster or two, heady playoff appearances, early playoff exits, a stalling of progress, and then signs of trouble between the coach and his players.

Trouble with a coach can be concealed in the NBA only so long as a team keeps climbing and the coach enjoys, in turn, the leverage coming to any Svengali. When the climb stops, the players' grievances flow like lava. It did not help Collins, in Chicago or Detroit, that he had irked key club officials. As setbacks mounted on the court, word spread that his players were alienated by Collins's emotional swings and criticisms, leaving management in both cities to conclude that he had lost the capacity to lead the teams any higher. In 1989, Chicago owner Jerry Reinsdorf dismissed him by saying that he didn't believe Collins could "take the team from point B to C," after which Jordan privately told an old friend that he never again would play for a coach so emotional.

As badly as Collins's Chicago days ended, his Detroit episode was worse. After waiting six years for another coaching chance, Collins inherited an underperforming team and transformed it by his second season, the Pistons winning 54 of 82 regular season games in a league where 50 victories marked a team as strong, sometimes superb. The victories triggered Collins's oversized emotions. He talked of loving players. He hugged players. He got dewy-eyed. He beat Chicago and Jordan in a nationally televised game, after which he began crying on the court, emotionally spent, as if he had just won the biggest game of his life.

A Detroit official came over to congratulate him, hoping to find words that would encourage Collins to put this single game in proper perspective: "Doug, enjoy it. It's a *moment.*" An expressionless Jordan glanced at Collins, then walked toward the Pistons' bench and found John Bach, formerly an assistant coach in Chicago and now back with Collins in Detroit. "Tell Douggie, 'Good game,'" Jordan said to Bach. "But tell him that next time, I'm really gonna give him something to cry about."

The Pistons became one of the NBA's best stories. With Collins presiding from the bench, and Grant Hill, Joe Dumars and Allan Houston starring on court, the club looked to be on the verge of entering the NBA's top echelon of contenders. But a fragile alliance existed between the coach and his squad. His demands and style wore on them. He sometimes shamed players in front of their teammates. At a team meeting during a tough stretch, a player cried out in hopes of inspiring his teammates, "We gotta play defense," to which Collins asked, "Does that include *you?*"

The peace could last only as long as they soared. Then, as swiftly as the Pistons had become contenders, they collapsed. By mid-season in

1997–1998, even the goal of making the playoffs, once a virtual certainty, looked unlikely. The team lost more than it won by then, and Pistons officials had begun worrying about Collins. He looked gaunt. It was the result, they thought, of stress, inadequate sleep, too many Diet Cokes and all his hours spent on a stationary bike.

Strung so tightly, he left those around him guessing about which Collins they would find from day to day. A Pistons staff member often arrived early on mornings to see Collins already there, peddling furiously on his bike, trying to work off his frustrations from the latest loss, confessing to barely having slept, worrying aloud about the players' feelings. Key Pistons had turned on him. One moment during a game seemed to say everything about his problems. An uncontested Joe Dumars had begun slowly dribbling the ball up the court and toward the mid-court line, looking to set up a play, when Collins shouted at him, *"Joe, get it over the line."* Dumars looked back at Collins, remembered a former Pistons official at courtside, "like he was nuts."

The coach had lost Dumars's loyalty by then, and Grant Hill's, too—a painful development on several levels for the coach, not least because Collins yearned for players to be close to him. In his worst moments, he was a walking grudge, suffused with self-pity. He heard reports of Jordan expressing "love" for Phil Jackson, and said longingly that he wished his players felt that way about him. The coach needed love too much, thought the former Pistons official.

That need conflicted with his autocratic style. He did not show much interest in input from players or even some of his assistant coaches, leading to conflicts in particular with proud stars who had ideas of their own. His basketball knowledge, everyone around him agreed, was prodigious. No coach in the league appeared more skilled during a time-out at diagramming plays that led to great shots for his stars. "If we could have called a time-out every minute, we might have won every game," recalled the former official.

But that same colleague urged him to permit his angry players a measure of individuality on the court. Having watched him halt practices to lecture individual players about a single mistake, he suggested to Collins that perhaps he needed to back off once in a while. Sometimes less was more, he said gently, adding that the best coaches seemed to say something quickly and then step away. An ear toward his players' concerns might help, too, suggested the official, who then spoke directly: "Doug, you can't be dictatorial or stubborn."

Collins replied that he didn't want to hear it.

Then came more losses, to be followed by more of Collins's emotional storms. The official saw so much pain in Collins's expression
that he began to fear the coach's misery might take down the entire
team. Others within the organization shared his view. Not much later,
only 45 games into his third season, the Pistons fired Collins.

He went into coach's exile, doing basketball commentary again for
a television network. But no NBA team beat down a door over the next
few seasons to woo him, and it seemed, just as likely as not, that his
days as a professional head coach had passed.

Then Jordan called him. Remembering their Bulls days together,
Jordan decided to opt for a known commodity he could command over
a wild card who might exert an unwanted authority. He had controlled
Collins during most of their time together in Chicago, enjoying the
power to pressure Collins into doing whatever he wanted done on a
court. Jordan told anyone who asked now that he thought Collins's
past coaching stints had revealed his ability to motivate and improve
young players. Jordan had made up his mind: Collins was his guy. Jordan offered him the job and a four-year, $20 million deal without con-
sulting Abe Pollin.

It was done. Not having worked in the NBA for three years, Collins
now owed his basketball life to Jordan.

His gratitude and their history together made Collins both an ideal
and dangerous choice to look after Jordan's comeback—ideal, in that a
confident Jordan believed he could work with Collins, and dangerous,
in that a confident Jordan believed he could steer Collins. Jordan
immediately became the shadow boss, free to make the decisions that
mattered most, at a cost in time to his own body and the respect of his
teammates for their volatile coach.

With Collins chosen, Jordan now only had one major decision left.
As the NBA draft approached, his big board bore more names than ever
of coveted college and high school players. But he hadn't seen many of
the players in person. He had a far less intimate and detailed understanding of players' strengths and weaknesses than many of his managerial counterparts in the NBA. Spain's Pau Gasol, to be drafted by
Memphis and quickly become a frontline player in the league, received
no serious consideration from the Wizards. Other notables fell off the
Wizards' screen. For Jordan and the Wizards, the best player for the
moment appeared to be a 6'11" high school center and power forward,
out of Glynn Academy in Georgia, named Kwame Brown, who, at 19,
had been named to all of the high school all-American teams that mat-

tered. He had glittering statistics—averaging 20 points, 13 rebounds and about six blocks a game in his senior year. Having collected 17 points and seven rebounds against other major high school talent in the McDonald's All American Game, he looked to the Wizards brass like the prize of the draft, someone with the potential to be groomed over a few years into becoming the next NBA phenom, a Jermaine O'Neal or Kevin Garnett.

A second player who caught their eye was another big high school man-child, Tyson Chandler. Jordan approved a suggestion that the Wizards bring both prospects into Washington, to be privately worked out together. They would perform the same drills and, finally, play a one-on-one game against each other. Jordan and the rest of the brass figured the workout would give them the best chance to study the players' skills and competitive fire in a pressure setting.

Brown wowed them in Washington. A smiling Chandler had amiably stuck out his hand for a shake before the one-on-one game, but a grim Brown responded by doing nothing more than grabbing the rival's hand and letting go, ready not to make a friend but to go to war. He destroyed Chandler in front of the private audience of Wizards officials. "Maybe that one workout impressed Michael and the rest of us too much," one of the officials said later.

With his dominant workout, Brown solidified his hold on the Wizards' imaginations. On the eve of the draft, Jordan and the other Wizards officials contemplated whether to try dealing their number one pick for All-Star forward Shareef Abdur-Rahim, who would soon end up in Atlanta. The imagined deal carried the Wizards' vision of making the team into an immediate playoff contender. But, in the end, the Wizards brass believed the cost of the deal to be too high and that, more important, Brown possessed the potential, as Jordan privately put it, to develop into one of the league's true stars. Maybe he wouldn't be a star immediately, Jordan cautioned. But the kid can *contribute* something this season.

Another official told Jordan that the Chicago Bulls might be interested in dealing young talented forward Elton Brand. Jordan didn't care. He wanted Brown, he said. The issue was closed.

That week, Kwame Brown became the first high school player ever selected with the first overall pick in the NBA draft. Jordan viewed it, along with his unloading of Juwan Howard, as a high point of his executive tenure.

In early 2001, as winter's sleet moved toward his spring's hopes, Jordan spent fewer days than ever in Washington, having made his great escape. He worked out seriously in Chicago, the comeback unacknowledged but in full flight, with Jordan and his personal trainer Tim Grover arranging for private games at Grover's gymnasium, Hoops the Gym, where Jordan first tested his skills against a contingent of mostly former college players now working in the Chicago area. Almost immediately, he exhibited the stiffness and pains of an overweight man who had not exerted himself in three years. The famous knees swelled during the first days of the private games in March. One of the scrimmages' participants, a former Harvard basketball captain, Arne Duncan, by then the CEO of the Chicago Public Schools System, saw ice bags around both Jordan knees at the end of contests, which Duncan and other players simply viewed as a consequence of normal basketball stresses.

The bags became fixtures. Grover was not yet worried, buoyed by Jordan's conditioning workouts before the private games, watching most of his excess pounds melt off, confident that Jordan was on schedule to play in NBA games by the opening of the Wizards' preseason, still more than a half year away. His game seemed largely intact, even when hindered in these early stages by a lack of leg power that limited his lift on jump shots. One afternoon, a Chicago business executive named John Rogers, a former Princeton basketball captain, enjoyed the thrilling sensation of leaping with the legend and getting his hand on Jordan's shot. "I was thinking to myself," Rogers later recalled, "I'm about to *stuff* Michael Jordan." Only then, with Rogers's hand on the ball, Jordan's strong arms continued rising and managed somehow to get off the jumper, which went in.

As much as he enjoyed scoring against Ivy League foils, Jordan knew he could not gauge what he had left without pitting himself against a tougher class of opposition. So, as the NBA regular season and later the league's playoffs concluded, he brought in new waves of players, a mix of friends, old protégés and former rivals who wanted this test as much as Jordan. Fresh from the Boston Celtics, his longtime friend Antoine Walker arrived, soon to be joined by Phoenix's Penny Hardaway, once thought to be among many possible Jordan successors when he starred at Orlando and outplayed Jordan in a playoff series that followed Jordan's return from his baseball sabbatical. Charles Barkley, retired and a good 50 pounds overweight, dropped in. So did a Jordan protégé, the Dallas Mavericks' talented Michael Finley, and an old Jordan rival and fellow North Carolina alum, Jerry Stackhouse, fresh from the playoffs with Detroit. Jordan's former on-court body-guard with the Bulls and off-court running buddy, Charles Oakley, showed up, as well as some current Bulls, including big forward Marcus Fizer. Another retired former teammate, Bill Wennington, played a game. Tyson Chandler, not so far off his thumping from Kwame Brown and headed to the Bulls' training camp, said he wanted in, as did a young, talented Wizards hopeful, shooting guard Courtney Alexander.

Then there was a young 6' 7" boulder named Ron Artest, a swift Bulls shooting guard with the determination and ferocity of a middle linebacker. Jordan loved his intensity, wished he had 12 Wizards with Artest's fight. With the arrival of Artest and the other NBA regulars, hard training began in earnest. Some days, particularly when he had the touch on his jump shots—the fadeaways especially—he dominated his millionaire practice opponents. On other afternoons, they schooled him, beating him downcourt, dunking over him, once in a while steal-ing his dribble. Wennington told a reporter that Jordan didn't seem to move as well. Charles Barkley eventually weighed in against his play-ing again, and, from 2,000 miles away, Kareem Abdul-Jabbar sounded no less pessimistic.

But, on balance, Jordan expressed satisfaction. He could feel it com-ing back, he told Grover, who had paced his workouts prudently, build-ing strength without overtaxing him. Aside from an occasional back spasm or some soreness in a knee that left him limping once in a while, everything appeared good, the comeback on course. Remarkably for a man coming from a three-year layoff, he seemed to be holding his own against men 10, 15 years younger, his fitness steadily improving.

Then, in an instant, he was hurt: two ribs broken by an elbow from Ron Artest during a summer game.

He needed at least four weeks to mend, four weeks during which he sat idle, four weeks in which nearly all the training he had done to that point went for naught—after which he maniacally rushed back into his workouts and scrimmages, trying to make up for time lost. Driving at such a furious pace presented its own danger, realized Grover, who warned Jordan that to play so hard after weeks of inactivity—and three years of indulgence before that—would leave him susceptible to ten-dinitis.

Jordan ignored him. They had become more than boss and employee to each other in the 12 years since Jordan had hired Grover, who was more responsible than any other person for having trans-formed Jordan from skinny wunderkind to strapping hulk. They were friends close enough to argue, and the trainer had felt emboldened over the years to chastise Jordan for choosing to skip a workout that Grover thought he had no good reason to miss. A 5'9" former college basketball guard, Grover even sometimes dared to tell the boss how he should play defense against a rival star. "You don't tell me how to play this game," Jordan snapped once during his Bulls days, and Grover backed off. But Grover didn't back down often, and he wouldn't now. He found himself in the odd position of urging his friend, client and boss to slow down.

Jordan told him he didn't want to hear it.

His workouts brought a measure of his strength and wind back, but his knees became steadily worse, as he pushed himself hard and then too hard. Jordan became plagued by a case of tendinitis. Grover was concerned that the comeback wouldn't even make it out of Chicago, then became convinced that the calendar wouldn't permit it. He told a couple of reporters that, due to the conditioning lost while Jordan's ribs mended, he didn't think it likely that Jordan would be able to play that season. Much of the media took Grover's words to mean that the comeback now looked impossible, that perhaps Jordan himself had asked Grover to brace the basketball world for sour news.

It was the rare moment when Grover did not understand his boss. Jordan was not about to return now to that Washington office. It became common in the weeks and months ahead for sportswriters to echo Jordan's line that he came back simply for "the love of the game." He didn't. He didn't love the game so much that he hadn't left it twice already. He didn't love it so much that its pressure hadn't made him consider getting out of the game a full year before his first retirement, back in 1992, when he told Grover to get a baseball training program ready. In the end, his father and Phil Jackson persuaded him to pursue a third consecutive championship, the first of his fabled three-peats, but the need for such coaxing underscored his need for a break from the pressures. He was not as immune from stresses as he liked having the world believe, citing his mental exhaustion on his way out the door following the 1998 season.

That retirement announcement had revealed only a piece of the truth. He privately knew he could not play the following season even if he wanted to; he had so badly cut his right index finger while trimming a cigar that he and Grover realized that the finger would be useless while it went through months of healing and rehab. Besides, with Jackson leaving and a new coach coming in, he didn't want to be around. The game had used him up. *Mental exhaustion* described his condition precisely.

He had looked forward to an office and the executive life, with all its new stature and authority. He had chased it, only now to realize that it didn't compare to what he once had. He felt empty without games, and so his comeback was never so much a tale of longing as it was of loss, which is a very different thing.

It was the difference in his case between wanting something badly and, on the other hand, going back to it because nothing else in his life looked half as good. It was the difference between having a compass and feeling adrift. "It's hard for anything to be as good as playing for him," a sympathetic Grover had said.

It was loss he felt—but loss was a dirty word in the Jordan camp; loss carried with it the image of a void, of something desperate. Jordan and his publicity minions instead talked about his love—"love of the game"—which sounded cheerier, as if he were responding to a calling instead of fleeing the void of an office. Love invested his return with the patina of a vocation and only the slightest hint of an addiction— what he winningly called an itch that needed to be scratched.

He had committed himself to playing now, regardless that he couldn't see what was coming. From its first days, his comeback was like stepping outside at night and running in pitch-blackness, risky but absolutely thrilling, in the not-knowing, in the equal potential for magic and catastrophe.

Finally listening to Grover, Jordan relented and took it easy for a few days, the tendinitis in his knees easing a little. In late September, a simple press release announced that he would be returning as a player. On October 1, wearing a black and red sweat suit that had JORDAN stitched across the front, he appeared before the press in Washington, sounding nothing so much as mortal, by turns reflective, defensive, determined, amused, fiercely competitive and lastly uncertain, entertaining aloud the possibility of failure. "If I fall, I fall," he said.

Then he headed for his hometown of Wilmington, North Carolina, the site of the Wizards' training camp, where a game awaited him as soon as he wanted one. Grover had the only comment that really mattered: "Michael's happy again. He's where he wants to be."

3

The New World

ON THE DAY HE RECLAIMED HIS OLD LIFE AND TOUCHED DOWN in Wilmington, he went to shoot baskets for an hour. His left knee ached, not a searing pain, but a pain not going away either. The press did not yet know about the problem, and Michael Jordan's silence on the subject was a tacit order to the coaches to be quiet about it, too. But the knee reminded his entourage and club officials about the precariousness of athletic comebacks.

At an advanced age, the body stops forgiving. It is particularly indifferent to aged ex-athletes who have taken off three years, forgotten about jogging, carried on passionate affairs with French wines and Cuban cigars, and rushed back into competition. Any success they have thereafter tends to be short-lived and to feel like a Faustian bargain. A weird doom hovers. The athlete oscillates between the bliss of being in the dreamy past and the melancholy of his realization that he will be forced to leave it soon. It was Michael Jordan's mood from the first day he arrived at the Wizards' training site, on the campus of the University of North Carolina, Wilmington.

Always, he seemed to be trying to make peace with the fact that he was terminal. Training camp had brought him back to the game, but there, at 38, he had to take his place amid raucously carefree, younger men—Hamilton, Alexander, Lue, Nesby and White, among them— who had been elementary school tykes when he began his career, so young that they might play into the next decade. The youngest, Kwame Brown and Brendan Haywood, had been two years old and four years old, respectively, when Jordan played his first NBA game. They were reminders of just how little time he had left. "They're the youngsters, I can see that, and they're the future when I go back upstairs, which I know is soon," he said in camp, and paused, wrapping his mind around the idea, then nodding, not at a listener but at something happening inside his own head. His voice became a mumble. "I know that."

He realized by then that his return would amount only to a flicker—a year, maybe two at most—and that, like all other flickers, it would then go out. When he momentarily forgot this reality, his body sent him reminders. In the three years he'd been gone from the game and sedentary, parts of him had atrophied and stiffened, a process hastened as he slid from his middle 30s onto the doorstep of 40. His old Chicago team doctor, John Hefferon, thought that Jordan's long inactivity—"deconditioning," Hefferon called it—made him particularly vulnerable to tendinitis if he failed to pace his comeback carefully. Hefferon was prophetic. As Jordan pushed harder, the tendons and joints in his knees quickly inflamed. For a while his left knee was considerably worse, but then the right knee felt afire. Back in Chicago, Hefferon privately thought there was only one sure cure for hurting knees—reduced practice time, including a day off here and there. Tim Grover thought the same thing.

Fuck that, just get me the fuck ready, Jordan responded. For a while, a moderately paced conditioning plan seemed in place: He would practice once a day, skipping the team's second daily workout session. But, after receiving lengthy treatment for his left knee, he felt so good in the early days of practices that, on day three—Thursday, October 4, with his old college coach and mentor, Dean Smith, observing for much of the day—he decided to participate both in a strenuous morning session that included lengthy defensive drills and in the evening intrasquad scrimmage off-limits to the media. Toward the end of the scrimmage, he was in pain, grimacing, taking a seat on the end of a bench. A trainer taped grapefruit-sized ice bags around both his knees.

Reporters waited outside, most of them unaware that Jordan had experienced any problem, writing off his stiff shuffle to common preseason soreness. After their admission into the gym, with practice finished, Jordan leaned against bleachers and the media crowded around him, a scrum of about 30 reporters. "See a little ice there on ya tonight," a smiling Carolinian said good-naturedly, gesturing at the big drippy bags. "How are ya feelin'?"

Jordan smirked a little. He made any reporter who casually broached the subject of the ice sound naïve about the realities of the basketball grind. "Always ice 'em. I ice every night. Obviously."

But his knees were no better on day four. He played some point guard, where he could pass the ball from around the top of the key and minimize his movements, but still he hurt. Even before the end of the practice, the ice bags were on the knees again, so big and stuffed with translucent frozen chunks that when he shuffled around, it called to mind the image of an ailing Thoroughbred outfitted with protective sheathing on his hooves. He gingerly walked around a bench for the last few minutes of practice, limping. Finally, one of the assistant coaches blew a long whistle to signal a finish, and the press scrum, trained like Pavlovian dogs, rushed to encircle Jordan, panting, jostling for position. Cameras and boom microphones bumped his arms. Jordan coolly adjusted an ice bag and flexed a knee. The questions about the knees and ice had to come, but they did not.

"What's up, Mike?" somebody began.

He talked about subjects he liked—how he wanted to lead the team by example, and how he did not mind if Richard Hamilton and Courtney Alexander carried the Wizards, offensively, on some nights, and how he thought he might like to play point guard sometimes.

"Two more questions, guys," a Wizards public relations person chirped.

"How is your knee holding up, Michael?" a local radio reporter asked from the side of the scrum.

Jordan ignored the question. He did this without a trace of irritation. His head did not even tilt in acknowledgment of the man on the side, so it seemed possible that the question simply had not registered amid the scrum's screams. The man tried again, shouting over 20 others. This time a silent Jordan blinked and pursed his lips, stealing a look at the persistent man, filing away a memory of an irksome face. It was, in retrospect, a telling moment—one of only three times, over the next two years, when he altogether ignored or brushed off a vexing question.

Now, like a thunderous wave, a dozen other shouted questions drowned out the man. None asked about the ice bags, the shuffling, the obvious discomfort. Such deference typified most of the media's approach around Jordan, where a studied servility was the rule, and a phrase like "sucking up" did not do justice to the level of subservience at work. If the pack sensed, as it did now, that he did not want to touch a subject like his knees, then that subject was generally dropped, lest Jordan penalize the offending reporter thereafter by being curt with him. Jordan enjoyed nearly all the leverage in the relationship. He knew the secret; he had become a source for a few trusted journalists and, with a smile, implicitly dangled this chance for others so long as they pleased him. It naturally left the whole incestuous process compromised, resulting in columns and stories rife with omissions. Reporters' worries about access trumped their eagerness to scrutinize the idol. It was a restraint bred in them long before Wilmington, a deference that had become second nature.

So on this day, as the radio reporter shouted the question about his knees, a more accommodating reporter caught Jordan's ear by asking what he wanted to see in the way of effort from his new teammates.

He pulled on his little goatee, rubbed at his tiny mustache, smiled, nodded and looked the guy square in the eyes—that intimate gaze he trained on people whom he welcomed into the front of the pack. Good professional question, the nod said. You got it. Way to show your savvy. The real story here is whether my teammates will take my lead and you were perceptive enough to see it. "The effort?" he asked solicitously, just in case anyone hadn't heard, which was part of what made him so good doing this. He framed a question and then delivered his theme of the day. "Just showing the *love* they have for the game—especially the young kids. You can't get better than being the first one out of the locker room or being the last one on the court. I don't want to have to tell them that. It's something you *gotta love*. . . . When I see that, they gain my trust, obviously. I've seen guys stay after and work on their games. But then again I've seen that guys *haven't*. So, obviously, they get a little whisper in their ear. . . . We gotta spend time workin' on our individual talents, and that goes for everybody, really."

Another radio reporter had a habit of familiarly calling him "Mike," as if they were longtime buddies. The guy shouted the same question every day—"Hey, Mike, I asked you the same question last night: How do you feel?"—but, just the same, Jordan could do something with it. He laughed, mixing a snicker in there. "The same as I felt last night: Good."

"Thanks a lot, guys," said the Wizards p.r. person.

That first radio reporter on the scrum's edge tried a last time. "Michael, about your knees . . ." His voice trailed off. Jordan was gone, the horde following him.

Nearby stood an impassive Tim Grover, who, for the moment, had a goatee like his boss's. The two men seemed to coordinate their dress and appearance, if only subconsciously perhaps. If Jordan wore black, so did Grover usually. If Jordan was in a houndstooth jacket and donned a silver earring for his left lobe, chances were as good as not that Grover would walk into a room sporting the same look. The clothes led to a perception that Grover was the entourage's Mini-Me. But Grover was neither a yes-man nor a hanger-on, rather one of the few men around Jordan who dared on occasion to be a contrarian voice, risking Jordan's wrath.

Grover gently confronted him in Wilmington, after Jordan had played in four hard intrasquad games in five days. Seeing his boss's movements increasingly hampered, knowing that he was suffering from a worsening case of tendinitis, Grover tried to cajole Jordan into doing what in the old days constituted a training sin in the Grover book: Think of going easier, or not at all—at least for a few days.

The boss shook his head. Grover tried a final time, this time in starker terms, painting a picture of the possible calamity awaiting. *Just get me ready,* Jordan ordered him. *I'll be fine, whatever happens.*

The story of Jordan's persistent physical troubles began in that moment. Privately, Grover believed that Jordan was favoring the left knee, which, if true, meant his right knee already had begun to compensate by absorbing more stress, leaving it vulnerable to tendinitis, too—physiology's equivalent of the domino effect.

It was the comeback's first real crossroads—Jordan's last chance to attend to his knees' problems before they escalated into something chronic and season-threatening. Grover persisted. Jordan nonchalantly resisted. The unspoken question hung there between them: Do you ease off the pedal or risk derailing?

Jordan found the press that weekend and made a vow: "I'll be ready for the opening of the season."

And the derailment began.

Which left only one man who could protect him.

The person always best suited to save a player from his compulsions is that player's coach, a man with presumed stature, hopefully a little sagacity, and, generally speaking, unquestioned daily authority. But Doug Collins had only a title; he demanded nothing of Jordan that the star did not wish to do. He owed his job to Jordan, whose wishes were fiats, and whose knees would be forever young, if Jordan told Collins so. He did not want to sit now, and Collins would just have to accept it—as well as to tell the press that he and Jordan were on the same page. Collins never dared to contradict him. In Wilmington, as throughout the season to come, Collins nightly served as Jordan's Ron Ziegler—the star's spokesman, concealer and protector who'd fall on his sword for the boss if necessary. No observer could even suggest that Jordan had had a subpar practice or scrimmage without Collins launching into a vigorous defense, just the beginning of a year during which Collins would shoulder the blame for many of Jordan's off nights by explaining that his coaching shortcomings were the cause: He had failed, he'd tell the press, to get Jordan the ball in the right place, or to concoct an effective strategy for coping with a defense.

It was never pretty to watch—from the beginning in Wilmington, you felt yourself slowly watching the emasculation of a man. In private, Collins sometimes read his Bible—lessons and homilies reflecting his conviction that, in life and sports, there was a right way and a wrong way. His piety did not help him much as a coach, nor did the unflattering contrast between his deference to Jordan and his rough-hewn treatment of other Wizards. He talked much about his young players' responsibilities and shortcomings, but he dodged truths about Jordan's worsening condition while wearing a silver cross around his neck. He insisted he knew nothing about Jordan's tendinitis, which meant that he was either naïve and sadly out of the Jordan loop or guilty of misrepresenting his player's condition—there was no other option.

Much of the Wizards' season hinged on what Collins did and did not do in the next couple of weeks about the Jordan knees. In not handling the issue of the tendinitis early—either by delaying the start of Jordan's play or severely restricting his minutes on the court during the first month of games and practices—Collins ensured that his star's performance throughout much of that first season would be erratic, and that eventually the pain and loss of mobility would sideline him. Jordan soared whenever his pain slackened, but a bad wave of tendinitis untreated is like the migraine that sporadically returns: When it strikes, its victim is useless. Even in Wilmington, Jordan could be brilliant one night and reduced to a hobble the next. It was a prelude for the season.

During training camp, Collins encouraged the belief that the pain in basketball's most famous knees was merely a normal, temporary effect of the team's rigorous workout regimen. He laughed dismissively when anyone uttered the word "tendinitis." The questions about it were few, but they wore on him just the same. This was part of his nature, too. He had a virtually nonexistent frustration threshold for topics that defied the theme that he wanted the media to advance. I stood alongside him one evening as he shook his head in exasperation at a reporter who dared to broach the matter of Jordan's knees. He wore his silver cross over a white T-shirt and black vest, and fingered it like a talisman. "You guys, you guys," he sighed, shaking his head gravely. "You guys." This did not sound good.

"My man," he groaned. "My man" usually served as a prelude to Collins's most irritated responses. *"My man,* he was going twice a day there," he barked. "You don't think everyone gets a little tired? Michael's fine."

He put up his hand like a stop sign then. No more questions. Enough. But as long as Jordan wore those ice bags and shuffled, the problem would not be going away, and, increasingly, there would be reporters posing variations of the same question. The next day, he was asked whether he was being careful to protect Jordan against a possible tendinitis problem.

The red lights of a couple of recorders flicked on. Collins took his time, answering but not really. "Well, I think his second night here he was awesome, you know. And then he came back the next day, and he went through the whole morning practice and it was very intense, and he went through the whole evening practice, and it sort of set him back a little bit. So I said, 'Michael, you got to trust me that, ummmm . . .'" His words trailed off. Collins would not be amplifying on whatever Michael was supposed to have trusted him about. He fingered his cross. He looked around and raised his hand slightly, as if poised to put up the stop sign.

One day, Jordan and Collins were watching tape of a Wizards intrasquad scrimmage when Jordan observed, "I look like I was in slow motion." He appeared hampered on some days to Tim Grover. But in the days ahead, Collins did not waver from his insistence that all was well with Jordan. "Michael is on progress, he feels great," he said exuberantly to the scrum, on Wednesday, October 10, the eve of the Wizards' first preseason game, a matchup in Detroit, for which Pistons fans had bought every ticket in anticipation of Michaelmania, but a game that Jordan announced he would be skipping. Collins supported his decision, nonetheless assuring reporters that Jordan had no injury or pain. "It's not like there's any setback," he said casually. *"There's no tendinitis. . . .* He feels real good right now, so he wants to keep building, and I'm all for that."

Collins declared that Jordan would not be playing later that week in

Miami either, and that it was possible he might sit out another preseason game against Detroit the following week.

Jordan added: "Even in '96, '97 [with the Bulls], I didn't really play heavy minutes in exhibition games. . . . It was my call here."

But he was just fine, he said.

The questions and answers could have ended there, but there was a part of Jordan that never could walk away from an issue without at some point hinting at the truth and then engaging in a little tête-à-tête with an inquisitor—hinting at what was real before qualifying it or shading it or explaining it away altogether. In such a moment, like now, he slowly leaned toward the questioner and closed the space between the two of them, never menacingly, but making the exchange feel like a gentlemanly test of wits and virility: He would not back down from doubters, would not be sissified by anybody, ever. He'd face the pad-toting skeptics on their terms. It seemed just one more test he'd laid down for himself.

So he started talking about tendinitis.

He mentioned the summer injury to his ribs and how, he said, "it set me way back. [Before that,] everything was on key, you know, no problems in the tendinitis, nothin'. I was out eight weeks [recovering from the injury]. Then I tried to rush back, without going through my fitness and strength conditioning. My tendinitis flared up, and then that kind of put me behind the eight ball, and now I just got to be patient and make sure I'm going through the necessary steps . . ."

He indicated that he had tendinitis *then*—but not *now*. "I'm getting there," he said.

And then he prepared for a flight to Detroit, where, though he did not know it yet, he would need to play in the game, because David Stern said so.

Detroit and Miami had complained to Stern's office: They had been able to sell out their arenas for a pair of meaningless exhibition games only because ticket buyers expected to see the first games of Jordan's return—and now Jordan and Collins were going to stiff them?

Stern's top-ranking subordinate, Russ Granik, spoke to Collins, informing him that the league wanted Jordan to play. The two men were friendly acquaintances, and Granik observed that there appeared to be no reason why Jordan couldn't or shouldn't play.

It was time for Collins to speak up: *He's struggling with tendinitis. His knees are killing him on some nights, and we're only a week into this. He could play in Detroit and Miami and might even play well, but it could set him back further if we don't ease the swelling in those knees right now. Consider him injured. We want him healthy for the start of the season, but he might not be if we don't take care of him. You wouldn't ask any other ailing player to risk his season like this for a game that doesn't count for squat.*

Had Collins said this publicly, the result would almost certainly have been different. If Jordan had called Stern with news of his problem, and followed up by briefing the press, he likely would have spared himself a week's worth of exhibitions. No other NBA star afflicted with Jordan's pains would have been asked to play.

But Collins didn't make the case, and Jordan wouldn't make a call. Jordan would have to play.

"People hold Michael to a different standard," Collins grumbled, but his complaint entirely missed the point. Jordan had to play because Collins didn't or couldn't talk about his player's condition. How could Collins report to the league that Jordan suffered from tendinitis when Jordan denied he was hurting and, moreover, did not want Collins to suggest he had a problem?

The handling of the tendinitis quandary presaged a far more damning problem for the Wizards. Over the next two years, whenever an issue critical to the team's well-being arose, Jordan bent Collins to his will—whether it was over Jordan's playing time, or who among his teammates deserved to start or not start, or what type of offense or defense to deploy. Collins's lack of power illustrated the dangers in allowing any team's Zeus to rule over a coach and franchise.

When it came to Jordan's physical well-being, only one man refused to be subservient. His private warnings had gone unheeded, and now they spilled from him publicly. In the beautiful coastal town of Wilmington, where it seemed like nothing could go wrong, Tim Grover acknowledged Jordan's problem one evening while in a restaurant picking up food for the Jordan coterie. "We've worked through every challenge except the tendinitis; we know we have to deal with it," he said.

But Jordan continued resisting much of Grover's advice. He wouldn't take time off to rest, because resting would involve a tacit admission that he had a problem, and Jordan would never allow that. Jordan's instinct, thought his old Chicago doctor, John Hefferon, would always be to conceal. Early in his career, he had hidden the news of a broken facial bone from the press in Chicago, where he played through the slow healing without a protective mask and ordered that Hefferon and others in the Bulls organization say nothing, determined that the news of his injury not leak to opposing teams. He did not want rivals believing he was vulnerable and gaining even the slightest of psychological benefits. Now as then, opponents had to be braced to lose. Now as then, Jordan believed in his ability to conceal nearly any problem, on or off the basketball court. Secrecy was an ethic to him. He did not so much lie to others as deny to himself; it was Jordan believing that Jordan could overcome anything. So now that he knew he needed to play in Detroit, he had developed an upbeat line intended to let everyone know he would be coming to Motown armed. "I think we've had a good training camp," he said. "Good effort by everybody. . . . I feel very confident."

Jordan looked around. Off to the side, in sweat clothes, Kwame Brown stood alone, under a basket, trying to palm not one but two basketballs. The kid grinned and waved one ball in Jordan's direction, as if to say, Hi, hi, look over here.

Jordan never saw him, moving gingerly in the other direction with Grover, out the door.

Brown put the basketballs down and just stood there, watching.

To be the first high school player ever selected with the number one pick in the NBA draft meant that 19-year-old Kwame Brown arrived in Wilmington as the Wizards' baby deity, the player with the second most value on the team, right behind Jordan. In any other NBA training camp but for the Los Angeles Lakers', the media would have mobbed Brown daily, reported on his every doing. But the relentless focus on Jordan enabled the 19-year-old Brown to undergo most of training camp away from intense scrutiny, a lucky thing, as Brown was struggling in Wilmington—both on the court and in his relationships with the two most important Wizards, Jordan and Collins.

No one among the Wizards had expected him to perform like a star at the outset, or be skilled and savvy enough to start. The team's officials understood that, without exception to that point in the league's history, players drafted out of high school had struggled in their first couple of NBA seasons, including those who since had become marquee stars in the league—Tracy McGrady, Kobe Bryant, Kevin Garnett, Jermaine O'Neal. Typically, it took a year or longer for a teenager to develop a body strong enough to compete in the NBA, and even more time to acquire the finesse and signature power moves that tended to separate the survivors from mere street-ballers. While understanding that Brown likely would need an extended development period, Jordan and Wizards officials hoped that he would be a productive reserve in his first season, immediately rewarding their faith by displaying intense effort, concentration, discipline and glimpses of the kind of play that marked a 6' 11" future star. In short, they wanted to see an inkling of a future O'Neal or Garnett.

None of that seemed to be happening in Wilmington. It was scary for some Wizards officials to see just how befuddled and often listless Brown appeared to be. The second-guessing over Jordan's choice of Brown began almost immediately. Swiftly, Brown became a case study in the risks of angering Jordan, a man famously intolerant of slackers and mediocrities.

When Brown arrived at training camp in October out of shape after spending part of the summer recovering from back spasms and an illness, Jordan had been patient for about a week, draping his arm around Brown and praising his ability to Wizards officials. For Brown, it seemed nothing had changed. In October, he appeared to be the only Wizards player who enjoyed a real friendship with Jordan, which had begun during the Wizards' courtship of him prior to the 2001 NBA draft. For a while in Wilmington, Jordan simultaneously played the roles of buddy, mentor and Professor Henry Higgins to Brown's Eliza Doolittle. He lectured Kwame on clothes and nutrition, took him to dinner and asked him if he felt like hanging out with him in the trainer's room. He wanted Brown to see the brilliance of the life that awaited him if he worked hard and succeeded. One day after practice, having noticed Kwame palming yet another basketball in solitary amusement, Jordan palmed two balls, extending his arms and shouting to Brown: "Hey, Kwame, you know what the difference is between you doing this and me doing this?" Brown looked stumped. Jordan laughed and yelled, "They pay me thirty-five million when I do it."

It was as if, in Brown, Jordan saw the possibility of a kinship with a future star so luminous as to be deserving of a bond with him. "When he got to camp, it was like Kwame already had the credentials in Michael's eyes to be a part of Michael's group," said a Wizards official who observed them daily. "So Michael let him in. For a while at least."

Jordan's infatuation with his protégé waned. He thought Brown was cocky and disrespectful sometimes, particularly when the teenager nagged him about playing a one-on-one game, hinting that doom awaited him. Finally, Jordan agreed to the game, Brown grinning on the court, convinced his youth and height would be indefensible weapons against this shorter man twice his age. Early in the game, believing he had a lunging, jabbing Jordan off balance, the kid dared to say, "You reach, I'll teach."

Jordan snapped, "You teach and I'll knock you on your goddamn ass."

He proceeded to humiliate Brown, mocking him while scoring at will, declining to help him up when the teenager fell hard to the floor, winning lopsidedly and, at the end, yelling at Brown to acknowledge his superiority in front of the team: "You better call me 'Daddy,' motherfucker."

"Michael was breaking him down," one observer recounted, "probably to build him up. But there was a lot of breaking down."

Things deteriorated quickly thereafter. Brown didn't work hard enough for Jordan's taste, and it did not help that many in the Wizards organization, from officials to teammates, thought that the kid showed no capacity for either accepting criticism or honoring an old basketball tenet that said rookies should play hard, accept bruises and complain about nothing.

With the criticism mounting and his play getting worse, Brown became maddeningly frustrated, a kid convinced he was being repeatedly fouled in intrasquad scrimmages by two veterans, Christian Laettner and Jahidi White, who weren't quick enough, Brown believed, to stay with him. He would drive toward the basket and feel himself being bumped by a hard hip, sometimes losing the ball, infuriated that the referees wouldn't blow a whistle. "*That* was a foul," he finally groaned.

Play stopped. There was an electric silence. A wide-eyed Jordan was walking toward him. "You fucking flaming faggot," Jordan exploded. "You don't get a foul call on a goddamn little touch foul, you fucking faggot. You don't bring that faggoty shit here. Get your goddamn ass back on the floor and play. I don't want to hear that fucking shit out of you again. Get your ass back and play, you faggot."

A stupefied Brown could say nothing. He looked close to tears, thought a witness.

"It was not a mortal wound," the same Wizards official said. But the man believed that Jordan's words left Brown numb for several days thereafter, observing that Brown appeared to be increasingly tentative on the court.

For as long as Jordan would remain in his life, Brown would be diplomatic. Even so, some memories he had difficulty holding back. "It was pretty rough," Brown recalled later of the scrimmage. "But that's Michael Jordan. You deal with it. You learn you're a rookie and you're not going to get calls. . . . But sometimes I felt all alone out there, like I was surrounded by sharks."

Famously hard in the past on many of his Bulls teammates, Jordan saw his approach in the Wizards camp as part of the toughening process for rookies and others who had not yet learned how to win in the NBA. He liked testing people, even when it ran the risk of temporarily breaking their spirit, certain that the strong would become better for it, and that the intimidated were unworthy anyway. He rode Tyronn Lue hard for not passing him the ball in his favorite place down low near the basket and for not being positioned at the right spots to take Jordan's passes and shoot long jumpers: "What are you doin' runnin' around? Get me the ball, get set, catch my pass and shoot. *I don't give a shit how far out you are.* Shoot out there. If you're open, don't be drivin' down in the lane and gettin' that shit swatted away. *Shoot.*"

He would be flabbergasted watching Brendan Haywood drop balls, and scornful when Courtney Alexander and Richard Hamilton got burned on defense or didn't fill the proper lane on a fast break. But he saved his most withering looks and words for Brown, with whom he didn't seem to know what he wanted to do, lavishing attention on the kid in one moment, skewering him the next. Freely admitting to having had his ass kicked on many days, Brown had taken refuge in his video games. He loved these solitary contests, his head bent with a concentration so complete that teammates calling to him sometimes couldn't get his attention. Jordan sporadically continued trying to play the role of mentor. It was not something that came to him naturally. He regularly approached Brown in locker rooms, whispering to him, earnestly patting his back for a couple of seconds. But they were separated by a full generation, and nothing linked them other than basketball and their passion for games. One afternoon after a practice, Brown rushed up to him, having heard that Jordan played poker and tonk with other players.

Can I play with you guys? Brown asked.

You want to play cards? Jordan sounded at once dubious and intrigued.

Yeah.

Jordan chuckled. You'll bring your money? he asked, making clear the rules: People have to bring their money. No owing. Gotta bring your money.

Okay.

We can do that, rook'. Just make sure to bring your money.

Assistant coach John Bach interrupted, warning Brown: "Kwame, there're some things you don't do in life. You don't eat at a place called

'Mom's,' you don't play poker with a guy named 'Doc,' and you don't play cards with Michael Jordan."

Jordan groaned at Bach. "Why did you have to say *that?*"

Others observed Brown happily playing with Jordan a couple of times, but no card game could be a substitute for a real relationship. Theirs was suffering new strains all the time. As Brown's on-court performance and practice habits continued to lag behind other players', Jordan and Collins began losing what was left of their patience. There would be no good cop–bad cop arrangement between them, no one from whom Brown could count on receiving a little sympathy after the other had eviscerated him.

Collins began sharing his misgivings about Brown with the media. Not many businesses permit their supervisors to publicly bad-mouth and sometimes humiliate their workers. But in professional sports, and the NBA especially, coaches and the media have a mutual interest in seeing a few players embarrassed. Media receives something to gab and write about; coaches get to vent. Good and bad coaches alike tell reporters who on their teams shoots too much, or who is out of shape, or too emotional, or not emotional enough, or not seeming to grasp the offense, or slacking on defense, or who—in the most damning criticism—*looks totally lost out there.* Coaches use the media as a conduit for turning up the heat on underproducing players, and Collins was using the training camp to put the flame under a 19-year-old. "I *begged* him this summer to understand what kind of condition you have to be in to play at this level," he said, sounding alarmed, and no coach was more talented at sounding alarmed than Collins. He invested *begged* with the force of a parent who said he'd *begged* his child not to drink and drive. He made *begged* sound like a mournful plea, the last fruitless attempt of a caring and beleaguered elder, adding, "And he came in *woefully out of shape.* And he's trying to catch up at the wrong time."

Collins's approach toward Brown was confusing and contradictory. He would say something stinging about Brown early in a week, and later, as if trying to put a salve on his criticism, comment that he "loved" Brown and that the teenager was doing everything asked of him. He'd call Kwame over, in front of the media, and say he had a video for him to watch. "Kwame's been great, he's been great," Collins said during week two. "He's working hard. I couldn't ask anything more from him. He's got a *great* spirit and attitude . . ."

Soon, Collins was publicly perturbed again: Brown, he said, was seven pounds overweight; the young man was *stubborn;* he didn't listen well; his conditioning was still subpar. "He's in great shape," Collins said sarcastically, "to play a high school game."

It was an early look at the erratic style that had plagued Collins elsewhere. Less than a month into his NBA career, Brown found himself in the surreal position of having to deny that he had a problem with his 50-year-old coach. Jordan was ill-suited for mending things. "These young kids should take it upon themselves to prove that they deserve to be in a winning program," he said, pursing his lips as if pained, "because they haven't thus far."

Kwame was his potential nightmare. Kwame might be his *Ishtar*. Kwame, he knew, might be the only thing people remembered of his executive days, if they weren't all careful. Why couldn't the kid handle the ball? he asked people in his entourage. Was it just his imagination, he asked, or did Kwame's hands look *small?* What the hell was happening?

Jordan tried to stay upbeat, but he wafted doubt. Where was Kwame's head right now? somebody asked him.

"Kansas, somewhere," he answered.

Hearing laughter, he tried to soften that. "A kid, nineteen years old, getting a dose of what NBA basketball is all about: I imagine his head is spinning. But he has to be willing to make the commitment. . . . He's walking around with a headache, I'm pretty sure . . ." He posed a rhetorical question. "Could [Kwame be showing] resistance? Could be. Could be."

Meanwhile, the young man with the headache had spent the training camp and preseason perfecting his look of serenity. No matter how bad it got, Brown told others, it would get better. He had been a poor Georgia kid just six months earlier and now he was a multimillionaire and this was much better, he thought. I bumped into him by accident late one afternoon. He stood smiling just outside the gymnasium in Wilmington, saying things were going okay and that he tried not to read much in the papers about himself or anything else. Didn't want to know what people were saying about *anything.* Just wanted to relax at night when he was done. Relax, play his video games, be left alone. Alone. Not needing to know anything more than what they'd stuffed in his head that day. Alone. A nice peaceful feeling.

And you could do that, Kwame Brown said. "That's the good thing. You can really be alone in your room if you want and people can't get to you. Just rest. Get ready for the next practice. Not having to think about anything else. You can like tune out. That's a good feeling. Nobody can get to you. Nothin'."

Even with all his on-court hassles, he liked it, the life, he said. He was an affable young guy, engaging to be around and at that moment delighted to see a big collared German shepherd crossing the path in front of us, being led by a policeman. *"Damn,* that's a *big* dog," he said happily. "Why do people bring a dog to a gym?"

They're here to do a search, I said. It's just precautionary.

He looked at me.

Search the place for bombs, I said. Before your intrasquad game. Just routine. Precautionary.

His mouth opened into an oval, a big O. His face went slack with surprise. Not shock or worry, but surprise just the same, that big puzzlement that comes when you've thought all along that something can't touch you and then you get an inkling that somebody else thinks it can. He'd heard a lot about the thing, as he called it. The thing in New York, the thing in Washington. Terrible thing. He was puzzled that anybody thought that the thing might ever get this close. Nothing but basketball ever got this close. "Big dog," he mumbled.

The dog was already sniffing at stuff.

"They really gonna look for bombs?"

He stared, his mouth wet and open, a kid's mouth.

They looked for bombs.

Never when I was in Wilmington for the 2001 training camp did I hear Michael Jordan or any other Wizards player mention September 11. It wasn't that the subject was too sacred to broach in a place of games, or that the Wizards were indifferent to the horror or ignorant about the magnitude of the terrorist attacks that had occurred only a month earlier (a fair number were TV addicts and, day and night, TV showed live pictures of the still smoldering Pentagon and the tomb that was the World Trade Center). It was that the players lived in a tube, and unless one spends a season inside or on the edge of the tube, it is impossible to know just how insulating it is, how nothing else but the game counts after a while. What matters in the tube is limited to basketball and practice times and the media cattle calls where, among other important matters, the press asks the players twice a day whether they're going to make the playoffs ("Time is short, right? You need to make it before Michael leaves, right?"), until this begins sounding like a national imperative. What matters is the latest trade and who around the league punked whom. What matters is the second practice that day, and somebody shouting he needs ice bags for his knees like Mike, and three more guys asking for ice, and soon the whole locker room looking like an ice house, young bodies growing old in a hurry.

It is a world apart. There is no thought of Afghanistan in the tube. There is no Osama Bin Laden. There are no Middle East conflagrations, no suicide bombers. There are no bad Washington schools or even fawning season ticket holders to bother the players, no lines ever to stand in. What they need, somebody will get for them. Just play. Play, get on the bus, get on the plane, move to the next city, play again.

The police dogs sniffed the whole gymnasium, everything from bathrooms to trash cans to seat covers, and then the local police went back over the bleachers and thrashed through the trash cans some more. Only then did the ushers admit a crowd of locals and college students who watched the intrasquad scrimmage for which Abe Pollin had flown down—Abe Pollin who, not living in the tube and having just come from Washington, was absorbed by 9/11, full of thoughts on what he hoped Jordan's presence might mean to Washington and the country in the aftermath of the nightmare. He proudly talked about a special scrimmage that the Wizards would be staging back home in MCI Center for Washington-area firefighters and police officers involved in rescue efforts at the Pentagon on 9/11, noting how special it would be for the heroes to be able to watch Michael Jordan in a command performance. He envisioned Jordan buoying spirits nightly, in his packed arena. "The terrorist attacks have been such a tragedy, but I think the fact that Michael has come back is giving the folks sort of a lift," he said. "I think having something positive with all the negatives is a good thing."

That was the Wizards line, the NBA line and David Stern's line. Stern associated Jordan's comeback with the soothing power of a welcomed diversion, observing, "Our fans look to us to provide some sense of normalcy."

Normalcy, perhaps, except that Americans were nothing close to normal, riveted by death, transfixed by a jagged mountain of broken concrete. It was strange to return in the Wilmington evenings to a hotel room and discover that prime-time television commentators— once part of the faithful legion of Jordanphiles—had no time for the idol. Aside from cable sports stations, TV seldom talked about his comeback. The networks were unmoved by athletes for the time being. Even Barry Bonds, who broke the majors' single-season home-run record on Friday, October 5, was eclipsed by the national trauma—no hero for now, rather viewed, in the new perspective, as simply a con-

summate athlete. America seemed to be rethinking what merited adoration. "Daring" and "courageous": Such adjectives suddenly seemed
absurd when attached to millionaire ballplayers. "Daring" described
that intelligence officer doing reconnaissance on the Taliban in Kabul.
"Courageous" was meant for that cop who had craned his head up
toward an inferno of jet fuel in a building ready to tumble, then rushed
into the burning tower anyway. The theme began finding a voice in the
public, sparking questions that professional sports usually avoided:
Had America associated athletic prowess with heroism for so long that
it could no longer recognize the real thing?

The self-serving hoopla of sports suddenly felt silly and out of proportion. America launched air strikes in Afghanistan on an October
Sunday morning, the news reports of it preempting National Football
League games. A New York telephone operator talked on CNN of
receiving a call from a man under the rubble at Ground Zero. A woman
spoke of a brief, casual conversation she had with her fireman-husband
before he went off on his last day.

At some point, if only out of sheer randomness, the horror had to
intersect with athletics. So it was that about 100 New York Giants football season ticket holders died in the World Trade Center. And 25 days
after his son Brian lost his life on the 97th floor of the Trade Center's
North Tower, Lee Jones, a former NBA referee and now the league's
supervisor of officials, briefed the Wizards coaches in Wilmington on
rules changes for the upcoming season.

While young men flew missions over Afghanistan and the National
Guard patrolled tunnels, bridges and train stations in New York City,
Michael Jordan joined the Washington Wizards in another practice.
Suddenly, for many sports fans, his return felt oddly irrelevant. His singular focus on the game, a quality that once spoke wholly of his commitment to winning and training, now seemed to some to border on a
middle-aged man's self-absorption.

The world to which Michael Jordan had returned was a different
place. It had been enough for him once simply to be a relentlessly
hardworking, charismatic, law-abiding demigod, especially in the '90s,
when the most pressing matters on Americans' minds were the O. J.
Simpson murder trial and the saga of Bill Clinton and Monica Lewin-
sky. He was the welcomed athlete who did not kick cameramen in the
groin or get arrested. It was a low bar to jump over.

But, after September 11, 2001, he was unmistakably diminished as
a cultural symbol. During his training camp and preseason, the only

viable sporting metaphor in the country became the team that New Yorkers most identified with for the time being, the Yankees, who had begun another playoff run.

Traditionally, the Yankees are the team that America loves to hate, the symbol of imperious, crushing victory, about as warm as a military junta. But for a while, the most thrilling sound in sports became that of a post-game Yankee Stadium crowd, 56,000 strong, singing hoarsely "New York, New York," in unison with a recorded Frank Sinatra—"It's up to you, New York, *New York* . . ." It was a sound more stirring than the crack of any bat or any basketball rippling a net, so moving it could leave a man, hundreds of miles away, feeling a chill in his hotel room.

Such a feeling Jordan could no longer tap, if he ever had. His commercial importance outside of basketball arenas had waned, said a host of marketing analysts. He continued to have an immense audience, but now, no longer a mesmerizing force, he was simply a venerable attraction. His hold on imaginations had loosened, at the same time his body was betraying him.

But he was still Jordan, and so still a symbol of something colossal and American to the rest of the world. That alone was reason for concern about his safety and that of anyone around him. At The Palace, located in the Detroit suburb of Auburn Hills, the director of arena security, Timothy Smith, had been preoccupied for weeks by Jordan's appearance. Jordan's first NBA basketball game in three years, he knew, would take place on the one-month anniversary of the terrorists' attacks. The entire sports world would be watching. Could a wanna-be terrorist ever have a larger audience or a better-known target? he wondered. Michael Jordan, he knew, was more than a man; he was the personification of American wealth and glamour. A corporate icon, he was more American than Mickey Mouse.

You had to prepare for the worst, Smith said.

In the past, he always had employed extra security when Jordan came to town, but now he meticulously prepared for a myriad of new, more terrifying contingencies. He was trained to view remote chances as real chances. A paved, steeply sloping ramp led down to The Palace's loading dock and garage—the very entrance through which Jordan and the other Wizards would be arriving on their team bus first for the game-day morning shootaround and later for the game itself—and Smith, whose job it was to envision *everything*, could envision the possibility of terrorists sending a truck-bomb hurtling down the slope.

On the morning of the game, in a pattern he hoped wasn't obvious,

Smith arranged for parked trucks and SUVs to be staggered near and along the ramp, a barrier that he hoped would discourage anyone with a bad idea, and at the very least prevent an explosives-packed vehicle from gathering momentum down the slope. Bomb-sniffing dogs checked out the arena. Extra security personnel were slotted for positions behind both team benches and Jordan in particular. More personnel would be patrolling the farthest reaches of the arena. Everybody, including press and team personnel, would go through detectors.

Smith shrugged, smiled: He had a sharp eye for detail and a good security man's stoic ease. "Think we've done what we need to, everything we can," he said at about 9:45 a.m., and his eyes darted, taking in faces.

We stood on the garage's smooth gray concrete, just beyond the bottom of the ramp and the entrance to the loading dock. The Wizards would be arriving in a few minutes. Security personnel furtively eyed pads, recorders, cameras. "Hey, check that guy out, will you?" Smith shouted to a guard, and a check was made for a press credential.

And then, without warning, the gate opened and there it was, the bus, and off it stepped Jordan, wearing a floppy little black golf hat and sweats and dark sunglasses and his silver headphones. Seventy journalists jostled with one another for position, cursing, yelling, glaring, shouting threats to other guys. There was something manic and crazed about it, and the security people, like skittish horses, bucked and shouldered some people back. Jordan walked a few yards, stopped in a tunnel between the locker rooms and the court, slid his silver headphones off his ears and took a place in front of a banner with the Pistons logo.

The howling began. Jordan couldn't hear nine-tenths of the questions. Somebody was asking whether the league had pressured him to play. "I didn't know the expectations of the fans . . ." he said. "But once I got the response of people in terms of tickets and whatever, I felt compelled to play. I didn't want to disappoint anybody."

Was he nervous? "No, no . . . I'm gonna play the game. Whatever happens, happens. I don't think anyone can take anything away from what I've done over the years in Chicago. . . . At the end of the day, it's still my life and I still have to do whatever I enjoy doing, which is to play basketball."

"Gotta go, guys," said the Wizards p.r. man, and they were gone, Jordan off to shoot with his teammates for a half hour behind a black curtain, and then ride the bus with the team back to the Townsend Hotel, where he rested for two hours.

Ride the bus, shoot, ride the bus back to the hotel, rest, ride the bus to the arena, play: the rhythms of his old life. His, again. The moment was here. And the knees still hurt.

The Wizards arrived at the arena shortly before 6:00 p.m. Jordan entered the small cramped visitors' locker room, licked his lips and looked around.

He sat on a stool while a dozen strangers stared at him. An NBA locker room is, by rules, a sanctioned peep show before a game, open for 45 minutes to anyone with the right pass. The strangers waited for him to change into the Wizards traveling blue and black trunks and jersey, which lay on a stool next to him. When this happened, it would be regarded as the instant of his passage from the Chicago Bulls, the moment of no return. It would be a piece of hot pricey film for the TV cameramen present.

Jordan was not going to give it to them.

He wanted this transition to happen in private, so he gazed clear through people with a stare he perfected two decades ago. He sat there on the stool in a black silk T-shirt and sunglasses whose light-sensitive lavender lenses were turning charcoal, his eyes dark and occluded. Then his bass voice punctured the silence, admonishing a cameraman: "Man, no pictures."

Some guy just walked up to the stool, looked down at him, holding a microphone. "Do you want to say something to people in Spain?"

Jordan looked up. "No. I don't do interviews before the game."

The guy backed up. Everything was quiet for the next five minutes.

Then somebody must have twitched. A stocky security guy barked, "Hey, get that camera away—he doesn't want any filming."

"Can't I get a shot of him putting on the jersey?" The cameraman talked as if Jordan couldn't hear, like his subject was sitting in a sound-proof booth, like he wasn't just five feet away. "Just one shot of him? *Just one?*"

"No. Not sayin' it again."

Everybody was quiet.

"Six-twenty," somebody shouted from outside.

Jordan looked down at the floor, looked up. "Spain, huh? What part of Spain?"

The Spaniard said something. Jordan didn't seem to hear. He looked at the floor again and stroked his chin, where he had trimmed that goatee short. People walked in and out of the room—a few reporters, a small knot of Jordan friends. No one said a word. Tyrone Nesby walked by, wearing a black headband. An ignored Christian Laettner was getting dressed.

Finally, Jordan fingered the Wizards trunks and jersey. "It's not the Bulls," he murmured, faintly wistful. Then, as if hearing his own voice, he quickly added, "But it's not bad."

He stroked the trunks' fabric some more, looking for a different tone, and then he found it, something more upbeat into which he injected a small snort—part laugh, part curt assessment. "It's an improvement," he said, meaning the design of the uniform over some old Wizards model. He rubbed the fabric against a silver bracelet on his wrist. "Not bad—okay."

He put the trunks down and gestured with a finger. Now an old friend was allowed to approach, a brief audience. Jordan's talk was about anything except basketball.

"You know, I shot three-under not long ago," he said.

"Come on," the man muttered, snickering.

Come on is not something Jordan appreciated. Skepticism pushed his buttons. He lifted his charcoal lenses to set his eyes on the guy. "Man, I shot *three-under*. I played so good I was afraid to go back out." He softly laughed. He took a slow breath, resumed looking at the floor.

A couple of journalists entered the room, men who'd written flattering things about him since he was young in Chicago. The relationship between the NBA and reporters is usually a symbiotic one. But around Jordan, power flowed one way. Reporters were sharecroppers: They tilled him only at his pleasure, and in this moment, preoccupied by what awaited him outside, he had nothing to say. The two men left. *Sports Illustrated*'s Rick Reilly, who had predicted his comeback amid much disdain, sidled up, patted his arm and said, "I didn't get any apology letters."

"Don't expect any either," Jordan said, unwilling to give Reilly a morsel tonight either. "You ought to know that."

"Ready?" Tim Grover asked over his shoulder.

"Move back, move back," the security man barked at a TV guy.

Jordan's tongue darted unconsciously, not the long tongue of a million game posters, but a tiny snakelike tongue. In, out, in, out.

"No pictures," the security man bellowed.

Jordan got up from the little stool and took a seat a few feet away on a training table. A Wizards trainer rolled up his trousers and applied a translucent film of gel to his knees; its smell, like Ben-Gay, filled the locker room. Jordan, sniffing, leaned his head back. No one talked. Grover's gaze did not leave Jordan's face, as if he was measuring his boss's reactions behind the charcoal lenses.

It was a reminder, if anyone needed another, of how everything hinged on knees aching badly. The trainer wielded a foot-long black cylindrical instrument that had a silver-dollar-sized disc on its tip, and the ultrasound treatment began, the trainer rubbing the knees with the patch, making a circular motion, like a man with an electric sander. The hope was that, in stimulating increased blood flow and oxygen to the knees' injured areas, the ultrasound would expedite healing. But no one really knew how effective or worthless the treatment might be.

"Hmmmm," Jordan mumbled, eyes closed. "Hmmmm."

No one else said anything for the next 10 minutes.

At last the trainer rolled down his cuffs and Jordan stood, breaking the quiet. "Gettin' the feelin', feelin' it now, feelin' it," he said, mock serious, hearing the laughs he wanted. He took off his sunglasses and smirked, rolling big brown eyes at the scene—the hyper-rumpled strangers, the cameras, the hysteria. "It's been three years," he observed sideways to a friend, "but nothin's much changed. Nothin'."

"Feelin' it," he yelled, laughing, and then went off alone to put his uniform on in a side room, alone meaning only he will know what it looked and felt like when his transformation was complete. "Feelin' it," he shouted from behind a wall.

At 7:19 p.m., he emerged in his new uniform and a pair of Air Jordans with mustard trim, adjusting a black support sleeve around his left knee. He left the locker room and took his place in the hallway among the other Wizards, in a loosely formed huddle. A half-dozen security guards stood close. "What are we lookin' for?" he demanded of his teammates.

Richard Hamilton quizzically stared at Courtney Alexander and a couple of other guys. When no one responded quickly enough for Jordan, he shouted, *"Respect."*

Nods, a little mumbling. Right. Respect.

He tried again. "What do we *want?*"

"Respect," they yelled.

Jordan nodded. "Yeah." He looked around. Grover gave his right shoulder a last pat. And Jordan led everybody out.

The first jolt of apprehension came before the game even had begun. A woman walked onto the arena floor, strolled over to Jordan, pulled out a cell phone and shouted into it: "I'm standing next to Michael Jordan."

An alarmed Grover wheeled, not knowing who the hell she was or what she might do next. He shouted at others to remove her. Bodyguard Larry Wooten wedged himself between an unruffled Jordan and the woman, who turned out to be simply the evening's overenthusiastic Anthem singer, bragging on the phone to her boyfriend. Jittery, nearly everybody felt jittery. Tim Smith had five security guards sitting close to Jordan whenever he came to the bench, and Grover, Wooten and George Koehler, Jordan's longtime driver and now in charge of his security, kept an eye on the crowd.

Jordan kept flexing his left knee. After 40 months away, at 7:43 p.m. Eastern time, amid a couple of thousand camera flashes, his career resumed. He did not play badly; he did not play great; somewhere in between, like a mortal, like a 38-year-old man a full step slower. The other nine players on the floor at any time were so incidental that it felt less like a game than performance art, a one-man show helped along by the stage presence of a few antagonists. These others seemed mindful of the script in the opening minutes. The first shot of the game came from the Pistons' young talented big man, Ben Wallace, an easy layup, except that Jordan came out of nowhere to block it, The Palace delirious: *Jordan putting the hurt on Big Ben.* Grover leaped. The boss missed his opening shot, a long-distance three-point try, but he scored the game's first points on his next trip down the court when, in a move that would become his style against younger, stronger, higher-leaping defenders, he pump-faked to get the Pistons' Corliss Williamson to leap. As Williamson fell to earth, Jordan ascended, connecting on a 17-foot jump shot. Then he signaled to his teammates that he wanted the right side of the court cleared out for him. He posted up Williamson, caught a pass, leaned his strong back and trunk against the younger man, backed him down a foot, then leaped and fell away from the hoop, lofting a jumper from 13 feet. Swish. The Palace was a din.

Only, the moment could not last. A minute and a half later, Williamson beat Jordan on a cut to the basket, grabbed a pass and scored himself. Wallace impudently swatted away his only real drive to the basket. Then came the play that spoke most powerfully about how much had changed. Moving without the ball around a screen, he lost Williamson with a bit of trickery and darted to the basket. Courtney Alexander threw a pass toward the rim, and there it was, the moment, the chance for the frenzied 20,000 to see Jordan catch the ball on his way up, up, and throw down a dunk or, even better, what he liked to call the "beautiful tomahawk dunk." He took a last step and was aloft. The crowd screamed, expectantly. The ball was waiting for him, suspended just above the iron, and one watched for the elongated arm to pluck it and do what it always had done. But Jordan could no longer reach it. In the air below, he waited a nanosecond for it to descend to his hands at rim level. There would be no no dunk at all. He simply let go of the ball over the rim, gently depositing it in the basket the way a man might drop a garment into a clothes hamper. The crowd softly groaned. And some of the air went out of The Palace.

It was a jarring night. With about three minutes left in the first quarter, the officials briefly interrupted the game. The crowd looked toward the big TV screen overhanging mid-court. Tom Brokaw intoned, "Here in the Red Room is the president of the United States . . ." and George Bush provided an update of the military campaign in Afghanistan.

The crowd was rapt in a way it seldom gets for politicians. Jordan—who had given away his $1 million salary that year to the relief effort for families of September 11's victims—sat on the bench, alternately looking at the court and down at the floor, sometimes studying the back of his hand. It was not a sign of disrespect but merely one more indication of something decidedly apolitical and task-oriented about him: He was a man, now as in his beginning, almost solely about games.

Meanwhile, the Pistons looked him over, formulating silent judgments about his game—some kind to him, others not. He was on his way to respectable numbers that night—hitting four of eight shots, for eight points, in 17 minutes—but Detroit reserve guard Jon Barry thought his reactions looked slower than in the past. How could they *not be* at 38? he asked. Barry thought that Jordan had become the most unthinkable of things—vulnerable. "[Rival players] are going to take it to him," Barry said. "Going to try to *take* the throne. There's going to be no mercy. There's never mercy in this game, but there's especially not going to be any for him. He showed none. He was the king in exile, and now he's back and they want payback and want what he has. And until they take it, they can't have it, so they're going to take it to him."

He talked some smack to Jordan on this night, seeing this as his own payback after Jordan, he thought, had shown little regard for his offensive skills by largely leaving him unguarded on the court. He howled at Jordan after making a long jumper: "Hey, you don't respect me." In the past off-season, when Barry had been a free agent interested in playing in Washington, Jordan had dismissed the possibility of signing him, Barry said, by telling him that he didn't need any slow white guys. It was just *a line,* Barry said to himself, intended by Jordan to be *funny,* and it was a little funny, and so there were no hard feelings there, though neither, it seemed, had Barry forgotten that Jordan thought him to be a tad slow. The league was full of Jon Barrys, guys wanting to prove Jordan wrong about something, guys wanting to let him know what losing felt like. Barry was a swirl of conflicted feelings when it came to Jordan. "I just don't see how he can be *that* Jordan," he declared matter-of-factly, a remark certain to get back to Jordan within hours, infuriating him.

Almost to a man, the Pistons were weary of Michaelmania. Detroit's star guard, Jerry Stackhouse, had spent much of the day casually saying, without edge, that he wasn't focusing on Jordan, that Jordan was "playing cat and mouse" about his conditioning, that he had no concerns about Jordan. A fellow North Carolina alumnus, Stackhouse had been a rival of Jordan for years, almost from the time he stepped off campus as a looming star taking his place with the Philadelphia 76ers, another candidate in a long line of aspirants thought to have a chance to reach Jordan's heights. Of course, Jordan needed to check him out, to measure the younger man's game against his own, out of public sight. Early in Stackhouse's career, he beat Jordan in a summertime one-on-one game whose outcome, rumor had it, Stackhouse mentioned to a few people. Jordan exacted revenge by scoring 48 points against him in their next meeting, a Bulls trouncing of the Sixers, leaving hard feelings for a while on both sides. The years since had been up and down for Stackhouse, who had starred only briefly in Philadelphia before his play slipped and a trade sent him to Detroit. He had been an All-Star in Motown, but Jordan's return to an Eastern Conference team now made another All-Star selection unlikely, unless he had a spectacular season.

Stackhouse seemed torn over Jordan. They had repaired whatever rift might have been there, with Stackhouse helping Jordan get in shape over the summer by flying to Chicago and participating in his private scrimmages at Grover's gym. But like Vince Carter, another star North Carolina player, Stackhouse had learned about the limits of Jordan's affection: Jordan wanted no one, particularly no North Carolinian, to get the best of him ever. People talked all the time, he said privately, of the need to be loyal to Michael. But how about Michael being thoughtful to everybody else? Stackhouse seemed to tire of singing Michael's praises, and today was one of those days. "We have no concern about Washington or what Michael Jordan is doing," he said. "We're more focused on what we're trying to do. . . . It doesn't matter if he comes out and is playing well or if he comes out and he's struggling . . ."

But Stackhouse thought that if he shined against Jordan, it would help him. It was what every talented player around the league thought, he guessed. "I know some people think Michael coming back is gonna take attention from young guys," he observed, "but I see it as a way to get attention, too. If you play well against him, that's gonna change things. I've played against him a lot. . . . If you don't go for his fakes, you can defend pretty effectively."

Stackhouse did not have a reputation as a great defender. But no one needed to motivate him to play defense against Jordan. When play resumed and he found himself briefly matched on Jordan, he bullied him. Jordan badly missed a fallaway over Stackhouse's long left arm. Stackhouse felt good. Maybe Jordan's return would actually have the unanticipated effect of highlighting the play of young guys, he thought. You'd have to beat him before the change happened, he thought. "We play them a lot," he said. "I'm looking forward to it."

Aside from their few feverish minutes, Jordan stayed away from Stackhouse most of the night, and the Wizards trailed throughout, with most of the offense coming from sleek 6' 7" Rip Hamilton. During time-outs, Jordan gave the young guard pointers on how best to fake defenders in the air. He was avuncular with his teammates on this night. Before leading the team out onto the floor for the second half, he tried to gather everybody around him again in the hallway, looking for Hamilton: "Everybody out of the locker room? Where's Rip?" Waiting on Hamilton, he turned to the young rookie center from North Carolina, Brendan Haywood, pumping him up, dispensing praise. "Hey, *come on.* Hey, you already have a *dunk.* You ready? *Come on.*"

But Stackhouse and the Pistons couldn't be contained on this night. Detroit won 95–85, with most of Stackhouse's 30 points coming at the expense of Hamilton, who, while scoring 19 points, had been outmuscled and outfought on defense all night, raising the concerns of Jordan and Collins.

As for Jordan, Collins hadn't expected him to play more than eight minutes. But, characteristically, once caught up in competition, Jordan had stayed out on the court longer than prudent, logging 17 minutes, thwarting any attempt to give his knees a rest.

Afterward, much of the 300-member press contingent opined he looked old and markedly slower. Words like "foolhardy" filled the air.

"Let's give him four or five more weeks, to get himself where he wants to be," Collins said cheerfully.

"I'm on schedule," Jordan said ebulliently, back in his lavender sunglasses and wearing a houndstooth jacket that matched Grover's. "I was surprised how *intensified* I was."

He sat next to Grover on the plane ride down to Miami, never moving from the back of the plane, where the rest of his retinue—Koehler and the bodyguard Larry Wooten—gathered. His teammates rode up front. A few Wizards hoped to get to know him better, but he was as enigmatic to them as to everyone else. Down in Miami, Tyrone Nesby had not gotten over the scene in Detroit, trying to imagine what Jordan must have felt. "It was wild there, *wild*," Nesby said. "So what did Mike say about it? Mike don't be talkin' much, you know, not about things like that. It's just ball with Mike. He'd be helping you with ball, you know. When it's about other things, you go to Mike and maybe ask, but he don't want to talk about it maybe. What he think about Detroit, man?"

No one knew what he thought.

In Miami, that Saturday night, Jordan sat on a folding chair in front of his locker, sockless, wearing Carolina-blue shower slippers, but otherwise with his uniform already on and another ice bag on his left knee. Grover sat alongside him, in the next stall over. No teammate approached, but a smiling man with a tape recorder came up to him speaking a torrent of Spanish.

"No hablo español," Jordan said.

The man kept talking. This kind of thing was not very unusual. It was as though a fair number of foreign-speaking visitors and journalists assumed he had powers like those of the visitant in the film *Starman,* who arrived on Earth knowing greetings in 54 languages and dialects.

The smiling man pleasantly raised his recorder.

"No interviews before the game," Jordan said, dropping his head, and the man, finally understanding, backed away.

A smiling Nesby walked by on the other side of the locker room, wearing a black do-rag wrapped around his head. "Hey, Mike," he called out, as if he might walk over.

Jordan looked up at Nesby, nodded and looked down. He turned back to Grover, the two men's heads bowed. People understood: This was Grover's spot. On the road, Grover or Koehler used the stall adjoining Jordan's whenever the boss wanted it. Teammates just had to understand.

Nesby stopped, reversed direction.

Jordan did not yet know what to make of Nesby, or the rest of his teammates, really. For all their raw physical talent, some of the players were stunningly green, while others, even the most promising, appeared to have major holes in their games. At that moment, they sauntered in and out of the locker room, young men laughing. The best player among them was 23-year-old Richard Hamilton, nicknamed Rip, beginning his third season in the NBA, after leading the University of Connecticut to the 1999 NCAA championship, scoring 27 points in the title game victory over Duke and being chosen the Final Four's Most Outstanding Player.

Like nearly all the era's best young players, Hamilton had left college early as a baby-faced All-American, selected by the Wizards in the first round of the 1999 NBA draft, with the seventh pick overall. In the 2000–2001 season, playing both as a guard and a small forward, he had averaged 18 points a game, but that number tended to obscure his real offensive prowess after he became a full-time starter in the season's second half and the club traded away the shooting-minded Juwan Howard. He scored 30 points or more in eight games over the last two months of the season and, at home, bombed Detroit for 40 points and Golden State for 41. He was slender verging on skinny, long-armed, long-legged, and shockingly quick, the fastest of all the Wizards, so speedy that no one could ever remember him being caught from behind. He blew by defenders and, with his reed-like frame, could slither between foes and contort his body in the air to score on awkward-looking, improbable shots. If turned loose, he could get a dozen points a night on fast-break baskets alone and possessed a better than average three-point shot. But his best weapon was his pull-up jumper from anywhere between 12 and 16 feet. Many hard-eyed observers, including Collins, thought he might already possess the best mid-range jumper in the league, a move that required speed against tough defenders, a nimble ability to stop abruptly and elevate, a balance in midair that would allow the shooter to be perfectly vertical and steady and, finally, an ineffable touch that couldn't be taught.

A great NBA mid-range jumper was a gift—an amalgam of silvery quickness and a shooting stroke born of superb coordination—and

Hamilton was gifted. He knew it, as virtually all the best ones knew it of themselves in the NBA; no one arrived there by being self-effacing. He had been a star everywhere he played, and parts of his wardrobe trumpeted the places where he had left his mark. He sometimes wore his old Connecticut sweats to Wizards practices. Leaving evening games, he often donned a long platinum chain at the bottom of which hung large block letters, *CV*—which stood for the Pennsylvania town of Coatesville, for whose high school he had been a schoolboy hero and a McDonald's All-American.

Never having failed anywhere, he could not imagine falling short now. His precocious rise made him like dozens of young NBA players who viewed it as a near inevitability that they would swiftly acquire NBA starting jobs and, soon afterward, become leaders of their teams, a go-to guy, the Man. The starting job had come; but leadership would have to wait, given Jordan's arrival. Hamilton worked hard in training camp to please Jordan, listening patiently in Wilmington when Jordan told him where and how best to cut down into a lane or run around a screen being set against him, deferring to Jordan in scrimmages when, late in a close contest, Jordan indicated that *he* wanted the ball for a shot or that *he* wanted to inbound the ball, that *he* wanted to take control—that it was time to win now. Hamilton obeyed.

Jordan had been toying with phrases to describe their working relationship, referring to himself as Tonto to Hamilton's Lone Ranger, a way to illustrate Jordan's premise that he had returned to the court only as a supporting player. But no one on the Wizards was naïve enough to believe that Jordan would be satisfied with being anything less than the hub of the offense. Hamilton told people that he could wait. He was only in season three, playing with a god, and he well understood his role for now, diplomatically acknowledging this so frequently that in time his various explanations and reasoning had melded together in one fast-talking rush: "We want to learn from Mike, 'cause he gives us a great chance to win and make the playoffs. It's an honor to be playing with the greatest player of all time. And we're gonna learn from him because we know it's gonna help us, because we know we're the future of the team."

Hamilton often found a way to drop that last line in there, a reminder to listeners and teammates that the status quo certainly could not last forever, and likely not beyond two years. Then it would be his time. And maybe Kwame's, too, or Courtney Alexander's. He sometimes referred to himself and the other young players as "the New

Jacks," a phrase borrowed not only from the film *New Jack City,* where it connoted young pride and power taken, but from other young ballplayers who used it to assert their own expectations and style. Hamilton did not favor Jordan's shaved head or impeccable suits, preferring cornrows and chains and the look of a hip-hop artist on occasion, as did a host of young players, from Allen Iverson to Hamilton's teammates Tyronn Lue and Tyrone Nesby. The younger Wizards were "coming," Hamilton liked to say. He believed not only that he was a future leader of the team but that he was a player who could immediately fill up a basket. "I've proven, I think, with last year, that I can score in this league," he said.

No one on the Wizards staff doubted that. Still, his game troubled them. For all his speed, he was a disappointing defensive player, they thought. Too many opponents exploited his frailness, pushing him around, muscling him out on drives and post-up jumpers, sending him sprawling with screens and hard elbows. His upper legs weren't big and strong enough, which hindered his ability, they believed, to sustain a proper defensive stance, to move and spring from a bent-knee position low to the floor. They wondered if he had stopped seeing the urgency in being a tough defender. Collins made it clear to Hamilton that he wouldn't be able to rely on his scoring to compensate for poor defense. "One thing I've tried to establish is, If they're going to play only one end of the court," Collins declared, "then they're going to come over [to the bench] and watch for a while."

Worst of all, the coaches worried that Hamilton's body might in time restrict him offensively. They had noticed defenders disrupting his balance by merely bumping him, sometimes making it difficult for Hamilton to sustain his dribble and convert drives to the basket. If the problem wasn't corrected soon, word about it would make its way around the league, and more foes would try to knock Hamilton off his dribble. He had to build his body, and the coaches and Jordan pushed to get him into the Wizards' weight room. Hamilton did not say no, but neither did he spend much time there. "You have to chain Rip to get him into a weight room for long," said one assistant coach. "It's just not his place. He's pretty headstrong that way. He sees himself as a pure scorer."

At best, Hamilton was a work in progress, like 24-year-old Courtney Alexander, who had come as a rookie from Dallas early in 2001, as part of the Juwan Howard trade, another young player thought to represent the Wizards' future. Like Hamilton, he had enjoyed big offensive numbers in the 2000–2001 season's final two months, scoring 33 in the last game, and the club had shown its excitement in the 6'5" guard by hanging a banner bearing his image at the Jordan comeback press conference. There he was, as Alexander proudly noted later of his banner, flanking one side of the idol while an image of Hamilton flanked the other. "An honor," he said solemnly; he said nearly everything solemnly. Then he borrowed a Hamilton phrase. "We're the future of the team helping Michael; it is an honor. I know much is expected of me and Rip."

His past had been murkier than Hamilton's. He had begun his collegiate career at the University of Virginia, where he had started until being convicted for the assault of his then-girlfriend, with whom he had a child. Suspended from the team, he transferred to Fresno State, where he became an All-American, leading the nation in scoring his senior year, coveted for his beautiful-looking, generally uncontested jump shots. But his defense had to improve, Collins declared. And players had to be in shape to play defense, he warned. This did not bode well for Alexander, who had arrived at the camp out of shape, after suffering a summer virus.

Jordan privately raised a question: Alexander could jump, but couldn't he get a few rebounds? If Jordan suggested anything about underperforming players, chances were he would soon get around to letting them know. Alexander wasn't intense enough, thought the coaches, who concluded that even his touted offense looked spotty in Wilmington. Collins thought a great leaper ought to be driving to the basket more and utilizing his physical advantages over smaller or less athletic guards, getting easy shots and drawing fouls. Instead Alexander remained a jump shooter, only now a jump shooter discovering that, unlike in his heady days at Fresno State, he could no longer shoot at will over defenses. Quick NBA defenders, including his teammates, anticipated his moves and got hands in his face as he rose. He couldn't seem to find his shot, and on the other end of the floor, he couldn't seem to guard anybody. Whether it was due to being set back by the virus, or his failure to get in top shape, or a refusal to fight, or a lack of talent, no one could be sure. Collins and Jordan soured on him quickly. With no place to turn, Alexander despaired and his performance further plummeted. It was a bad but familiar NBA spiral.

Alexander liked to hang with another 24-year-old, Tyronn Lue, the six-foot reserve point guard whom the Wizards had signed as a free agent during the off-season. Little known when he graduated from the

University of Nebraska, Lue had made a reputation during the 2001 playoffs as a Lakers reserve guard who so tenaciously guarded the league's Most Valuable Player, Allen Iverson, throughout the NBA Finals, that it looked like the two pugnacious little men might brawl on the court. His three years with the Lakers had provided him two championship rings and a reputation for backing down from no one. The Wizards coaches loved his intensity, convinced at the start of preseason that his Lakers stint had proven his ability to direct an offense, play ferocious defense and shoot the three-pointer, hopeful that he might prove himself worthy of a starting position during that season or next. But Lue's play at training camp had disappointed the coaches. "Ty Lue has gotta play better," Collins said. "He's a much better player than what he's played here. I told him, '*You played in the NBA Finals. You played on the brightest of stages and performed. You gotta play here.*' He's just sort of playing paralyzed."

Lue seemed totally out of sorts, for reasons entirely different from Alexander's. He arrived at camp, everyone agreed, in terrific shape, only to be befuddled by what Jordan wanted him to do. The commander told him that he was too far out front on the break and *too fast,* that he wanted Lue to slow it down, give up the ball sometimes and step back, to be ready for the pass and an outside shot. *You're in the wrong spot again,* Jordan barked at him. *You're too low. You're not getting me the ball in the right place.* So tentative had Lue become that he nearly stopped shooting altogether when teamed with Jordan. Collins thought the player looked worried. Lue's best trait now seemed a hindrance: He badly wanted to please people, and if he didn't, it shook his confidence terribly. He was, for all his toughness and determination, a sensitive young man. Collins went to him again and said, "Ty, when Shaq and Kobe kicked you the ball, you hit six of nine three-point shots in the Finals. You can't play like that ball is a hand grenade."

Lue said he understood. But nothing changed. Collins would get so upset about it that he'd scream in the middle of a play, and Lue would turn to see Collins's shoulders slumping in abject frustration. Lue wasn't nearly ready to play big minutes, decided the coaches, who agreed that the veteran Chris Whitney, an occasional starter in the past—unflashy, not particularly fast, but a reliable ball handler who understood the offense and had an excellent three-point shot—would be the starting point guard, with Lue to be groomed slowly.

At 30, Whitney never had been anybody's prodigy and so never had expectations beyond the present. He had graduated from Clemson eight years earlier as just another in a vast pool of 6'0" college point guards, and then experienced the heavens and hellholes of professional basketball, being waived after playing as a reserve during two seasons for San Antonio, toiling during the mid-'90s in the minor leagues, the Continental Basketball Association, with the Rapid City Thrillers and the Florida Beach Dogs, until he arrived in a Washington locker room with a 10-day contract during the 1995–1996 season.

He never left. This would be his seventh season as a Wizard, the longest stint of anyone on the club, during which he had been generally used as a backup. But no other Wizard had proven as adept a survivor as Whitney. His stability had ensured his safe place year after year. He could be counted upon to protect the ball most of the time, provide adequate defense, and know where to position himself for a three-point shot. He shot the three so well that he had a chance to break the club record for lifetime threes.

Whitney did not brim with fire, but he was a competent workman at ease with his place on the team, a stable personality never yearning for anyone's affection. In a locker room, he did not crave Jordan's attention like some of his teammates, usually quietly dressing or softly chatting with another player or two, well-liked, respected, smart and already looking ahead, at 30, to a life out of basketball. He had talked to his agent about not moving into coaching but perhaps being an elementary schoolteacher. His agent thought that yes, he could see that. The teaching profession would play to Whitney's best strengths—an amiable poise, and a capacity to show others how to learn and endure.

For now, Whitney would preside over a court, or at least for as long as Lue's game did not vastly improve. For insurance, Collins and Jordan also had brought 31-year-old Hubert Davis to training camp, still another player to come from Dallas in the Juwan Howard deal. A 6'5" shooting guard who starred at North Carolina a decade after Jordan, Davis had played for three other NBA teams. The consensus was that he had a fine outside shot and, like Whitney, a model attitude, but otherwise was a limited player. He had little quickness left and sometimes could be exploited on defense by younger guards, but Jordan and Collins knew he played hard whenever asked, believing his attitude would be an asset among younger players. Davis planned on becoming a minister, but he didn't proselytize. He worked tirelessly to improve himself, spending long hours alone working on his jump shot and three-pointer, which Jordan pointed out to the younger guys, while reminding people that Hubert was related to Jordan's boyhood hero, legendary North Carolina star Walter Davis. "A *nephew*," Jordan said, the way other people say *prince*, as if lineage counted for everything. To be a nephew of Walter Davis was akin to having the bloodline of Man O'War. Hubie Davis had a job.

That left just one last guard, powerful 6'7" Bobby Simmons, more a forward-guard swingman, who, at 21, had left DePaul a year early and whose status seemed uncertain. Jordan liked his speed and loved his toughness, which reminded him a little of Ron Artest's; Simmons was another big fearless kid who could put the hurt on people without even knowing. Jordan had picked him up in a deal with Seattle, and thought he might have an uncut jewel. Still, almost everything about Simmons's game seemed raw, so that no one could be sure if he would make the squad or find himself toiling in basketball's minor leagues.

Raw: that seemed to describe so much of the squad, starting with Kwame Brown and including 7'0" rookie Brendan Haywood, another North Carolina grad whom Jordan had gravitated to and acquired in a trade. About to turn 22, Haywood had a nice hook and an ability to block a shot on occasion, but he had come out of North Carolina with people believing that he had a weak inside game and, worse, played *soft*—a damning term in basketball parlance, suggestive of someone who lacked strength and/or toughness—a reputation that he had done little to dispel early in the preseason, with Collins and Jordan both demanding he rebound better and show he could get tough baskets.

It was about to get worse for Haywood: He would tear a ligament in a thumb and find himself in a cast for several weeks. Most of the team's big men found themselves being challenged to return from physical problems. Second-year power forward Etan Thomas, a strapping 6'9" shot-blocking machine at Syracuse, had missed his entire rookie year with a toe injury. Jahidi White, beginning his fourth year with the Wizards after being drafted out of Georgetown in 1998, had undergone knee surgery in 1999 and been on and off disabled lists.

White seemed in many ways to symbolize the old Wizards, a massively built 6'9" center who fought hard when physically able, but generally was frustrated by taller, quicker foes. The Wizards' public address system often played a parody of Cab Calloway's blues classic, "Minnie the Moocher," when White made a basket, to which fans could sing along: "*Ja-hidee-hidee-hi, Ja-hidee-hidee-hi . . . Ja-hidee-hidee-ho, Ja-hidee-hidee-ho . . .*" It had the unfortunate effect of making White, like his losing team, something of a cartoonish presence, evoking memories of

other endearing foils, like Marv Throneberry of the wonderfully awful
1962 New York Mets. Sportswriters and even Collins often referred to
White as simply "Ja-hidi-ho."

Fairly or not, White seemed to be part of what the new Wizards
wanted to forget. In the Howard trade, Jordan had obtained two big
men to whom he looked for a new consistency and savvy—Popeye
Jones and Christian Laettner. Unheralded when he graduated from little-known Murray State in 1992, Jones was as gritty a player as could be
found in the NBA. Four years before coming to the Wizards, he suffered
a complete tear of the anterior cruciate ligament in his left knee, underwent surgery, and made it all the way back. At a burly 6' 8", he inhaled
rebounds when healthy, having collected 28 on one night alone in
1996. But he was a 31-year-old who had gone through eight seasons of
NBA wars on a vulnerable knee. No one knew what Jones had left.

The same could be said of the 32-year-old Laettner, who had graduated from college at the same time as Jones but whose path to Washington could hardly have been more different. Laettner had left Duke
after being the star center on two of its NCAA championship squads
and receiving college Player of the Year honors in 1992, the same year
he collected a gold medal on the United States Olympic basketball
team. At 6' 11", he was the rare college big man who could pass with
aplomb and regularly connect on long jump shots, a legend in collegiate basketball precisely because he had made just such a jumper,
turning and letting it fly at the buzzer, in an epic NCAA tournament
victory against Kentucky.

He had been the third overall pick of the 1992 NBA draft, the same
position in which Jordan had been drafted eight years before. But that
was where all comparisons ended. Laettner's professional career had
been nothing short of a major disappointment. Some wondered how
far being a white man had carried him; for he had a reputation as a
"cerebral" player that tended to obscure the limits of his skills and lack
of growth as a player. He never had led a team anywhere close to a
championship, never averaged 20 points a game in any season, never
became a stellar defender or rebounder, never much improved his game.
He did not turn into Larry Bird and would never be confused with Dirk
Nowitzki, Dave DeBusschere or even Jack Sikma. He could not dribble
and drive to the basket, or make many jumpers with a defender in his
face, or show off a power move, or inspire his teams. He had a problem
with coaches, having gone through several, and now had a reputation
as something of an arrogant head case around the league, finding him-

self after nine seasons on his fifth team. His value having plummeted, he was, amazingly, merely a journeyman now. Teammates had stopped accepting any nastiness from him long ago. During his two years at Detroit, he had crossed swords once too often with Jerry Stackhouse, who had punched him out over a dispute in a card game.

Even the Wizards coaches couldn't be certain whether Laettner would be an asset or a liability. Collins, who had known him when Laettner was a senior at Duke and his own son was being recruited there, still appreciated his passing skills and outside shot, still liked the way he could read a court—an undervalued skill, he thought. But he wanted Laettner to rebound better and be more aggressive offensively. He tried challenging him: "You know, you come out of college as one of the greatest players there of all time. Your pro career has been up and down. This could be a great opportunity for you to leave your mark on a franchise. What have you got left? Four years?"

Collins understood the risk, admitting one evening that if Laettner didn't feel good, "he can be a coach's nightmare."

Throughout the preseason, Collins and Jordan projected an air of guarded optimism. They had a ragtag bunch—a loosely formed collection of talented but unproven kids, and veterans in their twilight, and a couple of guys given up on elsewhere, and one aging god, and a 6'6" man walking around the locker room in Miami at that moment with his cornrows completely covered by a black do-rag that made him look like a 21st-century pirate.

Tyrone Nesby appeared serene at this moment, a good thing. Several officials had questions about his temperament. It was thought he could go absolutely *off* if someone miscalculated around him. Off, as in *off the edge.* The impression largely stemmed from a single incident back in January of the previous season. Removed from a game, Nesby began loudly cursing at the Wizards' doomed coach Leonard Hamilton. Courtside fans gaped. Players tried to coax him to sit down. Hamilton and assistant coach John Bach told him to be quiet, but Nesby's tirade at Hamilton had just begun: "Motherfucker . . . Fuck you, motherfucker . . ."

Bach told him to shut up. Leonard Hamilton agreed to a suggestion to have Nesby ejected, calling upon arena security to escort him to the locker room. Nesby later apologized, promising never to misbehave again. But there were doubts about him, compounded by the fact that his life had messes: The previous season, he had been arrested in Indianapolis on an outstanding charge of failure to appear in court and pay child support he owed. At season's end, Nesby told friends that he would do everything possible to redeem himself in the eyes of management, Jordan especially. But he was still an excitable guy. Every now and then, when something went bad on a court, he would look up and begin cursing the air. His nickname was T-Nez but, behind his back, some people still referred to him as a psycho. At 25, Tyrone Nesby understood he was looking at his last chance with the Wizards.

He had made the most of his preseason. No one else at training camp worked harder to impress the new coaches and Jordan. Nesby arrived in camp 12 pounds lighter, his speed and superb conditioning evident from the first day, thought the coaches, who loved his ability to slash through the lane on offense and particularly his defense, which could be smothering. In Wilmington, he rebounded, he blocked shots, he did not call anybody motherfucker, he threw his body on the floor for loose balls, he set hard screens, he stole balls, he swooped down for dunks, he still had not called anybody motherfucker, he did extra work, he complained about nothing, he outplayed Courtney Alexander, he came back even harder in evening practice without once calling anybody a motherfucker, he harassed Rip Hamilton, he dunked on Jordan: He was a dervish. The only thing T-Nez couldn't do well, apparently, was shoot consistently from the outside. One assistant coach said that watching T-Nez fire long jump shots was like watching a blind man in a shooting gallery. But Collins loved what he had seen. Not only would Nesby make the team, but T-Nez, said Collins, ought to be rewarded with the occasional chance to be in the *starting lineup.*

Nesby was happy to the point where he got misty-eyed talking about it. He knew he would not be a frequent starter, but it was enough for him that he had succeeded in training camp and seemed to have a good chance of receiving respectable playing time. Walking around in his do-rag, he exuded gratitude. He wanted to do everything to keep this goodwill, to show the coaches and Jordan he would be forever cooperative, to prove himself deserving of everyone's faith.

Jordan would continue to be hard on him, he thought. Then again, he thought Jordan tested *everyone,* and that the test never ended. "I mean, it's hard playin' with Mike," he said. "Mike is one of them aggressive players, hate to lose, always talkin', always keepin' the players focused, and that's what we need: someone who's older, who's gonna continue to kick—" T-Nez stopped himself. The new T-Nez tried not to say any of those words unless they just happened to fly out on their own. ". . . *stand* on us. Make sure we keep our heads on straight."

T-Nez said he was cool with that.

Maybe life was a test, he said. He had grown up the last of 14 children in southern Illinois. He thought he was meant for tests. Besides, he liked the idea that maybe he'd be on a good team for once. He had played college ball for a decent team at UNLV, but then he found himself on pitiful NBA teams, like the Los Angeles Clippers. In having been traded from the Clips to the Wizards, he moved from basketball's equivalent of Sarajevo to Lebanon. Welcome to Hell East. "I ain't had the opportunity other guys had, to play with good teams," he said.

He knew he was a player on the bubble, not the most gifted, not the smoothest, so a player who needed to play hard every moment and make something happen. Jordan said as much to him one day, even mentioning something about dying, which T-Nez didn't quite know how to take. Jordan's advice had been this: "T, keep your gun loaded and go out shootin'. Die shootin'. Don't die with any of your bullets."

T-Nez liked a story with a gun. In Las Vegas, in the off-season, he did some real shooting with his guns. The only thing better than a story with a gun was a story with a gun and bullets. *Die shootin'. Don't have any of your bullets.* That's cool, decided T-Nez. He thought he understood Jordan's point. "Mike's sayin', Don't give him just eighty or seventy percent; he won't take that sh—" T-Nez stopped himself. Hell, reporters cussed more than he did now. ". . . that *thing* . . . He wants everything from you. That kind of motivated us. . . . He hate not seein' one hundred percent. That's the reason why he's got everything he's got. He's got a lot of stuff."

In the locker room, Nesby had taken off his black do-rag and his street clothes and put on his Wizards uniform and his black headband. He glanced at Jordan, who still had the ice bag on his left knee and was basically alone alongside his open stall, inside which his clothes neatly hung on hangers, a cream-colored suit tonight. It amazed Nez and other players how it seemed he never wore the same thing twice in six months. Mike knows how to dress, T-Nez said. Had the right things to wear every time. Suits. Shoes. And those tight Jockeys.

Tight Jockeys: That's what T-Nez called them. The Jockeys that kind of looked like bicycle pants on Mike. T-Nez chuckled, a kind of snicker-giggle, when he talked about the tight Jockeys. Once or twice, T-Nez and a couple of the other guys messed with him about the tight Jockeys: "Mike, why are those tight pants on you?"

Maybe, said T-Nez, you got to know Mike better if you joked with him. He couldn't tell if Mike liked the messing or not. But since Mike always messed with people, he thought this was probably okay. Especially because Mike knew how much T-Nez and everybody else respected him, T-Nez reasoned. Whatever advice Mike had for him, he would take it because no one knew more about basketball or the way to handle things than Mike. T-Nez admired everything about him—right down to the way he put himself together for games and after the games, always having the right colors and everything brand-new and stuff. Now he overheard Mike yelling something to somebody about his shoes, the Air Jordans. T-Nez loved the Jordans. He walked over and sat down on the closest stool, the one Grover had been sitting on. "Hey, Mike."

Jordan was surrounded by an Imelda Marcos–like pile of shoe boxes, all Nikes with his likeness on the instep. "Size thirteens?" Nesby asked.

Jordan looked at him. "Thirteen and a half, actually."

Nesby pointed at a pair with the same mustard-colored trim that Jordan wore in Detroit. "Those the mustards, Mike?" he asked. "I like 'em."

"You like 'em."

"Yeah."

"You sayin' you're gonna get some of these mustards, T-Nez?"

Something in Jordan's tone already had Nesby off balance. "Y'all talkin' about the shoes. Just sayin' I like 'em, like the mustards."

"The mustards are for a starter."

"What I'm just sayin'—"

"You gotta get sixth-man shoes."

Laughter from across the locker room.

Nesby tried coming back with a line of his own, but his words got tangled up. Against Jordan, nobody won those games anyway.

The laughter rolled.

Nesby went off to get ready.

Jordan donned his silver headphones to listen to a CD, and turned his attention toward a TV set, where a tape was running of a recent Miami game. Kwame walked by him. Jordan clasped the kid's arm, motioned for him to bend. When Kwame complied, Jordan whispered something in his ear and rubbed the top of his head. Kwame immediately lifted his head and straightened up, out of the stroking hand's reach. He did it without anger, but he did it: He didn't want his head rubbed. There would be more similarly awkward moments in the weeks ahead, as Brown began asserting a distance born of independence and frustration. He was not here to be somebody's prodigy in one moment and abused the next. If Jordan had hopes of forging a close bond, his task would be far more difficult now that he had called Kwame a faggot and threatened to knock him on his ass.

The older man had returned to a different game, one with a new breed of promising players, like Brown and Hamilton, accustomed to steadfast respect and sensitivity from the time they hit grade school. They had grown up in an age where others felt your pain if you had a sweet jump shot. None of that meshed with the approach of Jordan, who humbled, even baited, people until they earned his respect, who dispensed and withdrew affection, depending on a player's performance and attitude. In Chicago, he had regularly humiliated Horace Grant, but Jordan's admirers insisted Grant had improved under the whip and that Chicago's championships proved the worthiness of the idol's leadership style.

But Kwame's silence now suggested that Jordan's approach might have run the course of its effectiveness. Jordan wouldn't give in. He'd ridicule his teammates publicly if he thought it might make them better. On that very night, he would show a wave of fresh contempt for Kwame and the rest of the kids, telling the media that they hadn't demonstrated they even *deserved* to be in a winning program.

There was something drop-jaw outrageous about the next half hour. A man four months shy of his 39th birthday scored 18 points in the first quarter, playing in only his second game in three years. The press row underwent a collective conversion: Okay, so maybe this was possible. Miami ran three defenders at him—Rodney Buford, Ricky Davis, Kendall Gill—and Jordan made each look ridiculous, head-faking, pump-faking with his arms, eyebrow-faking, scoring on jumpers of all kinds, fadeaways, turnarounds, pull-ups, even an old-school floater. He rebounded, he stole the ball twice, he started talking to fans in the courtside seats. It was about the time when an old nemesis, Miami's coach Pat Riley—who had been at the helm of the Knicks in 1994, when Jordan came into Madison Square Garden during the first week of his first comeback and dropped 55 points on the patsies—started groaning. Riley yelled at him: "This is not gonna be another New York, is it?"

Jordan laughed. "No, I'm not gonna play that many minutes."

He sat down after the first quarter. The Wizards won by 20. Making the most out of his rare start, Tyrone Nesby had 10 points, six rebounds, one muted "shit" and zero acts of weirdness, to go along with a stint of fierce defense. Courtney Alexander came off the bench to light it up offensively and be lit up himself, and Rip Hamilton had 18 points but hit fewer than a third of his shots. Jordan was in every way the story, except for the moment when Miami's star center Alonzo Mourning stepped to a microphone to say a few words about September 11 and the country—"I think everyone out here is blessed . . ."

Mourning's moment reminded everyone traveling with the Wizards that Jordan never did that sort of thing. The team flew home that night, to get ready for their intrasquad scrimmage at the MCI arena on Tuesday night for the Washington-area cops and firefighters who had been part of the rescue effort at the Pentagon. Jordan decided he wouldn't play. No one could have rightly blamed him. He said his foot bothered him, though it just as well could have been the knee, the point being he needed rest and not another game of any kind.

The hope became that he would simply join a few other Wizards players in briefly addressing the honored crowd and praising the many heroes present for all they had done at the Pentagon on September 11. But he told the Wizards brass and Collins that he didn't want to talk, not about September 11, not even to explain why he wouldn't be playing.

He turned to Collins. "Doug, will you speak for me?"

Others could see a looming public relations problem. Susan O'Malley pressed him to reconsider. Collins coaxed him: "It would mean a lot more coming from you than it would from me."

Jordan grudgingly agreed. But when he took the microphone, he uttered not a word about the horror or the heroism, saying only that he regretted he would not be playing because his foot bothered him and he had a long season ahead. It was left to his teammates and, in the days ahead, to his rivals, to stand up in arenas and express sympathy for the victims of September 11, and appreciation for rescue workers. He would give money but say nothing.

Jordan's manner did not reflect rudeness, only self-absorption: He was a man who let nothing interfere with his preparation for games. He revered order and routines. He generally ate at the same time each afternoon, he folded his own jersey and shorts, he laced his own shoes. Though the NBA did not reveal the identities of referees until shortly prior to a game, Jordan wanted their names brought to him on a card 45 minutes before tipoff, so he could have an idea how tightly or loosely a game would be officiated. There was *so much* to do in the hours before a game, he told aides. *Didn't people understand that?* He wanted no autograph signings, no posing for photos, no interviews, no distractions. Anything that took him out of his pregame routine was a potential hindrance to his play, so the idea of his participation in pregame September 11 activities was out.

The contrast between his lack of involvement and other celebrities' passion could only be unflattering. Paul McCartney flew over from England to do a benefit concert in New York for families of the city's dead firemen and police officers. In time, while in New York for a game, Jordan consented to opening the Stock Exchange and paying a quick visit to Ground Zero. But his interests always lay elsewhere. For a growing body of observers and fans, his relentless talk about his passion for *winning* seemed silly and unseemly; he looked to them like a middle-aged man hungry for a last adrenaline rush. A school of pundits derided his comeback as vainglorious. He knew this had not gone as planned. "My head is on a block," Jordan said softly.

Increasingly, he took refuge in his tube. He had a *small comfort zone* with people, he admitted, not needing or wanting many people around, not even teammates. If not with Tim Grover or George Koehler, he sat by himself most of the time before games, listening to whatever streamed through those silver headphones. Only boredom interrupted this ritual. In Greenville, South Carolina, where the Wizards had gone to play a preseason game, the media crowd was so small, and the locker room so quiet, that Jordan began talking to a few reporters before the game. He slid the headphones off his ears and said that he was listening to a Jill Scott CD—Jill Scott live from Constitution Hall—and that he had a Marvin Gaye CD waiting. For a few seconds, he sounded like any other fan of music, talking about voices and acts he liked, who could sing, who couldn't. Somebody asked him if he listened to Nelly, a hip-hop singer so many of his teammates liked. He laughed, rolled his eyes. "I can't listen to rap. I don't know how those young guys can listen to that. If I did, I'd be too"—he laughed and clenched his fists, bobbing his head as if on a caffeine rush—"amped, you know. I'd go out and throw up air balls and shit and have turnovers."

The reporters laughed. He smiled, relaxing a little. His thoughts turned to the long season in front of him. "Where do we play on Thanksgiving?"

"Indiana," somebody told him.

"Indiana?"

"Uh-huh."

"Hmmm. All right." He dropped his hand on his chin. Another holiday came to mind. "This will be the first year I can remember that I don't play on Christmas." He seemed to be trying to decide whether this should please or bother him. "I almost always played on Christmas. Almost always."

He wanted to hear about the new arenas, those that had been built after his last retirement. "Toronto?"

Toronto's nice, everybody told him. The Air Canada Centre.

"Los Angeles. I never played in the Staples Center. Never been—"

George Koehler sliced in to clarify. "He's *been* there, just never played there."

Jordan gave him a sideways glance. "Right."

Someone mentioned Atlanta's new arena and he nodded, making a little more small talk, but already he had begun slowly sliding the headphones back up toward his ears, a part of him, it seemed, wanting to return to Jill Scott. He had his routines and never deviated long from them. His whole existence as a basketball player encouraged routines that he associated with order—and the firmer the routines, the greater his sense of order and serenity. He had found the tube.

One day, I saw the perfect metaphor for the tube—perfect because it was a real tube, or as real as a carpeted 6-foot-wide, 10-foot-high tube can be. It was in Grand Rapids, Michigan, the site of another preseason game. Jordan and his teammates stayed in an Amway hotel that enabled them, if they wished, never to step foot outside when it came time to leave for the arena, about a half mile away. If the team permitted it, the players could walk through an all-weather, clear plastic tube several stories off the ground that would take them all the way to the arena, a labyrinth that ran through open sky and shops and office buildings and in which the players could go undisturbed by the evening's cold and any annoying fans, groupies, autograph seekers, process servers, anybody. It was a sealed sanctuary.

But they already had their own tube. Their lives were a tube, and they knew it. On the bus ride over to the arena, most wore headphones that shut out people's screams, the perfect way to burrow deep into themselves and psych up without distractions. Getting off the bus, only Kwame Brown stopped to sign autographs, and the rookie learned soon enough that if you didn't want to sign, all you had to do was keep your headphones on and never slow down, never really make eye contact. Just keep walking. "You watch the way Michael deals with it," Brown said, "and you see he's the best at blocking off things."

Just two nights after he told the Washington crowd of cops and firemen that he was hurt and couldn't take part in the special scrimmage, Jordan played a grueling 33 minutes in Grand Rapids, against the Pistons and Jerry Stackhouse again, who dominated him. About midway through the fourth quarter, Stackhouse isolated him on the right side of the floor the way he might a hapless defender, posted him up, easily shot over him and drew Jordan's fifth foul. Their personal battle had taken over the game—a part of each man back on a court in North Carolina. Jordan responded by posting up Stackhouse at the other end of the court, palming the ball, extending it, raising the stakes, leaning his back against Stackhouse and pushing, pushing, Stackhouse pushing back, Jordan elbowing him with his right arm and dribbling with his left. Nothing there. Later he missed a fallaway jumper over Stackhouse, who soon posted up Jordan and hit a turnaround jumper over him. A steal led to a Stackhouse dunk. Bedlam in Grand Rapids.

Collins's gaze met Jordan. Jordan shook his head. There might be meaningless games, but for Jordan there never was a meaningless battle for supremacy against someone like Stackhouse. He kept struggling on his sore knees even when the exhibition game slipped out of reach, unable to let go of the fight. Collins let him play on.

Two nights later, the Wizards faced the New Jersey Nets in the year's first preseason game at MCI and, as he had in Miami, Jordan torched the opponent, on his way to 41 points. After a seven-point New Jersey victory, Jordan went off for more ice and electrical stimulation treatment on knees that had gone another night without rest. Now Collins had to face the fact that he had permitted Jordan to play 33 minutes in another game that counted for nothing. He had turned to some of his assistant coaches during the game and said, "I don't want to do this. I don't want to keep him on the floor."

But he did. It scared him, all the minutes Jordan kept playing, Collins said. We gotta change that, he told his assistants. But then he'd tell people, No, it's not the *33 minutes*. It's that he's working *so hard* during those 33 minutes—it's the effort he expends. Somebody out there has gotta help him.

But *that* was the problem, he thought. Not enough of the other players helped. If Jordan didn't score or make something happen, then the team struggled, Collins told his assistants. *When Michael isn't on the floor, we're bad.* They had no choice, Collins concluded, but to leave Jordan out on the floor for long stretches.

The coach's self-interest now merged with Jordan's insatiable appetite. Jordan had license to play as long as he wanted.

As the preseason losses mounted, so did Collins's frustrations with the rest of the team. Kwame was lost, he said. Courtney Alexander had to do more than just try to score, particularly when he was shooting so poorly. Laettner had to shoot the ball more and rebound. Rip would sit if he didn't play defense.

After the loss in Grand Rapids, Collins strongly implied that his players had not competed. Then, characteristically unable to stop himself, he just came out and said it: "I thought we caved in tonight."

"He said *what?*" Alexander muttered later, not yet angry, but visibly shocked.

An NBA coach did not talk about his players quitting in a game without running the risk that they would think he had questioned their toughness and professionalism. To talk about it was to light the match, and a coach could never know what would happen after that—whether the players would immediately stamp out the flame with inspired play, or fan the flame in hopes that the coach would be consumed in the inferno. The last scenario had claimed Collins in Chicago and Detroit. Now already there was a new flame.

The players felt divided over him—some, like Brown and Alexander, stifling their dismay, letting it fester, their anger to be revealed later. If sensing the bad will building, Collins did not show it, unable to change, knowing only one way. He screamed at players during games. This was not unique among NBA coaches either, except that Collins typically did it longer and louder than others, especially when scrutinizing the defensive flaws of a player: "Kwame, get over. KWAME. Fuck." A player could turn to see Collins's shoulders dropping in desolation, his head jerking up with disgust. Collins's despair was usually a quite public display of misery. His exasperation grew with Hamilton: "Tight, Rip. Get on him tight, Rip. Tight, Rip. TIIIIGHT. Shiiiit." Alexander's plight sounded hopeless, listening to Collins: "Courtney, get up on him. Tiiiiiiigt. Tight, tight, tight. *Come on, Courtney.* Oooooohh."

The whole bench could hear, as did much of the press and many fans. A player's shortcoming would, in effect, be announced to this audience, like a child being yelled at in a crowded classroom.

"Nez, get on your man. Nez, get on your man. Nezzzzzz. Shiiiiit."

Tyrone Nesby, so appreciative of the chance he had received, did not mind Collins's yells. He knew that Collins had told people that T-Nez impressed the coaches in training camp, a bit of praise that Collins had extended to Whitney and Hubie Davis, but had conspicuously withheld from Hamilton and Alexander. Nesby felt that Collins had helped to tap something good in him. He never before had felt a strong hand guiding him in his NBA career, felt ready to listen to absorb all of Collins's yelling if it could make him a better, more disciplined player. But T-Nez wondered how much all of them could take of losing and the early disappointments. "Mike and Doug, they hate to be losin', it's hard, man, you know," he said. "Doug takes 'em hard. We all do, but he hate it, losin', it can be real hard on a coach. Doug gets—it's just hard, he takes it real hard. You want to do good for him so it ain't hard for him. I want to do good for him 'cause there's lots of pressure."

Collins did not have a face capable of concealing pressure. Some faces are masks, but Collins's betrayed his every joy and irritation, all his pain and agony especially. It was a face well suited for a body that had undergone a series of knee surgeries and still suffered from 15 years of amateur and professional basketball wars, one left with a chronic limp that would require a hip-replacement operation at season's end. Sometimes, leaning against a wall, he grimaced, as if he had made a wrong movement, but then he would straighten, nod, throw out a how-ya-doin'. Sometimes his eyes darted to survey a crowd of reporters, especially if a couple of out-of-town strangers appeared, his suspicion creeping in. One glance at that face usually told his mood—good, bad, leery, extra leery, or tense to the brink of combativeness.

It was still a lean and boyish face at 50, despite its folds and crow's-feet and a deep line of unknown origin beneath his right eye. It went well with his graying hair, worn in a youthful crew cut. He grinned like a carefree, mischievous frat kid when feeling on top of things. On those days, he'd pop out of an office, limping over spryly, shaking a few hands, delivering a one-liner or two, laughing, slapping a shoulder, calling out the names of reporters he liked, maybe addressing one or two with nicknames he bestowed on them, sharing old stories from his playing days, regaling the pack, his hazel eyes glistening with the happiness of a man who'd rather be no place else. He'd giddily exchange how-ya-doin's with visiting rivals from old wars and hang nicknames on whomever he wanted, leading to the day when he would laughingly dub a young Asian-American man working in the

Wizards' public relations office as "Oddjob," as if a quarter century of political correctness never had happened. Even after two firings, his was still the privileged life of a star in the basketball firmament. He loved coming to work, loved speaking about the games and players to the press, loved his life, he said. He spoke much of love. He was an emotional man given to great highs, and sometimes got choked up when talking about a victory, or his family, or a player. He loved his players, he said. He loved Michael. He loved Kwame. He loved so many people and things, so that no life, it seemed, could be better. And then the losses and stresses started creeping in. Almost immediately, people saw a change come over him; for he was a man prone to great lows, too.

Even before the end of preseason, he began exhibiting signs of the moodiness and anger that had damaged his career in Detroit and Chicago, and questions arose as to whether the strains and irritations might already be taking a toll on him. Facing the media after another preseason loss, this time against the Philadelphia 76ers on the Penn State campus, Collins flared and ranted when he thought a young local reporter had asked a question already posed about Philadelphia's defense against Jordan, angrily lecturing him on his responsibility to listen. For the Washington press corps, it was their first glimpse of the Collins whom some Detroit observers had talked about, the Collins whose temperamental outbursts made him look like a man on the verge of coming unhinged.

"Thank you," a Wizards p.r. person said, hoping to end it.

He left people in those moments to wonder what might happen when the pressure grew, as it doubtless would when regular season play began. "It's not like I've been exiled," he said irritably in Toronto, later that week, in response to a question about his own return to the NBA coaching ranks. Now reporters began taking it easier with him, trying to read his moods, fearful of a blowup. October's preseason had not even ended. Six more months of this seemed a volatile proposition.

His behavior stuck out all the more because of the contrast to Jordan, who projected an air of cool. "I'm okay, I'm okay," he said to an acquaintance, about 45 minutes away from taking the court in the Air Canada Centre for the first time. "Just another game, just basketball, enjoyin' myself. You know me. Nothin' about anything's gonna get me worried. Feelin' it, feelin' relaxed."

Then, with a shout, he summoned Collins, who quickly walked

over. Jordan whispered something in his ear, wagging his finger, wagging it some more. "It's gotta be, Doug, *gotta be*," he mumbled, not sounding so relaxed.

Collins nodded, took a deep sigh and opened his mouth, as if about to make a point. Jordan, already finished, had settled under his headphones.

In the Air Canada Centre, Jordan would find himself playing for the first time against Vince Carter, whom he'd dreamt aloud of being matched up against, 10 months earlier, when he'd envisioned "the insanity" of the event, the fans' frenzy. The Canadian press had asked him to elaborate on a comment he'd made about the importance of Carter improving his defense, Jordan's suggestion being that Carter was an incomplete player. But, upon arriving, Jordan tried cutting back on the personal stakes: "Uhh, I'm not going to take it any different than I would against any other player. Times when we'll be matched up against each other, and that's what everybody is gonna be lookin' for . . . Everybody is tryin' to make it a one-on-one situation, which it's not."

But it was. The Centre was packed, Canadian officials and actor Michael Douglas sat courtside; the night had the feel of a duel. Jordan struck first—eight points in the opening four minutes to go along with a block—but then, in about a six-minute span, Carter single-handedly annihilated the Wizards. About midway through the first quarter, a switch on defense left Jordan guarding Carter, who stared him down, leaped straight up and hit a long jumper. Then came a barrage. Carter hit a jumper over Hamilton, whom he next proceeded to dunk over. Jordan missed a jumper, and Carter hit a three-pointer over a retreating Alexander. Toronto was on a 16–1 run. Carter picked up a dribbling Jordan, corralling him as the 24-second clock ticked down, Jordan pump-faking, Carter not biting, Jordan forcing up an air ball. Carter had 18 points at the end of the quarter, 26 at the half. Jordan had been reduced to a spectator. The crowd trained their delirium on him during a time-out.

"This is Carter's house."

"You move like a very nice goalie, M.J."

"You've been drinking a few Molson's, Mike?"

"You're an egomaniac, Jordan. Vince is the man."

"Is there still time for *Space Jam Two?*"

"Easier to lose your shirt on a golf course, Michael."

"What, Jordan—you scared?"

"Mike, he's *beating you.*"

Toronto won in a 17-point rout that really didn't feel that close; the second half was so lopsided that Carter contented himself with 31 points and an early exit. Jordan's statistical line was dreadful: five field goals out of 17 shots, 22 points, and one jump shot in his face. Carter had dominated, said Americans and Canadians alike. Then, moving gingerly on knees overused, Jordan appeared in a green-gold jacket, gold tie and gold hoop earring ("resplendent," a woman over my shoulder mumbled into a recorder).

He shrugged, smiled, his attitude suggesting, No big deal; this counted for nothing; it's early. He conceded that Carter had played well, before taking a backhanded swipe: "I think he is gonna learn and improve from a defensive standpoint . . . As a fan and a North Carolina grad, I want him to continue to improve as a player."

He sounded in reasonably good spirits, until someone mentioned the Wizards' struggles. Questions about the woes of his handpicked team dominated a portion of every press conference now, a line of inquiry that he never before had experienced. "Losing is definitely not something I can adapt to," he said, though softly adding later, "Whatever happens, happens."

Only one preseason game remained, and the Wizards lost that one, too, on the following night, in the casino town of Uncasville, Connecticut. The Boston Celtics, led by their young stars Paul Pierce and Antoine Walker, seemed to toy with the Wizards, who, with the exception of Jordan, did not look particularly inclined to fight, maybe because the team already had begun thinking ahead to opening night in New York. Jordan had played too long again. He had only finished the exhibition campaign, but with no chance to rest and heal, his knees were effectively at the mid-season point. He had taken three years off, only to try making himself whole in one month of pointless wars. He was hurting, so badly he wouldn't even be able to practice before the New York game.

Self-assurance had bled out of him. He was into stoicism suddenly. Like a general who found himself in deep snows with inexperienced troops, he was a man trying to make peace with his fate, as if able to see a cold winter ahead. "Whatever happens, happens," he said, having found his mantra.

He did not want to talk anymore about basketball that night. Finding himself in Uncasville, he wanted to relax at one of his restaurants alongside the Mohegan Sun casino, and there he had a drink, and another.

A man made the mistake of asking him what he thought about the upcoming season. "Whatever happens, happens," he answered, his way of saying, No more for now. He sipped his drink and, as someone present recalled, just stared through his glass for a while. Then he looked around and, as he did, a wave of noise from a distant party rushed over the Jordan group. Word spread that somebody over there had won big at the tables, *big*. It was not long afterward that Michael Jordan and his entourage left the restaurant and strolled toward one more game. He could not pass on a game.

4

When Supremacy Ends

CARDS. CARDS SLIDING HIS WAY ACROSS A GREEN FELT TABLE.
Aces, kings, diamonds, spades—losers, all losers. The man in Pit 21 had
been losing for a good hour by then, losing what for most people
would have been their life's savings. "Yeah, give 'em to me; give 'em to
me," Michael Jordan commanded, pushing another $5,000 chip for-
ward. He loved games but craved risky games more. He feasted on
adrenaline, the big jolts that mortals never experience. Besides
accounting for his comeback, his appetite had pushed him to this high-
stakes blackjack game at the Mohegan Sun casino, just hours after his
final game of the 2001 preseason, in the party town of Uncasville.

"Give 'em to me," he said to the dealer.

More than mildly addictive, his many games over 18 years necessarily had meant that real life, so devoid of spectacular risk, so steeped
in tedium and low on euphoria, had been hard on him. On the other
hand, a big gambling night, he'd told a friend, was "insane"—*insane*
being reserved for the highest order of thrills in the Jordan kingdom,
for scary slides and otherworldly highs, *insane* meaning that a great
game of risk approximated the competitive rush of a tight ball game.
The allure of it led him, a little after 11:00 p.m., past a cacophony of
clanging slots and to Pit 21, where he was escorted behind a red rope
designed to keep $100-a-hand plebes at a distance.

At the sight of him, squealing crowds surged toward the table, security shooing them along. He sat alongside young Boston Celtics star
Antoine Walker, whom he'd known since Walker was a promising ju-

nior-high kid in Chicago, and across the table from teammate Richard Hamilton, with whom his relationship had yet to define itself. Jordan played blackjack into the early morning hours, down half a million dollars at one point, refusing to quit, sinking deeper into the red, trying to recover his losses by succumbing to the sucker's gambit—raising his bets and playing multiple hands simultaneously.

Around 3:00 a.m., about the time his prospects looked the dreariest, he called for coffee to replace his drink, and lit another cigar. The Jordan party—bodyguards, teammates, his personal trainer and friends—settled in for what appeared to be an all-nighter. Hamilton could be seen yawning. Someone in his party whispered to Jordan that it was getting late, that his body had greater needs than his wallet: Perhaps it was time to call it quits. Jordan didn't seem to hear. Maybe he ought to consider getting his rest, the companion gently added, particularly as, in only three days, he would be in Madison Square Garden, playing in his first NBA regular season game in three years. He didn't want to go sleepless, did he? He himself had said he needed rest now more than ever, hadn't he?

Jordan ignored the questions, the veiled admonishments. A casino night never mattered a decade earlier. That was a time when he could go to Atlantic City during a break in a playoff series, play the tables all night, come back to New York the next day, eviscerate the Knicks like a mackerel, mock the opposing coach, trade smack with Spike Lee, get his 40-plus points, and still be woofing about that blackjack hand on which he'd doubled-down his bet, 18 hours earlier. No one ever had pressed him then about his lifestyle; no one pressed him now. It spoke of the bargain that basketball long before had made with him: Coaches and executives agreed to take on the burdens of his appetites. They lived with his vicissitudes, realizing that the very restlessness in him that triggered whispers was the flip side of a bottomless resolve without rival. He regularly subjected himself to grueling private workouts while his teammates slept. He arrived at regular practice before anyone else, did more stretching, came alone into the Wizards' MCI Center practice gym after a red-eye flight to shoot for an hour, and then another hour, a solitary figure attempting to regain the old touch of his three-point jump shot and turn back a clock. He was, in most things, a portrait of excess.

And any loss was a shaming for him. "Cards," he called, and a dealer in Pit 21 flicked out three more hands to him—three more busts, as it turned out, at about 10 grand a hand. He was hemorrhaging cash and chips now. Walker occasionally whispered to him. Jordan said nothing, absorbed by a fresh set of cards and his dwindling pile of blue $5,000 chips. He raised the stakes, playing $15,000 hands, drinking more coffee, finally turning the game around at about 4:00 a.m., drawing about even.

He rebuffed another hint that he should quit, moving ahead by breakfast, winning three hands at a time, going up about $600,000, exultant, manic now. Wanting his victory proclaimed, he began happily trash-talking, "Give me those cards, give me those damn cards . . . You're gonna have to rob a register to pay me"—not quitting until about 8:00 a.m., when he walked toward an exit of the Mohegan Sun with arms raised, as if he'd won Game Seven of a playoff series. Chattering. Woofing. Sleepless in Uncasville.

The whole night had been a gamble—the risk always present that his bank account might be emptied of a considerable sum, that the media would find out, that he would be tired in the days ahead and might be embarrassed in the opening game. But he had stayed in Pit 21 anyway. Money won excited him; money born of risk was the sweetest of all. Any reference to gambling, no matter how unrelated to the immediate subject at hand, eventually elicited his reasoning for why he liked to master games of chance, and how to do it. Almost anything could trigger his instructional talks. One night, in a locker room, away from his teammates and sitting alongside his retinue, someone said to him, "Did you hear about your boy, Dennis?"

Dennis was the Dennis who frequented casinos, the Dennis who had pulled down at least 15 rebounds for him on a good night in Chicago, the Dennis who had once enjoyed wearing a pink boa and dressing as a shapely blonde in stiletto heels, the Dennis who kicked a cameraman in the genitals and, for that matter, seemed preoccupied with genitals. An all-world maverick, Dennis had no job left in the National Basketball Association but several exotic legal problems. The mere mention of Dennis Rodman made Jordan smile. "I heard Dennis has gotta pay eighty grand for that casino thing," the person went on.

Jordan was sitting on a folding chair, dribbling a basketball around its legs without looking down, his concentration split on two planes, as if his hands were apart from the rest of him. "Is this the woman and the breast thing?" he asked, referring to an incident in which a woman had claimed that Rodman fondled her.

"No, it's the one where he rubbed dice on some guy's head or something," chimed in Tim Grover. A Nevada civil jury had ruled in favor of a Las Vegas craps dealer who charged that Rodman had, among other things, rubbed dice on the dealer's stomach and genitals. Rodman said he'd done it in hopes of finding luck. Grover winced. "*Humiliated* him, the guy said. Eighty G's."

Jordan laughed his deep bass laugh and rolled his eyes. He had his guys around him—Grover, George Koehler and bodyguard Larry Wooten—whose presence at that moment, as throughout the two seasons ahead, went a long way toward explaining how Jordan could stay happy and entertained amid a team as comically aberrant as the Wizards, the pink boa of basketball. His guys understood what interested him in ways his teammates never could, knowing, in particular, how much he loved a gambling story. Jordan tried to probe. "Was he thinkin' rubbin' would help him?"

"It's *Dennis,*" Grover said.

"Seems kind of minor," said Jordan, who did not yet know that Rodman had stroked the dealer's genitals. He laughed, his eyes finally falling toward the floor where his hands dribbled the ball. Now, still seated, he lifted the ball and shot it straight up in the air, over and over, studying its spin, watching his right wrist bend as he flicked it. "Hmmmm," he sighed, still trying to picture a man rubbing another man's head, wondering how desperate you had to be to look for luck that way. *"Hey . . ."* he exclaimed. He suddenly thought he saw the larger meaning to the Rodman story, the real lesson here for all gambles—blackjack, craps, basketball. "That rubbin' shit never works," he said softly. "That's *luck . . .*" The word sounded contemptuous. He thought Rodman had missed the point. "You gotta have a *feel* at the tables," he went on, "and be smart. If you have the feel, you can win. That's how I do it when I do it. I get the feel."

"Sometimes," Koehler tried joking. "Not *all* the time." This seemed, in part, a reference to losing so badly through most of the night at the Mohegan Sun.

Jordan looked around, as if checking on potential eavesdroppers. His voice lowered. "I came back," he pointed out, laughing.

"Yeah," Grover said.

Jordan wanted the outcome clear. "I *came back*. It's a *feel,* it's a feel. Not luck. You can do it if you have a feel. Feel and brains."

"How much you win at Mohegan?" another friend asked.

"Can't remember," he said, looking around, and it was hard to know whether he was being coy or truly did not care about exact sums. "Won, that's all. I won."

"How much were you losing before you got hot?"

"I don't even think about that shit. Never think of it. Wrong way to think. It's the feel; I had the feel. That was a good night. Insane."

Reporters always scraped for information about Jordan's gambling and partying. When it came to grandiose partying, journalists could write about such things but seldom do them, which always left us vulnerable to piety and a secret envy. I could be sanctimonious and tell you that I had an aversion to blackjack tables that preyed on weak people's illusions of easy dollars. But, in truth, I simply didn't have enough money to gamble anywhere except at the low-rent tables, which, given their unglamorous company and plebeian risks, held no allure for me. Nor did I have enough in my bank account to make a habit of clubbing in limousines or dropping a few hundred in an evening on champagne and rounds of lemon martinis. I couldn't afford the after-hours life of some of the basketball figures I was writing about, and this can be dangerous for a journalist on two fronts: (1) He can mistake the unusual for the immoral, at a cost to fairness and accuracy; and/or (2) He can go a little nuts and become self-pitying and resentful, for life on the road is surprisingly ascetic and lonely. If this is not enough to drive you into bouts of depression during at least seven months of chain-hotels and 6:00 a.m. commercial flights that follow 4:30 a.m. airport security lines, you need to make a life out of your long-standing compulsions.

Or at least I did. I fell into a routine on the road: I transcribed my interview tapes each night, called my wife and son, wrote a little and watched late movies. I turned on cable sports, I stared open-mouthed at highlights of a bass-fishing tournament, I watched a women's billiards match, I became an insomniac. In my new fuzzy state, I saw a few things more clearly—among which was that no one should be appalled that Michael Jordan would find himself down hundreds of thousands of dollars in blackjack games—alarmed maybe, but not indignant; he had broken no law, the money was his alone, and it represented only a minuscule fraction of his fortune, which was thought to be in excess of $400 million. (His possible losses that night at the Mohegan Sun were roughly akin, in terms of percentages, to a guy worth $500,000 dropping $600 at Caesar's Palace.)

What had come to trouble me about his gambling foray at the

Mohegan (just one of many in his life) was not the money risked, or that it raised the possibility that he might someday, with more time on his hands, squander huge sums (like Bill Bennett or, far more sadly, the late, tapped-out Philadelphia Eagles' former owner Leonard Tose). What was disturbing was that Jordan would so need the thrill. That he would stay up all night to get it. That the man who prepared harder and longer than anyone else for a basketball game because his ego couldn't tolerate the possibility of being bested, who preached discipline and rest as commandments, would go sleepless, with the Knicks and the rest of the NBA waiting three days later. What did this say about how helpless he seemed to be against the pull of his appetites?

It was not a new character trait. Magic Johnson recalled how, during the 1992 Summer Olympics in Barcelona, Jordan would go from a basketball game or practice straight back to his hotel room for an all-night card game, then nap for no more than about an hour before hurrying off for a round of golf and finally racing over to the Olympic arena for a game.

Uncasville served as yet another reminder of the impossibility of relying on Jordan to know when it was best to stop playing a game. Least of all in basketball could he be trusted to recognize when it might be necessary to sit, to cut his playing time, to give his swelling knees a chance to heal. Having a strong coach able to force him into thinking beyond the immediate game would be critical. This never could be Collins, who himself had difficulty thinking beyond an immediate stretch of games, so anxious to win big from the outset.

By then, with fluid building on his right knee, Jordan hurt so much that he couldn't practice. From Chicago, his old Bulls doctor John Hefferon prescribed some medication for the knee, only it didn't help much. Jordan wouldn't touch a basketball at all in the last three days leading up to the opening game in New York. He couldn't run or work up a sweat, which hampered his conditioning. And he had just come off his casino night, 72 hours earlier, and who knew what effect that might have on him.

Jordan said he was ready to go.

The evening arrived, the final Tuesday of October, and Madison Square Garden had the kind of security associated with a presidential appearance at a political convention. Bomb-sniffing dogs went through the two teams' locker rooms. A guard howled at a reporter for not producing his laptop quickly enough, pulling him off to the side for everything but a cavity search. The Garden had that audibly charged air that you normally associate with a major prizefight, a primal buzzing, 20,000 waiting on Jordan to score a great knockout or fall spectacularly.

Out of the locker room came Collins. He had coached his first regular season game here, 15 years earlier, a nervous-looking figure upon whom perspiration and something chalky on his face had conspired that night to leave unsightly gunk around his mouth. Late in the game, Jordan had taken a look at his sweaty rookie coach during a time-out and said, "Doug, drink some water and wipe that crap off your face. *Don't worry*—I'm not gonna let you lose your first game." And Jordan didn't. Collins had liked the Garden ever since. Tonight, he had a nice Nixonian layer of perspiration going. He told the assemblage that he was not going to monitor Jordan' s playing minutes that evening or, for that matter, anytime the Wizards had a chance to win; that Jordan might play 39 minutes or more. Gone entirely were his assurances that Jordan's minutes would generally fall in the range of 32 to 35. "We can't get to a point where I say, 'Oh, geez, he's played thirty-three minutes— I better get him out of there because we have to play tomorrow night.'"

He was upbeat. He talked of love, of course. "I love Kwame," he said. He loved Kwame's potential. He said he even loved Kwame's stubbornness; it was the empathetic Collins.

He wanted to stay on love and steer away from discussions of Jordan's health, even as his star, back in the locker room, was receiving yet another electrical stimulation treatment on his knees. But Collins acknowledged the evening's hard fact: That they were in New York guaranteed the stakes would be higher for Jordan. "One thing I've always said about New York," Collins said, "is that you're either going to be a king here or you're going to be down low—because there is no middle ground here. And Michael has made this a stage for his entire career."

And then the curtain went up.

Here was the sum of the evening: He had a dreadful shooting night; he threw balls away; he had nothing left in the stretch, when he appeared to tire badly. Sometimes double-teamed, he missed the only two shots he attempted in the third quarter, and hit only two of six in the fourth, while Latrell Sprewell was hitting 10 points down the stretch, on his way to 28 points. With about five minutes left in the game, in between Sprewell's baskets, Jordan elevated with his tongue out, in that pose of 1,000,000 posters, and missed a jumper over a tightly defending Shandon Anderson. He clanked another jumper against Sprewell, with

3:30 left and the Wizards down by just one. He threw an errant pass, intended for Popeye Jones inside, which led to an Allan Houston basket, increasing the deficit to four. He hit a jumper to bring them to within a single point with 1:30 left, but then he threw another pass away.

A couple of times he smiled wanly and shook his head, like a man befuddled over why an easy puzzle he had put together hundreds of times was suddenly so hard. It was the look Sugar Ray Leonard wore when the leather started pelting him, or Willie Mays when the fastballs began moving at warp speed. He couldn't even lay his fingers on the puzzle's pieces, sometimes starting down its middle and driving toward the basket, only to find it cut off from him by defenders quicker than anyone could ever remember. They were not swifter; he was a step slower, and jumping a few stories lower. All that most spectators remember is how great shooters shoot, and how gods soar or look old in trying. He looked grounded.

Still, after all that futility, there remained a chance. The Knicks' ineptitude and turnovers gave the Wizards a last opportunity to tie the game, and the ball was swung around in the last 20 seconds to Jordan, who found himself briefly open for a three-pointer from the right side. He knew he was hindered on any shot of that length by the tendinitis in his shooting wrist. Not far away stood an utterly unguarded and excellent three-point shooter, point guard Chris Whitney, who had enjoyed a productive night, efficiently stroking long jumpers. But Whitney had not yet earned Jordan's trust. Jordan lifted and took the shot, on a flat arc, as defenders ran at him. It was short.

The miss ended the Wizards' chances. Whitney hit a three-pointer with a second left, but that would only benefit bettors with an especially tight spread. The Knicks won, 93–91. Jordan had a "quiet" 19 points, sportscasters declared, and New York newspaper editors prepared headlines. "Jordan's Return a Sad Sequel" screamed one. "Stale Air" read another.

Collins had his own problems. Hoping for extra offense, he had started Courtney Alexander, who scored only 6 points and contributed so little else that he never received a call to come off the bench in the fourth quarter. Richard Hamilton played only three minutes in the last quarter, Collins annoyed by what he regarded as Hamilton's poor defense. Laettner looked awful, missing 8 of 11 shots and getting abused inside. There were a few solid performances, but nothing sterling. Popeye Jones pleased the coaches with 13 points and a strong effort on the boards. Whitney scored 18, and Nesby came off the bench to be productive in a short stint. But more characteristic of the team was the erratic play of Kwame Brown.

Still, the focus was entirely on Jordan. He had played a hard 37 minutes, hit only 7 of 21 shots, hid the pain in his knees, and left the court shuffling. "I knew people were going to rip me," as he put it later. He faced the press in a brown suit, gold tie, and sunglasses with blue-lavender lenses, expressing self-satisfaction. Someone asked him about his right knee, and he answered, "Yeah, my knee is bothering me a little bit. But—" He stopped himself in mid-thought. He rephrased his words; he could not be seen as hurting. It was not so much a matter of self-denial; he simply couldn't have upcoming rivals view him as vulnerable. "But I felt *good tonight*," he went on, changing the theme. "I didn't have any pain or aching *at all*."

In the back of the room, some New York reporters reminisced about that playoff game where he whacked the Knicks after running hot at the blackjack table the night before. But at 38, his body could no longer keep the hours that marked his life as a twentysomething without suffering a marked decline in productivity. That he now missed critical shots down the stretch and seemed to have nothing left in the fourth quarter left at least one Wizards official privately wondering what price Jordan had paid for Casino Night, as it had come to be called by some in the Wizards' sanctum.

No one in the organization referred publicly to Casino Night. At all times, Collins portrayed him as the eternally selfless player with perfect work habits. "He's so coachable," said Collins. "No one works harder than Michael Jordan. . . . He just wants to get better."

But better at what? To what end? What, if anything, was left for him in a game other than a way to score another adrenaline fix? Was there still time for a grounded comet to inspire, or had America moved on, looking for someone new? There, in the Garden, the crowd had cheered Jordan but roared at the mention of the firefighters at the World Trade Center. He waved, eclipsed for perhaps the first time in his professional life, overshadowed by tragedy, by ghosts, by an America rethinking what he and other idols meant. Still, he looked content to be there, happiest in his life, after all, when he'd found a game. You left thinking, That might have to be enough. That might be all there is.

Everyone flew to Atlanta. At the airport, I stood in line and took off my shoes for a security inspection and murmured I don't know to a worried-looking elderly woman who kept asking me whether I'd heard a wild rumor about al Qaeda and a terrorist strike somewhere in Europe, though it might have been Australia, I wasn't really listening. I wished she would pipe down. I was in deep contemplation mode. I was studying shooting percentages and offensive rebound statistics, and so I really did not need this tiny al Qaeda distraction right now. I was deep inside the tube.

In the tube, it was easy to forget that there was another life out there, that there were questions besides whether Michael Jordan's new team would make the playoffs, or how he would do against Kobe or Vince or Tracy, or whether his legacy would be enhanced or diminished when this thing was over. It was the cost of being in the tube.

The thing most easily forgotten is that, at all times, life goes on outside the tube—not only public life, but intensely personal things happening to you though you're not there. It was happening now to Jordan. As he prepared for more basketball, an Indiana woman privately resumed her effort to get money from him—for what, she claimed, was a promise he had made to her, in the early '90s, not to publicly disclose their two-year affair or to file a paternity suit against him, at a time when she was pregnant and neither could rule out the real possibility that he was the father. The media knew nothing yet about her past with Jordan, or her legal maneuverings. Now at 38 and a hairdresser, Karla Knafel wanted the $5 million that, she insisted, he had pledged to pay her.

Jordan already had paid her $250,000 in hush money, years earlier. She had come looking for more money after he last retired from the Bulls, finding him, as she told the story to her attorneys, in a Vegas casino, where she claimed to have sat down alongside him at his invitation, watched him play blackjack, quietly reminded him of their agreement, and listened to his assurance that he would attend to the matter after talking it over with his attorney. Now Jordan's attorney tried negotiating a private resolution of the matter with Knafel's attorneys, one that, if the Jordan side was successful, the American media would never learn about. The negotiations were not going well. Knafel had become a headache.

Behind the scenes, Jordan's problems were multiplying, exacerbated by unlikely people. In Cleveland, a man named Robert Mercer, who made his living as an exotic male dancer, had mailed off registered letters to Jordan and Wizards executive and Jordan friend Rod Higgins, claiming that Jordan had carried on an affair with someone in Mercer's family for five years after Jordan himself had married. Next, Mercer sent a similar letter to a secretary at Jordan's Chicago-based company, Jump, Incorporated. Word of the dancer's allegations began privately spreading, creating the specter of a serious public relations problem. Jordan's high-powered Chicago attorney, Frederick Sperling, dashed off a letter in which he denied the allegations and threatened Mercer with legal action if he made his claims public. Mercer angrily answered with a letter of his own, vowing he would not be scared off. He had begun preparing a letter to Jordan's wife, Juanita, mournfully writing that he had information "embarrassing to both our families."

Robert Mercer's station in life could hardly have been more different than Michael and Juanita Jordan's. He had no fame, no wealth, no great prospects. Self-dubbed "The Rumpshaker," Mercer could boast only of a brief appearance on HBO's lurid little slice of Americana, *Real Sex,* where naked people regularly filled the screen and the Rumpshaker shed clothes and shook his stuff for smiling women. He had big ambitions, but things had flattened out.

A male exotic dancer's career was not a lucrative one, he said, and he did not have money for what he insisted he needed—a psychiatrist for his loved one, who was fixated on Jordan, he claimed. Mercer wanted Jordan to pay for the psychiatrist. Sperling suggested this was tantamount to a shakedown. Indignant, Mercer said he didn't want a dime beyond what it would cost for a doctor and that he would "need to think about telling" his story publicly if Sperling and Jordan refused to help him. This meant he might be calling the tabloids, which would have money to dangle for his story.

As Mercer contemplated what he would say in his letter to Juanita Jordan, Sperling urged him to stop all such activity and obtain legal counsel. All the while, the man at the center of the mess remained preoccupied with his right knee. "If I can keep the problems with it under control, things would be about perfect with where this team is going," Jordan said.

In Atlanta, as everywhere else, people waited to exalt him. The exalting took on odd forms. The media assembled in a sweaty rugby-like scrum. The press scrum is as old as American sports, as old as college football games played in leather helmets, or baseball games on fenceless crabgrass fields. As the cult crowds grew, modestly but steadily, so did newspapers' interest in capitalizing on the commercial possibilities of writing about the contests. To grasp those origins is to grasp what matters most, to understand that, from the beginning, the table had been set to glorify, and in time to cater to, a Ruth, a DiMaggio, a Jordan.

When fledgling teams recognized the indispensability of the press to their promotion and growth, a symbiosis was born. Publishers sold more newspapers and, in benefiting from daily publicity, ball teams drew more fans and gained the imprimatur of institutional importance in a city's life. With baseball and football then, as with basketball now, the whole arrangement depended on an understanding: media would deliver widespread coverage in exchange for increased access to players and locker rooms. To succeed, both the games and the stories required high drama and moral symbolism—the elevation of some players and coaches to the ranks of heroes, the fall of others to goat status or despicable bums. The games were part news, but much more soap operas: overheated stories of triumphs and disasters, celebration and mourning, deliverance and damnation. They still are.

So profitable was the coverage of the games that the standard sports page became a sports section—reams of paper in search of stories to fill them. Ever since, newspapers, magazines and the rest of media have needed to feed the beast, so that in the modern age, it is common during the basketball season to find a spate of stories—on cable TV programs, in magazines, newspapers and digests—about such compelling topics as the NBA's top ten rebounders, or the top five point guards, or the ten best ways to guard the top five guys, or about the latest wave of gifted but troubled players, or the most promising underachievers, or about the caring, misunderstood point guard who didn't know the gun rested on his backseat at the time of his arrest, or the one-time spousal abuser who has reconnected with the Lord and rediscovered his game. We romanticize the banal, and catalog the silly. We have churned out so many of these stories, competently, even artfully, that at some point long ago we succeeded in making the ridiculous relevant.

But not even a sea of those tales could matter if sports leagues and media did not have gods. The two businesses need athletic heroes because the games themselves are seldom enough; fans need to be inspired by heroes' ascension, to dream of possibilities for their own lives.

Once a sport has a hero, it has everything—reason for people to stay tuned, most of all. A Jerry Reinsdorf or Abe Pollin markets him as a hero so long as he is around, hanging his portrait all over an arena in order to sell as many souvenirs and future season ticket packages as possible. Not even when the hero slows, or suffers a backlash, is anything lost, so long as he remains active. A hero like Jordan offered his sport and the media all kinds of dramatic possibilities, including the chance that the hero would someday succumb spectacularly or fall from grace, so that he would be as good a story at his end as in his beginning. Jordan presented all the scenarios, a hero whose hold on the world was reflected in the cold, hard ledgers of TV ratings, league revenues and Nike's sales. Even Hollywood used him. He was a male Marilyn. He was Ruth without the belly.

No one ever did a more cost-efficient job of orchestrating attention for Michael Jordan than Michael Jordan. He courted the media from his early college days—excitedly pushing to be on his first *Sports Illustrated* cover, allowing himself to be photographed dancing near a CBS Sports banner in his college dorm, talking to reporters and TV people whenever Dean Smith permitted.

It was an inclination that he brought to the NBA, where in his early years he made himself available to the media before games and lingered in locker rooms with reporters long afterward, a charming, quotable young man selling image and a shoe line. On the road, he regularly invited writers to his hotel room to play cards with him, and on planes that reporters and Bulls players rode together, he gave them time when they needed it, between poker hands, after happily taking their money. So close were the star and the reporters that, after the birth of his first child, Jordan persuaded them not to print the news, as it was a delicate matter: He and Juanita Savoy had yet to marry, and Jordan thought that news of the birth could damage his image.

There were limits to what could be kept from the public, however. In the early '90s when news broke of his gambling forays on golf courses, where he had been the easy mark of slick hustlers, hard-news reporters surrounded him to ask about his disreputable companions. He retreated, told his old friends there would be no more pregame interviews or invitations to his hotel room, and his rules for dealing with the media changed forever.

The unauthorized disclosure of information offended him, and offenders became pariahs. During his comeback, that reality left much of the press, which tends to grovel for access anyway, reluctant to chronicle incidents unflattering to Jordan, or to press hard about anything that he regarded as private. It was a virtual guarantee that almost all high-profile coverage would be slavishly favorable, on Jordan's terms.

Simultaneously, he used the cameras to promote what he wanted.

After practices or on game-day morning shootarounds for which he made himself available to the media, he donned for the cameras, without fail, some garment from his array of Jordan Brand gear. He wore floppy hats with both the outline of a dunking Jordan and the name JORDAN stitched in big letters across the front. Occasionally, he sported a big fez in Carolina blue (it looked like something off the head of the cat in *The Cat in the Hat*), and once, a beanie in the same hue. He was a walking mannequin for Jordan Brand wear.

The free on-air publicity for the apparel was the realization of the full use of media by Jordan and his advisers, part of a marketing machine that had run for the last 17 years without interruption. To the extent that a journalist safeguarded or bolstered his image, Jordan remained open to the possibility of a discussion with him. In turn, most reporters understood that the disclosure of anything unflattering about him would be regarded as blasphemy. That would mean being barred forever by Jordan and his minions from receiving any nugget of inside information about him—or the chance, however infinitesimal, of getting an audience with the god, of going home with chunks of gold in the form of exclusive Jordan sound bites. At its best, a journalist's relationship with Jordan was akin to a struggling gold miner being allowed to take a small pan and sift in the overlord's stream for a few minutes so long as he did not cross him. Few did.

They were grateful for whatever they could get from him. "We need to come out fast," he murmured, and the scrum loved that, not so much his words—as he had used much the same words countless times before—as the fact that he had said something, *anything*. Now they had his face and voice, and that was far more important than meaning or lack of meaning. They would have a canister of film footage and reams of notes for a couple of days' worth of stories. "He gave it up," a few reporters would say in the aftermath, a line with a vaguely sexual ring—the implication being that somebody in the pack had seduced him into giving it up—something that seldom happened with Jordan. Jordan generally pulled the scrum's strings.

Early in the season, during this honeymoon stage of his comeback, he had the media under control, able to avoid tough questions—about Collins, about his relationships with Kwame Brown and other teammates and, certainly, about anyone like Karla Knafel, about whom the media did not yet know. He left people like Karla Knafel and Robert Mercer for Frederick Sperling to deal with; he made sure he would be left alone. He was in the tube, thinking only about games for the time being, particularly the long bad one he'd had in New York, trying to dismiss worries about his knees and playing time, telling the press in Atlanta that the long 37 minutes in the Garden actually had *helped* him, that one night did not make a comeback. Quite assured for a man being written off by a school of basketball writers, he sounded serene, expectant: He had no doubt he would get payback for the disappointment of New York. After all, when had he failed to get payback? He would score big in the next game. It was that simple. He had a god's presumption. It was his greatest power.

Jordan never worried that a personal slump might be anything more than an aberration. He fretted neither over having missed a shot at the end of a game ("Only two things can happen when you shoot: You can either make it or miss it. I've missed a lot of shots."), nor about having committed a slew of turnovers. ("Sometimes I've lost my concentration, too.") Instead, immediately after having a disappointing performance, he began thinking about vindication, as if this were destiny—the vindication to come immediately. Jordan loved talking about a retired Washington guard named LaBradford Smith, who one night in Chicago had scored 37 points, most of them off Jordan, after which an amused Phil Jackson rode him mercilessly: *LaBradford Smith dropped 37 on you. LaBradford Smith.* Unfortunately for LaBradford Smith, the Bulls were scheduled for a return match the very next night on Washington's home court. Jordan told Jackson on the flight to Washington that he would have Smith's 37 by *halftime.* "And I would've done it," Jordan chortled, "except I missed a free throw with a few seconds left in the half. But I had thirty-six. At the half. That's the competitor in you. You believe and you know that you're going to get it. There's always a next game."

But, before a next game arrived, he generally took sanctuary in an impromptu game—say, a challenge that he created for himself against a teammate in a practice—or, if he thought teammates were to blame for a loss the day before, in venting at or about them. He would never be a man on his way to an ulcer, because he bottled up nothing. In Atlanta, he told Laettner, among others, that he wanted him to be more aggressive. And then he looked for a game, exchanging some trash talk with his favorite new foil, Tyrone Nesby, who could take it; for Nesby felt happy and reasonably secure. A consensus had emerged among the coaches that Nesby had played not only competently but quite well in New York, playing a tough defense that Hamilton and Alexander didn't. Nesby would be getting more playing time. Feeling good, the reserve dared to trade smack with Jordan, who baited him, pointing to the half-court line, Nesby yelling, No way, *no way,* could Jordan sink a half-court shot with just one try, no way.

So Jordan had his game for the day. He stepped to the half-court line, 47 feet away, and, with a little flip of his wrist, let it fly.

"*In,*" he shouted, as the ball came down.

Swish.

He strutted, he shook his shoulders, he shimmied.

He read the stories out of New York, and burned. He flashed irritation the next morning at a brief press conference: "I'm entitled to have bad games, and not be able to find my rhythm." That night, Atlanta ran a pack of young, mediocre defenders at him, and Jordan punished them for a half. He had 11 points in the game's first six minutes, on his way to being the high scorer, with 31. He had a dunk in the first quarter, albeit at low altitude, lifting 20,000 into delirium, and hit five of his first eight shots. After trailing early, and being subjected to an angry Jordan lecture at halftime, the Wizards won by 10, and so it did not attract much attention that he missed 14 of his last 22 shots, or that he wore down so badly in the fourth quarter that he desperately threw up three straight off-balance shots that did not so much as touch the rim.

He played 40 minutes in Atlanta, at least 10 minutes too many, his falloff in performance stunning by the fourth quarter, the throbbing right knee denying him even a semblance of the lift he had at the game's beginning. He was slowly being driven into the ground, waylaid by his stubbornness and Collins's acquiescence.

Afterward, Collins expressed gratitude that Jordan had spoken up at halftime, guessing that the Wizards would have lost that night if he hadn't deferred to Jordan at halftime and let him lash the team: "When you have a player like that, who comes in and lets the guys know that this is what we're going to do, then I can come in and calm everybody down. . . . I've never had that before."

But the young Wizards never sounded as enthusiastic as Collins about Jordan's pep talks and tirades. Nor, unlike their coach, were they content with being characterized as bit players in the idol's supporting cast. The first hints of faint displeasure came in the next 48 hours, after a game when a young lion starred and Jordan struggled. Having arrived home in Washington, they played their first regular season game at MCI Center against undermanned Philadelphia, which was missing its star, Allen Iverson, on the mend from elbow surgery, and two other injured frontline players, forward Aaron McKie and point guard Eric Snow.

The game had the makings of a Washington rout. But these were still the Wizards, and they found themselves trailing by 13 points early in the second half, with Jordan still unable to find the touch on his jumper and Collins berating Laettner for his passionless play, within earshot of the media and fans. Kwame Brown came into the game, and Collins couldn't leave him alone, sometimes just howling his name: *"Kwame . . . Kwame . . . Kwame."* The mood along the bench was sour and Jordan frustrated. His only memorable moment to that point had come in a brief scrap underneath the basket with Philadelphia's tenacious Matt Harpring, after the two became entangled and exchanged elbows. Harpring, who had not yet played in the league when Jordan last retired, was free of awe, part of a new generation of NBA players unaccustomed to bowing. "What the fuck are you doing?" Jordan blurted at him, but Harpring did not back off and Jordan missed another jumper.

Virtually alone, Richard Hamilton led the team back, scoring 11 points in the third quarter, guiding a 29–8 run that vaulted Washington into the lead by the quarter's end. Courtney Alexander left the bench long enough to score 11 points, and Popeye Jones effectively smothered Philadelphia's formidable center, Dikembe Mutombo. Motivated by Collins's lashing, even Laettner responded, blocking a couple of shots and holding the Sixers' Derrick Coleman to one point in the second half.

Jordan made only a third of his 21 shots (one-third became a fairly typical Jordan fraction on mediocre nights), trying to compensate for his offensive problems by assuming point guard duties at the top of the floor, a task that involved less running and therefore was a key to revealing when his knees particularly bothered him. He played 38 grueling minutes, looking gimpy at times in the second half, putting up a hand on a couple of occasions to slow his teammates, wanting to settle into a half-court offense. In part for that reason, he preferred playing with Chris Whitney—*C-Whit* or *Whit,* as he called him—over Ty Lue for the time being, believing Whitney understood, among other things, when *not* to run. Jordan did not want to play with racehorses. On this night, with bad legs and a worse jumper, the boss contented himself with setting up younger men, several of his passes going to the cutting Hamilton, whose speed bedazzled Philly. He slithered around and between defenders in the lane, his quick jumpers and 29 points rescuing the Wizards.

Afterward, Jordan placed himself at the center of the team's success, suggesting that his teammates were the beneficiaries of a Philadelphia defense that concentrated on him: "I was creating such a focus. . . . I kept moving the ball. . . . When I'm at the top of the floor, Rip and Courtney usually can get shots . . . The post-up is how I usually utilized Whit. . . ."

He alone "utilized" people; he created the "focus." His judgments, in turn, formed the basis of media questions posed to his teammates, who found themselves regularly asked to expound on the honor of playing alongside Michael Jordan. After the Philadelphia game, Hamilton showed signs that the theme had begun to wear on him. This was *his* night, but now somebody asked him what he thought of being referred to as one of the "Jordanaires."

Hamilton's expression remained neutral, unfazed. "I don't, you know, think we're no type of Jordanaires. I figure we're all special athletes; we all want to win." He tried his best to sound respectful. "I think playing with Michael is one of the greatest experiences I'm probably ever gonna have."

But he was not a young player who would be content for long in a slow-pace offense, particularly if fast-breaking opportunities were being squandered because one player sometimes became fatigued from playing so many minutes. Hamilton tried being tactful about it. "We don't want to burn [Jordan] out . . ." he said. "We don't want him playing forty, forty-five minutes a game." And then, without pausing for a breath, Hamilton said it: "One thing we want to do is *keep the tempo up; we got guys on this team who know how to play.*"

He waited for questions about his 29 points.

"Richard, how much pressure does Michael take off you?"

"Richard, did Michael say anything at halftime tonight, similar to what he said to everybody in Atlanta on Thursday?"

Hamilton's expression never changed. He had a good mask. He said of Jordan: "He didn't say anything. He shouldn't have to say anything."

Hamilton was careful. Still, he wanted to make a point here. "Everybody wants to make a mark for himself," he said softly.

For all his offensive productivity, most of the coaches had no greater regard for Hamilton's overall game now than they did at the start of training camp. Collins openly questioned his commitment to improving his defense, while another official thought Hamilton often sought refuge in the memories of his championship collegiate and schoolboy days, a perception enhanced one day when Hamilton drew attention to the worth of his platinum necklace, the one with the big block letters paying tribute to his hometown. Fingering the big *CV,* he asked, "You know how much this cost?"

No, the answer came back.

A Wizards official recalled Hamilton telling him the chain was worth about $30,000. The official smiled. He had doubts whether Hamilton was tough enough to keep that chain protected. "Rip, in Brooklyn, they'd rip that thing off your neck in five seconds."

Why do you say that? Hamilton complained.

He seemed so young, thought some of the Wizards officials. During breaks in practices, he sometimes pulled up his workout jersey or T-shirt to his mouth and began chewing it, like a small child with a pacifier, the portrait of nonchalance. One of the coaches finally blurted: "Rip, why do you do that? You look like you're sucking on your mother's titty."

He went on chewing.

The coaches still thought he needed to get stronger, to put some muscle on that reedlike frame. But, while they waited for his strength to improve, all agreed that Hamilton could at least rebound and play defense with more passion. They thought he ought to be fighting through screens harder, mixing it up on the boards, using his quickness to swipe a dribble, do *something* defensively. The next night, they played in Detroit, and Hamilton found himself assigned to guard Jerry Stackhouse, which was like dropping a minnow in a bowl with a piranha. Stackhouse feasted, scoring 15 points in the first quarter, and with Hamilton struggling offensively, the Wizards collapsed, down by 24 at halftime.

Collins's patience with Hamilton was running out. Euphoric just 24 hours earlier, the young player looked grim coming out of the locker room for the second half, staring down at the court, receiving whispered encouragement from assistant coach Larry Drew. Jordan was having his own problems, trying to ignore courtside spectators shouting that Stackhouse could punk him at will. "Why won't *you* guard Jerry? You're scared, you're *scared,*" a man in a sports jacket, with a towheaded child on his lap, screamed.

The thought that Jordan feared anyone was ludicrous. But playing relentlessly hard on defense against an aggressive foe now left him vulnerable to foul trouble and the possibility that he might become too tired to be productive offensively. Collins and Jordan agreed that he should avoid guarding Stackhouse for most of the night. Nevertheless, with so many screens and defensive switches in an NBA game, no defender can be hidden for long stretches, and Jordan found himself briefly pitted against Stackhouse in the second quarter, the younger man clearing out a side of the court for himself against Jordan. Few rivals in Jordan's career ever had so brazenly tried to exploit him. Jordan fouled Stackhouse as The Palace howled, after which Jordan, determined to exact some revenge, missed a fallaway jumper over the younger man.

Early in the third quarter, with Stackhouse having his way against all the Wizards and the Washington deficit only growing, Jordan called it a night, putting on his sweats as Stackhouse cruised toward 28 points and fans waved signs. JERRY STACKED THIS HOUSE, NOT JORDAN; JERRY CRUSHES MICHAEL; JORDAN: NO ONE'S SCARED ANYMORE; A derisive singsong came: "We want Michael, we want Michael . . ."

And then came the jeers from only a few rows behind the Wizards bench: "Don't embarrass yourself anymore, Mike."

"You look tired, Michael . . ."

Precisely because he looked so tired, his early exit, after only 22 minutes of play, was fortuitous: His knees could get some rest. With the game's outcome decided, Collins turned his attention to scrutinizing the young players, yelling at Courtney Alexander when he badly missed another long jumper, barking at Hamilton for not trying to rebound his own miss, his voice carrying: *"Shhhiiiit."* After the 22-point loss, he again questioned his team's commitment. "Tonight, we did not compete," Collins said, in what was becoming a familiar refrain, delivered in a self-pitying tone.

In the Detroit locker room, Stackhouse, who had his sore left foot in a tub and a wry grin stretching across his face, disagreed with Collins's assessment. "They're *trying;* it's just that they have a young team," he said.

In the meantime, he didn't feel sorry for Jordan. He took pleasure in the realization that now a Jordan team had to make adjustments in preparing for *him.* It had been no surprise, he said, that Jordan did not guard him. Collins, he observed, knew that the matchup would only put more pressure on Jordan, "because I'm gonna attack him, try to get fouls on him."

Somebody shouted at him, "Happy Birthday." Stackhouse smiled: His birthday would be coming the next day. He noted that he would be

27, in his presumed prime as a basketball player, while the man who once had used him as a foil was three months shy of 39 and getting older every day.

"But," he added, covering himself, "you gotta play well."

What makes professional sports, and particularly basketball, so different from nearly all other celebrated occupations is that room at the top is excruciatingly limited, narrowing like a funnel, leaving space for just one player at its tip. It is not at all like the rest of the entertainment business, where, say, in the film industry, there is always room for a great new actor: Pacino and De Niro can exist in the same pantheon as fellow graybeards Nicholson and Hoffman, and younger stars like Sean Penn and Denzel Washington and Russell Crowe, and whoever else will emerge next year. The Hollywood list is forever elastic.

Not so in sports. There is an immutable law in basketball: someone must fall for someone else to rise. Those at the top stay there only by beating down those just beneath them. The hagiography of Jordan, with its heavy helpings of solemnly told tales about Jordan's commitment to the team concept and winning, always obscured why a team meant so much to him. It was, in the end, always about self-interest, as it is in the case of nearly every accomplished athlete: Jordan could not have what he wanted—the acknowledgment of his athletic supremacy—unless his team won. Nor could he be the greatest if, in the view of the public and the media, other stars bested him in mano a mano confrontations. He needed at once to win and to dominate personally.

In his prime, arriving in a city to find that its big gun at guard had suddenly come down with an injury or illness, he often privately dubbed the foe's malady "Jordanitis." It was basketball's version of an early TKO: He had scared the foe into sitting on his stool, instead of coming out to fight him. These were victories inside the victories, and they mattered no less to him than the real thing. That need explained why playing against young stars like Stackhouse so mattered, and why he had begun steeling himself for a challenge in Boston, where an even younger star, Paul Pierce, awaited him. He wanted to remind any doubters that, at least for the time being, the young rival belonged on a lower rung.

Pierce had not even begun playing in the league until after Jordan's second retirement. He was 24 and cast from the physical mold of many young players challenging Jordan now—lithe, broad-shouldered, slightly taller than Jordan at 6' 6 ½" or 6' 7" (he was listed at 6' 6", but few people believed this, looking at photographs of him alongside the 6' 6" Jordan) and about five pounds heavier at 230 or so. He had grown up on the rough streets of Inglewood, California, becoming an All-American at Kansas, and leaving school a year early to enter the NBA, where he immediately flourished with the Celtics, progressing to score more than 25 points a game and become an NBA All-Star in the 2000–2001 season, just his second in the league. Soft-spoken and earnest around media and fans, he nonetheless enjoyed a reputation for toughness, an image enhanced, as is the case for so many modern players, by an enigmatic off-court life. The victim of a stabbing in a Boston nightclub, he had healed and returned quickly to the court, which gave him added *street cred,* which would be another useful attribute in the marketing of Paul Pierce. While a streaky performer, he had a complete game, able to drive to the basket, hit a three-pointer, play tough defense, deftly pass and tenaciously rebound. Now, in his third season, he was seen not merely as one of the best guards in the league but as someone with a chance to join the league's elite, a perception to be dramatically bolstered were he to have a series of big games against the idol.

The framing of the Jordan-Pierce encounter by the Boston media— Jordan, as the aging king, against Pierce, the gifted young prince— stoked Jordan's fires. No "young dog" would be making any climb at *his* expense, he told people. During his private summer games at Grover's gym, he had told Pierce's teammate and Jordan's longtime friend, Antoine Walker, that he badly wanted to play against Pierce, his excitement implying absolute confidence, thought Walker, who told Jordan the matchup might not be so easy. "Paul's strong, Paul's really tough," Walker said, on the day of the game. "Paul's going to stand up to whatever Michael brings him. Michael might score on him, but Paul will score on him, too; Paul will come back right at him, and be all over him. And once Paul gets used to his tricks, it gets better for Paul. I love Michael; Michael's great. But this ain't the young Michael anymore. I don't know if Michael knows all that. And Paul's got lots of heart."

They had matched up for a few minutes in that last meaningless preseason game in Uncasville, a sloppy confrontation that left each man dissatisfied. While trash-talking, they had thrown a few elbows at each other, and Jordan, who always rankled at signs of perceived disrespect, had done nothing since to downplay talk of a challenge. He wanted to humble Pierce, to whom he casually referred as a "kid," on the eve of their game. "He's a young kid looking to come at me hard," he said. "I would *rather* have him come at me hard than to sit back and be scared of me," he added. Was he suggesting that Pierce once had given off the whiff of fear? Jordan left his listeners wondering. And while they wondered, he wrapped up: "He's got to realize I'm coming at him, too."

The Wizards coaches cautioned reporters not to make too much of the Jordan-Pierce encounter, particularly as Jordan, they said, would not be guarding Pierce for much of the game. Assistant coach John Bach, always the most publicly candid of the coaches about Jordan's physical limitations at 38, said, "I don't think you can expect Michael to guard Pierce and then do all that we expect of him on the offensive end. It's more than a matter of fouls. He'll just be too tired. He could do that when he was young; not now. But I'm sure he'll want Pierce at some point, and then, of course, he'll have him. But we'll try to see that it doesn't happen too often, too early."

Before the game, Jordan sat on a folding chair in the visitors' locker room at Boston's Fleet Center, watching a game tape of the Celtics and drinking a cup of coffee. His teammates already had changed into their uniforms; a few had drifted out onto the court to shoot. He still had on gray dress slacks and a white dress shirt. A friend walked into the locker room. Jordan glanced back and forth between the friend and the TV. There was Paul Pierce on the screen, scoring. Like Jordan, Pierce had many admirers in the arena tonight, including this friend, it seemed. "Just don't leave my man Paul wrecked in the desert," the guy mumbled to Jordan, half-jokingly. "Don't be too hard on him."

A chuckling Jordan whispered back: "I'll give him a drink before he dies."

Another familiar face came by, the television sportscaster Dick Stockton, earnest and friendly, but a member of the media just the same. Jordan wouldn't be dropping any provocative one-liners on him, didn't need any give-him-a-drink-before-he-dies gibes being quoted on television. Predictably, Stockton hoped to get a comment from the king about Pierce, a little grist for a story about the new rivalry. Before Stockton could even raise the subject, Jordan began steering him in another direction. "Let me show you something," Jordan said to him. He reached back into his locker stall, pulled out a narrow canister from a suit-jacket pocket, opened it and removed two cigars.

Stockton's face brightened. "Ah. Where did you pick those up?"

Jordan smiled. "Not gonna tell you that. You don't expect me to tell you that, do you?"

The word "Cuban" seemed to be hovering, but it wouldn't be touching down. Stockton laughed. "That's why I came back, Michael: to get those cigars again. We gotta do it sometime."

"All right," Jordan said amiably.

"So how're you feeling?" Stockton was maneuvering toward business. "How are—"

"I just want to be happy with it," Jordan said.

"Sure."

"I just want to be happy at the end. If I'm happy, that's okay. Just want to be happy with it."

"And Pierce?"

"Good player."

"Uh-huh. But—"

"Very good player."

"But how—"

"How's your golf game, Dick?"

It was a life whose first responsibility turned on not making a public misstep, on not raising the stakes against a young lion who had everything to gain and little to lose. "Just want to be happy," Jordan repeated, and soon Stockton was gone. His old basketball friend came back for a last word. "Don't be too hard on Paul now," the man muttered, to which Jordan whispered, "I'll let him have a drink."

Jordan stopped looking at Paul Pierce and began removing his hoop earring, flexing his right knee, flexing, flexing, flexing. "Strong," he said softly to something on the TV. Then he strolled off to get ready.

He had only his resolve and savvy that night. But Pierce looked strangely passive, perhaps overwhelmed by the stage, guarded most of the night by Hamilton, who received aid from a double-teaming Jordan and other Wizards. In those rare moments when Jordan and Pierce matched up during the first half, Jordan throttled the young rival, using his wiles and ball fakes to keep Pierce off balance.

By contrast, Jordan scored against whomever the Celtics put on him, on his way to making 12 of 26 shots and scoring 32 points, in his best shooting performance of the young season.

With Laettner rediscovering his outside touch and contributing 29 points, and Hamilton adding a solid 19, the Wizards looked poised for an upset. Only the 31 points of Antoine Walker kept the Celtics in the game at all.

With just under seven minutes to play, the arena buzzed: Pierce assumed the duty of guarding Jordan for the remainder of the game, and their contest was joined. Pierce missed two jumpers, and Jordan got the best of him twice—first when a Pierce foul against him led to two free throws and next when Jordan isolated him on the left side, waved the ball the way the matador waves the cape, drove and hit a 15-foot pull-up jumper, to tie the game at 85.

If the contest had ended in the next few seconds, Jordan's control of it would have been deemed absolute. But the game still had about five minutes left, and now Pierce at last demonstrated that he had begun learning from an evening's worth of pump fakes and small humiliations. He blocked Jordan, who, in turn, at the other end of the floor, stripped a dribble from Pierce, the ball bouncing to a streaking Tyronn Lue, whose layup tied the game at 87. In the next minute, Jordan had the ball again, alone with Pierce on the right side, an entire arena watching as Jordan faced Pierce, staring at him, facing him down, Pierce leaning back on his heels, Jordan simply rising without a dribble and hitting an 18-foot jumper.

The Wizards bench leaped. Somebody growled, "Fuck him up." But that would be Jordan's last basket on this night. He had exhausted his tricks, and Pierce had been studying and processing his fakes. When Jordan next drove to the basket, Pierce forced him into throwing up an air ball and then, with 2:55 left, came payback. Jordan drove down the right side, stopped, pump-faked once, twice, and then jumped. Pierce blocked him. Hard. A stuff back in Jordan's face. The ball was rolling. Pierce dived to get it, passing it while on the floor to Walker, who fed it ahead to teammate Joe Johnson for a dunk, a seven-point lead and, effectively, the game.

Pierce's last block would be the focus of Boston media stories. But Jordan knew that, on balance, he had outplayed the kid; the evening was not all lost. He relaxed as the final minute ticked down, and during a break for free throws, he began chatting with referee Nolan Fine, both of whom golfed on many of the same courses in North Carolina. Fine shared a story about his elderly father endlessly searching for lost golf balls in the woods. Courtside spectators and a national television audience were treated to the unusual sight of Jordan, at the end of a loss, bursting into laughter. The moment reflected his good mood: He had drawn a split in his battle with the Celtics and Pierce, who acknowledged that he had spent most of the night being outplayed, declining to accept kudos for his blocks: "I was just tired of him shredding me."

By contrast, the losing team's leader sounded like a winner. "I played good," Jordan told the press. "I got into a good rhythm at the end of the third and into the fourth. . . . My legs are starting to come back around." He talked of his defense against Pierce: "I just tried to deny him the ball and stay in front of him, and he really couldn't get into a rhythm, and I didn't want him to get into a rhythm." It was as close as Jordan came to declaring victory in the matchup. Walking away, he repeated his central theme: "Felt good, played good."

He realized the young and ambitious were out there waiting for him, one every week at least—Pierce, McGrady, Carter, Bryant, Stackhouse, Ray Allen. The young, they kept coming. Even on his own team, they pushed him, not only Kwame, but Hamilton and Courtney Alexander especially, the duo hopeful of more opportunities, more attention. Jordan thought his young teammates needed to bide their time, learn respect, speak less, listen more, work their asses off and get better; he saw holes in *all* their games. And now he took a subtle shot— actually, not so subtle, the more his listeners thought about it—at Hamilton's defense, alluding to how the Wizards had needed to double-team Pierce to protect Hamilton: "Early on, we tried to get the ball out of [Pierce's] hands so he couldn't take advantage of Rip."

If Jordan was perturbed over Hamilton's defense, this meant Collins would be as well. Hamilton had become a vexing issue. His defense might be shoddy in moments, but if Hamilton ever left the starting lineup, there could be an offensive drought. Aside from Hamilton, Jordan and the sporadic Laettner, no Wizard on this night had contributed more than seven points. Hamilton had scored 19, a good offensive game, but Jordan sounded unimpressed: "We couldn't get Rip or Courtney going."

In the Boston locker room, Antoine Walker assessed his old friend. "Michael played good," he said. "But you could see Paul learnin' out there. I think Michael is still trying to get his legs under him. He's got to get his legs used to the wear and tear, and I don't know how that will go. He played *a lot* of minutes tonight. . . . How many minutes he play?"

"Forty-one," somebody told him.

"That much?" He sighed. Jordan was his friend, gambling buddy, mentor. Never would he express pessimism about his friend's future. But concern leaked out of him. "Forty-one is a lot. I don't know how that will go. . . . It's a long season. If you play a lot of minutes, your legs gotta be used to wear and tear. I don't know. *Forty-one?"*

Forty-one.

"He'll keep tryin'," Walker said softly. "He missed doing this, man. You should hear him talk, always talkin'. He'll keep tryin'."

Two nights later, the Wizards' losing streak continued against the mediocre but physically imposing Golden State Warriors, who dominated every matchup. Christian Laettner reverted to form, scoring only three points. Kwame Brown and even the normally fierce Popeye Jones received a thumping on the inside. Jordan spent much of the game trying to guard young 6'9" Antawn Jamison, a fellow North Carolinian who scored on him with outside jumpers and inside post moves, woofing a little until Jordan told him to cool it. The kid obeyed, though abusing Jordan just the same with that jumper, moving irresistibly toward 28 points for the night, grinning, living the most pleasant of dreams. Collins looked apoplectic, furious at everyone except Jordan, yelling at Hamilton, *"Rip, are you going to get a fucking rebound tonight?"*

Hamilton was scoring effectively, on his way to 16 points in a limited stint, but pulling down only one rebound, in what would be his last game as a starter for the indefinite future. Collins played him only five minutes in the second half, turning to heavier, stronger, more intense players—like Tyrone Nesby and rookie Bobby Simmons—for the tough defense that, he intimated, Hamilton wouldn't or couldn't deliver. Hamilton's absence meant the Wizards needed to rely on Jordan all the more for offense, and the risks of this strategy became apparent early in the second half, a tiring Jordan struggling with his jumper, missing 12 of 19 shots through three quarters, the heavy minutes catching up with him. One of the Warrior's guards, Bob Sura, thought that Jordan sounded winded. By then, the Wizards' offense moved like a glacier, the fast break an afterthought. Jordan briefly got hot in the fourth quarter, padding his point total to 32, but by then the game was out of reach, the team leaving the floor to boos.

Afterward, Collins let everyone know his guys hadn't competed again, but that he had had little to say to his players because he worried "they'd turn the tables and *put that on me* and I'm not gonna let that happen."

He took a shot at Hamilton and unnamed others: "There are two ends of the floor, and we're gonna make sure that everybody plays both ends. . . . And it's not just Rip; it's a lot of our guys. I'm not gonna just point the finger at Rip." And then he pointed the finger at Rip ("But Rip especially . . ."), who began the next game on the bench as the Wizards resumed their spiral, headed toward an eight-game losing streak, the longest of Jordan's career.

It was the worst of times for him. Among the NBA's top ten in scoring, he also topped the league in shots taken and missed, shooting at a career-low 41 percent. Two days after Golden State, in an afternoon game against the Seattle Supersonics, he started horribly again, his problems complicated by the tough defense of second-year pro Desmond Mason—the reigning NBA slam-dunk champion who was just seven years old when Jordan began his reign. Even while giving away an inch to Jordan, the 6'5" Mason enjoyed all the advantages in athleticism. With his callow team plummeting, Jordan had begun looking for victories in whatever form he could find them, a little nourishment to feed the ego. Early in the game, he stopped his dribble, raised the ball in the air, and Mason took the bait, jumping prematurely and then falling to earth as Jordan began his ascent. Jordan ran down the court grinning. "Don't go for the pump fake, don't go for it," he whispered to Mason, chuckling.

It hardly seemed to matter that Jordan's rushed jumper—its arc too flat, too low—had missed, again. His small, Pyrrhic victory against Mason would have to do on this afternoon, when Jordan would not make a single basket during the first half, when he would miss all 14 of his shots during that stretch—most of them against Mason, who effectively blanketed him on most possessions. "Don't go for the pump fake," Jordan repeated, as they bumped each other for position. "Don't go for it."

He had become basketball's equivalent of a junk pitcher who, having lost his fastball, now counted on feints and changes of speed to keep younger, stronger, overanxious opponents off balance. But the more that a skilled defender like Mason saw him, the better he could time Jordan's moves, as sluggers time slow pitches. Seattle's coaches had provided Mason with a scouting report that had three recommendations: Wear down Jordan by making him work hard to get the ball early in games; stay on your feet until he jumps; and crowd him, as size and strength now seemed to bother him.

In turn, Jordan had adopted the lines of frustrated stars everywhere: No one had stopped him, he said; he had stopped himself. "I wouldn't say I had *bad* shots, I had *great* shots . . . *easy* shots," he said after another loss. On other nights, he had an altogether different explanation: "The *whole* defense is focusing on me . . ."

In reality, it was just one guy guarding him most of the time now. He'd put on a spin move and there was Youth waiting for him at the rim. Mason shackled him on that Sunday, with Jordan hitting only 5 of 26 shots for a measly 14 points.

"Twenty-one missed shots, really?" Mason said afterward, as surprised as anyone, surprised but not stunned. He had followed the scouting report. "I waited for him to go up and tried not to go for his ball fakes. . . . We got up on him. We jumped *late,* stayed on the floor. He was talking, but you could sometimes see the frustration on his face."

The Wizards had lost four in a row, and kept losing on their home floor—to Milwaukee, Utah, Charlotte—on their way to going winless for 20 days. *What the fuck is going on?* Jordan privately asked coaches and others in the organization. *You're watching us, what the fuck do you see wrong?*

He was livid, shouting: *These motherfuckers think I'm gonna just take losing?*

Then, just as suddenly as he'd snapped in an alcove off the main locker room, Jordan fell silent, which worried those closest to him even more than his tirades—for a quietly brooding Michael Jordan held the hint of a volcano ready to erupt. An assistant coach, Larry Drew, told a colleague that he thought he had seen the first doubt in Jordan. His expression, thought Drew, bore a question: What did I get myself into here?

Nearly everyone with whom Jordan spoke counseled calm and patience. In his despair, Jordan was virtually alone among the players. Most of his young teammates, already accustomed to losing as Wizards after gilded college careers, were sad but philosophical, having perfected that impassive and amiable mien of trampled athletes everywhere, a glazed look that said, *I work hard but this is my fate.* It was a jarring reminder to Jordan of how easy it is for people to lose, to roll over and find satisfaction in sentimentalists' bromides about fighting hard but unfortunately falling short. "I don't want any motherfuckers talking that shit," he seethed privately. "Feeling good because you played hard: That's shit. These motherfuckers gotta play."

But several of his young teammates reeled from their diminished roles. Courtney Alexander, so heralded only two months earlier, now struggling with his jump shot and psyche, generally found himself consigned to the bench. A season earlier, as a Wizards starter, he had averaged 37 minutes a game; now he played less than half of that, and had seen his points plummet from 17 a game to fewer than 5. In some games, he didn't play at all.

Collins's discussions of his "rotation"—his starters and reserves who would see meaningful playing time—did not even include a reference to Alexander. Jordan's tutelage of Alexander had been brief, remote and off-putting, which was Jordan's style: He derived much of his power, on and off the court, by keeping people off balance. One night in the Wizards' locker room, Alexander eyed a mound of shoes and Nike boxes around Jordan's locker. "You like those?" Jordan asked, pointing to a box of Air Jordans.

Alexander nodded.

"Hey, Charlie," Jordan called to the team's equipment manager, Charlie Butler. "Can you get a pair of Air Jordans in Courtney's size?" He looked over at Alexander. "Size thirteen? Thirteen?"

Alexander nodded.

"Size thirteen, Charlie. Yeah, give Courtney a pair." And then Jordan muttered sideways, just loud enough for Alexander to hear, for this was the whole point: "Maybe they'll help him get a rebound."

Alexander said nothing.

The moment reflected Jordan's many sides around teammates, avuncular and needling, instructive and insulting, and always bent on sending not-so-subtle messages of dominance. Fealty was rewarded. Transgressions were never to be forgotten. Just the same, Alexander did not back down from Jordan. One night, listening to Alexander talk to a teammate about what he liked to put on his oatmeal and grits, an eavesdropping Jordan said disdainfully, "You don't put sugar on *oatmeal*. Defeats the whole purpose."

Alexander told him he didn't know oatmeal.

Jordan cackled, his voice booming. "I'm at least thirteen years older than you. You don't tell me—"

Alexander shouted, "That doesn't mean you know oatmeal and grits."

"*You* don't tell me what's right on oatmeal. You . . ." It sounded like an uncle dressing down an impudent nephew. In their heat, you could feel the distance between the idol and his underachieving understudy; theirs was a gap of generations and temperaments, and nothing would bridge it. The young man needed a mentor, and the older man did not know how to be one, if he'd ever wanted to be.

Alexander knew he had made mistakes from the beginning of training camp: "I think I made it tougher on myself—I didn't make the adjustments I should have made." He told himself that the season was young, but he also knew he had plummeted far in Collins's eyes. At 24, he worried about his future in Washington. In the past, amid his mistakes on basketball courts and in his personal life, he always believed that his athletic ability would save him. Now he was riddled with doubt. "I don't want to go backwards . . ." he said plaintively one night. "The scary thing is I don't know how to find a rhythm now . . . My confidence isn't there. That's never happened to me before."

In less than two months, he had gone from budding frontliner to disposable disappointment.

Richard Hamilton, out of the starting lineup, faced a crisis of his own. Amid TV microphones and reporters' notebooks, Collins shared stories about his personal chats with Hamilton, whom he depicted as befuddled: "It was almost like, *Coach, what do I have to do?* kind of thing," Collins said, recounting one of their talks. "And I said to him, 'Rip, I want you to be a complete player. I want you to be able to defend. . . . I want you to expand in every phase of your game. I don't want you to be considered a guy who can just put points on the board.'"

Then Collins linked Hamilton with Alexander, which sounded ominous, like being associated with bubonic plague. "Especially with Rip and Courtney, . . . what I see happen is that they'll go for a while [hard on defense], and then all of a sudden, they get a little tired and they'll lose a man."

Nesby had replaced Hamilton in the loss to Seattle. Then powerful 6' 7" rookie Bobby Simmons took the starting spot from Nesby against Milwaukee. Simmons was bigger than Hamilton by an inch and 20 pounds, and Collins revered his size, muscles and seeming commitment. "Bobby is solid as a rock," the coach gushed. *"And you can trust him."*

Affable and hardworking, Bobby Simmons had one small problem: He couldn't throw a marble into the Potomac River. His jumper looked like something shot from a bazooka. Simmons might have provided marginally better defense than Hamilton, but, offensively, Simmons couldn't produce in five average games what Hamilton's points and assists gave a team in one. For a coach to play Simmons ahead of Hamilton was to invite ridicule, the proof of which was that Simmons wouldn't even be on the regular roster by the opening day of the following season, dispatched for a period of needed seasoning to the gulags of the NBA's development league.

But coaches fall in love with players, and Collins had fallen for Simmons. The rookie moved ahead of Hamilton in the pecking order, and the Wizards lost three more games. That meant four straight losses since Hamilton had become a reserve, four games in which they discarded his 20-plus points a game starting average, four games in which Jordan's knees endured too many minutes and his shot failed him late in games. Hamilton did not complain, and when Jordan found himself unable to hit a shot for the better part of three quarters against Seattle, Hamilton came off the bench to score 23 points and collect a game-high five assists to keep the game close. Then he had 15 points as a reserve in a loss to Milwaukee. He politely deflected questions about his demotion. Caught in a young player's crucible, he seemed to sense that some of his similarly downgraded peers, shocked and embittered, wouldn't come out the crucible's other end. His body did not tell the whole story about him. For all the doubts about his toughness, he was a survivor. "I'll just keep playin' hard and hope good things happen, and not in no way be complainin' about it," he said.

Hamilton endured more Jordanaire questions, more questions about his and his teammates' responsibilities not to fall short in playing alongside the legend. One night, after a game, the questions finally became too much. A radio reporter, hanging out at his locker, asked, "What can you do to support Michael a little better?"

Hamilton arranged his Coatesville chain around his neck, looked down at the floor and said softly, "I'm not going to answer that."

He would not be anybody's sycophant, nor, on the other hand, a sucker taking the bait and lashing out at reporters. After a week and a half, with the losing streak at seven, Collins stopped talking about Bobby Simmons being solid as a rock. Hamilton was back in the lineup, as if he had never left it. "We have young guys here who can play," he said, just in case anyone had forgotten that he would never be a Jordanaire. "And young guys want to get some time and show they can play. I mean, *we're* the future."

On the other hand, Kwame Brown had stopped talking of the future. Collins had given him a rare start in the loss to Milwaukee, during which Brown struggled, thoroughly outplayed by men, five years older and 25 pounds heavier, who did whatever they wanted against him. The exasperated coach howled his name nearly every trip down the court. Brown looked spent afterward, mumbling that he didn't know exactly what went wrong, that maybe he was thinking too much out there. Collins told the media that he regretted ever giving Brown the start: "I rewarded him when he didn't deserve it."

Given their target, his words were cruel, even abusive. They amounted to a humiliation of a young man by a coach, 30 years older, who ought to have known better in the first place than to start a 19-year-old devoid of experience and confidence—his confidence badly shaken in no small part because that same coach had publicly detailed his shortcomings since the first week of training camp. And what was anyone to make of a coach who, on a patronizing whim, handed out a start to an unprepared teen and then, mockingly, let the world know it was an undeserved gift? The next day, Collins backtracked, pointing out that other young high school draftees, like Tracy McGrady and Jermaine O'Neal, had struggled like Brown in their early NBA years, and vowing to work more with his hurting teenager. "Consistency" and Collins did not often collide in the same sentence: He "loved" a player one day, only to be disgusted a week later.

Like Alexander, Brown had arrived in poor shape at training camp. His purported summer illness and back spasms had been only half the reason. He came into Wilmington overweight and, by his own admission, undermotivated. He had begun improving, only to roll an ankle, and be set back further still. He was a kid, and he knew he often acted like a kid. He had a likable teenager's self-awareness of his screwups: "I wasn't giving a hundred percent effort, or maybe my best isn't good enough because I'm out of shape. . . . I gotta get my legs back. I'm doing extra work now."

Thus the challenges of drafting someone 19.

Publicly, Jordan projected a cool on the subject of Brown, observing that his top pick was, not surprisingly, being manhandled at the power forward position by older, stronger men. Sometimes he radiated sympathy while simultaneously suggesting that Brown's presence on a court constituted a burden on himself and other Wizards. After a confused Brown blew three straight defensive assignments early in one game, Jordan cited the mistakes in his post-game press conference. "So I mean right then we were *off-key*," he said, adding that Kwame might *never* have been a proper choice as a starter, a statement certain to reach Collins's ears and ensure that, barring Armageddon, Kwame never again would start in a meaningful game that season.

Jordan had not forgotten Kwame mouthing off to him at training camp, talking *that shit,* he said, talking about *teaching me: Who the fuck did the kid think he was talking to?* Brown's remark irked him into late November. "He came in here, a rookie, and he thought he was gonna kick my ass," Jordan said apropos of nothing one night before a game, glancing over at Brown. With the embarrassment settling in, Jordan eased up—Kwame was his pick, after all; you couldn't destroy the very thing you'd created. Smirking, Jordan decided to throw the kid a bone. "But he's coming along." Pause. "I think."

Brown's protégé days were over from that day Jordan called him "faggot." Then, early one afternoon at a practice in Houston, it all became too much for the kid—the doubts, the ridicule, the poundings. He had been working out with Popeye Jones, Christian Laettner and Jahidi White, all veterans who seemed to genuinely care about him, though frustrated that he hadn't progressed more rapidly, and bothered that he hadn't grasped their work ethic. They took turns that day knocking him around in drills and one-on-one games.

Popeye Jones realized that Brown was taking a beating. In a three-on-three game with other big men, Jones made a point of matching up against Brown, telling him, "It's time to grow up."

Jones roughed up the rookie. Other Wizards screamed at Brown, questioning his commitment and guts.

A disgusted Collins told him to sit down.

Finally, Brown broke. As he sobbed, Jordan tried to comfort him, but by then, with the season less than four weeks old, Brown's rookie year was in tatters.

Jordan stopped talking about the brilliant future ahead for Brown. "Michael [had] shunned him for a while," a Wizards official said. "Kwame went from having the biggest guy on his side to having nobody. It was a long freeze. Michael helped him later when Kwame broke down and cried. But things were done by then."

Nearly all the young players struggled. A discouraged Lue still didn't always know where Jordan wanted him on the floor. Brendan Haywood, waiting for his thumb to get better, had yet to show anything to justify the Wizards' early excitement about him. Alexander seemed to be regressing further. Collins resumed questioning the mental toughness of his "sensitive" team, wondering aloud what would be needed to get his players to compete, declaring that his frustrations with their play were "driving a stake through my heart."

Brown felt himself being especially targeted for criticism. "I don't think I'm too sensitive," he said. "I know I've gotten confused sometimes, but I go out and try playin' hard all the time. I think it's just sometimes I go out now and I'm afraid of making a mistake. One mistake and then I'm thinkin' about it. I think too much maybe, and then it gets worse. If somebody says you're sensitive, that sounds like—" He stopped in mid-sentence, his head drooping. "That doesn't sound good."

Through the losing streak, Jordan's mood grew darker. He used the media to put his teammates on notice: "They take that paycheck twice a month, and along with that comes accountability. . . . And if they're not ready for that, then give back the money and go to school. . . . There's not much love amongst each other when you lose."

The Wizards' streak threatened to claim the rest of November. Few things for Jordan could have been worse than losing at home to the Utah Jazz and a trio of old foils—Karl Malone, John Stockton and especially Bryon Russell, over whom he had hit his final shot of 1998, an 18-foot step-back jumper in the final seconds of the NBA Finals—to give the Bulls their sixth championship. There was a measure of controversy to what the media had dubbed The Shot. Whether intentionally or not, Jordan had used his left hand to push off Russell, who slipped, leaving an undefended Jordan to shoot his jumper while Russell could only look up from the floor. Russell had tried putting the moment behind him, good-naturedly saying that Jordan's latest comeback meant at least that The Shot wouldn't be his last highlight, though sometimes his resentment got the best of him. Overhearing a reporter talking to one of his teammates about the challenges of playing Jordan, he blurted, "I'll tell you a challenge of playing Jordan. *Shiiiiiit.*"

It was hard to know precisely what this meant.

Russell snapped, "Do you think Jordan gets calls because he's Jordan?"

What do you think? he was asked.

"What do you think I think?"

Russell had arrived in Washington with an injured groin. Even slowed and hurting, he wanted to take on Jordan, so he was out there in the first half when Jordan hit a long improbable fallaway jumper over him and laughed loudly, woofing at Russell all the way downcourt, "Did you miss me?"

With Russell limited by injury, the chore of guarding Jordan mostly fell to 24-year-old Quincy Lewis, who never had played against Jordan, having graduated just two years earlier from the University of Minnesota, where he'd landed after starring as a skinny high school player, in Little Rock, Arkansas, where I'd known him.

I'd spent time with Lewis and his family during his senior year of high school. Now six years had passed, and here he was, 50 feet away, taking his place alongside Jordan. The moment had a *Twilight Zone* improbability. But Lewis looked unawed. Since his high school days, he had put on 30 pounds of muscle and grown another inch, so that he weighed 215 pounds and stood an inch taller than Jordan at 6' 7". He would not let an attacking Jordan muscle him, if he could help it. "I need to try to get through his first move," he said, "then try to use my feet, use my chest, get position and not let him be Jordan."

It did not go so well. Jordan was Jordan. He was on his way to 44 points, hitting 17 of 33 shots, having his best game of the season to that point. He bulled Lewis down in the post, using his shoulders and trunk to knock him further back, then shooting over him.

Lewis did not give up, pushing back as Jordan bumped him more. His tenacity seemed to anger Jordan, who more than once threw an elbow at him. In the second quarter, Jordan barked, "I'm going to knock your teeth out."

Referee Greg Willard raced over, stepped between them and shouted, "What's going on?"

The moment passed. Slowly, Jordan's legs began tiring on defense. Lewis scored a career-high 20 points, sometimes beating Jordan to the hoop, but more often losing Jordan around screens and freeing himself for outside jumpers. By the fourth quarter, Lewis was receiving help in defending Jordan. With the game tied at 89 and 4:40 left, Jordan tried to maneuver around a triple-team, only to have his 12-foot jumper blocked by Andrei Kirilenko. It was shades of Boston and the Pierce stuff. The block led to a Utah basket, triggering a 7–0 run. Jordan had forced the blocked shot while a teammate—this time Hubert Davis, who already had hit two three-pointers—stood open on the outside and Collins shouted, *"Michael, there's Hubert."* Jordan failed to hear, or failed to heed. The Wizards lost by nine.

Everyone looked drained afterward. Jordan shuffled off for electrical stimulation treatment and ice, dragging his right knee a little once he got into the tunnel. Lewis had heard that, at the end of games, Jordan sometimes complimented or offered advice to a young opponent. But, no, Lewis said, Jordan never said anything like that to him; nothing at all, really, besides telling him he'd knock out those teeth. Lewis didn't sound broken up about it. No big deal, said his gestures. But, just the same, never again would Jordan be exactly *that* Jordan to Lewis. He was simply Jordan now, a name that came off the young man's lips differently. Lewis shrugged. He was a new player in a new age, an age from which all 38-year-old players talking of mashing your teeth passed eventually.

In the third week of the streak, which had reached seven games and five consecutive home defeats, Jordan said it was probably good that the Wizards would be leaving Washington for a couple of days.

Collins's confidence in his other players sounded shakier than ever. He admitted going to his assistant coaches and asking them: "How many of these guys are saying, *Another season down the drain?* I don't want that to seep in. . . . It's easy to drift back to the abyss."

He wished everyone in the media a Happy Thanksgiving.

That startled me: I had no idea it was Thanksgiving week.

By then, I sometimes wondered whether, in its rhythms, my life had come to mimic those of the people I covered. The life is more than a little weird sometimes. At the door on that Thursday morning, just before my taxi left for the airport, my 12-year-old son said to me, *I don't understand*—why do you have to leave *today,* nobody leaves on Thanksgiving, who's gonna eat with Mom and me, *what are you doing?* So that had me wondering. That had me wondering even before I stepped on the plane, and long before it touched down in Indianapolis.

Let me tell you how I spent my Thanksgiving. It was a little bizarre, it was a little demeaning, it is what I do. That evening I stood in a locker room at the Conseco Fieldhouse, in Indianapolis, furtively glancing at Michael Jordan, who over the last few weeks had mastered this way of looking clear through me, as he did most reporters, like I was a pane of glass.

He stared out, like he was looking at an ocean through my forehead—his expression blankly meditative, a trifle preoccupied. So tall and regally aloof, he had the bearing of an American baron, with people running around him like menservants. On this day, he had three, including a stout, short-haired blond carrying ice bags. Two other people were touching his knees. He had a thin wire running up a trouser leg to small pads on his bad right knee, which received more electrical stimulation—*stim* treatment in locker-room parlance. It didn't seem to help much. He was a relatively young man with an old knee. "Shit," he mumbled to himself, glancing out at something only he saw.

Ninety minutes away from playing, he sat on a drab army-gray metal folding chair in front of a locker, drinking a cup of coffee, dressed in a charcoal suit and a silver tie, which he kept on, even as, all around him, his teammates shed clothes. He looked down at tiny pads on the back of his right hand—more electrical stimulation pads meant to enhance blood flow and aid the healing of the tendinitis in his wrist. Sighing, as if restless, he listened to a jazz CD on his silver headphones. Next to him, Grover and Koehler muttered to each other. Otherwise, the locker room was quiet and perfectly still.

The popular conception of Jordan's life, fostered by TV footage and mythology, is of a galaxy of celestial bodies revolving around him at all times—luminous celebrity friends and pinstriped corporate executives. But once a basketball season began, he led a reductive life, an exercise in minimizing the people and distractions around him. Bored with his CD, he took off his headphones and resumed staring at the stimulation pads. "Need more coffee," he said.

I wrote this down on a small pad. Then I assumed my locker-room posture, which resembled that of a stiff little sapling, inanimate. More people like me strolled inside, complete strangers staking out places within 20 feet of Jordan. He didn't seem to notice, engrossed in whatever he was thinking, absently fiddling with the silver earring in his left lobe and all the while flexing that knee. I wrote this down, too. It's what I do. I found myself saying that a lot to strangers by then: *It's what I do.* I think I said it in hopes of convincing myself and others that what I did should pass for normal human behavior when, actually, it's very peculiar, even squirrelly when you think about it—to be forever stealing looks at a single human being.

Even as I scribbled, more people streamed into the locker room to stare at Michael Jordan, and you wondered where all this was going, why we were there. If you spend enough time covering any superstar athlete, you begin to see that cultures, like individuals, can develop their own obsessions, that they can become fixated on people for no better reason than that they do—until they've shaped a world that extols fame as a virtue, and exalts people for no reason other than that they are already famously exalted. Which was what my son meant earlier that morning without really knowing it: *Why are you following him today? What are you doing? Why are you leaving me on Thanksgiving?*

I was trying to figure this out.

As I glanced at Michael Jordan.

"You asshole," Jordan said to somebody. I wrote this down.

A woman representing a Japanese publication approached him with a half bow of sorts. It looked like a replay of something that had happened in Detroit; it must happen all the time. The semi-bow was an unconscious gesture from people of all cultures around Jordan, a kind of obeisance paid. Jordan gave her a pursed smile, then shook his head. *Sorry.* She didn't seem to understand immediately, misunderstanding that smile, pushing closer and smiling. He gave her a firm shake of the head now. No, no, no, no.

Tim Grover sat down alongside him, while Jordan waved his cup and mumbled to somebody that he wanted stronger coffee next time. He had an endorsement contract with Gatorade sports drinks, but Gatorade didn't have caffeine in it, so coffee, preferably Starbucks, had supplanted Gatorade as his pregame elixir. To write that would be unauthorized, a publicist told me. A Wizards public relations guy now warned a couple of reporters about looking at the contents of Jordan's exposed locker. To do so constituted an invasion of privacy, he said. *Look away.*

We all just stood there for a while. The next voice I heard was Jordan's. He barked in my direction, angrily. I raised my hands in a gesture meant to indicate I didn't understand.

It took me a moment to grasp that he was yelling at someone else.

"You don't get any special treatment, *no special treatment*," he snapped at a man.

Now and then, I jotted a few words on my notepad—*angry at man,* or *mocking man,* or *calling him asshole.*

A Wizards public relations aide tried to look over my shoulder. I flipped a page of my pad and wrote, *Deposit check.*

I didn't think this fooled anyone.

"You tried to talk to them, didn't you? *You tried to talk to them, didn't you?*" Jordan fumed at this other man, whose chief offense, apparently, had been that he tried to talk to Tim Grover and one of Jordan's security men without securing Jordan's permission. "Not a chance you're getting anything from me," Jordan yelled, wagging his finger at the reporter. "I got nothing for you." He shot a look at Grover and Koehler, then wheeled back on the reporter. "You tried to talk to *them*, didn't you? You don't talk to *them*. You talk to *me*. And if you talk to me, I say I got nothin' for you."

"Come on, Michael, I came all this way—how about if you just tell me whether it's true?" the reporter persisted. "About what Krause said?"

Krause was the Bulls' Jerry Krause, of course. Krause, according to the reporter, had claimed that Jordan spoke disparagingly of his Washington teammates, that he had suggested his teammates lacked commitment and were quitting on him.

Jordan looked like he was trying to decide whether to hold to his vow not to talk. If he stayed mute, Krause's comments would go unanswered for a while longer. He looked across the locker room at me. "Michael, you hear what he just said?" he asked.

I was doing my best sapling, rooted to the floor.

"Michael, you hear him?" he repeated.

"I did," I said, and moved tentatively forward. I stared down at him on that folding chair. Jordan cocked his head up, each of us aware of the strangeness of the moment. He regularly spoke to me, in answering my questions at scrum sessions. But that was business. It counted for absolutely nothing, otherwise. I had been, in all other moments, that pane of glass. This was the first time he had initiated conversation with me since we had met in his office the previous winter, proof on some level that he was not above using a writer, even one whose presence sometimes perturbed him, when it suited his interests. I knew what he wanted. I looked over at this other reporter, introduced myself and said, "I heard about the Krause thing. No, he didn't say anything like that."

Jordan scowled. "That's right. And if I *had* said anything like that, *he* would know about it. He'll tell you it's not true; he'll tell you. Go ahead and tell him, Michael. Go ahead. Tell him. Go ahead."

I already had said it once. He prodded me some more. I interrupted, not wanting to feel like his caddy here; it was easy to see how these seductions of journalists happened. "He said nothing like that," I repeated for this other man. Then I turned in Jordan's direction, smiling but thinking I needed to make a point here, looking back and forth between the reporter and Jordan. "If he had said it," I added slowly, "I'd have written about it."

Jordan squinted up at me. He gave me the slightest nod, as if in some vague acknowledgment of something—maybe that I'd helped him out a little. But, simultaneously, he scanned my face, and there were few expressions on the planet that could convey so much as that squint, with its puzzlement and suspicion, determination and weariness, all canceling out his grudging appreciation. "He would, too," he repeated to this Chicago reporter, a little bite to his voice now.

Then he trained his attention on this other man, wanting order restored here, a reminder of who enjoyed superiority between them. What was the point of being supreme, after all, unless someone else knew it? A quick sideways glance my way: "Michael, you know I used to play cards with this guy?" he said to me.

This other reporter stood directly in front of Jordan, smiling casually.

"Yeah, I used to play cards with him *a lot*," Jordan said. "Didn't I, Lacy? Didn't I—"

"Come on," the man interrupted. Smiling, the man was actually talking *over* Jordan now, not about to be belittled. "Come on, give me a snack, Michael—aren't you going to give me a pregame snack?" asked Lacy Banks, who had known Jordan since his rookie season, when Banks regularly whipped the world's greatest athlete in Ping-Pong and played long poker games with him on the Bulls' team plane, with the result that perhaps no writer in the world had ever enjoyed a longer, more intimate relationship with Jordan.

They were an odd pairing. Nearly 20 years older, bespectacled and round, Banks was a Baptist preacher when away from the *Chicago Sun-Times,* and Jordan an inveterate bon vivant in his off-hours. But those years of poker and their battles over information had resulted in a complex relationship—alternately caring and combative, with Jordan's annoyance creeping out now. He looked at me. "Hey, you know I played poker with Lacy?" he said, chuckling. "Yeah, we'd play poker and Tonk, stuff like that, and I'd take his money." Now he smirked at Banks. "There was this one night coming back on the red-eye where I took *all your money*—didn't I, Lacy? Yeah, took all his money and then he had to borrow money from me to get his car out of the [O'Hare airport] parking lot. Didn't you, Lacy?"

Banks wore a thin smile. Over the years, he had learned to endure most of these slaps, realizing Jordan craved dominance, remembering how after he had thrashed Jordan again and again in Ping-Pong, the star angrily called a halt to their games, never telling Banks that he then secretly practiced for weeks, simply summoning Banks for a rematch in which he whipped him thoroughly. Jordan laughed. "Yeah, Lacy *lovvvved* to gamble. . . . And then the next day, he'd be preachin'. . . . Gambling six days a week, and then asking for forgiveness on the seventh."

"Puttin' the fangs in pretty deep, aren't you?" Banks asked softly. He was no longer smiling.

"Oh, you know it always does my heart good to see you," Jordan said, and for an instant his tone became—if such a thing is possible—at once gruff and soft, mocking and conciliatory, a paradox, like the man himself. "You know it does me good, Lacy," he said, and this hung there. "But you're not gettin' anything."

He looked up, above everyone else's head. "I took all his money," he said softly in summation, to no one really, to air. "And Lacy made a long drive from Chicago tonight, and he's not getting anything. Not anything. Nothin'."

Banks fell silent. Jordan smiled. He had reestablished control. He went back to staring through me.

In a while, he returned his attention to the wires on his knee. Lacy Banks stepped forward and took a last shot: "Michael, what—"

"You get nothin', Lacy," Jordan said. He would protect all his private thoughts that night, particularly any news about the knee.

He went out and had a terrible game, now visibly shuffling on that knee, limping a couple of times. He played too long, shot too much, shot even when it was clear that he had no shot. He didn't make a hoop until about five minutes left in the second quarter, and went 2–11 in the first half.

Amazingly, the Wizards led by four at halftime. It was Hamilton's first game back as a starter, and he had been asked to defend the aging Indiana star Reggie Miller, whom he outplayed on both ends of the floor, chasing the fleet Miller around screens, impeding his shot and beating him on offense, on his way to scoring 19 points on the night to Miller's 15. But if that matchup was a surprise in the Wizards' favor, the Jordan matchups with a variety of Pacers had proven disappointing for Washington. Nothing changed in the second half, except that Jordan committed three turnovers and Indiana went on a 15–3 run during the third quarter, to erase the Wizards' lead.

Jordan had difficulty, in his twilight, with nimble, long-armed, taller defenders whom he couldn't post up. Indiana had alternated in throwing three such headaches at him—6'9" Al Harrington, 7'0" Jonathan Bender and 6'8" Jalen Rose. If the rest of the NBA had possessed the same kind of small forward trio, much of Jordan's season may have been a nightmare; for seldom, especially when his knees hurt, did he possess the speed any longer to blow by aggressive big men. Harrington and Bender were only 21 and 20, respectively, two more former high school phenoms who had never played a second of college ball, wanting only to get over on some old god as soon as possible. At 28, Rose was a longtime foe whom Jordan had abused in his early quicker days, but no longer.

In the second half, Jordan continued having trouble, but this did not stop him from jacking up shots. He went 8–26 on the night, while the Pacers' young center, Jermaine O'Neal, another baby star, controlled the lane, and another youngster, point guard Jamaal Tinsley, played brilliantly, setting an Indiana club record for assists. The Wizards lost by seven points, their eighth straight defeat. The team was now an abysmal 2–9. Jordan walked stiffly off the court.

Twenty minutes later, ready to face the press, Jordan walked by Collins, who asked him: "Everything okay? The knee, how—"

"Fine."

"Yeah?"

"It's fine, Douggie."

Collins backed off. "Okay."

Jordan entered a media lounge, where a reporter asked whether he could remember ever having lost eight times in a row at anything: Golf? Checkers? Dominoes?

And from the first row, getting the final word, Lacy Banks said softly, "Ping-Pong."

The Wizards public relations guy cut off questions after five minutes. Jordan stood, wincing a little, flexing the knee, starting off down a hallway with his crew toward the team bus, maneuvering through a phalanx of security men and a small knot of stunned Midwesterners. They were muted by shock, then exploded. Gruff shouts, female wails, small children's cries: *Michael, Michael, Mister Jordan, M.J., Michael, MICHHHAAAAEL.* Jordan kept moving, ever so slightly dragging the right leg.

"Happy Thanksgiving, *we love you, Miiiiiiiiichaaaaaaaaaaaael,*" a woman squealed, triggering more screaming. *"M-Jaaaaaaaaaaaaaaaaaaaaaay."* The howls were maniacal, and security personnel were telling people to step back, *get back, back,* and he was moving, and moving, and moving, and then he was there, on the bus, safe in the tube.

Back in the press lounge, Lacy Banks said, "It's the only life Michael really knows. It's hard to know if his body will hold up, but this is the only thing he really wanted. I knew he couldn't stay away."

He should not have been playing, of course, two nights after Thanksgiving, at MCI. He needed a game off. By then, the severity of his tendinitis was impossible to conceal. By the fourth quarter against the Boston Celtics, he seemed to be jumping off one leg, looking like a man badly tilting on stilts, wincing during his short descents. Somehow he managed to score 17 points and, more amazingly, collect 11 rebounds, not so much by jumping as by blocking off foes with his body. But the effort had taken nearly everything he had to give, and he had nothing left by the fourth quarter.

It seemed that, at least on this night for the Wizards, his pain and struggles would not matter: Washington led by 15 points with less than seven minutes to play. Hamilton had played well, en route to 16 points, six assists and eight rebounds. For Boston, Paul Pierce was playing respectably, on his way to 23 points, but he had not yet exploded in either of the two meetings with the Wizards. The game seemed under control.

Then Washington went into a coma. How else do you describe scoring only two points in the game's final six and a half minutes. The lead plummeted to three as the game ticked down toward the last minute, but the Wizards had Jordan, who never had been part of a team that blew such a large advantage and lost. He called for the ball. His teammates spread themselves out on the floor so he could work alone against Pierce, bury the shot, restore order and make the upstart look foolish.

His reign had lasted the better part of two decades, but passages in sports come in seconds, in the flicker that it takes the eye to process something shocking and mind-altering. If a moment definitively signaled the end of Jordan's supremacy, it came in that instant when he lifted on tired, hurting legs with 56 seconds left in regulation to shoot a jumper, looking to seal the Celtics' doom.

Once, in these moments, Jordan was basketball's version of the guillotine: He would rise high and higher still—suspended above the hapless, sometimes prostrate victim, his tongue jutting out, a scary inevitability in the air—and then the ball would leave his fingers and the ax would come down.

So he rose again, though not nearly so high, to be met at the apex by Pierce, whom he had so thoroughly outplayed in Boston. But Pierce had learned from that first encounter, having already blocked him once this evening, unwilling to bite on his feints any longer. Now

Pierce kept climbing, high above Jordan, and then, with a swooping slashing motion that was its own blade, blocked his shot again.

The disbelievers in the arena gasped. Celtics were running the other way. Pierce rushed down the court, got the ball back, rose alone and, as Jordan looked up at him, hit a 26-foot three-point jump shot to tie the game.

Scoreless for six minutes, having problems with his dribble, Jordan looked for redemption in the final seconds. Holding the ball in that familiarly splendid isolation at the top of the key, he waited as the clock ticked down from 10 seconds to 5 before dribbling, spinning and . . . missing yet again, badly, at the buzzer, barely able to get the ball over Pierce's hand. The line on his night: 17 missed shots out of 24. He made only 3 out of 12 in the second half and the overtime that followed.

The Wizards won, but Jordan had little, or nothing, to do with it. He missed a jumper late in the overtime and, on the next possession, committed a turnover. Others had to perform a rescue. Laettner hit the biggest shot of all, a 17-foot jumper with eight seconds left, on a pass from Hamilton, who then stole an inbounds pass to seal the win. The losing streak had ended at eight.

Afterward, the Wizards' locker room resembled a champion's party. Hip-hop blared from a speaker. Players hugged and slapped hands. Hamilton was near delirious with joy in talking about his steal in the final seconds: "I said, 'Okay, I'm going to get a defensive stop,' and that's what I did. . . . When it went to OT, we just said, 'Stay connected, take our time.' And that's what we made sure we did."

In the losers' locker room, Paul Pierce sounded pleased with his showing. He reconsidered his first encounter against Jordan up in Boston, and now decided that he had won both of their personal matchups: "If this was an individual sport like boxing, you could say that I'd be two-and-oh." He shrugged, catching himself, as if to say he had woofed enough. He tried refocusing on the Celtics, obligatorily adding that he wished his team had won the game. But his smile said everything. "Happy with the way most of it went," he concluded.

Jordan wouldn't be coming out of the locker room for at least a half hour, receiving ice and stim on the bad knee. Collins looked alternately happy, relieved, weary, irritated. He told the press, "Needless to say, it was a great win for our guys," and soon said of Jordan, "He was very tired. . . . I tried to keep his minutes down."

Reporters exchanged glances: *Tried to keep his minutes down?* Jordan had played 45 out of a possible 53 minutes, including overtime. He now had averaged more than 41 minutes a game over his last five outings. A radio reporter asked the coach about Jordan's problems at the end of the game. Collins flared: ". . . I'm going to ignore you. You're going to ruin my night."

Jordan was subdued. His knee had ballooned up, though, under his suit, he could hide it from the press. He walked with a shuffle to the scrum. He said nothing about his tendinitis, only that his legs didn't have their customary lift at the finish. The Celtics, he explained, had concentrated on stopping *him*, so his teammates had open shots. "Defensively, the focus came straight at me and, obviously, I kept trying to move the ball to everybody else."

Then, alluding to Hamilton's big steal, he paid a compliment that sounded like a backhanded swipe. "That was a big defensive play for Richard Hamilton," he said. "I'm pretty sure he was excited about it, because everybody has been crying about his defense anyway."

He spoke of himself a little in the third person ("This is the type of win we can build on. It wasn't Michael Jordan scoring forty-four points, you know . . ."), and then reasserted his place: "I have total confidence that I can make big baskets down the stretch."

There seemed little else to say. He finished and shuffled off. The music continued blaring. Afterward, most of the whispers were about Jordan, of something irretrievably lost. People understood that he would come back strong enough in time, that he would have many good games, probably even a few great nights. But some piece of him was no longer there, and it was not coming back. It is that way with magic: When it is gone, it is gone, and never does hard work bring it back, for work never accounted for the magic in the first place. It was just there. And at some point it is not—and Jordan could no more summon it now than he could have demanded it when it first touched him.

A part of him fiercely resisted the idea that anything had changed. He had not been stopped by any defender, if you listened to him. He had failed himself, was his reasoning. It was just a rhythm thing, he insisted, the rhythm off but the power still there.

Meanwhile, secrecy was crumbling. In the days that followed, Collins would be forced to admit that something was wrong with Jordan. Word leaked that Jordan had flown to Chicago to have his knee drained of fluid by John Hefferon, who in turn disclosed he told Jordan that his minutes ought to be cut to ease the tendinitis. When you run into games on successive nights, Hefferon advised him, you ought to think of taking the second one off. Jordan thanked him and said he'd think about it. Hefferon understood what that meant. "He wants to be out there and winning," the doctor said. He urged Jordan to consider the matter carefully, knowing this would be hard, because, without saying it, he was asking Jordan to acknowledge nothing less than the reality that time was winding down, that the end was slowly coming.

In Jordan's best days, no company profited more from its association with the star than Nike. In this October 1995 photograph, a wall-sized poster of the iconic Jordan decorated the basketball court at Nike Town in Chicago.

No bird soars too high
If he soars with his own wi
—William Blake

Their happiness would quickly give way to tensions, but everyone flashed smiles on January 19, 2000, the first official day of their partnership. At a Washington press conference announcing his arrival as the Wizards's new President of Basketball Operations, Jordan clasps hands with the Washington Wizards's majority owner Abe Pollin (right), and minority owner Ted Leonsis (left). Jordan joined Leonsis in Lincoln Holdings as a partner and investor in the team.

Jordan's teenage pick, Kwame Brown, celebrates his entrance into professional basketball. At the June 2001 NBA Draft in New York, the nineteen-year-old shakes hands with league Commissioner David Stern after becoming the first high schooler ever chosen with the top selection in the draft.

On October 2, 2001, Jordan is surrounded by the media as he holds a news conference following his first day of training camp at the University of North Carolina, Wilmington. The chairs separating Jordan from the media on that day were rarely employed thereafter, enabling jostling reporters to crowd around him.

Standing alongside Jordan, Washington Wizards guard Richard Hamilton chews on his T-shirt and listens in on an impromptu team meeting following an evening practice in Wilmington, on October 4, 2001.

Jordan chats with a visiting Dean Smith, his former coach at the University of North Carolina, following a Wizards's morning workout in Wilmington.

With ice bags affixed to sore knees becoming riddled with tendonitis, Jordan meets with reporters after an evening workout in Wilmington, on October 6, 2001.

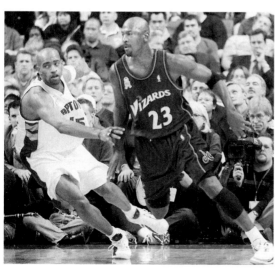

Jordan tries to shake himself free of Toronto's heralded Vince Carter during a 2001 preseason game in Toronto. It was the first NBA encounter between the two former North Carolina stars.

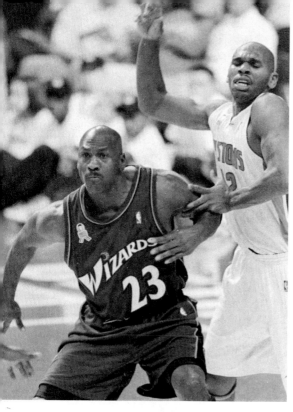

Jordan battles then-Piston Jerry Stackhouse for position, on November 4, 2001, in Detroit. Stackhouse dominated the Wizards that night, scoring 28 points as Detroit routed Washington, 100–78. In an early concession, Jordan sat out the game's final 19 minutes.

In Boston, the Celtics's young star Paul Pierce applies pressure as Jordan drives to the basket during the third quarter of the two players' first regular season matchup. Jordan scored 32 points, but the Wizards lost, 104–95.

Jordan talks to Wizards coach Doug Collins during a game in Miami, on November 30, 2001. The Wizards fired Collins as head coach on May 30, 2003, less than a month after Abe Pollin's decision not to rehire Jordan as the team's chief basketball executive.

Jordan hits a game-winning jumper over a beaten Latrell Sprewell (right) and Allan Houston (left) with 3.2 seconds left in the fourth quarter, as Washington defeated New York, 87–86, in Madison Square Garden.

In a victory over the Charlotte Hornets on December 29, 2001, Jordan connects on a short jumper in the lane against a flummoxed Lee Nailon, en route to scoring 51 points, in his greatest offensive game as a Wizard.

Jordan tries maneuvering around Lakers's star Kobe Bryant during fourth quarter action in Los Angeles on February 12, 2002. Jordan played a solid game, scoring 22 points. But Bryant was the superior player on this night, with his 23 points, 15 assists and 11 rebounds leading the Lakers to a come-from-behind victory, 103–94.

Having rushed back to action too soon after surgery on his right knee, and wearing a dark synthetic legging known as a circulation sleeve in a futile effort to alleviate the knee's swelling, a gimpy Jordan shuffles near Kobe Bryant during second quarter action in Washington on April 2, 2002. Jordan scored a career-low two points, and played only 12 minutes, as the Wizards fell, 113–93.

In Atlanta, Jordan acknowledges cheers during a halftime tribute to him at the 52nd annual NBA All-Star Game, on February 9, 2003. The game was Jordan's fourteenth, and last, All-Star appearance.

The aging idol and a young lion: Michael Jordan and Orlando's Tracy McGrady—a would-be successor to Jordan's title as the NBA's greatest player—pause during a break in play on March 11, 2003, in Washington. McGrady had the better of their on-and-off matchup that night, scoring 43 points to Jordan's 23. But the Wizards won the game, 106–105.

Jordan and Washington Wizards teammate Tyronn Lue raise fists to acknowledge a good Wizards moment against the Sacramento Kings during an April 2, 2003 game in Washington. The Kings triumphed anyway, 105–99.

Jordan briefly waves during a ceremony following his final home game in Washington, on April 14, 2003. Jordan scored 21 points as the Wizards lost to New York, 93–79. Alongside Jordan are team owner Abe Pollin and the owner's wife, Irene. Just twenty-three days later, Pollin informed Jordan that he would not be rehired as the team's president of basketball operations.

5

Resurrection

THE MEDIA AND THE WIZARDS' OPPONENTS KNEW NOTHING
about it yet, but Doug Collins understood that, soon enough, everyone
would learn that Jordan's bad knee had been drained of fluid. The
draining made clear that his tendinitis was far worse than Collins and
Wizards officials had led the media to believe, or perhaps believed
themselves. There would be more questions about why Collins had
allowed Jordan to play for such long stretches.

"We gotta get his minutes down," Collins said to another Wizards
official.

The official agreed.

"We just have to do it," Collins declared, resolute now.

If they didn't get the minutes down, they would be inviting disaster. On the other hand, the tendinitis alone was not disastrous. It simply meant what the word suggested, an inflammation of a tendon, and
Jordan's inflammation in this case was his knee's way of indicating that
it had been overworked or underprepared for the exertion being
demanded of it. It was equal parts a consequence (Jordan had failed to
give himself adequate time to prepare his body after suffering his broken ribs in summertime) and a warning (he better heed the message
before genuine catastrophe struck, in the way of chronic tendinitis or
an even worse problem).

Jordan had made a decision to keep secret his trip to Chicago,
where his personal doctor John Hefferon presided over the draining
and treatment of the knee. Someone close to him asked how they

could possibly prevent news of a trip from breaking, and Jordan said, Don't worry about it. The world always tried to keep tabs on him, but he ran it around screens and p.r. decoys and always lost it. Other than a few Wizards officials, no one outside his circle knew about his plans for the trip to Chicago—not even most of his teammates. Successfully guarding the secret would protect him against opponents who might otherwise try to prey on him, as well as the media mob who would howl: *What's wrong with the knee, Mike?* But now his advisers, watching him badly limp, realized the obvious could not be hidden much longer.

Aside from rest, no surefire cure exists for tendinitis, making it among the most stubborn of man's maladies. The knee's primitive defense mechanism against the problem is unsparing, designed to take away most of the injured man's mobility. When the tendon becomes inflamed and a nearby joint is irritated, the knee produces a clear substance called synovial fluid, which, as it accumulates, swells the stiffening knee, severely hampering movement. The accompanying pain represents the body's attempt to halt all exertion, so that the knee will be permitted the rest it needs and the tendon's inflammation will have a chance to subside. It is an old, crude and perfect little system of torture, like the rack. And through millennia of medical progress, little about tendinitis's misery has changed. When it hits, and synovial fluid flows, even a 94-foot run down a basketball court becomes a teeth-gritting exercise. Afflicted stars will hurt just as Cro-Magnon men did. The stricken are best advised to sit, and most do. They embrace common sense, in the interest of protecting careers. With his left knee throbbing, even 21-year-old Bobby Simmons, unusually young to be hit so hard, deferred to the advice of trainers and coaches, and rested until his tendinitis passed like a bad storm. But somebody would need to sell Jordan on the idea of rest, a concept that he generally resisted.

Jordan wanted his movement immediately restored so he could play, and for this to happen, he needed his knee drained of the synovial fluid, which required the insertion of a needle into his knee. "It's kind of a barbaric process to remove it," said Wizards trainer Steve Stricker. He did not mean unethical or dangerous (drainings occurred now and then in basketball), simply that the approach was old and crude relative to modern tools and techniques in 21st-century sports medicine, and that, for all its discomfort, the procedure didn't heal the knee, a point on which Hefferon and Wizards team doctor Stephen Haas completely agreed. There was only the illusion of a remedy. After the draining of his knee, Jordan could move again. But the tendon remained inflamed—a draining could do nothing for inflammation. If he did not rest, the pain would be coming back, along with more inflammation, more swelling, a nastier case of restricted movement and a heightened chance for other injury.

Hefferon had supervised the draining of enough knees to understand a driven athlete's compulsion to get back onto a court. But always he advised rest—first, a little time off, followed by a new, less demanding schedule of activity. He knew that, for older athletes especially, the supporting muscles around the knee weakened over time, and that, in Jordan's case, the muscles had atrophied even more during his three-year layoff. His age, layoff and past wars all conspired; his 13 years in the NBA meant his body already had absorbed a career's worth of stresses that left his knee far more vulnerable than a young one. Hefferon didn't object to the draining of the knee, but he saw little hope for a cure that season unless Jordan committed himself to a program of occasional rest.

Jordan sat out a Monday practice, but he traveled to Cleveland, to play on Tuesday night, determined not to miss a start during the 82-game season. Collins told the skeptical media, "I have to get Michael's minutes down to thirty-four, thirty-five minutes a game," which would represent a sharp reduction for a player who, through these first 12 games, had played less than 37 minutes in only one game. What Collins didn't tell the press was that his new talk of reducing Jordan's playing time had come only after he learned of the knee's draining.

Jordan jogged out to the floor, played a tentative 31 minutes and went 9–24. The Wizards lost by 19. Jordan's play had been abysmal for three games now. He had made less than a third of 74 shots over that span, still shooting too often for a man who couldn't get lift on his jumper. Something in Jordan snapped afterward. He publicly lashed out at his teammates for the first time during his comeback. "I just think we stink . . ." he said. "I don't see anybody covering my back. But everybody, I'm sure, expects me to cover theirs. That's something I'm not going to live too much with." He hinted that he was not right, physically. "It's not fun to go out there and not see the effort, especially if I'm not one hundred percent."

At 3–10 and with newspaper headlines screaming JORDAN: WE STINK, the team seemed on the verge of coming apart. They traveled to Philadelphia for a game the next night, in what seemed the worst of all possible scenarios for Jordan, a game immediately following another game, a burden aggravated by the presence of a foe good enough to have played in the NBA Finals just the year before, and led by the small but gifted Allen Iverson. If the Wizards' chances didn't seem dismal enough, Collins chose this moment to disclose that Jordan had had his knee drained, earlier in the week.

Jesus, said somebody in the press horde.

Is he okay to play? somebody asked Collins.

"Oh, yeah, oh, yeah, he got it drained and checked out," Collins said casually.

Jordan, wearing a black support sleeve around his right knee, was noticeably restrained during warm-ups, careful not to leave his feet when shooting jumpers. It was one of those games that observers deem a blowout before a ball ever goes up. Then the Wizards surprised everyone in the arena. Jordan had 30 points, including the Wizards' last 14 in the first half, substituting quickness for lost jumping ability, rising without warning off his dribble to hit uncontested jumpers.

In the second half, badly tiring on the fragile knee, he missed 9 of his 13 shots, but by then, other Wizards had taken over. Playing tenaciously, Hamilton pulled down a career-high nine rebounds and scored 28 points—13 of which came during a third-quarter run climaxed when he got a step ahead of the pack and dunked to give the Wizards the lead. He held Philly's Aaron McKie to just two baskets, a performance so sterling that even Collins was moved to put an arm around him and say that now Hamilton was giving him what he wanted.

Brendan Haywood's left thumb had healed, and he outrebounded everyone matched up against him. Tyronn Lue—who, as a Laker a season earlier, had almost gotten into a fight with Iverson during the NBA playoffs—came off the injured list to nearly brawl with him again, so angering Iverson that, even en route to scoring 40, the star came apart in the second half when it most mattered. "Motherfucker, I'll fight you after the motherfuckin' game in the tunnel; kick your punk ass; c'mon, bitch," yelled Iverson, and Lue, fierce but cool, came right back: "I'll fight you *right now.*"

After that exchange, Iverson was helpless to find self-control, his mission now to punish Lue, the game an afterthought, the Sixers' lead melting. He threw up a series of off-balance jumpers that led to Wizards fast-break baskets. His rage played into the hands of Jordan, who, double-teaming the frazzled star, forced him into disastrous turnovers. Iverson lost the ball nine times, and the Wizards won by seven.

But Jordan had played a hard 38 minutes. In just 24 hours, Collins had abandoned his expressed goal of allowing his star no more than 33 or 34 minutes. Afterward, Jordan remained in cover-up mode. The knee was no problem, he said: "I felt *good*. I rested it, iced my legs a little today and I felt good."

Two nights later, in Miami, he scored 22 in a victory, and then the following evening at MCI, just six days after the draining of his knee, he played his fourth game in five nights, in an NBA version of a death march. It had been exactly a week since Paul Pierce had taken him apart down the stretch. Now came an even swifter and bigger young lion, Orlando's 22-year-old Tracy McGrady, who, having come into the league straight from high school, was already an NBA star who would match up against Jordan from the game's start. "T-Mac," as the league had dubbed him, was generally thought to have the most talent of any young shooting guard in the league, with the possible exception (though this was by no means certain) of Kobe Bryant, some McGrady devotees insisting that, in an individual matchup, Bryant paled against the bigger, taller T-Mac.

No other opponent could have been worse for Jordan at this stage. McGrady stood 6'8", but even his listed height didn't reflect his true size. In the NBA, scouts and observers talk with reverence about a player who is "long" or, in a nifty bit of adverbial praise, "plays long." *Long* is homage; long refers to the player's unusually long arms that, coupled with his leaping ability, enable him to reach up in the air just as high as players considerably taller. Long is a gift, just as great Ups are a gift. With his lengthy arms elongated in flight, Tracy McGrady was the personification of Long. He swooped and dunked with either hand over seven-foot centers, and posted up any rival at his position. He was 6'8" but he played at 6'10", at least. So easily did he abuse guards on the inside that it made them hesitant to guard him too closely on the outside, out of fear that he would embarrass them with a short bank shot or a dunk or a no-look pass to a teammate left unguarded because nearly every defender had been forced to pick up the slashing T-Mac. The result was that he could always step outside, catch a pass, simply rise and cast up sweetly arcing three-point shots over intimidated defenders. He had too many physical advantages over Jordan now and languidly hit a jumper over him early in the game just to prove the point.

"Allnight long," a voice called out from the Orlando bench.

Only on defense did McGrady seem to have any shortcomings. The offense from a healthy Jordan might have presented problems for McGrady, but that right knee was slowly locking up now. He was *on fire.*

It meant something different now. Different from those days when he hung 55 on the Knicks or 63 on the Celtics and someone like broadcaster Marv Albert nasally shouted, "Jordan on fire." Now it was no longer so metaphorical. His inflamed right knee felt afire, as if somebody stabbed it with a scorching poker. He spent most of the first half pump-faking McGrady, doing it slyly enough that the young star leaped, committed two silly fouls and found himself languishing on the bench for much of the half.

In the second half, McGrady dominated, on both ends of the floor. Jordan already was giving up two inches to him in height, another inch or so in arm length and at least a couple of more inches in leaping ability. The younger man saw him grimacing and knew he could beat Jordan on the dribble: "I just tried to put the ball on the floor and make him move his feet. Then I'd shoot a lot of jumpers." Jordan seemed to stumble a couple of times on the knee. Collins left him in, with the Wizards still within 10 points. By then, Patrick Ewing, now an Orlando role player, noticed Jordan wincing badly. "I knew it was the knee . . ." he said later. "It's hard to play on something like that."

During the fourth quarter, Jordan pump-faked from about the same spot on the floor where, a week earlier, he had tried fooling Pierce. McGrady stayed down on his feet, waited for Jordan to lift, and then went up. He didn't need to jump particularly high, just lift that arm. His big hand swatted the shot away. MCI sounded like a tomb. Jordan lurched, buckled. His pain and limp became impossible to hide, and Collins stared hard at him. Something passed between the two men. Collins lifted him, though a good 15 minutes too late. Jordan quietly took a seat on the bench, and limped off at the end, the Wizards losers by nine, Jordan having gone 6–19 in 33 minutes.

The knee's problem was so obvious now that not even Jordan could deny it. In the locker room, he admitted that it had begun swelling again, and added that he would be returning to John Hefferon the next day. The knee would receive another draining and undergo an MRI examination. He counted on a swift remedy: "I don't think it's gonna be something that's gonna linger. I have to make sure that there's no ligament damage, get it treated, get it drained and see what the doctors say."

Then somebody broached what he didn't want to hear: Would it be best for him to sit out some games?

He paused, allowing as to how he might sit. "I'd rather continue to play, but if it's not going to get any better [without] me sitting out, then I guess I gotta do that. . . . If Dr. Hefferon and Dr. Haas come to an agreement, I may [sit out]," he said.

But Hefferon was not so sure that Jordan would commit to a lengthy rest. "When have you ever seen Michael just say he's willing to stop playing?" he observed. "There are just some things in life that don't easily happen. He understands risks, he understands what is happening to him, and he understands he wants to play. Which of those does he appreciate more? He wanted to play; he had to play."

Back in 1985, during his second season, Jordan trusted Hefferon with his career when he broke the navicular tarsal bone of his left foot and found himself under the care of the prominent Chicago orthopedist. The rehabilitation, scheduled to last six to eight weeks, ran considerably longer, until it became maddening for Jordan, who at one point during his rehab, to the disgruntlement of Jerry Krause and others on the Bulls staff, played pickup games in North Carolina, angrily arguing that the foot had healed enough for him to rejoin the team. He needed *to play,* he told Hefferon; he needed *a game.*

Forced to play dual roles of doctor and diplomat, trying to coax patience from the young star, Hefferon finally decided that the team risked alienating Jordan forever if it made him wait any longer. Estimating the chance of reinjury to the foot at 10 percent, Hefferon recommended that Jordan be allowed to play. "I think he appreciated I listened," Hefferon said. "I could talk honestly to him and he could talk honestly to me. . . . That's not as common as you'd think."

Hefferon came from an athletic background, a former Triple-A pitcher in the Oakland Athletics organization who understood the code of discretion in locker rooms and knew that certain secrets remained inviolate. But he was not blind to things. He had come to believe that Jordan needed games more than any athlete he'd ever worked with, believed even during his retirements that Jordan would come to regret his departures, that he had retired before he was truly ready, that there would be a void there. Hefferon had been right, on all counts. Now he knew that Jordan's appetites might make any doctor's advice to him pointless; that, in the end, Jordan would do what his appetites drove him to do.

On Monday, December 3, a little more than 36 hours after the Orlando game, Hefferon gave Jordan an MRI exam and presided over the second draining of the knee. He saw no structural damage but significant tendinitis. He urged that Jordan immediately cut his minutes; that he pick and choose what back-to-back games to play and bypass; and that he sit out the next several games until the swelling in his knee diminished and the pain of his tendinitis eased.

Jordan was noncommittal.

No surprise there, thought Hefferon.

Hefferon saw no quick fix to Jordan's problem. He believed that age and many hard years on unforgiving basketball courts inexorably grinded the knees of thirtysomething players, and here his patient was two months from 39. He didn't see severe tendinitis in 20-year-olds, only in older players whose knees, over the years, had passed some threshold of "wear and tear," as he put it. "There was a lot of wear and tear on Michael's knees, and human beings' knees aren't made for wear and tear forever." Add in his high school glory days, he said, and Jordan had experienced more than 20 years of wear and tear. So the knees had been at risk from the beginning. But then Jordan had likely added to the risks, Hefferon thought: So many minutes of playing time so early in the season had likely spurred more irritation and inflammation, he thought. He reminded Jordan of this point, gently urging him to back off.

Jordan listened intently.

Like Tim Grover, Hefferon believed that the knees would have probably fared just fine but for Jordan's long layoff and then his rush to get back. The doctor and the trainer understood better than the sycophants: Jordan was not a god but a man—a stunning athlete with a remarkable body but a man just the same—and a man whose muscles were in decline at about the same rate as other athletes his age, only Jordan had more talent and, likely, far more fast-twitch muscles to begin with, Hefferon thought. Jordan had fallen out of condition during his time away, and the leg muscles providing core strength and stability around his knees had lost much of their protective force, atrophying from inactivity and age. Had Jordan never retired, he still would have faced a degree of decline, Hefferon pointed out: "By 38, a person already has lost some strength in the legs. The muscles aren't as good at 38 as they are at 25. Your thigh muscles aren't as strong. You have fewer fast-twitch muscle fibers and a lower percentage of fast-twitch fibers. . . . The time is ticking down on your athletic career."

But Jordan's long layoff hastened the atrophy, Hefferon said. Jordan had worked out less in those three years away than the typical American fitness club member—lifted weights seldom, ran less, developed a gut. The pain he experienced now was common in anybody of his age who rushed back to physical activity after being dormant for so long. Even when a thirtysomething athlete walked away from a game for only a year, it meant that leg strength, speed and durability would be significantly reduced when he began a comeback, raising the risks for pain and injury. That lack of strength left him vulnerable to other problems, like a painful hyperextension of the knee, which had happened when he tried to reach back over his head and snag a long rebound during the last preseason game against Boston.

But Hefferon and Grover remained convinced that, given enough time to get ready, Jordan still had an opportunity for a sustained, relatively successful comeback. He had the gift that mattered most, a spectacularly athletic body that never had been abused. His vices were, physically speaking, minor: late nights, cigars, a few drinks now and then. Outside of fitness buffs in a monastery, the body was about as well preserved as any 38-year-old's could be after doing essentially nothing over three years other than occasionally walking a golf course. The main challenge for Jordan would be in remaining patient, in not rushing either the tendinitis rehab or the training program. Pushing the pedal so hard after suffering the broken ribs had been a serious mistake, the doctor and trainer ruefully concluded. If Jordan held down his playing minutes now and adopted a prudent conditioning program, then he could still thrive on the court. On the other hand, if Jordan did not reduce his playing time, his chances for failure rose significantly, believed Hefferon. The doctor advised him to find periodic games where he could play brief stretches or not at all.

For the most part, Jordan listened impassively. Hefferon knew what this meant, too. "He understands he's older and that, philosophically, he has to deal with it. But he hates being told he shouldn't do something. . . . It kills him when he cannot play. . . . But my goal is to get him better. . . . I was honest with him. I don't know how many other people say it to Michael, but I have to tell him what I think."

Jordan liked to know bottom lines, and Hefferon repeated his: He preferred that Jordan sit out several games. Hefferon understood that, for competitive reasons, it was a tough decision for an athlete (or a coach, assuming Collins had any say in the decision) to make. If the Wizards, at 5–11, went on another losing streak, it might bury the team for the season. On the other hand, Hefferon viewed an NBA campaign as a long one (the Wizards had completed fewer than one-fifth of their games), remembering how Jordan had come back from his foot injury during his second season to lead the Bulls into the playoffs. That first rehab had been a lengthy ordeal. Addressing this tendinitis problem would require only a small fraction of that time. He lobbied Jordan courteously but vigorously.

His patient committed to nothing, and flew to Texas.

Jordan had decided not to sit out several games but just one, in San Antonio, the next night. He decided he would try saving his knees by barely practicing, or not practicing at all—then play against Houston, two nights later. Hefferon could offer no assurances about his future, particularly if Jordan rejected his most important advice. "If he plays fewer minutes, there'll probably be fewer problems with the knees," Hefferon said. "But the problem with all this has been that, in the heat of battle, he wants to play. In the fourth quarter, he doesn't want to talk of minutes. . . . Realistically, if he says he's feeling good and wants to play thirty-five to forty minutes, how are you going to tell him he can't? . . . You would need to persuade him, and who's going to do that? Who's in a position to do that?"

Doug Collins?

Hefferon didn't directly answer. He always had gotten along with Collins. "I don't know that there's anybody around there who can say to Michael, 'You can't play, you shouldn't play.'"

By then, Doug Collins faced new questions about both the minutes he had played Jordan and about his denials in Wilmington of the tendinitis problem, which, in turn, raised issues about his candor and powers. Increasingly, he seemed to be not a normal coach but a nominal coach, and the real issue was no longer a knee but who led a team. The question was who had control of any team with Michael Jordan on it—over matters of personnel, lineups, playing time, game strategy and team morale—and whether Collins could ever be fully trusted to put the interests of his team above those of one player. The question had been there since the start of training camp in Wilmington, when Collins casually and sometimes smugly denied that Jordan had any serious physical difficulties. Had he been in the dark about Jordan's knee problems? (This was, in retrospect, difficult to imagine.) Had he concealed the truth about a player's health? If so, why? What did the matter say about his authority, or lack of authority, to do what was best for his team? Had he been instructed to be quiet or shade the truth since training camp?

I needed to ask him about what he had known, which raised the possibility that he might become very angry. I'd heard the stories of his battles with journalists in Chicago and Detroit; how, at some point, things became ugly enough between Collins and particular writers that relationships ruptured. During Collins's days at the helm of the Bulls, it had gotten so bad at one point between the young coach and *Chicago Tribune* reporter Sam Smith that not only did they stop talking to each other for a while but Smith stopped *writing* about Collins during the period, so that *Tribune* readers were treated to daily Bulls stories surreally devoid of any reference to the Bulls coach.

Collins was easily triggered. Understandably, the media around the Wizards treated him gently, the way you would treat any volatile man, with the result that some questions had not been asked as aggressively as they might have been around another coach less prone to eruptions. It was a consideration that seldom arose in political reporting, where the moment that anything becomes an issue, the media zestfully confront the candidate or official, who blows up at his peril. By contrast, coaches, like athletes, have license to be loutish. They vent with impunity. On live television, the head football coach at the University of Michigan, Lloyd Carr, testily responded to an ABC sideline reporter's politely phrased question about a bit of Carr's play-calling this way: "Why would you ask a dumb question like that?" A variety of coaches in all sports periodically blow up or lash out at reporters, who in turn generally accept the blowups as the cost of doing business, trying to learn for the sake of their professional survival when it might be best to approach on discomfiting matters, and when to back off. There is a great deal of backing off.

Collins always had difficulty with questions that were not in keeping with his message for the day. Now, with the most famous knee in sports drained for the second time in eight days, Collins was back to talking about yet another plan to cut Jordan's minutes, from an average of 38 down to about 32. In retrospect, he said to the scrum, he wished he hadn't played Jordan so many minutes. He nodded and smiled, as if to say, *There it is; the matter is closed.* But the matter wasn't closed.

To have a sense of what it is like between journalists and a coach when the subject of discussion is an athlete to whom the coach owes his job, it is instructive to know what happened between Doug Collins and me during a 24-hour period in early December, when the Wizards were on the road in Texas. It was the rare time when things did not feel sanitized around the team, perhaps because, away from Washington, the usual p.r. safeguards weren't in place. In Houston, three days after the latest draining of the knee, I asked Collins when he had first learned about the tendinitis, reminding him of Jordan's and his trainer's version of when the ailment worsened: "Tim Grover and Michael now both say they felt the tendinitis coming on in training camp, that it was something of a problem then. When did you first become aware of it?"

Collins took his time answering, stammering a little, not a sign of defensiveness, just his way when speaking especially carefully. "Uhh-mmm, oh, before the New York game [the opening night of the regular season]," he said. "I thought right when we played in the [Mohegan Sun] casino [in Uncasville, Connecticut, the last preseason game]. I thought he tweaked his knee . . ."

I asked whether Jordan exhibited any signs of knee problems before the preseason game in Connecticut.

Collins didn't say no or yes. He looked over my head and answered slowly: "Well, you know what? I would basically go on just how he was playing and what he would say. Michael's never gonna tell you."

And Collins *never* asked Jordan how his knees felt during training camp in Wilmington—or so, again, he was asking the media to believe.

He moved on to a question about Kwame Brown, and I never really finished asking about the subject that day—nothing unusual, as reporting on sports figures goes. You work in a question here and there. You bide your time, city to city. Matt Williams, a Wizards p.r. official, came over to say hello, and I casually let him know I would be asking Collins a couple more questions about Jordan's knees, hoping that he might convey my intention to Collins, so that no one would feel blindsided. Williams said okay, tersely. This reaction was not auspicious. There seemed to be a tension welling. It is always palpable if, as a journalist, you are on the wrong end of things with a professional sports team. If a superstar like Jordan and his coach have become disenchanted with you, you can quickly be made to feel like a troublemaker. It was happening now, signs being sent among some of the Wizards employees that I was pushing too hard, some signals less faint than others, a few trivially amusing. I walked into the locker room and heard an equipment man, in a voice not meant to be overheard, call in warning toward the coaches' quarters, "Leahy's here." That night, a Wizards assistant trainer, a stout blond woman, walked around the press row passing out sticks of Big Red gum (Jordan seemed to like the product). It was something she occasionally did, and now she gave sticks to the reporters on each side of me, and then all around me, but not to me.

"Hi—may I get a stick of gum, too?" I called out.

She looked at me, and moved on.

"Just a stick?" I said. "That's dynamite gum, that Big Red gum."

She kept walking.

A tiny thing, but the Big Red gum was a little red flag.

For a reporter, this is when, perversely perhaps, you think you are making headway. But at some point, you need to finish, and the time to finish was the next day, at a practice in Dallas, at the American Airlines Arena. Waiting for Collins, I began worrying about the possibility of a scene were he to become angry at my questions. I asked Matt Williams whether Collins might prefer it if I spoke to him away from the rest of the media—off to the side, after he had finished with the scrum.

Williams said he'd prefer that, too, and walked over to Collins to ask him about it.

Williams came back and shook his head. "He said no."

I told Williams I thought I would be asking the questions anyway.

Williams just nodded.

Now here came Collins, running a hand through his gray crew cut, shuffling over on his bad hips. The scrum enveloped him. He stood on a practice court, at the other end of which Jordan was shooting with Brendan Haywood. Jordan occasionally looked over, spinning a ball on his fingers, throwing up a hook shot, glancing back at us, tossing up another hook. Collins was saying he loved Michael, and that his knee looked good. I prepared to ask my questions toward the end, after reporters who had stories to write that day had had a chance to get all they needed. But then the session ended abruptly. As Collins walked off, I strolled over to him.

This may or may not have been a good move.

But we were alone at least. The television microphones were not around him. Maybe he would feel less besieged. He stared at me. I told him I just had a few questions, only needed a couple of minutes. He kept staring. I asked him about training camp: "Did Grover and Michael not tell you about the tendinitis?"

Collins folded his arms across his chest. "We never discussed it."

Did you think his problem was just part of the normal aches and pains associated with any training camp?

"Yes, yes. I don't know where you're going . . ."

You thought it was just normal aches and pains?

"I didn't think *anything*."

Were you concerned that if you talked about it that the media would be on a big tendinitis watch?

He sighed. He turned slightly and bent his head, as if contemplating what to say next. He quickly turned back, having settled on something; he was going to say it. "Michael is in a situation where, you know, if he gets tendinitis, then everybody says, *See, you're too old, you shouldn't have come back.* I mean, he gets it no matter what he does. He gets it from every direction."

He shook his head, as if angry for having said this much, angry for being prodded. His head had that familiar little tremble that it got when he was deeply emotional, a shake like a tuning fork's.

I could see Matt Williams walking over. Time to finish. "Just a last question," I said. "On—"

Collins cut me off. "You're trying to run me into a circle . . . *You guys.* You guys are having this guy under such a microscope. I mean, day to day, all you're doing is watching this guy's every move, and imagine if we turned it around?"

It was a good point. How much weirder and more scrutinized could a life be?

Williams had arrived. I tried wrapping up. "The question—"

Collins exploded. "I'm done with you for today. God dang it, I'm done. I mean . . ." He paused, looked up and shouted, not so much at me, not so much to Williams, but to the air. "This guy, this guy's *a stalker.*"

At the other end of the court, Jordan and some other players wheeled and looked at us.

Collins stormed off.

By contrast, the man in the storm's eye seemed unruffled, even looked a little amused. As Collins was fuming along the practice court, Jordan spun his ball, whispering something to Haywood, then glancing at me. He looked in a fine mood. "Doug," he called out, softly, the way a man would call out the name of a comrade just to acknowledge a job well done. Collins was one of his buffers to the world, a defender who freed Jordan to concentrate on his pleasures, one of which was about to take place, Jordan preparing for the briefest of one-on-one confrontations with the 7-foot Haywood. He stood on the left side of the floor, at a diagonal to the basket. Teammates cleared the court.

"Let's go," Jordan said to Haywood, faking a jump shot, then bursting along the left baseline toward the basket, where Haywood met him in the air and swatted away his reverse layup. The kid bounded around the court, he whooped, he raised the ball like a trophy.

"That's a foul," Jordan cried.

"Block, block," a happy Haywood yelled. "That's it, that's it."

"Foul," Jordan said, but he did not argue strenuously, or for long. A smile worked at a corner of his mouth. He sidled over to Haywood, whispered in his ear and patted his back.

All the while, his head bowed, Collins stood off to the side, shouldering his burdens. Matt Williams told Collins that he couldn't be screaming at reporters. I privately wondered if I would be reporting on this moment if the coach involved had been more successful. After all, Collins wasn't the only coach who became upset with the press. A variety of sports pooh-bahs (football's Bill Parcells, a two-time Super Bowl winner, sprung to mind) sometimes turned ugly and abusive around writers, and (Bobby Knight's flameouts aside) almost always the incidents went unreported, especially if the coaches won. If they brought home championships, it was said that they were "generals," whose volatility stemmed from their high standards, their fire meriting our accolades. Winners received exemptions. Only second-tier coaches like Collins who flew into tirades ran the risk of being written off as jerks, but even they generally received passes for their behavior. I had tired of the charade in any case.

They were not esteemed "generals." They didn't lead armies, save countries or implement the Marshall Plan. They presided over *games*. They called for plays, they cut rosters, they screamed at young kids like Kwame Brown, and they tried to keep Michael Jordan and other superstars happy. Collins was simply another guy accustomed to screaming.

Nonetheless, glancing at him, I felt some sympathy. I never had the sense that he took pleasure in erupting at anybody. Usually his outbursts were instinctive and defensive, Collins intent on protecting Jordan, on demonstrating his gratitude and loyalty to his benefactor. It was a constant burden. I looked across this Dallas practice court and saw the toll it took on him. Some men fray more easily than others. *"This shit,"* he was saying.

Power relationships between superstar athletes and uncelebrated coaches do not need to be one-sided from the beginning. Someone must give in to create a relationship's imbalance, someone must cave. Under pressure, Doug Collins had yielded to Michael Jordan more than a decade earlier, during the coach's turbulent stint at the helm of the Bulls. Deference swiftly became habit. It was difficult to point to a single event in Chicago that triggered Collins's subservience, but several people in the Bulls organization remembered a closed-door intrasquad scrimmage during the 1987–1988 season when Jordan began complaining that Collins, the scorekeeper, had deprived his team of points. No, the score's right, said Collins. Like hell it is, Jordan yelled back, the argument escalating.

The issue seemed minor to the point of silliness to everyone else on the floor, but Jordan fumed, stomping out of practice. Collins called to him: *You just can't leave a practice, Michael—come back here.*

Jordan kept walking, a stunning act of petulance and defiance, an enfant terrible moment rivaling anything that a young Wizards player would later do to Collins. That evening, the Bulls, scheduled to fly to Indianapolis for a game the next day, sat shocked on a plane, aware that Jordan had not shown up. The players stared at Collins, who, though outwardly calm, had his head down, in the posture of a condemned man who knew the fate awaiting him if a reprieve did not come. If the plane left without Jordan, there would be a furor, stories of dissension, and Collins, not Jordan, would soon be gone. A former Bull, Brad Sellers, remembered the rapt fascination aboard—the plane sitting at the O'Hare gate at 5:09, scheduled to leave at 5:10, Collins saying nothing, most of the players staring at the plane's open door.

In the next few seconds, Jordan appeared and coolly walked past Collins without acknowledging him. "Maybe Michael was a little late, but it was a power play, too," Sellers said. "It made Jordan's point about who was in charge. . . . Nothing was the same after that. The guys knew who had control."

In that moment, the relationship between coach and star changed forever, the pecking order established—Jordan the star, Collins to serve at Jordan's pleasure.

Careful not to offend thereafter, Collins frequently turned to others to confront Jordan about sensitive matters, one day dispatching an assistant coach, Phil Jackson, to press Jordan about Jackson's conviction that a star became great only when he sublimated his desire for individual accolades in the interests of bettering his teammates and winning championships. Emissaries on Collins's behalf were always useful. Even when trying to be helpful, Collins sometimes said the wrong thing, plagued by a tin ear for what caused offense, cursed by poor political antennae. Prior to the start of the coach's first season with the Bulls, he had wanted to help guide Jordan through whatever rehabilitation might remain for his still questionable, if seemingly healed, left foot. The broken foot had been a sensitive issue. Jerry Krause, in trying to bar Jordan from playing at the end of the previous season so as to extend his rehab, had told his star that his return to the court was a matter for the club, not Jordan, to decide; that Jordan was the Bulls' "property." An insulted Jordan played anyway, and never really forgave Krause. Good political sense dictated avoiding the issue if one wanted to remain in Jordan's good graces. But Collins raised it, trying to project empathy. He told Jordan about his own foot injury at the height of his career and how he believed he had rushed its recovery to his detriment, offering the recollection as a cautionary tale about the risks of subjecting a foot to stresses too soon.

It was the last story his listener wanted to hear. Jordan replied frostily: "That's your foot; this is mine."

After Jordan's tirade at the intrasquad scrimmage, Collins was even more careful around the star, with assistants like Jackson assuming an increasing role in working with Jordan. Collins earned Jordan's tolerance and friendship, though eventually the coach's mood swings wore on Jordan, too. In the end, with his volatility having alienated several players and key Bulls officials, Collins was out the door, and Jackson on his way to becoming a coaching legend. Never had Jordan accorded Collins the regard he soon paid to Jackson, whom Jordan more than once said he loved, adding that he could never play for another coach.

Never is a short-lived thing in sports, however. So here was Collins again, gratefully referring to Jordan as "my boss." From the viewpoint of players and at least one Wizards official, he sounded subservient, emboldening Jordan while undercutting his own authority in the locker room. Never did he have the confident bearing of most coaches, not their easy banter, nor chin-raised magisterial ease, instead always seemingly a trifle leery around people, looking around furtively, especially amid strangers: He was a congenitally suspicious man.

He had had a life of basketball disappointments that left their marks. He might have been an Olympic hero but for a rank injustice: In the gold medal game against the Soviet Union in 1972, with the United States trailing by a point in the final seconds, he had stolen the ball, been fouled, and hit two free throws for the apparent victory, only to watch Olympic referees give the Soviets three inbound attempts to make a basket, after the last of which the great robbery was complete and the Americans the losers. Collins wept afterward and, for years afterward, sometimes teared up in private when discussing the loss. But the heartbreak seemed to stiffen his resolve, if anything.

No one could question his steeliness as a player, nor the source of his commitment to preparation and standards. When he was a small boy, growing up in Benton, Illinois, his father had been the local county sheriff, and the Collins family lived for several years in a two-story county house adjoining the jail. The bedroom of young Doug Collins was on the upper floor, with only about 30 feet and a wall separating his room from the second-story jail cells that his father presided over. The son embraced tough standards early in life. He acquired a lawman's sense of rigid propriety, of *right* being a path from which a winner could not stray. *Right* meant practicing hard, meant staying after practice to work harder, meant year-round conditioning, meant agonizing so much after a loss that it was unbearable. *Right* meant agonizing as much as your coach, and Collins as a player had agonized more than anybody.

Playing when hurt, he likely sacrificed years off his career. A *Sports Illustrated* cover boy while a college All-American at Illinois State, and the first player selected overall in the NBA's 1973 draft, he had been a 6'6" All-Star guard for the Philadelphia 76ers, though his playing days were characterized by frustrations—a near-miss in the 1977 NBA Finals, and a series of debilitating injuries. He left with no championships, despite playing with Julius Erving and George McGinnis. He had suffered a series of knee injuries, and now was scheduled to receive his hip replacement in the next off-season, moving in the shuffle of a man 20 years older. He had given everything and expected nothing less from his players in Chicago and Detroit. Six years as a head coach had brought him young stars but no loyal disciples or NBA titles—Phil Jackson had shown the Bulls how to win.

Now Jackson did television commercials and was America's favorite Zen master, and Collins was barely hanging on in the basketball profession, trying to please a player whom he called his boss. Jordan's status as his professional savior meant that Collins—even after Jordan the player ostensibly gave up all managerial authority in accordance with NBA rules—would take his cues from him.

That meant, among other things, that the shadow boss told Collins about what he hoped to see in the way of game strategy. Collins's submissiveness left a Collins friend in the organization fearing that it might undermine the coach's authority with his other players. *Why don't you treat him like any other player?* he asked Collins, whose silence suggested to his friend that he didn't want to hear such advice again; it would do him no good.

He routinely deferred to the star in front of his squad. One afternoon, during a scrimmage at a closed-door practice, Collins casually said, "I'll let the players keep the score."

Jordan could not resist having his one-upsmanship: "I haven't found a damn coach yet who could do it."

Collins knew his limits around Jordan. He worked hard at remaining his friend, buying cigars as a present for him, sticking up for him around the press. When it came to the issue of playing time, Jordan seldom sought out Collins directly. Usually, Tim Grover approached the coach, bearing a message from Jordan. "Doug, he's feeling good," Grover often said, which was code for, *Don't cut his minutes down, don't interrupt his flow.* During games, when Collins readied himself to take Jordan out at prearranged points, he looked at Jordan. If Jordan stared hard and long back, it meant, *Don't lift me, I'm feeling good. I'll let you know when I'm ready to come out.*

A shadow coach, Jordan guided the most important decisions. His control over personnel was absolute. If he wanted Kwame benched, Kwame was out. If he was dissatisfied with Courtney Alexander's play, then Alexander sat. If a point guard didn't get him the ball often enough, or in the right places, the point guard faced demotion. Once the coach talked semi-jokingly about being "lasered" by Jordan if he made a move that offended the star. Such obsequiousness was unseemly, thought the worrying Wizards official. "Doug jeopardizes the respect of the younger guys for him when they think that Michael can run him that easily," the official observed. "Maybe Doug thinks there's no other way."

One frequently heard the argument that Phil Jackson would have handled Jordan differently, a criticism that was not so much speculative as beside the point. It did not take a Jackson to wield influence over Jordan or any other headstrong athlete. Historically, professional sports have been replete with unglamorous coaches and managers guiding athletic gods. Joe DiMaggio, Ted Williams, Jim Brown, Joe Namath, Reggie Jackson, Barry Bonds, Roger Clemens, Magic Johnson, Larry Bird, a mix of testy, flighty and demanding personalities, all played, successfully and respectfully, for the little-known and charismatically challenged. Even now, the New York Yankees' manager, Joe Torre, skillfully presides over a team made up of barons whose salaries in some cases dwarf his own. Jordan and Collins's pairing bore no resemblance to the superstar-coach relationship of, say, Babe Ruth and Miller Huggins, the Yankee manager through all of the 1920s, who had no qualms about letting Ruth know who was in charge.

A leader needed to assert himself. Coaching, like so much else in life, turned on calculated risk, and risk was what Collins was reluctant to take when it came to Jordan. What would Jordan have done had Collins taken firmer hold of the reins and declared that the star would play fewer minutes, or that he would no longer be exerting so much influence over personnel decisions? Certainly, Jordan could have had Pollin fire the coach, but the move would have looked petty and spiteful, severely damaging the god's image. That reality alone always gave Collins more leverage than he understood. Perhaps it didn't matter. He wanted Jordan's affection. He would do whatever Jordan demanded.

With his knee drained and John Hefferon's key advice disregarded, Jordan sat out just one game, against San Antonio, where more than 35,000 fans—the biggest NBA crowd of the regular season—showed up hoping to see him play. It was the first game he had missed because of injury since the '92–'93 season, a streak during which, fans remembered, he had played through bulging ankles and a broken facial bone and an infected foot, as if impervious to mortals' agonies. Down to the last few minutes, Jordan diehards in the Alamodome believed he would suit up. Disappointed, they nonetheless applauded warmly when he walked out of the tunnel in a cream-colored suit. The ovation built as he reached his seat on the end of the Wizards bench, Jordan waving slightly, smiling. Then he plopped down on the bench and, laughing, ribbed Popeye Jones: "Don't get your ass beat." He seemed relaxed enough, and then the game began and he couldn't sit still. He fitfully flexed his right knee. He pulled on his gold earring, grimaced and covered his face at bad passes.

The young Wizards, particularly Richard Hamilton, weren't exactly despairing over Jordan's absence or the possibility he might need to sit out more games. "The guys take pride and want to show we can play without Michael," Hamilton said, even suggesting that Jordan could benefit by observing *them* for a night. "Hopefully, he can watch and maybe get an understanding of *our* games. The guys out here are the guys who played on last year's team with me. . . . We can't put all our eggs in one basket, planning on Michael playing. . . . We have to approach this as the team we're going to play with . . ."

Courtney Alexander replaced Jordan in the lineup and played well on the offensive end, hitting 8–17 shots, scoring 16 points to complement Hamilton's 24. But this would be a tough night for the young

Wizards to try proving themselves without Jordan. San Antonio's stars included the league's best young big man, Tim Duncan, and the classy veteran David Robinson. Jordan looked pained as San Antonio built its lead and exploited defensive mismatches, particularly one that called for Kwame Brown to somehow handle Robinson. Jordan groaned and jerked his head back a few times, as if to recoil from the horror.

The San Antonio fans appeared reasonably content: their team was winning, and they had a chance to see Jordan, who emerged to a new wave of screams before the second half, thousands of necks craning as he gingerly walked past, people leaping and pointing, ecstatic in much the same way that crowds once reacted to a sighting of DiMaggio on Old Timers' Day. Only this was bigger; he had a legend possessed by no athletes other than Ali and Ruth. He was equal parts man and Wonder now, and people paid big money and endured horrific traffic jams just to say they had occupied his air. His lure meant that financial forces changed wherever he went on the road. But a crowd could not change any team's on-court fortunes. The Wizards got pummeled, losing by 15, a margin unreflective of how lopsided the game felt. The team's record sunk to 5–12.

Thousands of fans hung around afterward, hopeful of getting one more glimpse of him. They waited an hour, two hours, long after the Wizards team bus had left. Jordan was sitting in an airport by then, deep in his tube. Privately, he already had put an end to any serious thought that he would rest the knee for another game. He was upset: He needed for the sake of everybody to get back to playing, why couldn't people see that? *Didn't everyone goddamn understand they couldn't afford to drop every fucking game in Texas? Hadn't everybody just seen what happened out there?* He repeated a refrain. *We're losing, we're getting our asses beat, this is unacceptable, losing like this is fucking unacceptable.*

Only it wasn't unacceptable, not really; very few things were unacceptable in the NBA so long as the big money rolled in. In Washington, more money poured into the Wizards' coffers than ever in the team's history—despite a team that already had experienced an eight-game losing streak.

All the normal gauges of sports—team standings, wins and losses, playoff possibilities—had a curious irrelevance by then. A Jordan game now was not basketball so much as a transcendental event, and the Wizards less a losing NBA team than a novelty act, a touring troupe led by a charismatic figure aiming for nothing less than his professional resurrection. It was basketball's equivalent of a fantasy Beatles reunion at Wembley Stadium; it was Sinatra at the Garden. It did not particularly matter how much or how little the show moved you so long as you saw it. You'd seen him, you'd done the Jordan thing, you had the souvenir jersey. Thus motivated, they poured through the turnstiles everywhere—worshippers of a man, addicts for big events, lovers of a game, moths to a flame.

The Wizards were on the way to leading the NBA in total home and road attendance for the first time in franchise history, selling out each of the team's 41 games at MCI, increasing the club's home attendance by a league-high 32 percent and banking what some industry experts estimated to be an extra $450,000 per home game in ticket revenue—which translated to a gaudy boost of more than $18 million by season's end, which did not include the bonanza in extra souvenir and concessions sales.

But even the team's new profits in the 2001–2002 season paled against what Jordan the gold mine meant to the NBA as a whole. In the last year of their contracts with the league, NBC and Turner saw their ratings climb, most importantly among 18- to 34-year-olds. Foreign TV ratings soared. Thirty-eight of the Wizards' 41 road games would be sellouts, with the only vacant seats coming on nights later in the season when an injured Jordan could not play. Coupled with a coming-out of new stars and a surge in NBA merchandising, Jordan set off a tsunami of new gate and ancillary income for the league.

Best of all, for several team owners, the new money sparked a casualty. The NBA's so-called luxury tax—the levy imposed on high-spending teams whose player salaries exceed a ceiling reflective of a defined ratio of league revenue—already had likely disappeared for the season, in large part because the jump in revenue from Jordan's presence allowed for larger aggregate player salaries, thereby pushing the year's salary cap beyond even the most profligate teams' expenditures. Three NBA big spenders originally projected to be hit by the tax—Dallas, New York and Portland—consequently would pay nothing, saving their owners an estimated $60 million.

In the end, Jordan's financial boost to the league would be ineffably high. "If the league wrote Jordan a check for $100 million, the league would still be getting the better end of the bargain," said Alvin Gentry, the Los Angeles Clippers' head coach, aware that Jordan was receiving only a $1 million player salary and donating it to September 11th victims (a contribution that simultaneously sparked praise and criticism as some observers felt it was a transparent effort by Jordan to compensate for his lack of community involvement—an issue that meant nothing to the league, which simply loved its bonanza).

Such gratitude toward Jordan sparked a powerful deference throughout the NBA, a reluctance to press Midas to do anything he didn't wish, even when his edicts meant the Wizards broke league rules. Wanting to minimize scrutiny of his practice habits, particularly as his right knee worsened, Jordan and the Wizards casually flouted NBA rules governing the relationship between the media and players, including those guaranteeing reporters the opportunity to observe the last half hour of team practices. The vast majority of practices were closed altogether by Collins and Jordan, the coach typically exchanging a glance with his star when a Wizards p.r. official asked whether the media could be admitted that day. Jordan would usually be riding a stationary bike by then.

"No," Collins said, dispatching someone to tell the media to stay put.

The media complained to Wizards p.r. men like Matt Williams, but Williams's ultimate boss had no complaints about Jordan or Collins, or at least none he would mention publicly. Abe Pollin's tone conveyed only absolute delight with everything. He had a two-faced quality during Jordan's best days in Washington, his public face radiating unqualified admiration for the star. To listen to Pollin was to believe that, on and off the court, Jordan had comported himself brilliantly and nobly. "Michael is showing everybody why he is such an inspirational person and a classy guy doing a great thing," Pollin said in passing one night.

Jordan was making Pollin a lot of money. "Michael's impact already has been dramatic," Pollin went on happily, telling people in days to come that, thanks to Jordan and the newly constituted Wizards, it looked like years of financial malaise had ended, that the franchise would actually be realizing a profit for the first time in many years. The Wizards season ticket sales had climbed to more than 14,000 seats, the luxury boxes were being filled, revenue both from ad sales in Wizards souvenir programs and from corporate signage around MCI had spiked. Jordan was as reliable as the United States Mint, and as long as he was, nothing would be permitted to impede the money machine.

But, beneath the public surface, the tensions between the two men's camps persisted. Susan O'Malley still wanted Jordan's occasional help in marketing and public relations activities. Her requests did not call for much of his time, but now Jordan tried minimizing all commitments other than those on the court. It did not help matters that it was O'Malley, so aggressive from the Jordan camp's view, who was asking for his time. Even her least-demanding requests were often met by Jordan's resistance, escalating the uneasiness between the two. One winter day, after a special practice staged on the MCI court for Wizards season ticket holders, she had approached him as he was leaving the court and asked if he might be able to take just a few minutes to chat briefly with a group of ticket holders. They stood alone together at the foot of the tunnel leading to the Wizards dressing room, alongside the overhang of seats behind a basket, Jordan towering over her, O'Malley lifting her head nearly straight up to make eye contact. Jordan said how, unfortunately, he couldn't do anything at that moment, citing something in his schedule. "I'm sorry," he could be heard saying.

O'Malley didn't yield. She kept softly but tenaciously pushing: It would just take a few minutes, Michael. They'd love to see you.

Jordan's body language was adolescent-like. He slouched, glanced down, rolled his shoulders, swayed, looked trapped. He had a commitment, he said.

O'Malley became firmer: Michael, it would just take a few minutes.

Now Jordan was shaking his head: Sorry, sorry, no, can't do it, sorry.

They parted after a while, with neither really saying, "'Bye," or "Thanks anyway," or "See you soon"—their conversation just ending, the frustration of each palpable.

Once he soured on someone, that relationship, for all practical purposes, was dead. O'Malley had become his new Jerry Krause. It guaranteed that the strains between the two, and in turn the tensions between Jordan and Pollin, would worsen. Meanwhile, flush with financial health, Pollin could not have appeared happier. "Everything Michael's doing is great for the Wizards—I'm so lucky, we're all so lucky," he said, anticipating another night inside his arena teeming with the well-heeled and free-spending.

Jordan wasn't thinking dollars at that moment. *What the fuck was wrong with all these people doubting he could take care of his body?* he asked. *Nobody knows me like me.* He had been miserable in San Antonio, but now, just two days later in Houston, he was on the court, his rehab having lasted all of one game.

Collins had told the media that the possibility loomed that Jordan wouldn't be playing in games on successive nights, and that he might occasionally be told to sit out games during particularly crushing stretches: "On some nights, we may *have* to say, 'Sit it out.'"

He hadn't cleared that comment with Jordan. Jordan had no such plans, so Collins wouldn't be publicly saying *anything* like that ever again.

It was Classic Collins, people joked. He veered off script, saying something that simply popped into his head. Jordan always forgave him, believing Collins had his best interests at heart, never bothered in the way he might have been had a Jerry Krause uttered the same words. Collins had passed the loyalty test, the proof of which was that, after a gaffe, he swiftly got hold of the Jordan camp's talking points again. Displaying his malleability in Texas, he voiced sympathy with Jordan's instinct to play until his body had nothing left: "You want to know there's not another pitch left in that arm or even one more time up and down the floor. You want to know it's all gone . . ."

Jordan hadn't practiced, hadn't even touched a ball for four days by the time they hit Houston, his conditioning a mess, his finesse gone, his gait stiff. Panting through a lung-scorching 33 minutes, he looked ungainly for three quarters, even during a baseline dunk when his leap was so precariously low that he had to rattle the ball off the back rim. His outside shot had lost all radar-guidance, clanging short and off to the side.

He was pitiable, and then he was not. A single play resurrected him in the fourth quarter. He beat two defenders and hit an improbable, high-arcing reverse layup (the basketball equivalent of a trick billiards shot, deftly executed with added English and assisted by no small portion of luck). Next he canned a couple of tightly defended jumpers. And the game swung. It was in such moments, at 38 years and 10 months—whittled by age, winded from inactivity, his skills maybe 25 to 50 percent of what they had been at his peak—that even a doubter could see that here was the most remarkable athlete ever to play on an American sports team. You could point to the erosion of his skills, obviously. But even great mountains erode. Erosion is the inevitability. The prize, if any is out there, is in the way men resist it. Jordan's decline only made what he did on a night like this so confoundingly supernatural. He was the aged athlete who could just as well have been playing in an old-timers' game, but instead was in Houston, scoring on a bum leg against a double-teaming defense, and humbling men 10 and 15 years younger. In all, he scored 10 of his 18 points in the final quarter and collected several assists on no-look passes, and though he hit only 9 of 23 shots during the game, his savvy made the difference down the stretch. Hamilton, who had led the team for three quarters, played superbly again, finishing with a game-high 26 points. Haywood had a big block in the final minutes. Lue hit two huge jumpers, and the grunting, bruising, indomitable Popeye Jones finished with 10 points and 10 rebounds on his own pair of pained knees.

The Wizards won, 85–82, which made their record only slightly less woeful at 6–12. What no one knew is that they had begun a long winning streak. The team flew to Dallas, where Jordan again couldn't find his shot for most of the game—a portent of disaster, it seemed, particularly against a team as offensively potent as Dallas. But the biggest Dallas gun, forward Dirk Nowitzki, sat out with an injury, and so even with Jordan making only 3 of 15 shots through three quarters, and Dallas once leading by as many as 20 points, the Wizards found themselves in the game late.

Jordan then picked up a couple of steals without seemingly moving. On defense, he seldom darted any longer. But, in his best moments, he read the court like Garry Kasparov scanned a chessboard, anticipating foes' moves and filling lanes to make interceptions. Some of it derived from his sense of fate, the conviction that good things were meant to happen to him on a court, a gift unaffected by his struggles in a game. He knew that basketball was an aggregation of disappointments. What distinguished Jordan from mortals by then was less his talent than his refusal to back off on a bad night: He didn't cower like beaten prey and disappear in the midst of a 3–15, not even with a throbbing knee. The doctor who knew him best thought it explained why Jordan had been uniformly great during his career's most formidable challenges. "Michael always thinks that the next shot he's putting up is the one going in; he's always saying to teammates, 'Keep putting it up, keep putting it up,'" Hefferon observed. "His belief is absolute, no matter how he's feeling physically."

And so it was that Jordan scored 15 points in the fourth quarter, and the shortest of win-streaks was alive at two. At the game's end, he draped a long arm around the neck of Lue, an amazingly intimate gesture for a man unknown for such displays. He walked happily, if a tad awkwardly, toward a trainer's room, where ice waited for his knee. He flexed it. Someone asked him how he was feeling. "Fine," he said. His listeners waited for elaboration. "Fine," he repeated. It was as much as he would give them.

They flew to Memphis, where they won again. Hamilton had a season-high 30 points, flaying Memphis's heralded rookie, Shane Battier, hitting 15 of 24 shots, just another indication of how befuddling his mid-range jump shot had become to league defenses since he returned to the starting lineup. Jordan contented himself for the time being with feeding Hamilton the ball in stretches, picking up nine assists to go along with 16 points. For the first time all year, the Wizards looked less like the Jordan Show than a real team. Other players seemed to be jelling. Lue and Chris Whitney hit long jumpers. Laettner played tougher defense. Haywood was spectacular, with 15 rebounds to go with 17 points, on a night when, along with Laettner, he helped to frustrate the league's eventual rookie of the year, Spain's Pau Gasol, who managed to pull down 13 rebounds but was limited to six points. The only disappointing note was Kwame Brown, who still looked confused, unable to score a point or pull down more than a single rebound. Courtney Alexander would not be a disappointment because Alexander did not play, placed on the injured list with an ankle sprain.

The team's starting lineup and reserve rotation finally looked set. Players understood their roles. Laettner had become more assertive. Hamilton did not need to fear an imminent benching. Morale was good, and the Wizards won at home against Miami and New York, the winning streak now at five, Jordan and Hamilton combining for 48 points against Miami, and 53 against the Knicks. After the New York game, Hamilton tried spreading the praise, saying he had learned much from Jordan ("It's wonderful listening to Michael . . .") and, especially, assistant coach John Bach, with whom he had spent hours watching tapes and working on his defense.

As for Collins, Hamilton said that he and the coach were "still trying to feel each other out," adding that, with every day, he had a better sense what Collins wanted. In between pleasantries, Hamilton slipped in his observations on what changes had benefited the team. The team's tendency to run most of the offense through Jordan *seemed* to be shifting, he said, pleased that he had begun seeing the ball as much as he wanted it: "At first, we used to throw the ball to Michael. *Play over.* Now we're running through our offense, starting to look at second and third options. . . . *Everybody's* benefiting now."

He seemed, wherever the Wizards went, to be the target of reporters who wanted him to say how much, as one reporter put it, "Michael's influence is sinking into your team." Hamilton deftly changed the premise, keeping his answer short: "I think the big thing is that we're learning to play off *each other.*" He would say the next day: "Michael is getting a better feel for me. He's starting to understand what *I* can do." As he starred in more games, he became emboldened. He was not going to be Jordan's sidekick forever: "The game is now more up-tempo, more younger players. . . . I think [Jordan] is willing now to allow us to go ahead and play *our* game. And we all feed off each other. It's not just us feeding off him."

Beneath the surface, there was a lingering tension. Jordan complimented Hamilton while portraying himself as the teacher finally getting through to an up-and-down student: "I feel good that he's accepted, you know, the education that I've tried to pass on to him, to where he's starting to see it within our structured offense." And then Jordan couldn't help himself: "And that [means] not isolating [going against defenders one-on-one] and alienating the rest of his teammates." He let the scrum think about that for a half beat. Jordan ended on a vaguely positive note: "I think he's understanding all-around play, and hopefully he can learn from that education."

Amid the win and tenuous harmony, one major thing had gone wrong on the night of the New York game. Laettner broke his left fibula and would be out for about a month, which meant, said Collins, that Brown would be starting the Wizards' next game in Toronto. Once there, Jordan effectively overrode Collins's decision, recommending to Collins that Popeye Jones start in Laettner's place, as Jones, thought Jordan, would be more effective against Toronto's toughest inside player, Antonio Davis.

The game marked Washington's first with Toronto since Vince Carter had so badly scorched the Wizards during preseason. Jordan decided to guard Carter one-on-one, and in the first half, Carter had 23 points, most of them coming on three-pointers. Carter simply pulled up and, with Jordan backing up, cast up rainbow jumpers. Jordan looked helpless for a while. ("He's a tough cover," Jordan said later. "It took me a whole quarter to learn his tendencies.")

With Carter already at 19 points, Jordan gave way for a while in the second quarter to Tyrone Nesby, who never made better use of his toughness than in the next six minutes. He had his best defensive stint of the year, bumping Carter, knocking him out of his rhythm, forcing the star to put extra arc on his shot. "My whole thing," Nesby said later, "was just tryin' to get [Carter] frustrated. . . . He didn't want to post me up because [opponents] kind of get hit with [my] arm a lot."

By the time Jordan got back on the floor, Carter seemed to have lost something, a new frustration gripping him. When he blocked a Jordan shot, only to be called for a foul, he snickered at referee Rodney Mott: "Yeah, bail him out. Way to bail him out."

Jordan shot a look Carter's way. In the second half, everything turned, and Carter wilted. Jordan shut him out completely—Carter scoreless for the remainder of the game, seemingly so discouraged that he only put up four shots, none of which was remotely close, Jordan smothering him, chastising him a couple of times when Carter complained to officials. He took delight in bumping the younger man late in the fourth quarter, Carter not bumping back, broken by then, Jordan now psychologically dominating the matchup that he had dreamt aloud about back in his office a year earlier. Later, Jordan would declare, with the understatement of a satisfied victor, that it had required some study of Carter to "take his rhythm away."

The Wizards came from 19 points down to win by five. Hamilton, who had been selected by the NBA as the league's Player of the Week, carried the team offensively again with 27 points, and Jordan added 21, even with another poor shooting performance. Having won their sixth straight, the Wizards were now only a game under .500, as hot as any team in the NBA's Eastern Conference. Amazingly, less than two weeks after having his knee drained, Jordan had played 36 minutes, already back to logging heavy playing time despite John Hefferon's warnings and Doug Collins's oft-repeated assurances that the minutes would be coming down. The Wizards were thriving, and everywhere around the NBA, and the MCI Center in particular, the registers were clanging with new money, and the expectations of more millions in Wizards' playoff ticket revenue. But it was a fool's gold. Jordan was about to play the best ball of his comeback while grinding down those knees against all reason.

The day after the Toronto game, on Monday, December 17, Abe Pollin threw a holiday dinner for the Wizards' players and coaches—part of a multicourse, weeklong lovefest, an owner's bacchanal. As the Wizards beat Atlanta at home to reach .500 and stretch the winning streak to seven, Pollin expressed gratitude for all his players and coaches, and his "luck" at landing two people as wonderful as Doug Collins and Michael Jordan. He reminded people that, before the season ever began, he had predicted the Wizards would make the playoffs. *I know people laughed at that,* he said. *But look at the players. Aren't they playing great? I still hold to my prediction they're going to make the playoffs. And people aren't laughing anymore when I talk about the playoffs, are they?*

He had high praise for Collins. "Doug is a smart coach and is doing a fantastic job," Pollin said. "He likes hard work, and I do, too. And he's showing the players the importance of it. Tough defense, teamwork and hard work, and they've all picked it up."

He had a *team* now, he happily emphasized. "Sure, Michael brings them in, but people coming to MCI are excited about seeing the younger players, too, because they're getting better all the time and winning. We're competitive, and I give a lot of the credit for that to Doug and Michael. . . . This is the place to be now. People want to see the Wizards. I'm so excited about the playoffs. I think we're going to get there. . . . I just say, Let's keep it going, let's keep it going. And, as I say to everybody, I know Michael's going to lead the way."

Do the two of you talk a lot?

"We keep in touch," Pollin said.

Inside MCI Center, any apparel or souvenir with the Jordan name flew off shelves. His jerseys, ranging from $35 to $169, sold briskly. In a game against Atlanta that week, as often happened at MCI, the crowd chanted his name—*Joooorr-dan, Joooor-dan*—less an exhortation than a feel-good mantra, more reverential than rabid. Sometimes fans booed when he laid a ball up for a gentle basket rather than dunked, a soft boo, not a display of anger, only comradely disappointment: Most of the booing came from good-natured, middle-aged fans who keenly understood from their own lives the new limits.

Still, the reality chipped away at his majesty. He could score 35, and some fans would leave the arena feeling strangely deprived, thinking they had missed something but having difficulty putting their fingers on exactly *what*. Their ennui had nothing to do with his productivity, only aesthetics: A night's worth of flawless fallaway jump shots never would have the impact on them of one tomahawk dunk. His art lay not in point totals but in his magic, only most of his magic was gone. Younger players best understood the inevitability of this, sympathizing with him, viewing the fans' disappointment as an injustice. "Jordan doesn't have the Ups to dunk all the time anymore," Tracy McGrady said. "*So?* I don't know why people get surprised . . . He's older now. He does different stuff now. He *has* to."

Nonetheless, the change in his game had a profound effect on the way audiences viewed him. His magnetism did not extend as far during his second comeback, his appeal among youth in particular not as strong as during the peak of his magic in the '90s. The new tableau of the comfortable American family at a Jordan game looked different. It was not uncommon to see a parent wearing, as a kind of sweatshirt, a fresh Jordan jersey purchased just minutes earlier, with two more jerseys slung across his arm for his children to don later perhaps if the mood struck them, which was questionable, as the kids had come to the game in their own favorite jerseys—an Iverson here, a Carter there, a Bryant, an O'Neal. The scenes reflected a shifting marketplace, the signs of which were everywhere. The first round of fan balloting for the All-Star Game had just come out, revealing that Jordan trailed no fewer than five players—Carter, Iverson, Bryant, O'Neal and Minnesota's young star Kevin Garnett. He had lost his hold on children and young adults, and, in turn, his grip on advertisers had slackened, said analysts. His core audience skewed older now, but, even in that group, people's fascination with him had waned. The new reality dented his appeal as a commercial spokesman. After an MCI commercial with him tested poorly, the corporation said it had no immediate plans for another Jordan television ad. Neither did Gatorade announce any role for him in an upcoming ad campaign. Nike indicated it would be using younger athletes to shill for Jordan's new approximately $200 shoe, ready to come out on the market in 2002. He was the best player in the history of basketball, but he was now old-school in a game whose fans, particularly the urban young, gravitated to the young and fresh. In a cruel truth, he was losing worshippers at the same pace he was losing Ups.

In most cases now, the curious came to see him for the same reason that people went to see Niagara Falls or stared up at a lunar eclipse—because they wanted to glimpse the attraction. They packed MCI, and, after games, they jammed nearby Washington restaurants and clubs. The businesses' owners were delighted, no one more so than Abe Pollin.

Jordan went out on the town sometimes with his crew—Tim Grover, George Koehler and other trusted friends. He had opened up an eponymous restaurant in Washington, but he generally preferred going to other restaurants and nightclubs, mostly Washington hangouts for the deep-pocketed and discreet. He liked Zola and Café Milano and sometimes a club called Dreams. He'd knock back a few drinks, settle in, maybe smoke a cigar, talk to some women, talk longer to others, accept a handshake from a club employee or two and chat for a bit with guys about basketball—not at all unusual doings, as evenings in the NBA go. Just the same, the regular media didn't see any of it. Reporters heard about Jordan frequenting particular clubs, but never did they have a chance to get close enough to observe him in such places, the security around Jordan essential for warding off not only voyeurs but also the potentially unstable.

The result was that no reporter or stranger could dare think of approaching Jordan and his friends at a club unless that person happened to know someone seated at the Jordan table. The male companion of a woman who had ended up at the Jordan table seemed to qualify, especially a perturbed companion. This meant, in turn, that the boyfriend or date saw and heard things that regular journalists covering Jordan couldn't. In time, an intriguing story would run in a Washington, D.C., alternative newspaper, *Washington City Paper,* written by an offended young man who told the tale of feeling somewhat jilted when his female friend had not only gone off to the Jordan table, he claimed, but had received a whispered invitation from someone at the Jordan table to join Michael and his friends later in the evening after she had separated herself from her date. Michael's limo would quietly pick her up, promised the Jordan friend. In time, without telling her friend about it first, she accepted the invitation, joining Jordan and a few of his friends on an extended outing somewhere in Washington. The young man was offended and more than a little angry at Jordan. He thought Jordan had acted arrogantly, particularly during their encounter, claiming that Jordan had been aloof to the point where he wouldn't acknowledge his presence, while simultaneously making a move on his date.

No reader could be sure of what happened, of course, and even if the worst was true, did it really amount to anything more than a story of bad manners and a trifling flirtation between a married man and an agreeable young woman whose upset suitor had lashed back? Probably not. After all, how many times in my life had I witnessed married male acquaintances try to woo women? Still, the story reminded me of all I couldn't see, day to day, in Jordan's life.

By December of 2001, I was about to hear another tale, another set of allegations about Jordan's off-court existence. In Cleveland, male exotic dancer Bobby Mercer was preparing to make contact with me over the subject of Jordan's alleged affair, years earlier, with a Mercer family member. He had come no closer, in letters and phone calls, to getting what he wanted from Jordan's attorney, Frederick Sperling—an agreement that Jordan would pay for psychiatric sessions for the woman, whom, he insisted, was still obsessed with Jordan, though their supposed affair had ended long ago. Still threatening legal action,

Sperling had warned Mercer to back off. Mercer refused, sending a letter to Jordan's wife, Juanita, which began:

> Dear Juanita Jordan,
>   Here's some information I think you should know about, that is going to cause embarrassment to our families . . .

Now Mercer planned to share his story with the media, formulating plans to hold a press conference to "expose" Jordan on the same day, January 31, 2002, that the Wizards would play in Cleveland. He already had plans to publish a flyer and send it to journalists at major newspapers. If Frederick Sperling wouldn't deal with him, the Rumpshaker was ready to take the next step.

A few hundred miles away, in Indiana, Karla Knafel still wanted the $5 million that she claimed Jordan had promised to pay her, in exchange for her silence about their old affair. The quarter of a million he already had given her would not keep her quiet much longer. Her attorneys were no closer to resolving their demands with Fred Sperling, both sides digging in their heels. If the negotiations did not result in a settlement over the next few months, Knafel was prepared to file a lawsuit. The story of the affair then would break publicly and Jordan would face a new p.r. headache.

Sperling's job included trying to minimize Jordan's p.r. nightmares, thereby freeing his client to think about nothing other than basketball and his other pleasures. Jordan spent late December happily finetuning his errant jump shot, receiving more stim treatments and hanging out with his crew, deep and safe in his tube.

Jordan still hadn't asked any of the young players to party with him. It wasn't going to happen. The kids understood his reluctance, said Jordan, who noted that going out with him would probably cramp their style anyway, given the security and seclusion he looked for. Beyond that, he wasn't anxious to have newcomers in his private circle, didn't have need for any more close friends in that regard, he added. Grover, Koehler and a few others from his crew: They made him comfortable. His comfort zone was small, he reminded people.

The young players did not look busted up about it. They had their own lives, and any life in the NBA, even as a grunt reserve, had its perks and pleasures. The Washington clubs and bars became frenzied whenever a couple of the players dropped in for drinks—they were young princes, imbued with a celebrity enhanced by their good performances and impervious to their bad ones. Hamilton, Lue, Alexander and Nesby made the rounds. "Fans like to talk to players—you don't have to be Mike for them to be wantin' to talk to you," Nesby said. "Some people just treat athletes special. Winnin' got nothing to do with it. If they are like that for players, imagine what they be doin' around Mike."

What *are* they like around him?

"That's what I was goin' to ask you," Nesby said, squinting, smiling, adjusting a black do-rag over his cornrows.

He thought about it. "Guys talk. You know, 'What's happenin' with Mike? What's happenin'?' But Mike don't talk much, not about that stuff. That's cool, I guess. You with him on the court. You here to play basketball. I just know the Mike with the basketball part. The other stuff is Mike's other stuff, you know, and nobody 'round here be knowin' that."

T-Nez was cool with knowing or not knowing.

He finished adjusting his do-rag and headed out with Lue and Alexander.

One morning, on the road, I walked into the gift shop of a hotel and bumped into a young Wizards player.

"Hey, dawg," he said. He was admiring some candy on a rack. "What's going on with M.J.?"

I said he seemed to be trying to get over his tendinitis.

The player fingered a candy bar. "People get real careful talkin' about M.J., huh?"

I guess, I said. Makes sense.

"People don't want to make mistakes. I don't like talking about the man's business."

Sure.

"M.J.'s a little hard to get to know," the player said. "But I respect the man. Just a little hard, you know—to get to know."

Does that bother you?

"No. I don't know if I'd want to."

Want?

"Goin' somewhere with him. The boss seein' you doin' *anything*, just bein' *playful*—dawg, you don't want that."

He shrugged, his mind momentarily erasing Jordan so that he could concentrate on this candy rack. He picked out a few bars and asked the cashier to bill them to his room.

"Sorry—you need a minimum purchase of fifteen to bill to the room," the cashier said.

The player sighed. Then something slowly ignited in his head. He glanced back and forth between the candy rack and the cashier, back and forth, the candy and the cashier, candy and cashier, candy, cashier, candy, cashier. It was like watching a *Beavis and Butthead* cartoon, when the two are trying to figure out where and how to get a TV.

A lightbulb went off in the player's mind. He walked to the rack and picked up a veritable mound of candy. It came to about $20, allowing him to bill everything. The cashier put it all in a bag for him. He happily bounded out, calling toward a teammate.

They were very young.

And their boss was not.

Hamilton went down early that Friday night in Orlando. One moment he was streaking past a beaten defender; in the next instant, making a cut, he was in agony. He partially tore his right groin, the injury reducing him to a hobble, with the early prognosis calling for him to be out for four weeks. If losing a 20-points-a-game scorer wasn't bad enough, Jordan had an awful night, scoring a season-low 12 points, on 3–16 from the field. The combination of Jordan's and Hamilton's setbacks would have typically guaranteed a blowout loss, except that Tracy McGrady was out with a strained back and the chronically ailing Grant Hill had undergone season-ending ankle surgery.

Hubert Davis came off the bench to save the Wizards with 19 points, hitting several long jumpers early in the fourth quarter, the winning streak now at eight. Collins was not exultant but worried: "We lost Christian to a broken leg. Now Rip's out. . . . We have to play through it. . . . But how much of this can a team take?"

From the players' view, winning with Hamilton out and Jordan's shot in tatters proved anything was possible. Much of the team slept on the red-eye flight to New York, where the next night, Jordan scored 26 points and led the Wizards back from 10 points down in the final quarter, hitting the game-winning jumper over Latrell Sprewell and a late-arriving Allan Houston with 3.2 seconds left. Sprewell had only six points, none of which came off Jordan in their matchup, Jordan rendering the Knicks star as impotent as he had Vince Carter, six days earlier, during the second half at Toronto. *"Look at the numbers, look at the numbers,"* Jordan shouted to the coaching staff, meaning *Sprewell's* numbers: 3–16 on the night, and 0–13 off Jordan, by most people's count. But the more important number on this night was nine, the length of the winning streak, which tied a Washington franchise record and catapulted a team once seven games below the .500 mark to two games above it. Jordan sounded supremely self-satisfied. Referring to Hamilton and Laettner, he said, "We have two key guys out and I stepped up tonight. Our defense kept us in the game. And I was able to make a big basket."

He had played 41 minutes in Orlando the night before, and labored as hard in Madison Square Garden. He insisted he felt great, but already the workload exceeded John Hefferon's recommendation. Hamilton's injury put more pressure on Collins, who did not want to sacrifice wins by sitting Jordan for too long but who understood the Wizards would crash if the bad knee broke down. The coach had options: He had Nesby and Davis to buy Jordan a few extra minutes of rest in each game, and also Alexander, who was coming off the injured list that week. But Collins seemed to have difficulty weaning himself off relying on Jordan to play heavy minutes. And, all the while, his star pushed to stay on the floor. Characteristically, Collins sounded conflicted, lurching between worry and his instinct to accommodate Jordan's desires: "I've gotta get Michael's minutes down, because when I didn't early in the season, his leg swelled up, it was the point of diminishing returns. We've talked about it. . . . He thinks he can play thirty-seven or thirty-eight minutes comfortably. . . . This is gonna be a judgment thing, where he and I have to look at each other. There's a real trust there."

So he had a plan in place, he said, shrugging, accepting the congratulations of old friends on the team's turnaround. He rode the league's longest win-streak. Things could not be much better.

Yet the game is fickle. The streak ended in Charlotte, where Jordan's shot betrayed him in the fourth quarter. The next night, December 27, the team found itself in Indiana, where Jordan played in his second set of back-to-back games in less than a week. He had difficulty getting lift on his jump shot, wincing after a few misses, making only 2 of 10 shots, calling it a night after only 25 minutes of play, when Indiana turned the game into a rout and Reggie Miller began clapping his hands together and woofing. There seemed to be a foul mood in the air—players on both teams tired, tempers short. When Collins started complaining about a ref's call, Miller snapped at him, "Goddamn, Doug, you worry about everything. *Just coach your team.*"

The weird vibe seemed to hover all night. Players began chewing out teammates for everyone at courtside to hear. Jermaine O'Neal beat Jahidi White on a move to the hoop, and Jordan yelled at White, "You gonna let that happen? Let him show you up like that? Let him kick your ass? What's wrong with you? What's wrong with you?"

White said nothing.

Collins jumped on Kwame Brown. "Tell me, what are you supposed to be doin' out there? What are we doin'? What are we doin'? What are we doin'?"

The kid hung his head.

"What are we doin'?"

But the weirdest moment came during a time-out with 2:45 left in the game. Popeye Jones, who worked hard with the young players, moved toward Etan Thomas, perhaps the most dedicated of the Wizards' young big men. They were two of the best-liked guys on the team, two of the most determined competitors. It had been a frustrating night for Jones, but even with the game's outcome decided, he wanted to exhort Thomas to play hard in the last couple of minutes. He mumbled something to Thomas, adding, "Do it."

The remark caught a nerve. The usually amiable Thomas flared. "Fuck you, Popeye," he said, walking back onto the court.

Jones's mouth fell open. Taking a seat on the bench, he said nothing, just glared at the younger player, who, in turn, stared back and slowly nodded, accepting a challenge. Once inside the locker room at the game's end, they began fighting, each landing punches. Tables toppled, players stepped between the combatants, pulling them apart, Thomas landing a last shot, Popeye still straining to get at him. Once order had been restored, Jordan told everyone, No one, *no one* should be talking about the incident. Ever. *No one.*

It had been an awful night all around. The Wizards lost by 27, and Jordan managed only six points, a career low, the first time in 867 games that he had failed to score at least 10 points, a streak that dated back to 1986. He just wanted to finish with the media and get on the plane. He strode into the press lounge, and it was then that he saw Lacy Banks, who had driven from Chicago with his special brand of mirth and a question about the problems of the Bulls. Jordan smirked. Banks grinned. It was impossible not to like Lacy Banks. He was the Will Rogers of basketball reporters, lighthearted, engaging, gabby, and usually posing a question that elicited something remarkably human from Jordan. Mischief oozed from him.

Banks was there to ask Jordan about the demise of Tim Floyd, the

Bulls' coach and Jerry Krause hire who followed Phil Jackson and who had resigned just three days earlier, on Christmas Eve. "Floyd was brought in to try to rebuild the dynasty that you built . . ." Banks began, and Jordan already had begun chuckling, trying to hide a smile behind his hand, ribbing him: "Lacy, you came *all* the way from Chicago for that one, didn't ya?"

Now everyone was laughing.

The cameras kept rolling. Jordan took a breath, and shook his head. He settled on an answer: "Well, I don't like to elaborate on other teams' miseries or lack of success"—a nifty shot at the Bulls and Krause; he was always happy to take one. "I like Tim. I thought he was a qualified coach. But some situations are not made for some coaches. Unfortunately, I don't think the Chicago situation was there for Tim. And, unfortunately, it took him four years to realize it. . . . I think he's going to get rid of that whole stigma of coming in after Phil Jackson and after the championship team. . . . I think he's better off. I hope you don't take that in a way that's very derogatory. . . . It's in support of Tim Floyd."

Then he took a last swipe at Krause and the rest of the Chicago management team who had declined to make him an executive. "I'm happy where I am."

The Wizards p.r. man said, "Thanks, folks. We gotta go."

The TV guys flicked off cameras.

Jordan started walking away, then turned to Lacy Banks. Smiling, he muttered, "You asshole."

The media roared.

Jordan looked like he felt a little better.

Media reports made much of his six-point game. By the time the team arrived back in Washington, he was angry again. Already, he had begun working himself into a simmering furor for a game two nights later at MCI, doing what Michael Jordan did better than anyone else in sports—convincing himself that he was being dismissed and disrespected. "Scoring six points, my career low, I'm pretty sure you guys were saying how old I was," he would say, 48 hours later. He shot a look at his inquisitors, searching for confirmation of his suspicions—a nodding head here, a telling chuckle there. Nobody around him so much as flinched, nobody said a thing. He wasn't through. "I knew with that game, you guys would say that I'd lost whatever I'd gained, that maybe [the comeback] wasn't a great idea."

That many of those voices were his own invention hardly mattered. Playing in a frenzy, he delivered a masterpiece against Charlotte that night, scoring 24 points by the end of the first quarter alone. Muscling defenders low in the post, he furiously motioned to teammates for the ball: *Give it to me, give it to me.* Everything worked. Finding himself guarded by bigger but slower foes, he faked and scored on fadeaway jumpers and tricky little up-and-under moves, where he would pump with his arms, get the opponent in the air, then take a long drop step and go under him for a short bank shot. He rediscovered his quick first step to the basket, bursting around defenders and finding space for easy pull-up jumpers and driving layups. He looked offended by miscues, berating referee Derrick Stafford after having one of his jumpers partially blocked by 6' 10" Hornet P. J. Brown: "Derrick, what game are you fuckin' watchin' out there? How's that not a foul on him? *What game are you fuckin' watchin'?*"

Stafford looked at him but said nothing, just one more ref reminded of the uses of Jordan's power. P. J. Brown stared slack-jawed at Stafford, as if incredulous that the ref quietly permitted such a lashing. On the other hand, Brown knew better than to say anything to Jordan ("He seemed to have extra motivation tonight," a diplomatic Brown would say later). Jordan abused Brown a while longer until, in mercy, the Hornets tried 6' 9" Lee Nailon on him. Nailon fared no better, and soon David Wesley, Jamaal Magloire and Stacey Augmon futilely took turns. By then Jordan was in ether, going over the rim and pulling down a rebound from Augmon, yelling, mouth open, tongue out, sweat running in rivulets down glistening cheeks, a thousand flash cameras in the arena clicking, Jordan reborn, yelling at somebody, his face a little wild, the crowd berserk.

A few times, Doug Collins looked over at him. Jordan gave him a firm shake of his head: *No, no.* Before the game, Jordan had told Collins that he didn't want to be coming out in the first quarter if he had his rhythm. "Let's ride me," Jordan said, and Collins complied.

Jordan had 34 points at half, a franchise record. Late in the third quarter, Collins briefly took him out, only to have Jordan swiftly countermand him. "Do you want to go into the fourth quarter with a big lead?" Jordan asked. "Or do you want them to come back on us?"

Collins put him back in the game. The decision was good for Jordan's point total, but risky for a gimpy knee. Late in the fourth quarter, with a last binge and a short fadeaway jumper, he scored his 51st point, the oldest player in league history ever to score as many as 50. MCI became a din—*Joooor-dan, Joooor-dan.* On his off nights, he had been a reminder of mortality. But on this evening, he was the flickering ember that would not go out—and so, transfixed, the crowd screamed.

After 38 minutes, slightly raising a hand, he called it a night. Following the game, he said of his doubters, "I'm pretty sure they're going to say *less* now, and tryin' to understand that I can still play this game, at 38."

When on a roll, he lost himself in basketball, and two nights later, on New Year's Eve, determined to prove that his gem against Charlotte was no fluke, he set out to decimate New Jersey, whose rising 6'9" young star, Kenyon Martin, was asked to defend him. Early in the game, Jordan was astounded when Martin casually told him that he was playing with a back injury that hampered his movement. Why, why, *why* had Martin been so naïve to tell him *that?* he asked later. Didn't Martin know he was a predator who *attacked* any weakened quarry?

He scored 45 points in 41 minutes, including 22 straight Wizards points early in the game, just one point shy of his own NBA record for consecutive points on a team. He might have had 50 again, but, seemingly tiring and with the Wizards leading comfortably, he took only two shots in the fourth quarter. Shortly after he missed his last—a three-point attempt—with about three minutes left, Collins looked at him, signaling he hoped to take him out, and Jordan consented with a nod.

He looked beatific after the game, in a way he never would again that season. Other players rushed out to New Year's parties. He lingered in the training room, finally emerging at 11:30 p.m. to face the media, his silver hoop earring glistening. He talked longer than usual and, even after saying goodnight, he hung around, basking in the good feeling, wanting to talk a little longer. Somebody in his retinue said, "Gettin' late. We better be goin', M.J."

Jordan raised an index finger like a sword: *Wait.*

He turned and told a few reporters that another 50-point game had been within his reach that night. There had been only five back-to-back 50s in NBA history and, though his name was already on that list, oh, man, he muttered exuberantly, how he would have loved to do it again, especially at age 38. "And I *would've* had it," he insisted, "if I didn't miss that last one"—an allusion to that errant three-point attempt, after which he permitted Collins to take him out. "If that one goes," he said, "I'm there [at 48 points] and then . . ." He grinned, and flipped his wrist, in a gesture that meant 50 would have been only a hoop away, a done deal.

The team was nearing the end of its greatest run during his comeback. Having begun with that win in Houston, the Wizards were on their way to winning 13 of 15 games, and no player in the league had enjoyed a more scintillating December than Michael Jordan—an older and grounded Jordan, certainly—but once again a Jordan who was being touted in some quarters as a candidate for another Most Valuable Player award, as improbable as that sounded. He emphasized that his legs felt great, answering a question no one had posed, talking about the bad knee though he'd spoken about it to the media horde two minutes earlier. "I'm getting treatment [for it]," he said. "If I can keep this tendinitis away, knock on wood"—he audibly conked his shaven skull with a half-formed fist, in what was becoming a favorite Jordan gesture—"then obviously, you'll see how I can move."

It was 11:40 p.m. Another voice began pleading: *Let's go, Mike.* He kept talking. No party could compare to being back in the firmament, with even the skeptical media singing hosannas.

Let's go, Mike. Please.

He finally relented. He happily started off on his night, yelling at something in the air, something only he could feel: "Yeah, yeah." Outside, by the entrance and exit of the players' garage, a pack of fans stood three deep, hoping for a glimpse of him in a fleeting SUV. "Yeah, yeah." The euphoria would last for all of one more week.

6

Secrets and Tensions

THE NEW YEAR BROUGHT TWO SLICES OF HELL—ONE THAT HE didn't see coming, and one he saw coming only too late. His right knee apparently sent no warning signals he could recognize. But a divorce petition seldom sneaks up on a man; a spouse's estrangement is a palpable thing. Juanita Jordan and her attorney signed and dated her petition for divorce the day after Christmas. A week later, she still had not filed it, its existence a secret to the world. As she privately resolved to file the petition later that week against a husband merely identified as a "businessman" named "M. Jeff Jordan," the soon-to-be respondent spent the first days of 2002 outwardly serene, finding his idyll, as usual, at an arena, getting ready for a home game against the Chicago Bulls, two days away.

After doing his strength exercises with Tim Grover that morning, he sat out another midday practice, deciding to rest his fragile knee for the approaching game, doing nothing more than ride the stationary bike and briefly shoot while his teammates drilled.

The media didn't see any of this. In accordance with Jordan and Collins's desire, virtually all Wizards practices were closed, despite NBA rules that governed the relationship between the media and players, guaranteeing writers the ability to observe the last 30 minutes of all practices. The closed practices were a reminder that few league rules applied to Jordan. Angry reporters in Washington called the NBA offices, to ask for enforcement of the media access rule, the violation of which by the Wizards was punishable by league fines. The response of the NBA's chief public relations official, Brian McIntyre, was always the same: We'll look into it, and ask them to follow the rule.

Nothing changed. No fine was ever administered. No edict from the NBA ever came. Abe Pollin never intervened. In the end, the league's rule meant nothing. Answerable only to Collins and Jordan, the Wizards' public relations staff played the role of gatekeepers, keeping writers at a distance. Washington reporters became resigned to being shut out of practices. But visiting writers, unaccustomed to seeing league rules ignored, were irked by Jordan's sway and the Wizards' secrecy. *Chicago Tribune* columnist and Jordan biographer Sam Smith had this *Looking Glass* exchange one day with Wizards p.r. representative Maureen Nasser.

> Smith: You're agreeing that there's a rule that says we're supposed to be allowed in, to see the last part of practice.
> Nasser: Yes.
> Smith: And that we're still out here.
> Nasser: Yes.
> Smith: And that it's time to let us in.
> Nasser: Yes.
> Smith: And you're saying that we're not going to be let in.
> Nasser: Yes.

"She's just going to keep saying yes," groaned a *USA Today* reporter.

"I think I see him; I see *twenty-three*," shouted a reporter who believed he glimpsed Jordan through a slit in the gym door.

"Move away from there," commanded Nasser.

"We never get to go in," the *USA Today* man mumbled abjectly.

"I think I see *twenty-three*," the other reporter said.

"Move away from there," Nasser barked.

The reporter obeyed. Such splendid seclusion for *23* required the constant vigilance of a large band of club and Jordan-hired assistants. Even with the tight controls, however, information seeped out. Jordan's knee still plagued him, according to insiders watching him walk gingerly at closed-door practices. The information landed in stories. Jordan's personal publicist, Estee Portnoy, made a phone call in an effort to learn the identities of those who had spoken about the boss without his authorization. She recited a favorite Jordan aphorism: *Those who know don't speak, and those who speak don't know.*

It was, among other things, a cryptic order to those in his circle: *Don't talk.*

Portnoy told writers that Jordan would look with dismay on any reporter whose Jordan stories might rely on information from people who "Michael thinks don't truly know his life." It left journalists hanging on the horns of a dilemma. As the Jordan camp's reasoning went, those friends who dared to talk about him were necessarily ignorant and not part of his inner circle, making any anecdote gleaned from them unworthy. On the other hand, if reporters wanted to do a legitimate story, they needed first to talk to those people who *really* knew Michael, except that journalists wouldn't be able to do that, Portnoy added, because the close friends couldn't and wouldn't talk in most cases, in accordance with Michael's wishes. And if they ever did talk, then by definition they were no longer in the inner circle and what they had to say was nonsense.

It was catch-23.

A large number of reporters continued to play the game, as if hoping that cooperating with Jordan would lead to an exclusive interview. It never happened. The simplest course was the most productive: Write whatever you had, ask Jordan whatever you wished, and be braced for the possibility of trouble.

That is what Sam Smith had done throughout Jordan's Bulls days. Now, never having gotten into the Wizards' practice, patiently having waited around until its end, he found himself standing in front of his old antagonist Doug Collins, about whom he had ceased writing, many years earlier. All that had changed. Amazingly, over the years, they had become friends, with a view taking root that Smith, among his many accomplishments, had broken Collins just as surely as a broncobuster tames a temperamental mustang. Now the coach was as compliant as the gentlest colt. The coach talked and talked and talked for him. In the case of Collins, Sam Smith was the NBA's Horse Whisperer. Maybe he could be persuaded to go out on the road with us.

Smith had a question: Doug, what do you think Michael expected versus what this season has been?

Collins happily nodded. "I think Michael knew, in his heart, that those rib injuries were going to get him off to a slow start. . . . As Michael has gotten better, it's given the guys a little bit of a swagger . . ."

Collins kept talking. From behind the locker-room door, Jordan now and then poked his head out, then swiftly brought it back in—in, out, in, out, like a prairie dog in a burrow. He stayed inside a few more minutes. Collins happily kept talking and talking to Sam Smith. He said that Jordan's young teammates needed to earn his respect by proving themselves on the floor, just as had been the case during Collins's days in Chicago, where players had responded by showing their mettle—John Paxson, B. J. Armstrong, Steve Kerr, Craig Hodges . . .

"You didn't say Brad Sellers," Sam Smith interjected, grinning—Sellers the former Bull who had so disappointed Jordan that the star had helped arrange to have him traded away, but not before Sellers had observed the Collins-Jordan blowup at practice and said that everybody knew that the real power on the team certainly didn't reside with the coach. Collins shot Smith a glance that looked like a faint plea, as if to say, *Please don't go there.* Not seeming to notice, Smith had moved on, anyway. It was all pleasant, a nice exchange between two old combatants; but no matter how pleasant, their friendship hadn't won Smith an invitation into practice because Jordan would never give Sam Smith special permission to attend a practice. And if Jordan didn't, Collins wouldn't, couldn't.

Now Jordan finally exited the locker room and walked over. He glanced down, expressionlessly, at Smith. In the old days, when Collins and Smith wouldn't speak to each other, Jordan talked to the reporter all the time. Like Lacy Banks, Smith had known Jordan in those early years when Jordan frequently invited the Chicago press corps up to his hotel rooms to hang out, play cards, get a few quotes. Jordan liked Smith enough at the time that he invited him to play golf. But after Smith declined an invitation from Jordan to bet during their round, Jordan, who liked wagering, never asked him to play golf again. Smith felt no keen disappointment. He never had sought to become another "Jordan Guy." Over the years, he reported what he saw, and in time wrote his book, "The Jordan Rules," which is when Jordan shut him out for good, limiting his discussions with Smith to press conferences.

"Michael doesn't like it when people make money off him," Estee Portnoy said of books about Jordan. But the Smith book, which chronicled Jordan's occasional abuse of Bulls teammates, especially irritated the Jordan camp. In some respects, the book was quite tame. In limiting its scope to Jordan's basketball existence, it acknowledged the kind of boundaries that athletes like to have drawn, steering clear of Jordan's private life and any questions about whether his behavior comported with his marketing image. But the book angered Jordan just the same. Nowadays, Smith asked his questions of Jordan without making much eye contact, and Jordan coolly stared over Smith's head in an exemplar of composure, courteously answering his questions but not offering Smith much in the way of insights.

It took the rare day for him to open up when Smith was part of a scrum, and it said much about the state of Michael Jordan's mind, 48 hours away from his first game ever against his old team, that this would be such an afternoon. Later, it would seem extraordinary that he had talked on this afternoon at all. He was fighting a heavy cold, and his wife had drawn closer to the day when she would make her move. At the instant Juanita Jordan's filing took place, there would be p.r. issues to address. There would be painful private matters involving his children and the prosaic question of where he would live full-time during the off-season in Chicago, with his wife and kids ensconced in the Highland Park manse. He had many personal reasons for excusing himself from the press scrum on this day, but he seemed anxious to talk. The Bulls would be in Washington soon, which meant that one of the men responsible for depriving him of an executive position in the Bulls organization and breaking up the triumvirate of Jordan, Jackson and Pippen would be arriving. Any press conference over the next two days offered him another chance to zing Jerry Krause.

His contempt for Krause had not stopped him in recent years from trying to use his old punching bag. A year earlier, when desperate to unload players in an effort to get the team under the salary cap and give himself room to acquire better performers, he actually had called Krause, extending the possibility that perhaps they could do some business together, that perhaps Krause could benefit from acquiring one of his veterans. Krause wasn't about to be lured into doing Jordan a favor by lowering the Wizards' bloated player payroll and taking a high-priced mediocrity off his hands. Krause offered nothing, embraced no deals, and Jordan's grudge remained fresh.

He never would stop taking veiled shots at Krause, whom he viewed as an egotist who had exaggerated his role in the old Bulls' successes. There seemed no shortage of Krause-related topics available now, especially given the state of upheaval in the Bulls' organization. With Tim Floyd fired as Bulls coach, Krause had elevated a former Jordan teammate, Bill Cartwright, from an assistant coaching position to the top job. If the Bulls kept plummeting, not only Cartwright would be booted but Krause likely would be endangered. Someone just had to ask Jordan about Krause, and he would do the rest. But no one raised the topic immediately after practice that day. The scrum barraged him instead with questions about the Bulls' young guard Ron Artest, the rock-hard kid who had inadvertently broken Jordan's ribs. In a monotone, he said he liked Artest and didn't blame him.

No Krause questions.

Now the scrum session was breaking up. "See you guys later," he said softly, turning his back and walking down a hallway toward an elevator, when he heard Sam Smith far behind him calling out a question. Jordan generally ignored questions once he walked away from the scrum. But this one, asking for his opinion on Cartwright's hiring, presented the opportunity he wanted. A good 50 feet away, he slowed, wheeled and shouted over his shoulder that, as recent club moves went, hiring Cartwright "was the best thing the Bulls did." He kept turning, stopping, facing the scrum now. He paused only for an instant, then thrust the shiv: "Now they need to fire Jerry and hire John Paxson."

What did he say?

Silence on both ends of the hallway.

As if uncertain whether he exactly meant it, or because they *knew* he meant it and wanted to convey ease so as not to scare him off a provocative quote that had fallen like manna from the sky, the reporters up the hallway casually laughed. But Jordan did not, his expression flat, eyes wide, body in a forward lean, as was his way when most serious.

Another question flew down the hallway, carrying a suggestion as to when Krause might be fired: "Maybe this summer?"

"I hope so," Jordan answered.

He had said it, and he meant it. He had pulled up the shade and, for an instant, he had let the world see much of himself, maybe too much, let them see just how much he could loathe somebody, how he did not have to go deep to tap his grudges. He turned and walked into the elevator.

On game day, the Bulls' new head coach, Bill Cartwright, spent much of his morning and late afternoon with reporters who seemed to be interested only in talking about Jordan. He'd had a complicated relationship with Jordan, dating back to the early '90s, when the 6'11" Cartwright had come to the Bulls from New York in a trade that sent Jordan's close friend and on-court bodyguard Charles Oakley to the Knicks. Jordan fumed in the aftermath, and Cartwright suffered under his digs for the next couple of years until confronting Jordan one day. Cartwright told him to stop it or he would hurt him. The exact remark varied depending on who, in the old Bulls' circle, was telling the story. Some people thought Cartwright had threatened to break Jordan's legs.

Others insisted he simply warned that he would fight him, or kick the shit out of him. All that seemed certain was that the moment had been ugly, and that, thereafter, Jordan had ceased to ridicule Cartwright, later grudgingly accepting Cartwright as the new man proved his worth on the floor.

Cartwright never had sided with Jordan in his battles with Krause, suggesting in time that he thought Jordan ungrateful and spoiled. "I don't get it," he would say to reporters. "'Guy was making thirty [million] and we won the championship and he is [critical of Krause]."

On this day, the two middle-aged men sounded like a pair of careful, stodgy senators when talking about each other. Cartwright offered a few diplomatic words, telling everybody that Jordan remained a great athlete: "I'd kind of like to have him now, playing for us."

There. He'd played nice.

He had the day's only humorous digs, an indication that he hadn't entirely forgotten the old harassment. Asked whether the Bulls' unwillingness to offer Jordan a managerial job amounted to a black eye for the organization, Cartwright exclaimed, mock-offended, "'Is it a *black eye?*' My God, *what* a question." The faintest hint of a smile curled at the corner of his mouth. Now he had some fun, elaborating on Chicago's decision not to offer Jordan either a share of ownership or an executive position, aiming to sound matter-of-fact. "That's not the [managerial] direction [the Bulls] went; we chose another direction." He affected a momentary look of puzzlement. "And Michael retired for the *what* time was it?" He smiled impishly. He said the next words slowly: "The *second* time, right? And here he is *again.*"

What did he think of Jordan in his blue-and-white Wizards' uniform?

"He doesn't look good in those colors. He looks really bad. His natural colors are Bulls colors."

Did he think he might be talking to Jordan?

Cartwright allowed as to how he wasn't sure, not sounding anxious about the possibility. "When Michael's out of here [the arena], he's hitting a golf ball. Most of us have to *work.*"

The press laughed.

He hadn't seen anything about Jordan's play that surprised him, he said. "If he gets going, he's trouble," he added. "Gotta make him a jump shooter. We're going to start Ron on him."

"Ron Artest, Rib Breaker," someone said.

Cartwright rolled his eyes, smiled. "I've learned that it's useful to *bother* Michael. . . . Hopefully, Ron can get up and bother him. . . . Bothering him is what you gotta do."

He believed in the power and respect that came to somebody who bothered Jordan. But just the same, Cartwright observed, the guy was still Michael Jordan. He might have gotten Jordan the teammate to stop hassling him, but Michael Jordan the player still worried him.

Jordan had spent much of the last 36 hours in bed, getting up only to play a basketball game. On the morning of Friday, January 4, while Juanita Jordan set out to file her divorce petition that day, Tim Grover busied himself monitoring Jordan's sinus cold at MCI, one of the few people to know what was likely to happen soon in Illinois, loyally safeguarding the secret, preoccupied at that moment with his boss's condition, as Jordan prepared to face the Bulls in a few hours. He worried about Jordan's endurance in the game's second half, if his sinuses got any worse. Jordan sat in a steam room for about a half hour, trying to sweat out the cold. It didn't help much.

Still congested and sneezing, he nevertheless told a trainer that he had a good feeling about the evening ahead. He looked not like a man sick or distraught but happy, as radiant as a man with a bad sinus cold could be. He didn't think another 50-plus point game tonight would be awfully surprising. Hell, he said, he could have had *60* the week before against Charlotte if he hadn't come out of the game with four minutes left. He'd have liked 60, but he'd done 60, done it more than once, he pointed out. So he could live with leaving at 51 points. But it just showed you, he thought, that another 50 was always a possibility, just like having several big games in a row was possible. He'd had three huge games in a row back in 1987: 53, 50 and 61 points, in successive games. He could recite the numbers: *53, 50, 61.* Check it out, he said. You get to 45 points in a game, he said, and 50 was right there waiting for you. Get to 50 and there was always 60. Ask the Celtics.

He was having fun now. Yeah, let the Bulls taste some. He didn't see it as personal. He didn't even know any of the young guys over there, with the exception of Artest and Tyson Chandler, and even in those cases, not very well. The only Bull with whom he seemed to have any real connection, his old running buddy Charles Oakley, didn't play much. He thought Oak would much prefer to be with him than in Chicago. Oak would understand why he wanted to put up a big number.

Whatever happened in the game, it was going to be a big night, he said. He'd hit a milestone tonight—*30,000 points*—and join the company of Wilt Chamberlain, Kareem Abdul-Jabbar and Karl Malone. Just needed 15 points. Nice to do it with Chicago watching.

He took a little more steam, showered, dressed and went off to nap. By the time he awakened and entered the locker room to dress for the game, his wife's petition, signed and recorded, was in the files of the Lake County Circuit Court. The press still did not know about her action, and the court was about to close for the weekend. But the documents were there; she had done it. He knew it had happened. The media would know soon, too, maybe today, probably Monday at the latest. In the locker room, he held a basketball, shooting it straight up, flicking his wrist, working on his form, studying the ball's spin. A tired-looking Tim Grover walked out onto the arena floor.

"How do you *think* Michael's feeling?" he asked rhetorically when prodded by a couple of reporters.

The reporters guessed this was a reference to the sinus cold. A Wizards assistant trainer rushed over and whispered something to Grover. He immediately started back toward the locker room. Jordan needed him again. "Nothing can stop Michael from playing in this game," he said, striding. Grover allowed himself a wan laugh. "What do you think could have stopped him?"

Nothing.

Nearby, in a courtside seat, sat Jerry Krause. He looked comically endearing, like a character out of Tolkien. His head was oversized. His body was short as a gnome's. His dark hair had matted itself to his skull and, as in a kind of parody, he had a couple of crumbs from some recently ingested processed food product on a sleeve. He had, of course, a gut. Just one look at him reminded people of why his problems with Jordan and other Bulls had so escalated. He was too easy to pick on for glamorous, graceful, handsome ballplayers. They were everything he was not, and, in turn, he was everything they had no interest in being. He had spent a career working longer and harder than anybody else around him, and all that labor had gone a long way, though not long enough, toward compensating for his stylistic shortcomings, including a tendency toward the fatuous remark; too often he had all the finesse of a caveman wielding a club.

Seemingly everybody had his favorite Jerry Krause story, which always meant the most unflattering Krause story. In wrapping up a 1997 deal with Phil Jackson, with whom his relationship had disintegrated, Krause told the coach's agent, Todd Musberger: *This will be the last deal we ever do with him.* People blamed Krause for Jackson's eventual departure, though Jackson had wanted out, too: The coach had a marriage breaking up, and this had factored into his need for a hiatus from basketball and the big city. Nonetheless, Krause received virtually all the blame, to be regarded by a wide circle of fans and reporters as the insecure egomaniacal jerk who had driven Jackson and Jordan away.

Jordan's enmity for him had raged since the early days, when Krause suggested that the Bulls' organization played a greater part in the team's success than any player. The executive's presence on long road trips hadn't helped matters, with several Bulls players making no effort to hide their contempt. On the team bus, they mocked him like they would a particularly irritable runt of a schoolmate—needling him for suggesting he had built the team, that he had made *them*. They regarded him as a pompous ass. Jordan joined in the abuse, as nothing Krause could ever do would earn back his respect. Krause responded by seemingly trying to ingratiate himself, as a Chicago official who rode the bus remembered. "That only made it worse for Jerry," the official said. "Michael can smell desperation. He doesn't respect desperation in an executive or a coach. After he smelled it in Jerry, that was it, he was unrelenting. Jerry didn't get it: Michael didn't forgive."

Once Jordan turned on people, his hostility was everlasting. Krause would be the butt of his scorn until his last breath. His fans freely vented at his archenemy, too. Incomprehensible shouts flew Krause's way from seats high off the MCI floor. Krause looked up at the stands, now and then, eyes darting. A few signs taunting him had begun unfurling.

"I have no animosity for Michael," he mumbled.

"You suck, Jerry," someone cried from the concourse.

His eyes blinked, but he didn't acknowledge the shout. He didn't have any animosity for Michael, he repeated. But, no, he wouldn't go so far as to say this game with Michael was special. Oh, come on, Jerry, somebody said to him.

"It's just one of eighty-two games," he responded, adding that he didn't see how he'd be able to exchange so much as a word with Jordan even after the game, given that the Bulls had to get on a bus and leave for the airport right away.

A kid shouted from somewhere high, "Bite me, Krause."

He didn't twitch. It was easy to see how he endured the abuse of ballplayers. He talked for a minute or two longer and quietly sat down. The teams were taking the floor. A half minute or so after the Wizards came out for warm-ups, Krause stood and turned his back to the players, choosing this moment to crane his neck and study an enthralling row of luxury boxes.

Jordan lashed the Bulls quickly, scoring 25 points in the first half and picking up his 30,000th point with about five minutes left in the second quarter on the second of two free throws, following a foul by Ron Artest. After being whistled for another foul on the next possession, the 6' 7" Artest, who before the game had spoken about his goals in the third person—"For Artest, he's gonna hopefully have respect"— punched the advertisement board beneath the scorer's table, screaming that he had done nothing more than what Jordan did to him on every trip down the court. He slugged the ad board again, pulling back his fist a third time. Jordan glanced over, slack-jawed. Collins, alarmed that the young player might break his hand, rushed over, urging him to stop. Artest shoved him away, cursing, punching the placard again.

With his young foe coming unglued, Jordan took advantage, torching him in the second quarter, leading fans to dream of another 50-point night. But his cold had him gasping for breath. He scored only four points in the second half, tiring badly, shuffling a little on his bad knee, missing eight of his last nine shots as the Wizards' 26-point lead sunk to just six in the final minute.

With less than 30 seconds to play, Artest blocked his jumper, and Jordan screamed, unable to believe the refs hadn't called a foul. With the Bulls on a fast break and Ron Mercer ahead of the pack, free for a breakaway layup, Jordan angrily raced down the court and the improbable happened. "I can jump when I have to, especially when I get pissed," he would say later. He took a running leap from behind Mercer, looking a little ungainly, like a man who had just jumped off a pier, his motion hurtling him forward. But he was climbing. He met Mercer at a point a foot above the rim. There, he didn't just block Mercer's shot but altogether snatched it from the air with two hands, pinning it against the backboard.

The crowd exploded, in that way people howl when they see something they do not believe. As a single moment goes, it was more thrilling than anything else during the entire comeback, save nothing, not a last-second shot, not even the 51-point game—this was a snarling Jordan in the cosmos, his shoes coming down and straddling the prostrate foe.

"Did you fucking see *that?*" a reporter shouted, pounding his laptop. The air was suddenly pocked by the profanities of happy cynics—*Fuckin' A, Get the fuck out of town, Motherfucker bitch-slapped him*—amid a roar that went on a long while: *Joooor-dan, Joooor-dan.* He held the ball aloft. His snatch sealed the Bulls' fate. The victors were momentarily in ascendance; the losers mired in basketball hell. "Sorry, gotta get to the bus, gotta get to the bus," Jerry Krause said, hurrying down a hallway.

The week represented the zenith of his comeback, a time during which talk so built of the Wizards' surge and Jordan's MVP chances, that I had begun tentatively writing a story about the possibilities of both, when my phone rang on Monday, January 7, three days after the Chicago game.

An editor said, "Juanita Jordan has filed for divorce. Just heard."

Within an hour, the stories came in a rush out of Chicago. They were staid, like Juanita Jordan's petition, steeped in the vernacular of well-heeled breakups: "irreconcilable differences," "25,000-square-foot mansion," a request for "half of the marital property," a reference to the respondent's "net worth of $400 million." Reporters abided by the conventions of celebrity journalism. There were the standard references to the eccentricities of the marital start. (The Little Wedding Chapel, in Las Vegas, at 3:30 in the morning, in December of 1989. Juanita had on a five-carat diamond; Jordan bore three-carats. The bride and groom wore jeans. Haste seemed in the air, a reasonable reader could infer.) Most of the stories ran old Jordan quotes suggesting an inconsistency between his words and his conduct during the 12-year marriage. After his first retirement in 1993, in explaining his desire to get away from basketball and spend more time at home, he said, "It's time to be a little bit unselfish." Within a few months, he had embarked on a baseball career. Less than a year after his second retirement announcement, he left for Washington.

I put the stories down.

The Jordan petition was rather unexceptional stuff—no threesomes, no domestic abuse, no attempted contract hits, nobody absconding with the joint assets.

TV could not get enough of it.

The next night, with Richard Hamilton still out with his bad groin, the Wizards defeated the Los Angeles Clippers, their fourth consecutive victory. Jordan played solidly for a man beset by personal strain—18 points, 8 assists, a team-high 10 rebounds.

After the game, in the Wizards' locker room, I took my usual place near a gold star on the royal-blue carpet. The gold star had become Jordan's unofficial mark during postgame press conferences, like an insignia you'd see David Letterman stand on during his opening monologue.

Because he had come out and faced the media on every game night for many years, it would have drawn more attention for him not to appear. So, as the game ended, everyone knew he would be out. While he received ice and stim treatment on his right knee in the closed training room, a petite, bespectacled woman maneuvered into the front of the scrum, almost on top of the gold star. Her name was Lynn Sweet and, as a Washington-based reporter for the *Chicago Sun-Times* who typically covered hard news, she found herself in the unusual position of having been dispatched to a basketball game, assigned the task of asking Jordan a couple of questions about the divorce filing.

You knew why she was there, before Lynn Sweet ever said it. One look at her quiet efficiency and lack of fascination with her environs made clear she had not come to study basketball, and you realized she would ask her questions of Jordan and likely never be seen in this locker room again. A group of reporters had spread out just enough to let Sweet have a good angle at her subject. She said thank you, she knew that others knew, she just wanted to do this and get it over with. She was an experienced professional who understood that some stories were more awkward than others, and knew that this moment had the potential to be terribly awkward. She would hold her recorder, ask her questions and be done with it. Hers was a reporter's life.

The wait was long. Sweet did not move from her spot. Then Jordan appeared, smiling as he approached the cameras, so familiarly resplendent in a tan jacket with matching gold tie and hoop earring that, for a long moment, as he began talking about basketball, it seemed that nothing had changed, nothing would ever change.

The illusion lasted all of about two minutes. Lynn Sweet leaned forward, extending her recorder. "What hopes do you have for a reconciliation with your wife?"

He looked her in the eye and answered swiftly: "That's none of your business." The line hung there for an electric instant, unsatisfactorily so for him. He decided to elaborate: "Quite frankly, I really don't want to talk about my personal life. . . . We have kids, obviously, and we want to make sure that's the focus. Everything else, when the time comes, you guys will hear it."

A half-dozen voices shouted basketball questions, but Sweet cut them off. "Michael, do you think your divorce is inevitable?"

"Excuse me?" His head bent toward her as if on a long crane, his lips pursed.

"Do you think your divorce is inevitable?"

He stayed composed, but it was an effort. "None of your business," he said.

"Thank you, folks," said the p.r. man, Matt Williams, trying to end it.

But Jordan did not move. He had more media savvy than anyone else in the room, knew better than to end a press conference on an unflattering note. He wanted one more question, and he got it, a valentine, an invitation to talk about his team's future: "Michael, how much better can this team get when Hamilton and Laettner come back?"

He nodded slightly in the direction of the reporter, as if to say, Good question. "I think we can be a lot better, obviously. You got a veteran player [Laettner] and you got another scorer [Hamilton], so it takes pressure off me. I just like our progress and our overall attitude. If we continue to take that attitude of improvement, we can move ourselves right up this ladder."

"Thanks a lot, folks," said Matt Williams.

"All right," Jordan added, walking off.

In a corner of the locker room, a fuming Tim Grover—his loyalty runneth over—wanted Lynn Sweet banished.

Nearby, a fairly large group of reporters and TV people seethed over Sweet's questions. "What a stunt, what a bitch," one muttered, believing the Wizards would be justified in tossing Sweet. "Shit, her questions had nothing to do with sports. Isn't he entitled to a private life?"

An American boomer had to go back to an event before his birth—the dissolution of Joe DiMaggio's second marriage—to find a time where America so cared about an athlete's marital problems. Even in DiMaggio's case, the comparison had limits: The country's interest in Joltin' Joe's woes had less to do with him than in his coupling with America's fantasy, Marilyn Monroe.

It was sensible to ask what could justify the intense speculation in Jordan's marriage. If divorce beset half the marriages in America, laid ruin to the domestic unions of prelates and politicians, athletes and accountants, the respectable and unseemly—nearly all of whom we allowed to suffer through their relationships' demises without intrusion—then why subject Michael Jordan's to special scrutiny? The Jordan camp never seemed to grasp the answer. The explanation lay not in Jordan's personal conduct so much as in nearly two decades' worth of his business representations: His people had held him up as a man to be emulated, making Jordan more than a half-billion in endorsement dollars in the process. If he carried a special burden, it was a burden of his own making. He had raised the bar on his behavior during 17 years of unremitting self-promotion, in campaigns approved by the Jordan camp and coordinated by Nike and other corporate sponsors that elevated him from great athlete to hero and, finally, to moral symbol.

Typically, celebrities do not offer themselves up to the world as the personification of an ideal. Mick Jagger does not appear on TV while somebody else in a voice-over says, "Be Like Mick." The cautious celebrity does not do a film scene in which, amid his friendships with cartoon characters in *Space Jam,* he plays himself immersed in the day-to-day stuff of real family life—using another woman to play his real wife, other children to play his real children—offering America the heartening Jordan family tableau, complete with the portrait of marital fidelity and attendant moral message. Most athletes and entertainers never engage in anything remotely so risky. *Risky,* because when you present yourself as virtuous in years of ad campaigns and TV commercials, you will be fairly held in time to that standard. Fairly held because you have sold your basketball shoes to people plunking down in excess of $100 not merely for a chance at better Ups but for a way to rub up against your aura, to feel a tiny sense of you in that admittedly silly way people feel when they wish to emulate anybody, to be inspired by your class and elegance, your morality and grace, as they've heard it told. And if some of that was artifice, then so, too, was everything you sold with your likeness on it.

No other American athlete had ever been so intimately involved in his own deification. Jordan, remembered Nike ad producer Jim Riswold, wanted to know detail after detail of proposed ad shoots, a bright young man with suggestions and occasional reservations. He balked on some things *because Michael Jordan just didn't do that.* He had a virtually flawless sense of what would be flattering and what wouldn't, of what would grow the Air Jordan shoe campaign and his image.

Most athletes, even the mega-millionaire stars, didn't aim so high. They balled, they collected big checks, they won games. They were just ballers, and their agents, advisers and shoe companies did not pretend otherwise. Neither American journalists nor fans were ever disillusioned by the behavior of, say, Shaquille O'Neal—the partying giant who, on the eve of being suspended for three games after an on-court melee a few years ago—happily talked of having three children out of wedlock, blithely adding he was "not pure" (he since has married his girlfriend, the mother of all but one of his four children today). The public's reaction at the time to O'Neal's statement, like that of disclosures about Mick Jagger's stray progeny, was that of yawning, smirking, chuckling disinterest. O'Neal, who had a well-earned reputation for being generous around children and never succumbing to drugs or any other great vices, was never marketed as anything other than what he was—a fun-loving, adolescent-like, occasionally foul-mouthed, unpredictable behemoth. Candor has its rewards.

Jordan became the league's, his shoe company's and sports TV's reliable guardian of the Ethic. TV children sang about him. The ditty "If I Could Be Like Mike" fused idolatry with consumerism, just part of a campaign to elevate Jordan into the ether of commercial deities. Now, with the divorce petition and the stories about his alleged affairs, more publications were paying attention to issues of his personal life, posing questions about whether his behavior amounted to hypocrisy. A measure of disillusionment was inevitable.

The Jordan p.r. machine cranked on. In the same week that his wife filed her divorce papers, there came word that suddenly he had plans for a *magazine*—like Rosie O'Donnell's, Martha Stewart's and Oprah Winfrey's. The publication, said a statement, would offer lifestyle pieces and advice. Nike released a statement promising that JORDAN would reflect "the inspiration of Michael Jordan."

What that "inspiration" might be was difficult to discern. What idea had he ever expressed beyond winning games? But even this was not the question that mattered most, at least not to anyone on the Jordan team who saw an annual cut of his endorsement money. The biggest worry was that the singing of the TV children might give way to a new question: Had most of this been a ruse? It was why news of a woman's legal filing in the quiet town of Waukegan, Illinois, triggered such seismic waves in the culture.

By that Friday, January 11, reporters chasing the divorce petition story had descended on the Bradley Center in Milwaukee, where the Wizards were playing the Bucks. Nobody asked him a direct question about Juanita Jordan's filing, not after Lynn Sweet. That night the Wizards got blown out, losing by 19 in a game far more one-sided than the score.

It was the start of a four-game losing streak. The next night at MCI, playing 40 tough minutes in the second of back-to-back games, Jordan scored 35, but visibly tired late, hitting only three of his last nine shots, as the Wizards lost by eight to Minnesota and Kevin Garnett. Three evenings later, the team fell at home to San Antonio and then was annihilated the following night in a 44-point loss at New Jersey, where the team's record dropped to 18–18, and Jordan spent the entire second half on the bench. The team's problems without Hamilton never had been so evident, and now came news that his torn groin was healing more slowly than expected, that his expected return had been pushed back from mid-January to perhaps as late as early February.

The team flew to Chicago for the first game since the comeback's start at the United Center, where a statue of Jordan stands at the front entrance, a shrine to which tourists flock every day of the year. By game day, hundreds of the ticketless had joined ticket holders in making the pilgrimage there. Quite a few bowed their heads, like people do in Arlington National Cemetery next to JFK's Eternal Flame. An elderly woman wiped tears from her eyes. A couple of younger women fell into each other's arms in sodden collapse. A nicely dressed child knelt on a McDonald's bag.

Inside the arena, a couple of hundred reporters stood outside the visitors' locker room. Jordan walked down a hallway, people squealing, tripping over microphone cords, throwing elbows, cursing each other, anything to get a position close. He bounded toward the locker room, abruptly stopping to say hello to a disabled woman in a wheelchair who said she had been coming to see him play for 13 years. He bent, hugged her, moved on. The Chicago reporters crowded into the little locker room, staring and pointing at his Wizards road jersey already hanging in his designated locker, right next to a plastic bottle of baby oil and his silver headphones and a single pair of white Air Jordans with black trim.

I saw Lacy Banks. "This is nuts," he said happily.

We walked out into the hallway, where we bumped into Jordan's longtime agent, David Falk, whom Banks called the "Bird of Prey." Agents typically find these monikers very flattering. The more menacing the moniker, the greater his status, the more demand for his services.

The Bird of Prey stood there grinning.

Perfectly bald *(wrong,* somebody corrected me—*once balding, now shaven)*, Falk looked like a skinny version of the Man from Glad (old school) or a skinnier version still of Austin Powers's archenemy, Dr. Evil, with a marginally better tan. He gave Bobby Simmons a power shake ("You ready for *today?*"). He put the shake on the two Jordan buddies who worked as executives in the Wizards' front office, Rod Higgins and Fred Whitfield. ("What a day *really.*") Falk had an unusual way of putting emphasis on words where emphasis didn't necessarily belong, but it made him sound enthusiastic and pugnacious. It seemed to work.

He had represented Jordan since his first contract negotiation, in 1984. His clients included Patrick Ewing and Alonzo Mourning. He would tell you this if you did not already know it. He also handled key Wizards over the years, like the jettisoned mega-millionaire disappointments Juwan Howard and Rod Strickland, dealing in the process with Abe Pollin, for whom he did not try hiding his contempt. "The only reason Michael came to Washington was Ted Leonsis," Falk said.

Falk noted that he had gotten along well with Bulls owner Jerry Reinsdorf, and so regretted, he said, that the tear in his relationship with Pollin had not been repaired, that Abe seemed so resistant to the idea of dealing reasonably with people who could help him. Jordan didn't permit Falk to speak about certain subjects related to Jordan, or to certain people about *any* subject, but Falk evidently had free rein to talk about Pollin whenever he wished.

Still, events suggested that Falk had fallen a ways out of the Jordan loop. Jordan's business seemed to be increasingly handled by an old Falk lieutenant, Curtis Polk. The reality left Falk with less to do in Jordan's empire, which seemed to be slowly downsizing anyway, with less new business coming in. The sports pages, which once boasted prominent articles about Michael Jordan's "super-agent," seldom wrote about him, and like most of the Jordan support staff whose stature derived largely from Jordan's, he would need to find something new in the coming years to keep himself from looking like a has-been.

Now here came a problem for him. He stood there in front of Lacy Banks when Mike Wise, then of *The New York Times,* strolled over and said hi to everybody, very casually, greeting Banks and me and, only then, turning to Falk and politely saying hello. This said less about Falk than it did Mike Wise, who was among the most skilled basketball reporters in the country and someone admired as much for his personal style as his professional talents. He did not genuflect before his subjects. Wise smiled at Falk and asked, "Is there a bit of nostalgia for you today, to have the media jackals surrounding you like this?"

Falk got a funny look on his face, the look fighters get when they take a jab on the nose and understand they might be facing surprises. "I love Chicago . . ." Falk answered. He rhapsodized about Chi Town and the old Bulls.

Wise tried moving him toward a discussion of Jordan's business relationship with the Wizards, particularly the circumstances under which Jordan had opted out of his managerial and ownership contracts with Pollin and Leonsis. Falk began frowning. Wise wanted to know if an agreement was already in place to have Jordan benefit financially in any future ownership contract, given that his comeback had raised the club's revenues. "Michael likes to say he scratched his itch," Wise said, "but he's also increasing the value of the franchise. Now [after his retirement as a player] he can buy back in and make money and—"

A smirking Falk cut him off: "If he does that, he's *gotta* buy back in at the higher price. See, that's why guys like you are writers, and other people do the financial stuff, because—"

Wise interrupted: "I heard he's got an under-the-table deal with Leonsis that I heard about. . . . You were cut out of the deal."

The Bird of Prey seemed to lose a wing then. He blinked, looked up and down, stared hard at Wise. The truth was already clear: Falk was no longer anybody's consigliere, just another agent with a new role whittled by the years and Jordan's shifting ambition. It was probably the natural order of things, but this made it no more pleasant for him. He raised his chin, in a show of dignity. "I can *handle* that," he said. "I took a very specific role, a non-role in that, because [Jordan] was in management. I wasn't allowed to negotiate his contract; it's against the rules. It wasn't a complicated deal."

Wise continued prodding, in hopes of obtaining details of any future financial and ownership guarantees for Jordan. In truth, there were none. What struck me in that moment was the uncertainty of Jordan's future, the utter absence of assurances for him, the risks being taken by the Jordan team, the assumptions made, the confidence that an ownership deal would still be waiting for their man at the end of his playing days. Falk admitted there was nothing ironclad in place, nothing even suggested, and added that Jordan didn't fret over it. "He's not worrying what will happen a year from now," Falk said. "I don't think he's worrying about what's going to happen *a week* from now."

Falk could scarcely have been more candid. From the beginning of his comeback discussions, Jordan had placed a far greater priority on playing than in taking steps to make certain his future was protected. His casualness invited danger. A savvy handling of the matter would have dictated that he extract guarantees up front from Pollin and Leonsis about his future, an action that would have required finesse, as the NBA's conflict-of-interest rules prohibited Jordan and the Wizards from having a future ownership deal and executive contract already in place for him.

But this did not preclude obvious public relations steps that would have locked Pollin into a position essentially guaranteeing Jordan's future with the club. Jordan's people had neither secured Pollin's private oral pledges nor, far more importantly, made certain the owner publicly suggested that he hoped to see Jordan back in the front office at the end of his playing days. Even a vaguely worded public statement would later have given Jordan both leverage and a moral claim. The Jordan team had secured nothing, the consequence of two decades of feeling assured, of believing Jordan always had the most leverage in a negotiation; that no one ever said no to their man. In the end, Jordan had given up his entire Wizards stake in exchange for nothing—nothing other than a chance to play ball. The headlong rush said everything about his priorities. "It was for his love of the game," Falk said softly, falling back on Jordanese to describe this need that overwhelmed all others.

Falk looked over his shoulder, power-shook another hand and turned back, folding his arms across his chest again, reclaiming his command pose. Another gaggle of basketball executives in suits swooped. "You're doing it *today*," he mumbled over his shoulder.

He muttered hi to somebody else. Keeping the face out there. Keeping the Bird of Prey flying. Nothing about Jordan's future was certain, he knew. Soon-to-be-retired athletic gods did not dictate terms once they stopped filling seats. He insisted that Jordan wanted to stay in Washington and work with Leonsis, though when I asked whether Jordan might buy into the Bulls if an ownership opportunity ever presented itself, he held up his hands, being careful. He understood his client's impulsiveness. "I don't rule anything out," he said.

The afternoon's solemnity was a bit overwrought, and one could have committed heresy by noting the presence of a few boos. But the ovation for Jordan was heartfelt, lasting more than two and a half minutes—and it might have gone into the following week had the Bulls not cut the lights. Conspiracy theorists blamed Jerry Reinsdorf and Jerry Krause, a bit of speculation plagued by just one problem. Neither of the two Jerrys had even shown up, exhibiting the kind of dreadful manners that we in the media love to note. It was a strange and dazzling day.

"It was the worst game I've *ever* seen," assistant coach John Bach would say later.

The afternoon start probably had something to do with the awfulness of the play. Bodies hadn't fully awakened. But the tension of Jordan's return explained more. Just before the tip, he looked down at the court, his arms extended and hands half-clenched, in a strangely meditative pose. It didn't help. After Ron Artest badly clanked the game's first shot over him, Jordan came down, lost his handle on the ball, regained it and missed an open jumper. Both teams spent much of the game handling the ball as if it had been rolled in butter. Jordan committed nine turnovers and made only 7 of 21 shots, with Artest holding him to 16 points. In payback, Jordan cuffed Artest, who missed 12 of 15 shots, looking half out of his mind sometimes. Once, in his daffy hyperactive way, he kicked Jordan, accidentally, or maybe not. Having the two defend each other meant a kind of mutually assured destruction.

Jordan looked exhausted by the end, having played too long again, 41 minutes. The crowd had commenced a mass exodus from the dreariness a couple of minutes earlier. The final seconds were played before perhaps half of the 23,500 there at the start. The Wizards won by eight, thanks to Chris Whitney's 20 points and Popeye Jones's 14 rebounds that accompanied his besting of Charles Oakley, whom he held scoreless. Reliable Hubert Davis started in place of Hamilton and played 38 minutes, while holding down Ron Mercer.

The Wizards looked like a tired team, but they had won their 19th game, equaling the team's victory total from the previous season, which had been the worst in franchise history. Collins made a big deal about it. Jordan sounded grateful just to be off the court. "When the crowd started that whole thing [the ovation], it was hard for me to play . . ." he said. He likened the city of Chicago to a brother. "In all the other games, I don't think I played against my brother. I owe a lot of gratitude to this city for what they gave me. . . . . It was a tough [day], tough, tough. I played like it, too. The motivation wasn't as high as I normally play with."

The mood was all too glum. Lacy Banks stepped forward with an observation that pushed the right buttons, telling Jordan that his eyes seemed to be tearing up during his introduction.

Jordan groaned, "You didn't see *tears*. They cut the lights out before you could see *anything*, Lacy." He shook his head. The press laughed. And then Jordan acknowledged he had almost cried. "I was getting close," he said. His eyes glazed over. He glanced at Banks, and laughed ruefully.

The Wizards' bus left a half-hour later. Players wanted to see his statue. Jordan groaned to the driver, "Keep going, keep going, keep going."

Pressured by everybody else, the driver ignored him. The bus slowed near the statue. Players moved to one side so they could get a good view. Lue and a few others began applauding. Jordan looked out the other side, stared at asphalt and said nothing. It had been a long afternoon, and finally they were gone.

Among those who had stared at the Jordan statue and politely clapped was Richard Hamilton, reduced to being a spectator at the games for the time being, still trying to recover from his injured groin. Collins thought the groin probably needed at least two more weeks of rehab, to be augmented by gradual conditioning. It didn't make sense to play Hamilton at 70 percent, he said. Hamilton's whole game was speed, and if Rip didn't have it, he couldn't fight his way free. Foes would knock him around like the waif he was, and batter him mercilessly. Rip had to stay on the injured list for now.

The next morning, still in Chicago, the team practiced at Tim Grover's facility, Hoops the Gym. Near the practice's end, Hamilton worked alone, doing light footwork, shuffling his feet laterally, trying to maintain some semblance of conditioning while being careful to protect the groin. He shot some jumpers, looking as though he was careful not to push off too hard on his legs. The shots went in anyway, jumper after flawless jumper. You could roll him out of a hospital bed and he would still make jumpers.

Across the court, a happy-looking Jordan casually called out to him: Did he want to have a shooting game?

Sure, Hamilton answered.

Their relationship remained murky. It was not volatile; it simply had yet to connect, and seemed by then that it never would. Around the media, Jordan still occasionally referred to Hamilton as the Lone

Ranger and likened himself to the loyal companion, Tonto. Hamilton, who hadn't been alive during the Lone Ranger era, never really knew what to make of the analogy. "The thing is, Michael said something to reporters about Tonto and it gets attention 'cause it's Michael, and we all respect that, but I didn't really know about Tonto, and the young players just want to show our talent and that matters more to me than this other stuff," Hamilton said. "We're not Jordanaires."

For Hamilton, it always came back to that: He was no Jordanaire. He appreciated being around a great player, but he wanted more respect from observers. He thought he could play with anybody, and aimed to get past this injury as soon as possible to resume his climb. Even injured, he knew he could make shots. "Hey," he yelled, and threw up a shot from 45 feet away. All net. He looked at Jordan and their contest was on, as a whole team waited for them outside.

No player but Jordan had the power to keep the team bus waiting. A few of the Wizards on the bus guessed that he had found himself a game, and they knew what any game meant. Cash was always on the line in a Jordan challenge—which on this day consisted of a shooting contest from mid-court, a distance of 47 feet from the basket. In the unfamiliar surroundings of Grover's gym, the Wizards p.r. representative had been unable to keep tabs on reporters, and I'd found myself able to walk unseen up to a viewing area behind glass, a floor above the practice court. It was a window onto a game and a relationship. Hamilton went up several hundred dollars early, happily yelling, while the attendants, a couple of ball boys and a Wizards staff member, kept glancing at watches. The competition dragged on. Ten, fifteen minutes. Someone finally said: "Probably time to get going, Michael."

No, he said coolly.

The game would not end until Jordan said so. The lean Hamilton, having to use his shoulders to muscle up shots, continued making improbable swishes and adding on to his winnings. Jordan's shots careened off the sides of the rim. He struggled with the half-court distance while expressing ever more confidence that the contest would soon turn, making this sound like fate: "Feelin' good—oooh, *almost,* there it *is,* startin' to *feel it,* oooh, *feelin' it.*" It was a nifty head game; he knew how to plant doubt. Three more Jordan shots went wide, and the swishing Hamilton tacked on a couple hundred dollars more. The bus had waited 20 minutes by then. Jordan began improvising, seemingly compensating for his wrist's tendinitis, adjusting his form, finally settling on a one-legged set shot that look borrowed from the

'50s and Bob Cousy, his left foot on the floor, his right knee lifted and bent. He gave the ball one bounce, did a little hop, got a hip into the shot and flicked it, effortlessly. Finally, he started finding his range— *"oooooh, oooooh, oooooh"*—hitting 8 of his last 13 mid-court shots to win more than $1,000 off the day's prey. At last, Jordan indicated that the game was over. He grinned and whooped—"coo, coo, coo"—a signal that he had fleeced another pigeon. He pointed in a gesture of amused supremacy at Hamilton, who, turning his back, walked to the back of the gym to retrieve his sweats, while a delighted Jordan fitted an earring into his left lobe, put on a black cap and kept teasing. "You knew you weren't taking my money, Rip," he cried, and when Hamilton didn't turn, he repeated it. Hamilton never stopped walking, never uttered a word. Jordan stared at Hamilton's back, calling out, "Rip, we'll do it again."

The moment revealed all his sides—his need for dominance, the compulsion to find another rush, his avuncular instinct to soothe the bruised foe. He had an alpha personality in a profession teeming with alphas, which necessarily meant that, from his early Bulls days, there always had been ebbs and flows to his relationships with teammates, particularly with other alphas. But his taunting and besting of other Bulls had been accompanied by his expert schooling of them in practice, where he sometimes preyed on the weakest during scrimmages in hopes of humiliating and browbeating them into raising their games.

He played a critical role in improving the games of several Bulls, most notably Scottie Pippen, who had arrived in the NBA with a reputation as a sieve on defense. Relentlessly abused in scrimmages by a merciless Jordan, Pippen lifted his play to become a premier defender. "You either sink or swim with Michael in practice, and Scottie made it," said Tex Winter, the architect of Chicago's famed Triangle Offense and a longtime Bulls assistant coach who had moved on with Phil Jackson to the Lakers. "You either work hard or Michael has no use for you."

The Wizards had hoped that Jordan's ruthless practice style might transform Hamilton and Alexander, two players still in need of improving their defense. But Jordan's bad knee made any hard practicing or hands-on tutelage impossible. In January, the knee began to show signs again of fatigue and strain. By then, he seldom played any basketball outside of games, participating in about one-quarter of the Wizards' practices, according to team observers. He would do a few drills—a series of sprints, some shooting on undefended fast breaks, a brief run-through of plays—before muttering to Collins, "I'll go to the bike." Or

Collins, wanting to save the troubled right knee for a coming game, would sometimes call to him, "I think you've had enough, Michael. Go to the bike."

Consequently, the Wizards seldom scrimmaged full-court, with one team observer saying he had never been part of an NBA organization that practiced so little under game-like conditions. Ultimately, Jordan gave the young players far fewer of the tough tutorials that he had brought to a Chicago practice. What he had left to give them was his dominant side: alpha man's periodic aloofness, his ribbing, his shooting games. Aside from his occasional chats with Ty Lue, he offered no key players any reason for affection. Alexander was lost. Hamilton's improvement on defense came from working and watching tapes with John Bach. The team's number two star resumed making the point, casually and politely, that Jordan would not be around in another couple of years. "We showed that we got the pride to win without Michael," Hamilton said. "We know we got a lot of talent, and we're going to be the leaders someday soon."

With every month, Hamilton voiced his conviction more directly. It reflected an ebbing veneration of the idol, a new daring among a few players making clear where the future rested.

It had become clear that the team could not win steadily without Hamilton. But if the team also lost Jordan, the effect on the Wizards' playoff chances would be fatal. Any plan for the team was meaningless without abiding by the only priority that mattered: Protect Jordan. Safeguard the knee. Make certain he received adequate rest during a game. Preferably, no nights longer than 38 minutes.

He had played 40 minutes or more in four of the last six games, or five to eight minutes longer per game than had been recommended by John Hefferon. His performance had plummeted. He had missed nearly two-thirds of his shots, and been guilty of a rash of turnovers. The team flew to Minneapolis, where he again played too long. He was brilliant for a half, hitting 10 of 19 shots, only to sink in the second half, missing 13 of 15 shots, and making only 1 of 11 in the fourth quarter, as the Wizards lost again, their fifth loss in their last six games. He had pulled down 14 rebounds, a testament to his tenacity, but no one could dispute his decline during the final minutes, when nearly all his shots hit the front rim and he labored defensively. Afterward, he was asked: Are the minutes taking too much out of you?

"I didn't feel that bad, actually," he said, dismissing the suggestion that the team needed to reassess his playing time.

A few hours later, he got off a red-eye flight back in Washington, arose early and worked on his shooting, alone. He could not go through a real practice on most days, but he felt the need to try honing his erratic shot after sleeping just a couple of hours. He received more ice and stim treatment. That night at MCI, against Philadelphia, the pattern of the Minnesota game was repeated: Another sensational Jordan beginning, followed by an abysmal, exhausted finish. He had 28 points in the first half, but hit only one of eight shots in the second half. In this, the second of games on back-to-back nights, he had played 42 minutes and scored only two second-half points, and the Wizards lost by seven. He now had made only 47 of 130 shots in his last seven games, shooting a miserable 36.2 percent and missing more field-goal attempts in that stretch than any other player in the league.

Meanwhile, I had spent the last few hours on my own flight, with nothing better to do than crunch more Jordan numbers.

He had gone 4-for-30 in the fourth quarters of his last three games, shooting a microscopic 13 percent.

"What are you doing?" a Wizards p.r. man asked me.

I had just come off the plane and arrived at MCI, hair askew. Unshaven and wired, I probably looked a little wild. I was sitting in the pressroom scribbling numbers, calculating shooting percentages, gorging minutiae, spitting out factoids, drooling banalities, buzzed after the road trip, deep inside my tube. *"He's four-for-thirty in fourth quarters over the last week, Dolph,"* I said. *"Four-for-thirty. What do you think of that?"*

"He's sure putting people in the seats, huh?" the man said.

His name was Dolph Sand. He had big, dark hair and a thick mustache and he looked like he could be related to the Marx Brothers. He was a very nice man whom everybody liked, and his job included bringing Jordan the names of the refs, when they were announced the evening of a game. Sand had worked in his Wizards job for many years, and he had been around through the good days and bad ones. He had seen the arena half-filled, and a third-filled, and sometimes as quiet as Lenin's Tomb. Everything was different now, Dolph Sand observed.

"He's packing them in," he noted, brightly and rightly.

Not that I didn't already know this, but hearing it kind of shook me awake. It brought me out of my tube and reminded me what this whole thing was about, bottom line. You get back into MCI and somebody like Dolph Sand innocently reminds you what it's always going to be about—and what it's about is stuffing these seats and selling goodies.

And Jordan had done it. He had filled everything, including the luxury boxes. He had attracted more advertisers who wanted their companies' names to hang somewhere, anywhere. To come back from a road trip and walk into MCI was to see advertising billboards on about every inch of space that couldn't be used to squeeze in another paying customer—signs for some companies that had been here before Jordan and some that hadn't, the old loyalists having to cede their prime positions if they couldn't pony up for the higher rate. There were signs hawking beer and cellular phones, and sodas and fast-food joints, and an internet venture and a supermarket, and whatever and whoever else had the money to pay. There was a toy blimp—about 15 feet long— that flew around inside the arena before the game, bearing the name of a health-care company. It hovered maybe 10 to 20 feet above the baskets. Kids loved the toy blimp, and their parents stared at the health-care company's name, and if they were sitting close enough to courtside, you could now and then see one of the kids toss a souvenir miniature Wizards basketball up at the blimp as if hopeful of blowing it out of the air, and if a ball got lost, go get another for $10 or so at a souvenir stand and another $70 jersey while you were at it. Cha-ching.

Jordan accounted for that sound. Knowing this as well, Abe Pollin had expressed appreciation in the way owners do, honoring Jordan at a halftime ceremony earlier in the month, presenting him with a trophy of a silver basketball to commemorate Jordan's arrival in the 30,000-point pantheon. To see the two of them stiffly standing together, surrounded by their coteries, was to understand that they shared so many traits, good and bad.

Both men worked hard, exuded public grace, and almost never made excuses. They were about as color-blind as men can be, with each having surrounded himself long before with capable people of different races. Jordan rewarded anyone who could help him, and as many of his closest friends and advisers (seemingly far more) were white as not. Pollin had distinguished himself early in his basketball life by ensuring that African-Americans rose to top positions in all sectors of his organization. Wes Unseld found himself in his sixth year as the club's general manager, and the hiring of Jordan as club president had ushered in Fred Whitfield and Rod Higgins. African-Americans held key managerial positions in everything from Wizards advertising and ticket sales to the public relations department. It was an egalitarian place, like so much of the NBA, a seeming model for race relations and social progress, and Pollin had played no small role in that.

Yet Pollin and Jordan also had a great need for loyalty and deference, and here neither man had yet to satisfy the other's wishes. The owner's handing of the silver basketball to the star constituted both an acknowledgment of the obvious (Jordan had changed the team's fortunes on every level) and a gesture of respect toward a man with whom his relationship had experienced serious tensions. But the gossipers around both men had made certain that the gulf between them widened. And the media offended Pollin by suggesting that Jordan had single-handedly advanced the franchise, whose fortunes, it was suggested, would be even brighter if Pollin did not stand in the way of Jordan's grand plans.

By then, the press in Washington and a few other cities had advanced a broader argument: Jordan, it was said, had begun transforming the city of Washington—particularly the community around MCI. Michael Jordan had done what Abe Pollin hadn't, what a city's worth of business people couldn't. Michael Jordan's arrival had sparked a renaissance. Michael Jordan meant new shops, new buildings, new jobs, new hope. Michael Jordan had lit a flame, and Abe Pollin and other Washington entrepreneurs were lucky to hold his torch.

The Jordan phenomenon was moving, it was transcendent, and it was nonsense.

The adoration of Jordan always inflated his role in a city's development. Simultaneously, it tended to obscure the community achievements of a businessman like Pollin, who had built MCI, five years earlier, in a tired, stagnant area of Washington, and absorbed all the attendant financial risks, a man whose life in the construction business made risk a daily part of his existence. The community surrounding MCI had been on a slow, steady rebound ever since, for which Pollin seldom, if ever, received kudos, any improvement generally credited to Jordan's playing comeback, which by then was only into its third month.

That slight, or hard luck, depending on your perspective, simply underscored what little magic the Pollin name had in either the city of Washington or pro basketball, despite his high profile in both venues. He was the Rodney Dangerfield of basketball owners. His commissioned biography remained unpublished. His reputation as a skinflint among basketball owners appeared unalterable. For all his money and clout, his quest for enduring respect in the sports community looked as tough now as it had been in his beginnings.

Since his boyhood, Abe Pollin loved sports. With a quarter in his pocket, the schoolboy regularly rushed to nearby Griffith Stadium in the early '30s to watch the Washington Senators. It was an age when major league baseball lorded over other American team sports, and a pre-television era in which to have a ticket to a ball game meant having a seat in an exclusive theater. The Senators were generally also-rans to the New York Yankees, and, watching Babe Ruth and Lou Gehrig swat the ball around Griffith, the boy was able to marvel over the New York idols in the flesh while mourning his beloved Senators' losses. A role reversal came in 1933, when the Senators soared to win the American League pennant. Young Pollin rejoiced. Never to be a great athlete, he had found a permanent place as a spectator, and dreamer. Silvery quarters and baseball tickets were aplenty for him. His family enjoyed a comfortable life, thanks to his immigrant father, Morris, who built a thriving plumbing and heating business from scratch and passed on, as part of Abe Pollin's and his brother Harold's Jewish upbringing, the importance of community involvement, charity, passion and achievement.

His father segued into the construction business, for which Abe Pollin worked in the '40s, before establishing his own company a decade later, building office complexes, houses and apartments, on his way to becoming a wealthy man. By 1962, he had enough money to explore the possibility of fulfilling a long-held wish to buy a professional sports team, attempting to acquire the NBA's Cincinnati Royals. A deal with the Royals never materialized, but the new part of his life had begun. His pursuit of the club that would one day be known as the Wizards began in 1963, the year Michael Jordan was born and the ailing franchise played its last days in Chicago. There, it was known as the Chicago Zephyrs, and its star was a superb young center named Walt Bellamy, who had failed to take the Zephyrs far. The team struggled for recognition in a sports-crazed town that belonged to Chicago's two baseball teams, along with the city's football Bears and the hockey Black Hawks. By the time Pollin and two partners bought the team for an NBA-record $1.1 million in 1964, it had moved to Baltimore and was renamed the Bullets. Four years later, Pollin bought out his partners.

The landscape of professional sports was changing nearby. Baseball's Senators lost their grip on Washington loyalties, the empty seats growing as the early '70s began, the team's attendance next to last in the American League. After the 1971 season, the Senators said goodbye to Washington, soon to become the Texas Rangers. A vacuum existed; the time seemed ripe for new Washington teams. In 1972, Pollin acquired the National Hockey League's expansion franchise in Washington. A year later, with his basketball team dropping Baltimore from its name to become the Washington Bullets, Pollin's two teams assumed residence in his new arena, built in the Washington suburb of Landover, Maryland. The '70s became the Bullets' golden days. The team regularly made the playoffs and reached the NBA Finals three times in the decade, winning the championship in 1978.

Then came 20 years of mostly misery. Losing became habit, a trend unbroken by the arrival of promising young draft picks and high-priced veterans acquired in the twilight of their playing days. By 1997, Pollin had changed the team's name. "Bullets" no longer had the right ring. The name worked in the '60s, when TV was inundated with all-American six-shooters and homey Westerns, when always a good TV sheriff had the good bullets. But the country had changed, and the nature of American cities, too. *Bullets* had come to have a lethal sound. Bad name for a city that had too many areas with too many real bullets and too much bloodletting. As names go, the "Washington Bullets" had come to make about as much sense as the Washington Nukes (and, across the world, in what was the final straw for the name, Pollin's close friend, Israeli Prime Minister Yitzhak Rabin, had been assassinated with a handgun).

It had become a loser's name besides. One heard the words "Washington Bullets" and immediately braced for news of the latest rout. Not merely a rout, but a down-in-the-dust ass-stomping, punctuated by comic ineptitude. Maybe you could get rid of the stench with a name change. *Voilà*: The too edgy, too-identified-with-losing, vaguely gang-banging name of Bullets gave way to the happy, prudent, vaguely Disney-sounding name that seemed born of a children's birthday party theme—the *Wizards*.

Along the way, Pollin gained a reputation for philanthropy and social activism that spanned a half-century. He had integrated Washington area construction crews in the '50s, and initiated a program in the '90s for feeding the Washington homeless called "Abe's Table." He helped to launch the area's "I Have a Dream" program, designed to pay the college tuition of impoverished Washington-area children. He personally aided a large group of fifth graders at a Maryland elementary school, later fulfilling his vow to pay for the college costs of the 20 students who graduated from high school. He was that archetype known as a kindly patron.

1997 was Pollin's makeover year, facelifts for everything. He had built another new arena, this time not in a suburb but on the edge of Washington's Chinatown, in a downtown area desperate for revitalization. No one could reasonably argue that he didn't tap into his wealth, or put himself at financial risk. He paid for everything, with the costs of construction over two years exceeding the projected $175 million budget by at least $45 million. For financing, he had borrowed from several lenders, offering as collateral his two teams and most of his land and properties, including his arena in Landover. Susan O'Malley's father, Peter, a Maryland attorney and longtime Pollin friend, handled the legal end of much of the project. In December 1997, Pollin moved his team out of Landover and into his new arena, the MCI Center, for which the telecommunications giant paid him $44 million for naming rights.

From the moment the arena opened for business, the area around the seedy east side neighborhood bordering Chinatown slowly, steadily changed. Pollin deserved the lion's share of credit. A couple of nice restaurants popped up here, and a couple of attractive night spots there, in tandem with all the new foot traffic coming to see the Wizards, the Capitals, his WNBA Washington Mystics, Georgetown basketball and rock shows. The mass of bodies, in turn, generated new cultural and business activity. A theater group began contemplating expansion plans in the area, later to settle on building a new stage across from the arena. The area around MCI became a hub of activity on game nights, requiring parking lots, small shops, still more restaurants. The influx of attractions, employees and revenue served as the stimulus for the construction of apartment complexes and the refurbishing of old buildings and surrounding streets. That is, by any measuring stick, an economic and social revitalization, which Pollin's money and risk had set in motion.

Once Jordan came to town, pundits around Washington tended to overlook or undervalue Pollin's contributions. It was Jordan, said the Jordanphiles, who stoked economic activity in the area. But in measuring people's relative contributions to the rebound of a dormant area, reason dictates that you begin with the man who gambled something, the one who put up considerable money from a fortune that paled against those of other NBA owners. Jordan was generally disinclined to risk his own money, outside of casinos.

Jordan looked to others to assume business gambles. Jordan did not provide the big money for deals, believing his presence alone constituted an investment, that it ought to be enough for a free stake in something.

What he did on his end was show up somewhere. The move generally made money for someone else. When he donned a Wizards uniform, it meant that about 5,500 more people a night came to MCI than the year before. By the start of the season, the Wizards had sold nearly 14,000 season ticket packages, an increase of about 4,000 from the year before. The surrounding shops, bars and restaurants benefited, with some eateries reporting sharp increases in business on game nights.

Still, many observers had hoped for and predicted a broader economic impact. The speculation was that Jordan's presence, and the increased excitement and business at MCI, would lure more technology companies and young venture capital firms to invest in the area, where they could offer employees the chance to be close to a city's vibrancy—to Jordan's games, trendy new restaurants, exciting clubs. A few businesses set up offices nearby, but there was no dramatic spike in investment after Jordan's arrival.

The economic stimulus could be likened on a smaller scale to what the Chicago arena area had seen during the early years of Jordan's ascendancy around Chicago Stadium, and later nearby the United Center, a trickle-down effect that benefited neighborhood restaurants and sports shops. But Jordan was never FDR, and what he brought was not the WPA. In Washington, mythologizers were so starstruck as to equate a man's mere presence with hands-on accomplishment. In truth, Jordan never invested in the Washington community around the arena. He was not an assertive force on behalf of a community. He was simply the wonder who landed there.

The contrast was somebody like Magic Johnson, who formed a real estate development company in Los Angeles and, in the wake of learning he was HIV-positive, began heavily investing in some of the toughest, poorest communities of that city, high-risk investments that created businesses and jobs. His chain of movie theaters meant more jobs for locals and more reason for outsiders to come to Southeast L.A., look around, eat, shop and pump more money into the area, forging a connection to places and people they would never have considered before. Johnson was a builder and investor who left his mark on places. Jordan's connection to a place was remote. In his old Chicago days, he had been involved with the Make-A-Wish Foundation. But such activity even with children had diminished markedly. While still club president, he did one community appearance at a Washington school, arriving for a photo op, efficiently posing, expressing thanks and departing quickly.

There were limits, too, to what Jordan would do to boost the Wizards, a fact clouded by the media's emphasis on Pollin's shortcomings, and fed in no small part by the Jordan camp's sniping. Word still floated around about how the Jordan people wished that Pollin had had the sense to accept Leonsis's supposed offer, a year earlier, to pick up the cost of the league's luxury-tax penalties on deals that Pollin had allegedly vetoed. Why couldn't Pollin, asked Jordan allies, allow an important minority partner like Leonsis to help? Moreover, why couldn't Pollin pay *on his own?*

The Jordan people carefully avoided discussion about why then-part-owner Jordan—if so enamored of the idea that his partners, Pollin and Leonsis, pay for luxury-tax penalties and added salary—did not see fit to offer money from his own fortune. That was always the essential contradiction to Jordan: He wanted ownership, but none of ownership's traditional financial responsibilities. He wanted the rest of Wizards ownership to invest more millions, but did not want to invest any money himself. He wanted other possible ownership groups in other cities to pony up huge sums if they wanted him, while sparing him any risk. He saw no contradiction in any of this. He did not bring money to a table; he was not a money guy. He brought *Jordan.* He injected *mystique.*

That so much was made of his economic and social impact on Washington evinced the media's willingness to graft a fairy tale on the city. But besides his free stake in the Wizards and Lincoln Holdings, his business investments in Washington were really confined to one. In the early part of 2002, his restaurant, Jordan's, opened in the Reagan Building on Pennsylvania Avenue, close to the White House. His sixth eatery in the country, it seated about 200 people, and business seemed brisk there for a while, despite restaurant reviews that characterized the fare as diner-quality disappointing. I ate there several times, once with a couple of colleagues, each of us struck on that afternoon by the same thing: There seemed nothing around to indicate that Jordan had anything to do with the place—no grand photo or artistic representation of the idol, no signature on a menu, no hint of his influence upon the ambience or décor, which had an unfinished, even vacant feel. It was as if he was there but not there, a feeling that characterized the sensation of Jordan in Washington.

While in Washington, he stayed in his tube from the moment he left his home in the Ritz-Carlton to when he returned. More than a few superstars lived that way, like a careful extraterrestrial: touch down, quietly reap the local benefits and return to the pod. The insularity of his life manifested itself in ways big and small. One night in the scrum, a visiting Chicago reporter asked Jordan about the perceived renaissance of the Washington area around the MCI Center, for which he was then receiving credit. Jordan was confused, believing the point of the question was about games and winning. The reporter rephrased the question so that Jordan might have a better chance of understanding that it had nothing to do with games, that its point was to elicit Jordan's thoughts, if any, on the neighborhood around the arena, and what he thought his role was in helping it. The clarification didn't help. Jordan's answer, swift and rote, underscored how little of his new city had dented his consciousness. "I think a whole new attitude is something that's needed with this [the Wizards'] organization, and winning does that," he said proudly. "And I think the fans are starting to see that."

To say that he gave much thought to revitalizing anything in Washington, other than his lethargic team, was to be party to a fiction. He cared about winning, and if a city's residents liked to win, then he was happy they were happy.

Once, when he was baby-faced, this was all right, part of a carefreeness granted to twentysomething athletes. But as he'd gotten older, the attitude had begun to seem so . . . *young.* What had once looked charming now struck many observers as evidence of arrested development, a sign that a nearly 39-year-old man had spent too much time in a world of games. The divorce petition and stories of his affairs only added to the doubts. He remained an idol to many fans, except now he had become a symbol of self-indulgence to a legion of others. America had come to be divided over Michael Jordan.

That reality went unadmitted by media forces. Television needed him for all that he could do for its ratings and future advertising revenues. In the three years prior to the 2001–2002 season, the Wizards had not appeared on national television. In just the first two and a half months of the new season, long before its midway point, the Wizards already had appeared in 13 nationally televised games. But Nielsen ratings could not mask the doubts about Jordan. He still trailed several players in the overall fan balloting for the All-Star Game. The greatest and most promoted player in the history of the game could not win a popularity contest against a group of twentysomethings? The numbers were not an anomaly. The following season, the fans would not vote him onto the starting All-Star team at all. How could that be, if he was, as his advisers and worshippers insisted, the most loved and admired athlete in the world?

Always, his popularity had been like that of the politician who has support thousands of miles wide, but only an inch deep. If he ever committed a misstep and his skills began visibly declining, the ardor couldn't hold, because most fans never had felt any real connection to him. He was an astounding athlete, but down deep, only an athlete. He was not, say, Muhammad Ali, someone whose intense appeal endured well beyond the ravaging of his physical skills, whose daring in asserting his religious beliefs, railing at racism, resisting the draft during the Vietnam War, withstanding the government's prosecutorial force and weathering the loss of his livelihood for more than three years, still inspired fans of diverse backgrounds. Ali's emergence as a moral and cultural symbol explained why his legend had endured his own old extramarital affairs, as well as the hubris of his career's twilight, when he fought on too long, at a horrific cost to his health. Fans remembered his sacrifices. Love was not too strong a word for what people felt for him. He enjoyed an infinite reservoir of affection and adoration that flowed from his commitment to something larger than championships and himself.

Jordan didn't. It hadn't mattered once. As long as he remained the comet, fans could still marvel. But now, looking at him grounded, hearing of his personal troubles, hoping to discover something new and more to him, they couldn't see it. Their embrace slackened. The occasional big game couldn't change this. His comeback, just as some of his friends feared, had begun diminishing him.

Away from a basketball arena, the dangers to his image always felt greater. I flew to Cleveland and saw Robert Mercer, a.k.a. the Rumpshaker, who had mailed his letter to Juanita Jordan, a month earlier, and had no idea whether it had any impact or if she had even read it. "But I don't wish bad things for anybody," he said, having heard about the divorce petition. He sat in a Hard Rock Cafe and told me he had decided against holding his scheduled January press conference, the one where he had planned to talk about Michael Jordan's alleged affair. He'd mailed out a lot of flyers for the press conference, he said, and hoped that a big press crowd wouldn't show up disappointed.

"Just isn't gonna be one," he said. "I changed my mind."

The phone calls and threats of legal action from Jordan attorney Frederick Sperling hadn't stopped him from going forward, he said. No, he simply had decided that this wasn't the right time to talk to reporters, that there might never be a good time.

The Rumpshaker looked relieved. He wore a gold chain and gold earring, and bore a striking resemblance to no one so much as Michael Jordan.

"Yeah, people say that a lot," he said casually. He sipped a bottled water, declining french fries, swearing off calories, wanting to keep his body taut. He mentioned a gig he had coming up, talking about the exotic dances he performed, a pleasant man in good spirits. He just wanted to get back to his life, he said, sighing, finished for the time being with all his talking about Jordan. "It's tiring," he said. "You just want to go on to something else. I don't know how people who find themselves in something like this can handle it for months and months, you know. Like how does Michael handle it? I don't know how he handles it."

So the Rumpshaker was out of the picture.

A few hundred miles away, in Indiana, the hairdresser Karla Knafel had heard nothing from Jordan's attorneys that satisfied her. With Bobby Mercer suddenly quiet, Frederick Sperling could even train more of his attention on the Knafel matter, if necessary. There remained time to stop the mess from breaking publicly.

Things were looking better for Jordan at all points on the personal front. He and his wife had spent time together, soon releasing a joint statement that they were reuniting. It had taken only a month for the divorce petition to disappear.

So brilliantly did Jordan play in stretches for the next two weeks as to leave observers wondering whether his morning leg-weight sessions with Tim Grover had solved his knees' problems altogether. He would be abusing a defender so easily. Then, in the time it takes for a man to turn with a dribble, he would jerk his head up, grimacing, bending, walking gingerly, not injured but clearly pained, playing through it, carrying on, jogging carefully for the next few minutes. Nonmedical coaches and some press-row observers would say, "He just tweaked something."

Tweaked is sports parlance, a nice catchall word used when nobody has the slightest idea what is going on with an athlete's body. *Tweaked* is to be employed when the grimacing athlete isn't writhing. Anything tweaked is thought to be no serious cause for concern, nothing more than a momentary pain. And there seemed reason to embrace the tweaked diagnosis when, within a half, Jordan would be running freely again, torching another opponent and playing the same grueling 40, 41 minutes.

"Just tweaked something," somebody would declare reassuringly.

The belief was as wishful as Jordan's workload excessive. He had 40 points in 40 minutes in a home win against lowly Cleveland, and two nights later at MCI, he scored 41 points in 40 minutes, as he hit 17 of 30 shots and the Wizards beat Phoenix by 10. With the Wizards' big men increasingly understanding where he wanted them to screen his defenders, he shot more unguarded jumpers than ever. Popeye Jones especially knew how to free a shooter. Jordan liked Jones's skill at picking off defenders—Jones's blind screens sometimes left smaller opponents feeling for their jaws. As a Wizard, Jordan never before had enjoyed such wide-open shots. "I like the way the guys are starting to set screens," he said, after the Phoenix game.

"The last four games, you've averaged 35," a reporter pointed out, making this sound fairly remarkable.

"Oh, yeah? That *surprise* you?" Jordan answered, a little testy. He didn't much appreciate compliments about 30-point averages, assuming reporters would know this had been commonplace once.

It was always surprising to see what pushed his buttons.

He had a couple of days off, then had 32 points in 42 minutes in a home loss to Detroit. The game came down to the final 18 seconds, with the Wizards trailing by one, when the Pistons' Michael Curry smothered Jordan during an inbounds play. The moment exposed a new Jordan limitation: He simply wasn't quick enough any longer to free himself from a defender as fast as Curry without the aid of screens. The Wizards never could get him the ball. Without Hamilton on the floor, the ball went to Hubert Davis, who missed a long jumper.

Once again, the absence of a second threat had killed the Wizards. Hamilton had now missed 17 games, but Collins announced that he would be coming back with his 20-point average to play that week in Cleveland. Jordan made clear to the media that, given his long layoff, Hamilton shouldn't be thinking of immediately reclaiming his old role in the team's offense. Hamilton's Lone Ranger would have to sit back and defer because "Tonto is gonna have to take the reins," Jordan said of himself. "And when the Lone Ranger is ready, then I can step back and I will welcome his offensive input."

Hamilton was asked about it. He smiled wearily. More Lone Ranger questions? "I'm feelin' good, movin' pretty good," he said. "I'm a team player, and I want to get back in a hurry."

But he would need at least a few days to get his wind back. He couldn't do much for long in Cleveland, back in Jordan's shadow. Jordan scored 26 points but played 40 minutes again, wearing down in the second half as Cleveland came back from a 15-point deficit. A rebound basket gave Cleveland a one-point lead with less than two seconds to play. The Wizards called time-out and Collins began drawing up a play.

"Everybody in the place knew where the ball was going," Jordan would say later.

What set him apart in all kinds of games was his fearlessness in the face of possibilities, good and bad. He had no worries about uncertainty, about randomness, about in-and-out shots, about dice rolls, about blackjack hands, about scoring or not scoring. The simplicity of what was about to happen in those moments put him at ease.

It was so different from the rest of life, he thought, where so many things could happen. When you took a shot, he'd tell people, only one of *two* things could happen: You were either going to make it or you were going to miss it. He'd missed loads of last-second shots in his career, he freely told people. And made loads—more than he missed— including one right here in Cleveland against Craig Ehlo to win a play-off series and vault the young Bulls toward greatness. But you never knew, he said. You couldn't do anything more, he'd say, than give the basket a good look, exercise solid mechanics, rely on instinct, let the ball go and not be afraid of what happened next. Give yourself over to the realization that the ball would be going in—or staying out. That this is how it was meant to be, whether in or not in. That randomness at some point took over. That sometimes you won and sometimes not.

He'd been able to grasp this truth even as a young man, and Phil Jackson had helped him to see it even better. Visualize the good. Execute. Accept the randomness. It left you blameless, whatever happened.

What you wanted to do, he believed, was always give yourself the best chance of making a jumper, and for this to happen, you needed to work constantly on the mechanics of your shot. And this he had done. He'd hurried off that red-eye from Minnesota and gotten into the gym to shoot for hours, the same thing he'd done countless times in Washington while other guys slept. No longer the game's greatest player, he still possessed its greatest work ethic on a court. He believed fiercely in a professional's accountability. Even if he took the court injured, his presence, as he saw it, meant that he had declared himself ready, and so there could be no excuses; he had to produce. With his hardest work already done, he simply fell back on instinct, without the need for assurance from any coach.

Collins knew what he wanted. He had learned from the Detroit game the other night, when he couldn't get the ball to Jordan in the final seconds because he had failed to use enough screens and cuts. He decided to utilize screens that would enable Jordan to find a free space. He wanted Cleveland thinking about possibilities other than Jordan. Now he brought back the tired Hamilton into the game, simply to serve as a decoy, another good shooter whom Cleveland would feel it could ignore only at its peril. Collins would have the fine outside-shooting Whitney on the floor, too, as well as Alexander, whose reputation as a shooter would at least force Cleveland to have a defender watching him.

Collins drew up the play. Popeye Jones would inbound the ball. Alexander would race to the outside, above Jordan, while Whitney would cut under him, toward the lane, and cut yet again. The cuts, and the prospect of either a wide-open Whitney or Alexander, would concern the defense just enough that Jordan's defender might be distracted for an instant, if not move altogether to cover a wide-open Whitney.

Jordan would be free.

It was to be Collins's finest moment in a huddle during the entire season, evidence of what one assistant coach had said earlier: that if the NBA allowed a time-out every possession and the team could huddle up like a football squad, the Wizards would have a chance of winning every game; that no one in the league was better at freeing up someone for a shot than Collins.

Now the players stepped back onto the floor. Cleveland's coach,

John Lucas, an old friend of Jordan's, walked over to him and began joking, trying to distract him. Jordan smiled and told Lucas the talk had to stop.

"It's money time," Jordan said. "No time for jokin'."

Lucas kept chatting, getting closer. Jordan gently pushed him away and walked toward a spot near the baseline. A young, strong Cleveland swingman, Bryant Stith, took a position in front of him. The Cavaliers' tough point guard Andre Miller hovered close. The referee handed the ball to Jones, who waited. An open Whitney darted under Jordan, who made a cut around the baseline, then raced back up the lane, headed toward a spot just to the left of the free-throw line, close to where he had buried Craig Ehlo. Seeing Whitney bolt free, Stith hesitated, then took a step toward the point guard. Momentarily unguarded, Jordan reached his spot, maneuvering around Miller. Jones had already let go of the basketball, a well-timed, precise missile. Jordan caught it, turned his shoulders toward the basket and simply lifted for a 15-foot jumper.

The shot went in at the buzzer.

Wizards, 93–92.

"Who did you think was gonna shoot the ball?" he asked Lucas afterward.

He had that look he only got after he'd hit a big shot—brown eyes wide and gleaming, his head bobbing. "*Everybody* in the gym knew I was gonna take the shot," he kept saying proudly.

However, the 40 minutes had left him feeling a little stiff, and the Wizards had a game the next night at home against Atlanta. He would be playing yet another back-to-back. He received stim treatment for the right knee and played heavy minutes again, scoring 28 points, the Wizards winning by seven. "I know everybody was tired," he said, "everybody" meaning himself.

Two days later, in a Sunday afternoon game at MCI, he played 41 minutes and scored 23, looking badly fatigued as the game moved on, getting outplayed in stretches by Jalen Rose, with whom he traded elbows to the head, the two having to be separated by officials in the second half. The Wizards won by 20 points anyway, a margin of victory possible only because Hamilton, in just his third game back, had rediscovered his legs, scoring 21 points.

Afterward, reporters asked Jordan what Hamilton's boost meant to the team. Jordan coolly talked instead about the lessons Hamilton had to learn in coming back. "It's good to have him back . . ." he said. "I told Rip that the game had taught him a lesson. He thought he could come in and pick up where he left off. Doesn't happen that way. You got to get into the game and try to get your rhythm and your timing and get your legs back."

The Wizards would need major production from Hamilton now, as Jordan was slowly but inexorably running himself into the ground. Two nights later at home, after stim treatment before the game's start, he played 40 minutes again, this time in a victory over Toronto, which received 29 points from Vince Carter. Hamilton played well, scoring 16 to go along with Jordan's 23 points. The Wizards had won their fourth straight. But Jordan stayed in the training room for about 45 minutes afterward, icing his knees for longer than usual, slowly shuffling out when the door finally opened.

It was only the first week of February. The team still had one game left before reaching the All-Star break, and 35 games to play after that, which meant more than 40 percent of the season remained. The Wizards stood four games above .500, suddenly a favorite to secure one of the top playoff berths in the Eastern Conference. But no one among the coaches knew that Jordan's season was nearly over, as a practical matter. He only had a few good games left in him for the year, and only 20 days before he would go on the injured list. In the eight weeks since John Hefferon had cautioned him, no one had reined him in, particularly Collins, who had let everyone know, again, that he would rely on Jordan to let him know if his right knee ever felt sore or tired.

He wanted to please Jordan, wanted to be his friend, admiring the star for never having run to him during the worst of the losing streaks and asking, *Why am I doing this?* No weakness there, no self-pity, said Collins. The only worry he ever detected in Jordan came in non-basketball moments—say, on plane flights, when sometimes he became quiet. He didn't know what Jordan was thinking then. Jordan didn't share much of that. But sometimes you could feel a sliver of the pressure in his silences, thought Collins, who didn't know that any other star alive could have handled that burden. Any other superstar was excused a bad night, Collins pointed out—any other player could ease into a game and have a scoreless first quarter. But if Jordan did that, Collins added, people immediately suspected that he had turned old overnight. He just wanted to help him, he told Jordan on the team plane. He loved him as a player, and appreciated him as a friend. "I just want to help you, Michael," he'd repeat.

"I'm fine, Douggie," Jordan said.

Collins said okay, and left it at that. He knew not to go too far.

7

The Costs of Pretending

AS THE SEASON PROGRESSED, A CAREFUL COLLINS LOOKED FOR
ways to guide Jordan during a game. If unable to communicate with
him, the team would suffer, particularly when a tired Jordan lapsed
into being a one-man offense. Collins sought a way to offer criticism
without being overtly critical. He wanted to correct without correcting.
Sometimes an assistant coach would ask him, *Why do you do that? Just
talk to him.* But Collins, so burnt during his early Chicago days when
blunt around Jordan, didn't act like a man confident in expressing his
worries directly. If bothered by an aspect of Jordan's play, he often
delivered his concerns cryptically, admonishing not Jordan but the
entire team, hoping that Jordan would catch on to his real meaning.
Sometimes he specifically excluded Jordan from his complaints,
though the intention of his remark was to influence Jordan alone into
changing something he had been doing. It was a weird mind game, but
it made for pleasant relations between coach and star. Noticing that
Jordan wasn't passing the ball often enough, he waited for a time-out,
stared at his other players and said, "Come on, guys, we gotta move the
ball. We can't stand around and watch Michael play."

It was Collins's way of saying, *Michael is holding the ball too much.*
Sometimes his messages were too opaque to be grasped by *anybody.* But
Collins thought that Jordan generally understood. He decided that his
new dialect, this evolving Collins-speak, worked. He settled upon
reserving his advice for matters mostly related to technique. If he saw
Jordan's jump shot losing its arc and turning flat because he wasn't

jumping as high, he carefully formulated a pointer. "Michael, lift a little bit," he would say. "You're getting a little flat with it."

"You're right," Jordan responded.

The coach was walking a fine line. Jordan wanted to be in control of everything he did. On the other hand, Collins knew that if he didn't coach Jordan enough that this could lead to trouble, too. On the day he'd hired him, Jordan privately warned that if Collins was ever seen as bowing to him, the other players would resent the double standard and lose respect for him. That would be the moment, Jordan added, when he would begin having his own doubts about Collins. "He told me he wouldn't respect me if I didn't [express a coach's occasional criticism]— because then I can't coach the other guys," Collins recalled.

Jordan carefully avoided any appearance of usurping Collins's power. Sometimes, Collins called to him, "Hubie was open," meaning that Jordan had forced a shot while Hubert Davis waited alone for a pass at his favorite spot along the three-point line. Jordan nodded agreeably, as he did when Collins expressed clipped concern about Jordan's shot selection. The tendinitis in his right wrist had increasingly made long jumpers, and especially three-pointers (he hit fewer than one in every five), doubtful propositions. Every few games, there came a moment when, watching Jordan badly miss a 25-footer, Collins gently indicated to him that it would probably be best if he didn't cast up another long jumper: "Michael, we don't need that shot."

Jordan nodded.

He deferred during practices, too, when Collins sometimes said he needed him on the floor to run through a play. But the limits of the coach's authority were always clear. One night during a time-out against Minnesota, Collins diagrammed a play that called for the ball to be rotated to Whitney on the outside. "This is where I'm going to put you," Collins said to Jordan, pointing at his chart. "I'll put you there so I can load up the other side of the floor and it can go to Chris over here and—"

Jordan interrupted. "Good, but how about having me over there?" Jordan said, pointing to the opposite side of the floor, Whitney's side, where the ball was going, and where Jordan wanted to be to get the shot himself.

Collins nodded.

He knew when not to push. But he realized he had to find a way to alter Jordan's game sometimes, in part because Collins could see physical problems with Jordan that extended beyond the bad knee.

He couldn't handle the ball with his old skill, Collins noticed. Some of that had to do with diminishing reflexes, and some with his lack of practice since the knee problems. But mostly, it was a consequence of his bad right index finger, which never had regained full movement after the cigar-cutting accident, in early '99.

He sliced the finger while down in the Bahamas, the victim of a cheap cutter that had malfunctioned, Jordan told people. A doctor in a local emergency room treated the injury, but the tendon was snapped, with the result that Jordan had a finger he could not move. Once back in Chicago, he went to John Hefferon, who, during surgery, also saw extensive ligament damage in the finger unrelated to the accident, the product of years of dislocations. Even in repairing the tendon, he couldn't hope to restore all of the finger's mobility and dexterity, he told Jordan. The finger would never again be able to handle a basketball with quite the same sureness. The rest of his right hand would need to compensate.

It never wholly adjusted, Collins knew. Before the accident, Collins had watched Jordan do anything with a basketball in his right hand— palm it, grip it like a grapefruit, wave it at a foe before blowing by him and dunking. Now Collins saw that Jordan couldn't reliably palm the ball, making many dunks problematic. Most seriously, he experienced problems for the first time in handling the ball against defensive pressure, especially late in games, when defenders often came at him in double-teaming pincers. The index finger would sometimes betray him, and the ball would come up too high off the dribble, leaving him exposed and vulnerable to a steal. He'd occasionally dribble a ball off his foot, or try to make a stylish move and have the ball squirt away from him. His turnover rate never had been higher—five or more, on many tough nights. "He mishandles that ball sometimes," Collins said, carefully noting that he thought the bad finger, not Jordan, was to blame. "He can't grip that ball and swing it."

But still, on his best nights, Collins marveled, he could be as productive as anybody else in the league. The trick, the coach knew, was in reining in his star when he played like a tired man. For a while, Collins had settled upon a plan to rest Jordan routinely toward the end of first quarters. But the plan was quickly shelved, under Jordan's pressure. Collins had reversed course again. Like a mariner sensitive to the slightest shift in winds, he was forever tacking. He allowed Jordan now to play 40 minutes on successive days, the part of the regimen that worried John Hefferon the most. "I thought Michael was okay with that tonight," Collins said blithely following the earlier home loss to Minnesota, the second of consecutive 40-minute evenings. "He felt pretty good."

Meanwhile, he sought in moments to lay the responsibility for Jordan's playing time on Jordan. Sometimes he would touch on Jordan's intransigence and, in the same breath, change course and say he needed Jordan out there to win. Asked whether he was thinking of shaving time off Jordan's minutes, he answered: "I'd *like* to. But you know how stubborn he is. Michael wants to win. . . . He doesn't want to be saving it for anything. So, ummmm"—long pause here, Collins already tacking— "that's why, you know, the score dictates a lot [about] his minutes. . . . We go into these droughts where it's so tough for us to score."

As Jordan's knee pain became more severe and his limp more pronounced in February, Collins was back to saying that he wished he could cut Jordan's minutes. But who would fill those minutes, even if Jordan agreed to the arrangement? Alexander could score, but the coaches still thought his offense erratic, his defense spotty and his intensity almost nonexistent. The hardworking, reliable Hubert Davis had done everything asked of him without complaint, filling in as a starter, making big baskets, later calmly reassuming his spot on the bench, scarcely playing at all until somebody else would be injured and he found himself playing 30, 40 minutes again. Davis had delivered, but Collins worried that Davis already was exhibiting signs of fatigue. At 31, Davis was thought to be in his NBA twilight, relatively old by league standards for any player not named Michael Jordan, and Collins worried that he could not ask for more minutes from Davis without seeing a sharp decline in his effectiveness.

That left Tyrone Nesby, who, though not an offensive threat, brought a defensive prowess that no other Wizard, aside from a healthy Jordan, could match. Having come off the bench to stifle Vince Carter during that second-quarter stint in Toronto, Nesby had so bothered an array of capable players that he seemed on the brink of carving himself a nice niche as a 6' 6" defensive specialist. In three successive victories, during late January and early February, he put the shackles on three talented foes down the stretch—Cleveland's Jumaine Jones, Atlanta's All-Star Shareef Abdur-Rahim and Indiana's Jonathan Bender. "We don't beat Cleveland or Atlanta without Nez," Collins said.

Nesby had nimble feet to go along with long arms, which he often spread and waved maniacally around an opponent, like an octopus enveloping quarry. He'd belly-bump foes, too, and push them with his strong upper legs and forearms. T-Nez could be maddening for a rival who had seldom seen him in action. A perturbed Jumaine Jones just put his hands on his hips at one point and stared at him, incredulous that Nesby was getting away with something that Jones had difficulty articulating to an official. T-Nez didn't seem to notice, taking a break during a change of possessions to stare off at something, mumbling at air.

Nobody on the Wizards possessed more motivation, as Nesby was playing in the last year of his contract. In the Wizards' next game, a tight contest at home against Atlanta, he harassed the Hawks' young star Abdur-Rahim into losing his grip on the ball with about a minute to play, the ball spinning free, with the Hawks unable to recover it before the 24-second shot clock expired. A pleased Jordan slapped him on the butt, shouting, "Don't leave yourself *any* bullets, Nez."

Nesby had moved high above Alexander in the rotation, having played about 20 minutes a night over the last two weeks. His versatility now made him the ideal person to enter the game when Jordan needed a breather. Nesby could play not only a shooting guard but also either of the forward positions, his speed enabling him to handle quick, smaller swingmen like Jumaine Jones or bigger, more powerful forwards like Abdur-Rahim. In the next game, at home against Indiana, he received a rare spot start at power forward, filling in for the rugged Popeye Jones, who wasn't thought fast enough to defend the athletic Indiana front line. Nesby locked up big, swift Indiana forward Jonathan Bender, led the Wizards in rebounding and had a double-double—10 rebounds, 10 points. Afterward, Collins lauded him: "He did a *great* job on Jonathan Bender."

Aware that Nesby was in the last year of a deal paying him more than $3 million a season, Collins had begun exhorting him with talk of his potential appeal to other NBA teams and how his future might hinge on the season's remaining three months. "Nez," Collins said to him alone in his office, "when you're in shape, you make us a totally different team. Think about this in terms of money. Bust your tail for the ninety days left this season and then you're a free agent. This could set you up for the next few years. You say to yourself, I'm gonna go to the wall every day for the next ninety days and establish myself. . . . Somebody has *gotta* pay you, because you have talent and you're only twenty-six years old."

Nesby tried not to ponder his contract running out or what he had to do to get a new one. "If you think about it too much, it can start to be like the only thing you think about, and that's just gonna get you upset," he said. "That'd just be havin' me thinkin' negative and nervous when I'm on the bench. I'd be angry I'm not playin' more, and I'm not that way, not angry, just tryin' to do my best."

He talked very fast—and what came rambling out of him was usually unfiltered, which accounted for why most of the media so liked him. He was that rare player who could be counted on to say whatever popped into his head, an affable guy hoping to stay in the league and make money, and if telling his story could help, he would tell it. He thought Collins liked him, he said, thought Coach liked *hard* players, and this he was trying to be, flying around the lane, snatching rebounds, cutting off bigger players even if it meant being knocked to the floor. Better to get hurt playin' hard, he said, than to protect your body and not get another contract. And he knew Collins appreciated guys who played hurt. "Doug wants to see you holding nothin' back if you want that money," he said. "And I'm tryin'. I think I'm showin' it."

In the locker room, he carefully fit his black do-rag over his corn-rows, looking over his shoulder as Jordan came walking out of the trainer's room. He knew he had to win over Jordan, understanding that he had begun the year with serious baggage after having screamed at Leonard Hamilton. He called the incident The Thing, like it was its own octopus. "I know Mike was wonderin', about The Thing and other stuff. . . . You know, like: 'Well, let's see, you know I hear Tyrone got attitude.'"

Attitude always meant *bad* attitude. It was like The Thing, something hard to get away from.

He sensed that Wizards officials had yet to make up their minds about him, including Jordan, who urged him to continue rebounding hard: "Go to the rack, man."

Nez thought the team could help Jordan best if it wasn't so reliant on him. At anytime in a game, he thought, when the score got close and players felt uncertain, the ball went to Jordan. Nez found himself often catching a pass and instinctively looking to put the ball in Jordan's hands. "I looked at tapes and saw that we basically only scored when Mike's got it going," Nez said. "When he wasn't on the court, everybody looked like: *What are we gonna do?* You can't be playin' like that. . . . So I said to myself, 'I'm gonna start goin' and takin' shots. I don't care if I only shoot three or four shots. I'm gonna try to help out.'"

Jordan wanted Nez to drive, dunk, use his power game for easy hoops. "If you have your shot, shoot it," he told Nez, the same thing he'd said in preseason. Nez thought the pointers were hopeful signs— *Mike's talking to me, Mike's passing on advice, Mike's wanting to help.*

But you never knew what was going down, Nez thought. He'd proven he could defend virtually anybody at his position in the NBA, but The Thing and all the old talk about his attitude might have had an effect he couldn't see, he realized. One Wizards official said privately, "He might still be a live firecracker," meaning it was possible, thought the official, that Nez might still go off. But the single incident with Leonard Hamilton was not an insurmountable barrier to another Wizards contract for Nesby, not by a long ways. If he played well down the stretch, his continued presence in Washington would be a real possibility, and if Washington took a pass on him, another NBA team might bite. However, the limits of Nesby's outside shot meant he would always be on the bubble, and bubble players, noted the official, enjoyed far less room for screwups either on or off the court.

This was a reality of the business. A superstar with a more offensively productive and crowd-thrilling game enjoyed far greater latitude for volatility and terrible behavior. Latrell Sprewell could choke his old Golden State coach, P. J. Carlesimo, once, attack him a second time, and, after serving a lengthy suspension, come back and make tens of millions, while being promoted as an anti-hero of sorts by a shoe company. But Sprewell, on his good nights, could easily score 30 points and more. The list of misbehaving players who had kept getting signed for many years, from Dennis Rodman to Isiah Rider, could have filled the rosters of a couple of NBA teams. Stars who assaulted women arrived at settlements and went on blissfully playing, the incidents quickly forgotten, at least in basketball circles.

But all those players could change a team's fortunes. Middling players lived by a different standard. At that moment, in winter of early 2002, Nesby was averaging slightly fewer than five points a game, in about 18 minutes per night. His reputation for defensive excellence had not spread far. He was on the bubble, and could go from his $3 million-plus salary to zero in the NBA if he couldn't prove himself in the next 90 days. "When I think about the contract, I just tell myself, *Show Mike, show Doug, and play hard and do it every night, 'cause not many nights left,*" he said. "I'm playin' my best ball now. Mike hasn't talked to me about it, but he's busy, I know. I think I still have a chance."

His motivation resembled that of any guy anxious to hold on to his job. The NBA earning window for a player like Nesby was about four to five years. There would be an opportunity perhaps in a European league, but the money there would be nothing comparable. This was not a reason for pity, only an indication that professional ballers did not live for terribly long as young princes. Nesby's hopes for long-term financial security hinged over the next 90 days on his defensive prowess, which might have been his ticket once to 10 million dollars, but still could be overshadowed by a five-minute incident, one year earlier, in which no one had been punched, pushed or threatened. Nesby simply hoped that league executives, when they heard his name, would not automatically think of a frustrated, screaming young man from a single game. He hoped they saw how hard he defended, how long he could run. "Ready to go through the wall," he promised.

If Collins needed him to play an extra five, six minutes to give Jordan extra rest, said Nez, then he was ready.

Five minutes or so a night was exactly the additional time that John Hefferon wished Jordan would take off. Nesby was the man who, defensively, at least, could serve as the adequate substitute.

But Jordan told Collins that he did not want any more minutes off. Jordan would keep logging 40-minute nights—until he couldn't. The decision meant everything to the idol's season and the bubble player's career. They were the two sides of the NBA reality—one always to be venerated, the other waiting for word whether he would stay or go.

If October, November and December had worn Jordan down, the early part of 2002 was the death march for his right knee. He played 41 minutes a game during one especially brutal stretch in January and early February. People close to Jordan all over the country worried. Phil Jackson privately told people that Jordan was playing too many minutes. Tex Winter, Jackson's highly regarded assistant, said it publicly: "I think he's running a real possibility of injury in the second half of the season if he keeps playing those kind of hard minutes. It's a risk."

The final game before the All-Star break was at home against the Sacramento Kings, who entered the night with the league's best record at 37–11 but had just played the night before, tired after a long road trip. "You gotta kill when you can kill," Jordan told his teammates.

The Wizards delivered their finest team effort of the season. Jordan had 25 points and nine assists. Hamilton led all scorers with 33 points. Popeye Jones had a mouth-dropping double-double—18 points and 15 rebounds—dominating the boards against a Sacramento front line that included Vlade Divac and All-Star Chris Webber. Brendan Haywood blocked a pair of shots and had 11 rebounds. Chris Whitney hit three-pointers. Etan Thomas ran down loose balls in key moments. Jordan and Nesby alternated in chasing Sacramento's superb three-point bomber, Predrag Stojakovic, stymieing him in the second half.

The Wizards won by seven, but not before a scare that portended trouble for the remainder of the season. In the second quarter, after hitting a jumper, Jordan turned and banged knees with big Etan Thomas. Jordan fell to the floor, grabbing his right knee, not writhing but not getting up right away either. Even as the staff dashed onto the floor, Jordan rose and motioned for them to get back: He was fine.

After the game, he shuffled out to the scrum with no more stiffness than he usually exhibited, not even mentioning the knee. He trumpeted the team's accomplishments, the Wizards having arrived at the four-day All-Star break with a record of 26–21 and a five-game winning streak. Washington already had seven more victories than a season earlier, and Jordan was leading the team in scoring, with more than 25 points a game.

He said that he looked forward to the All-Star Game, which many observers viewed as the first half of a doubleheader between Jordan and Kobe Bryant—the second game to come, about 48 hours later, in Los Angeles. Jordan downplayed both matchups with Bryant, particularly the All-Star confrontation. He tried joking: "If Kobe tries to make it a one-on-one game, I'm gonna foul him with every foul I got. I'm a competitive person, but I know we have a long second half of the season."

Collins said he hoped Jordan's All-Star minutes wouldn't be *too* high. Jordan assured Collins that he would keep his playing time short—somewhere around 12 minutes. It was basically the same thing he said to the Eastern Conference coach, Byron Scott. "Twelve to fifteen minutes, that's what he told me," Scott said, smiling. "Fifteen minutes. I think once the game *starts,* he'll probably change his mind."

Fifteen would not remain fifteen.

On Saturday, in the Philadelphia 76ers' home arena, the First Union Center, Jordan sat for a joint press conference alongside Allen Iverson, who sported a red headband with his nickname in large white block letters, THE ANSWER. Jordan wore black Jordan Brand/Nike sweats with a silver earring. What you had here was the perfect confluence of a charismatic young man's self-adoration and an experienced elder's marketing pose, and in that way the scene mirrored perfectly two forces that stoke the basketball industry's success—vanity and the skill to make vanity pass as class, to make money off vanity as a fashion statement. The two players spent most of the time carefully praising each other and trying to restrain journalists. Surprisingly, Jordan looked the edgier of the two. Some reporter in the first row asked him if he might play beyond his two-year Wizards contract if—

Jordan cut him off. "Slow your roll," he said to the guy, which mockingly meant, *Chill.* It was a Jordan whom you seldom saw in a press setting. This was the Jordan who had sliced Lacy Banks in Indiana. A few reporters chuckled. He pointed out to the questioner that he would be 41 years old if he played into a third season. *"No, no,"* he said, shaking his head, as if to say, Not a chance. "You guys gave me a lot of shit when I [turned] *thirty-nine."*

He fired a few zingers, declaring that he loved Charles Barkley but that Barkley never would be part of the elite class of players, instead relegated to "that second tier" because he never won an NBA championship. And he issued a challenge of sorts to Iverson, who had yet to win an NBA title. He pointed out that his own scoring titles hadn't won him inclusion into the ranks of players like Magic Johnson and Larry Bird until the Bulls won their first championship. "That's the kind of respect I *earned,"* he declared. "And that's something he's gonna have to earn."

By then the media looked restless, as if Jordan wasn't getting around to what they most wanted him to talk about. Finally, a reporter raised the subject: "This is for Allen. You played against Michael and Kobe both this year."

Jordan was already smirking.

The reporter went on: "Can you compare the two guys, and maybe think back on Michael before the retirement and compare the two [Jordan's and Bryant's] games?"

Jordan sliced in. "I wouldn't answer that question if I were you. But go ahead."

Iverson looked hesitant.

"That's an unfair question," Jordan went on. *"Truly."*

"You heard what he said," Iverson said to the reporter.

"Next," Jordan commanded, and the question was officially rejected.

Nearly every All-Star doing interviews at the arena found himself barraged by questions about what it felt like to contemplate playing alongside or against Jordan. One player seemingly had had too much of all the bowing at the altar. The Milwaukee Bucks' All-Star guard Ray Allen raised a point that no NBA official, or television announcer working the game, dared to make because it would necessarily raise questions about the strength of Jordan's appeal. Referring to Jordan's fourth place finish in the overall All-Star voting, Allen asked, "How could he finish [fourth] in voting? He is on TV more than any other player in the league. When he first started [his comeback], [ESPN's] *Sportscenter* showed [his] every play, every shot. Popularity is the biggest key in All-Star votes. So hearing he's [fourth] in voting is a surprise to me." He elaborated later: "How does that happen if it's all a popularity thing and he's so popular?"

It was a brave, perceptive question. No one connected to the NBA dared to venture an answer.

Magic Johnson had come to Philadelphia, on All-Star eve, to play in a three-on-three game involving celebrities and retired stars. He talked while getting ready in a locker room. He spoke to anyone about anything. A television man rushed up and asked if he'd do an All-Star Game promo. Magic said sure, taking about a hundredth of a second to prepare. He turned 90 degrees, looked into a lens and started talking: "And tomorrow the NBA All-Star Game—*whooooooo*—*Michael Jordan returns*. And so many other super super *super* great players."

"Thank you, Magic," said the TV guy.

"Anytime," Magic said.

"Oh." The TV guy wheeled back. "How old are you, if I may ask?"

"Goin' on forty-three," Magic said.

"Thank you, Magic."

"Anytime."

Do you miss any of this, Magic? somebody asked him.

He shrugged. He alluded to how his past had put everything in proper perspective for him: After being stricken by the AIDS virus, he had retired as a player, later to make a comeback that hadn't worked out.

He didn't refer to his mistakes but everyone around knew them: He had cheated on his wife, slept with too many women, engaged in unprotected sex, and recklessly cut his career short. Having redeemed himself since, he was a part-owner of the Lakers, but he reserved his greatest passion for his movie theaters and many other businesses in Southeast L.A. He was now the personification of what Jim Riswold, the producer of Jordan's famous Nike ads, had hoped to see Jordan evolve into, someone who cared deeply about something beyond games and winning. He beamed when a woman said that she had a friend whose teenage son worked in one of his businesses.

"Thank you; that's a *wonderful* thing," he said.

Another TV man asked him for another promo. Magic stared into another lens and said, "And tomorrow, the *NBA All-Star Game*. With Michael Jordan, Kobe Bryant and the most *super* players in the world."

"That's great, Magic."

"Anytime," Magic said. "Michael around?"

"No, he left quite a while ago, Magic."

Magic chuckled. "I'm sure Michael knows he's gotta get rest for what's comin' up for him after this weekend."

He meant the Wizards–Lakers game that coming Tuesday night.

"Everybody in the world is waiting on *that* game," Magic said, adding that he thought Bryant, like Jordan, understood he couldn't blow his wad on the All-Star Game and not have enough in the tank for Tuesday. "Probably more important for Michael to keep his playing time down than Kobe. Kobe's so young. Michael's gotta be careful. It's an All-Star Game, but the L.A. game is *the* game. He knows that."

So Jordan won't be playing for very long tomorrow? somebody asked him.

"I didn't say *that*," Magic answered, grinning. "You just don't know with Michael. You just don't know."

You really don't miss it, Magic? a woman whispered.

He looked at her with an expression made dreamy by all the pleasure and serenity in it. He returned her whisper with a voice not much above a whisper. "I really really don't. I love what I'm doin'. I'm grateful to get the message out. Oh." He seemed to have been reminded of something. "People really should be tested for AIDS. Really important. I try to talk about that wherever I go."

All men grow older, but only a few grow. Magic Johnson was the well-to-do athlete who had found his next life. Foreign TV people and grizzled American reporters jostled with one another to get close to him, their hands outstretched. He shook them all. He had a connection with people; it was what so separated him at that moment from Jordan, whom he liked, whom he cared about, but who, on the doorstep of 40, had yet to find anything beyond the game. Much time remained in a life at 40. Johnson's life spoke of the possibilities.

The next afternoon, Jordan arrived at the game, two hours early, to do extra stretching, feeling a little tight. It didn't help. He looked stiff throughout the evening—not hobbled, just not himself somehow. In the first quarter, he missed a breakaway dunk, a dunk when he was far out ahead of the field and had several seconds to think about it. He mistimed it, not getting up high or soon enough. His hand brought the ball down on the back of the rim, where it caromed off as a good 2,000 flashes recorded the moment.

He tried smiling. He knew it would be the only moment the crowd and media remembered about his day, understood it would be the first thing he'd need to talk about at the postgame press conference. Not long before his missed dunk, he had beaten Minnesota's Kevin Garnett on a drive and dunked over San Antonio's 7'0" Tim Duncan. But all that most people would remember from his performance would be the missed dunk, a defining embarrassment on a day when he struggled, missing 9 of 13 shots, scoring only eight points.

None of those numbers, however, would have an impact on the rest of his season. On the other hand, his 23 minutes worried Wizards officials, who regarded his playing stint as needlessly long, on a weekend when he needed as much rest as possible. Just as Byron Scott and others had hinted, Jordan found it too difficult to come off the court once a game was in motion.

His competitive instincts could not have been assuaged by the sight of his touted heir, Kobe Bryant, tearing up the game, scoring at will for the victorious West squad—31 points in 30 minutes—on his way to the game's Most Valuable Player award. Playing in front of hometown fans who booed him throughout the game—the venomous Philadelphians still smarting over the local schoolboy star's escape to warm and winning Los Angeles—Bryant was possessed by an on-court fury.

He could have scored 50 if he'd wished. The quality of his play only made the Wizards officials wish all the more that Jordan had gotten off the court sooner, so that he could begin resting for the Lakers. But in this garish game (an All-Star weekend is a modern-day Roman bacchanal), Jordan's pride did not permit him to leave any sooner than the third quarter. By that time, putting on his sweats, he seemed stiffer than ever, shuffling, displaying the telltale signs of his knee problems.

Afterward, he appeared before the press and handled the discussion of the missed dunk with much grace. No one had to ask him about the moment. He sat down, leaned into a microphone, smiled thinly and blurted, "Okay, who's gonna be the first to ask?"

The press chuckled.

"I laugh at myself," he said. "If I can't laugh at myself, I can't laugh at anybody."

Then he delivered the closest thing to a soliloquy on aging. "It was one of those situations where you got a wide-open dunk. . . . It's been a while since I've been in that circumstance. The wheels started turning. I started trying to figure out, What will you do?"

He hunched his shoulders. "At the last minute, you think, Well, just *dunk* it. And you lose concentration. As much as you want to be creative, you listen for all the signs and moves in your body. And you're just worried about something popping or whatever. As you get old, you just don't have the same kind of confidence. So you gotta go through a checklist."

Jordan paused and chuckled. The mood lightened in the room.

"And I went through the checklist, and by the time I was ready to dunk the ball, I wasn't there."

He sounded wistful. He mentioned that he had been talking about the missed dunk to NBC when Tracy McGrady made a spectacular dunk. "I remember when I used to be like that," he said softly.

A reporter asked him about Bryant being booed. Something in him changed in that instant, as if a switch had been flipped and he was suddenly thinking two nights ahead. He wouldn't be feeling sorry for a rival. "He's played on hostile territory before," Jordan said, observing that many players got booed somewhere, sometime.

"I'm always booed in Cleveland."

Shuffling a little, he was off to Los Angeles, where most of the questions for him were about Bryant, though Jordan seemed more absorbed by the shadow of Phil Jackson. "We know our friendship will outlast any battle we ever have on the basketball court," he said, on the morning of the game. "No matter what happens, there's a sense of love between us."

For all his talk of Zen and openness—or maybe because of it—Phil Jackson did not display much emotion or sentimentality. He seldom expressed the standard NBA coach's excitement and gratitude about things, the gushing about a player that took on this form: *He's been so important to our team, and I can't say enough great things about him, we really love the guy.* You never heard his voice trembling with feeling. His impassiveness and gray beard gave him the bearing of a $500-an-hour psychoanalyst who could take you or leave you but would probably leave you except for the business between the two of you. He gave off an air of being above sentiment, which meant he could scarcely have been more different from Doug Collins.

Love was not part of Jackson's public vocabulary. He'd smirk a little when a questioner used the word. Much of the time he had an amused disdain for the media, condescension radiating from him. His aloofness intrigued many reporters, and flummoxed the rest. He would not hesitate saying, after coming back from an off day, that he'd watched no basketball at all, and wouldn't waste his time watching basketball on an off day. That smirk encouraged the image that he was constantly evolving, and others weren't.

He had been a wild card of sorts during his playing days with the Knicks in the late '60s and early '70s. But, with his days of beads and heavy cannabis consumption in Greenwich Village long since over, he wore nice suits and natty sweatsuits now. He radiated élan. The formal scrum session over, he'd start moving away, amused he was still being pursued. He'd airily mention a book, something he ate, make a quick reference to something about spiritualism, smirk at somebody asking him about a no-name power forward somewhere and snicker "Don't know" because he couldn't care less about the no-name forward. "Okay, guys," he'd say then, done with them, smiling in amusement.

The press reveled in portraying him as a grown-up '60s flower child, but to spend time at his media sessions was to realize that he was no Peace and Love holdover but seemingly a guy emulating the ultracool of a Beat poet, consciously wry, detached, understated, confident he had *It,* whatever It was. His public air was hip: He was a little too good at making such things as the Triangle Offense sound like a spiritual epiphany (he had likened the Triangle to tai chi), and in trying to ground all of basketball into enlightened truths, as expressed in his book *Sacred Hoops,* where he proffered the chance for his players "to create something as a group that transcended the limits of their own singular imaginations." Okay, then.

Now he did a commercial for a national chain of hotels, in which, in self-parody, he spouted his own coaching version of Zen and New Ageism ("Surrender the me for the we . . ."), having arrived at that special place in America where one could turn a profit and still project purity.

He was on a 10-year roll, the coach nearly every other team coveted. More than a coach, Jackson had become a name in pop culture, rising to the status of American Winner, the counterculture's answer to Vince Lombardi, respected enough for his leadership skills that his old friend Bill Bradley had asked him to run his doomed presidential campaign. Jackson declined, having decided by then to take the Lakers job, but

this did not stop many Democrats from touting him as a possible political candidate in his native North Dakota.

The media, which loves theatrical archetypes and needs someone at
all times to be portrayed as Svengali, never could get enough of stories
about the Zen Master recommending tai chi, meditation, visualization
and Sun Tzu's *The Art of War* to his players. But the Zen label misled
fans. Jackson's passion for transcendentalism never had made him gentle. He didn't shy away from bruising people when he thought they
stood in the way of his winning, chewing out players about as often as
most other coaches did, having once booted out his starting power forward, Horace Grant, from a Bulls practice when Grant said that his tendinitis had become so painful that he didn't think he could perform.
Jackson told him not to come back until he got his head together and
decided to play. For the team's amusement, in front of Grant, he
screened a video of Grant making a bad play, the video then segueing
into a clip from *The Wizard of Oz,* in which the Scarecrow wished plaintively for a brain.

Jackson regularly zinged Bulls players with his film clips. He had
had no sacred cows, in film sessions or anywhere else, not even Jordan.
Early in his reign, he had signaled to the team that it would no longer
be Jordancentric: In selecting a new co-captain, he appointed the lone
Bull who had ever challenged Jordan and backed him down. Bill
Cartwright, thought Jackson, was a natural leader. That quality, in
addition to the benefit of making clear that Jordan did not run the
team, meant the upside of a Cartwright co-captaincy far outweighed
any possible problems presented by Cartwright's shaky relationship
with the idol. Cartwright had the job. Jordan would just have to get
over it, if he had a problem with it.

The Bulls' style of play changed during Jackson's tenure. Against Jordan's preference, Jackson implemented Tex Winter's more pass-oriented
and ball-sharing Triangle Offense, which Jordan had originally derided
as "an equal-opportunity offense" that sometimes placed the ball in
average players' hands at key moments in a game. The Triangle became
law. Jackson won his team's respect while leaving himself vulnerable. As
in Collins's case, had Jordan demanded a coaching change, Jackson
would have been out in days, hours even. Jackson moved ahead with all
his plans anyway. He had to persuade Jordan against single-handedly
attempting to dominate the stretches of big games, when Jordan had a
tendency to take virtually every shot. During the Bulls' first championship season, they led the best-of-seven NBA Finals series, three games

to one, against the Lakers who, trying to stay alive on their home floor, had kept Game Five close as the fourth quarter ticked down. Jackson was exasperated with Jordan's failure to pass to wide-open Bulls, particularly guard John Paxson, Chicago's best three-point shooter. During a time-out, with the Bulls trailing by a point, Jackson had had enough. John Bach, then an assistant under Jackson, felt Jackson was ready to say something. So did Bill Cartwright. The many accounts of the time-out slightly vary, and a decade's worth of apocrypha might have altered some memories, but everyone agrees upon the gist of what Jackson did next. With his team seated on the bench and his star toweling off, Jackson asked Jordan: "Michael, who's open?"

Jordan stared at the floor, did not answer.

Jackson demanded of Jordan, *"Michael, who's open?* Who's open?"

Jordan said softly, "Pax."

Jackson spoke evenly: "Then pass him the fucking ball."

Jordan complied. Suddenly the arena rained Paxson jumpers.

The Bulls won their first title. Jordan embraced Jackson, who had been resolute enough not to sacrifice any part of his vision to appease a player.

Jackson had demonstrated conviction since being hired by Jerry Krause in 1987, to serve as an assistant to Doug Collins. Jordan was only 24 years old, and a raw 6' 7" Scottie Pippen had just arrived as a rookie out of the University of Central Arkansas, where he had improbably progressed from the team's student equipment manager during his freshman year to the fifth overall selection in the NBA draft. Jackson tutored Pippen, not only honing his shots and defensive technique but encouraging him in the aftermath of games to consider what he had just seen on the court, helping him better visualize what would be coming later. Pippen quickly admired Jackson, as did Jordan, to whom Jackson spoke about the ethos of team play. Jordan thought Jackson had guts to make a point that the star might not have wished to hear.

Simultaneously, Collins began fraying nerves. "He yelled a lot," Brad Sellers remembered. "It wasn't that he was vicious, just that he wanted to win so bad, and wanted everything done in a certain way. He'd be yelling at everybody, not Michael, but everybody else."

The perception of two standards on the Collins-led team—one for Jordan and another for everyone else—did not help the head coach's position. Shying away from Collins, some players sought out Jackson, who filled an emotional vacuum. Stars like Pippen and Horace Grant made no secret of their loyalty to Jackson. Jordan did not then reveal a preference for one coach over the other, but neither did he send a clear message of support for Collins, whose relationships during his third Bulls season had disintegrated with Krause and later Jackson, who was already being viewed by Krause as Collins's possible successor and so had become cast as the usurper of power, in the view of Collins's few remaining allies. At the very least, Collins would need to bring the Bulls to the 1989 NBA Finals to keep his job.

He didn't. After Jerry Reinsdorf fired him with the explanation that the team needed someone who could take it the next step to a championship, Collins diplomatically stayed quiet, preparing the ground for a coaching comeback. In only his second season as head coach, Jackson led the Bulls to the first of their six championships. He had given Reinsdorf what Collins couldn't, using largely the same players, and the identical core of superstars. But Jackson didn't know any more about the game than Collins, thought associates close to both men. Jackson simply had the greater skill in managing people. He did not blink, and sometimes Collins did, which meant that one man was a coaching legend, and the other trying to hold on to a place in the profession.

But Jordan didn't know everything about Jackson. He had met at last a man with a penchant for discretion that rivaled his own. In 1998, as the Bulls stormed toward their sixth title and Jackson's last Bulls contract ran out, the talk around Chicago was, increasingly, that Jerry Krause had torn apart the Jackson-Jordan-Pippen trio, a line of thinking that Jordan adopted, not knowing the full story. Jackson's second marriage was in trouble, and the coach welcomed a sabbatical that would at least give him the chance of trying to repair his relationship with his wife. "I didn't know everything that was going on," Jordan would say of the Jackson departure.

By 2000, Jackson and his wife had split up, with Jackson coaching in Los Angeles and becoming involved in a relationship with Jeanie Buss, a Lakers executive and the daughter of the team's owner. Meanwhile, Jordan was in his Wizards executive office, contemplating the loss of what he loved most. Early during his comeback considerations, he chatted jocularly with Jackson about what it might be like if Jordan ever played for the Lakers, each man grinning, laughing, seemingly trying to avoid a seriousness that, as one witness observed, would lead the other to conclude he was being courted. The longer each could keep the conversation light and fanciful, the greater the possibility for discreetly measuring the other's possible interest. It was a no-risk, no-embarrassment dance. "Michael knew he could come here; things were kind of said; he *knew,*" said the sagacious assistant coach Tex Winter.

Blunt around Jordan, free of the crippling obeisance that character-ized most people's treatment of the star, Tex Winter was the rare Jordan coach, past or present, who did not see it necessary to be a caretaker of myths, who spoke matter-of-factly about the star. L.A. would not have worked as well as Washington for Jordan, Winter thought. "In Los Angeles, we have established players, and we'd already won. He would have had a different role here; we probably would have asked him to play fewer minutes. Things for all of us were different; things would have been different for Michael, too, if—" and Winter's voice trailed off momentarily. "The talk never got serious, only casual. Michael knew what the reality was."

The Lakers were already an extraordinary team built around two young stars, Bryant and Shaquille O'Neal, whose talents surpassed an aging Jordan's now, and whose own egos and needs left no room for anyone who might supplant their star status. If Jordan were to have seriously considered playing for the Lakers, he would have had to con-tent himself with the idea of playing a complementary role to a new generation's stars, and that, thought a sympathetic Winter, ran against everything in Jordan's nature.

You do not ask Zeus to be Mercury's attendant. "He needed a younger team he could help build and lead," Winter said, "and this wasn't a team that needed to be led. This team has leaders and stars. There were better places for him. The Wizards seemed like the right place. . . . Michael knew it; everybody knew it. He knew he could have come here if he wanted, but no one needed to say anything and no one did. I don't even know if he really thought of any place besides Wash-ington. The Wizards were the better place for him."

After the playing comeback had begun in Washington, Jackson called Jordan every few weeks just to check in, to ask Jordan how he was doing. Jackson, as much as anyone inside the Wizards organiza-tion, knew how Jordan was feeling and faring—which explained in part his concern about Jordan's playing minutes.

Jackson did not have any fondness for Collins, who in turn had regarded Jackson as partially responsible for undermining his standing in Chicago. But few people cared about the Collins–Jackson relation-ship. At the Lakers' practice the day before the game, virtually all the questions for Jackson had to do with Jordan.

What will it be like to see Jordan in another uniform?

Jackson smiled, a tiny smirk. "Well, I have to disinvolve myself from that, emotionally. It's just got to be a game where we play a team that's playing very well. It's not going to be about Michael versus Kobe or whatever."

Will it be hard for you to disengage yourself from all that?

"No. I'm pretty good at that."

Is Jordan a better player than he was in the '90s? a TV guy asked him.

Jackson looked beyond incredulous. "No, he's not a better player . . ." he said soberly. "Physically, I think it's hard for him. I see a period of a game where he gets really tired. And things don't go as well . . . when he gets tired."

He heard another question, but he was not through unspooling his philosophy on how to care properly for Jordan or any other aging veteran, in what sounded like a rebuke of Collins's style. He thought an average of about 35 minutes a game for Jordan probably suited his body best as he approached 39. "You get to forty minutes," he observed, "and the decline is really rapid."

A friend of Jackson's in the NBA coaching fraternity had an idea how Jackson would have addressed the idea of Jordan's minutes. "He sure wouldn't have gone to him and said, 'Michael, I care so much about you and I really think we need to lower your minutes and is that all right?'" the coach declared. "He probably would have said something like, 'Feeling good? Well, that's great.' Then he would have played Michael forty-six, forty-seven, forty-eight minutes. Michael would have gotten the message. It would've been the end of the forty-minute nights. And Michael would've respected it. . . . Michael always respected Phil's toughness. Michael liked toughness. Just so it had a purpose—and it won."

Jackson had said all he wished to say about Jordan's minutes. Somebody asked him about the best way to guard Jordan. He squinted. "Make him shoot jump shots in positions he doesn't like," he answered softly. "And that's not always easy. He can usually get the ball where he likes to shoot it. Okay, guys."

Somebody called out to him a last question, as he walked away, something about "Kobe and Michael." Jackson glanced at the guy the way a doctor would a mental patient. "It's *not at all* Kobe versus Michael," he said, shaking his head, shaking it, shaking. Even the Zen Master couldn't hide the pressure.

Jordan had much the same kind of relationship with Kobe Bryant that he had with many young stars, giving advice when asked. For a long while, Bryant had ravenously absorbed every suggestion. But given each man's nature, it was inevitable, as Bryant matured and needed Jordan's pointers less, that something said by one would sometimes push the competitive buttons of the other. Bryant had listened coolly once, during Jordan's executive days, when the mentor lectured him on defensive techniques. It was a day when Jordan bantered lightly about the fantasy of playing again. Chuckling, Bryant responded, "Stay upstairs, old man. You'll have more fun upstairs."

Jordan's circle had leaked Bryant's words, reflecting Jordan's mild irritation at the prodigy's impudence. Jordan, who looks for reasons to feel slighted, would use the comment as one more means for stoking his own fires. Many athletic relationships are like that, an oscillation between friendship and fury, off-court support and on-court sabotage. Great athletes typically view this as a normal state of affairs, and hold no lasting grudges. Jordan and Bryant were no different. But the weird yin-yang of their relationship meant that the older athlete, once on the court, would be trying to cannibalize the young man he guided. Likewise, Bryant, who at 23 already had won two championships and had a kingly sense of his powers, would be trying to slay the monarch, if given the chance. Both Bryant and Jordan understood this. So did their coaches, which explained why neither side wanted to see the personal confrontation happen.

Each coaching staff had other misgivings. The Wizards camp worried that an older Jordan would be left exhausted and useless on the offensive end if he guarded Bryant. The Lakers coaches, by contrast, had no doubts that Bryant could physically handle Jordan. But they worried that Bryant would be so psyched for the personal duel that the game itself would become secondary to him. "Kobe takes his defense against a great rival so *personally*," Tex Winter said. "It becomes too much of a personal challenge, and we don't like him to play that way. We're trying to get Kobe away from the idea that it's a one-on-one contest. . . . If he matched up with Michael, we [would be] a little afraid he would consider it a one-on-one game, instead of a five-on-five game. . . . And that won't ever be allowed to happen. Phil doesn't want that, won't allow it. It won't happen."

Someone close to Jackson insisted that the coach never would have put Bryant on Jordan for an additional reason: He wouldn't want Jordan believing that he had attempted to embarrass him. Winter doubted that Collins would expose Jordan to a Bryant matchup either: "I'm not sure Doug would want to put Michael in that position . . ."

The Lakers coaches informed Bryant that he would spend most, if not all, of the game guarding Richard Hamilton, whom they hoped Bryant's defense would shut down completely, leaving Jordan to assume the burden of making up for points lost. Bryant said he understood. But Jordan, holding all power that mattered over Collins, could decide for himself whether to guard Bryant or not. He had guarded Vince Carter for long stretches and Tracy McGrady. It was his call. Jordan didn't want the matchup, deciding instead to guard Lakers forward Rick Fox. The decision spoke more powerfully than any words about his respect for Bryant.

Although the press reported there would be no matchup, the sense of a personal confrontation only grew with the reports that O'Neal's sore arthritic toe would keep him out of the game. The main event would be Jordan versus Bryant, a fight that looked quite even, at least on paper. Jordan entered the game averaging 25 points to Bryant's 26; six rebounds to Bryant's five. Each man averaged five assists a game. They scarcely could have been more equal on paper—except that one man was 15 years older and the other had two good knees and a deer's speed.

The game was nothing special, Bryant insisted. "If I was going to get stoked about it, I'd tell you guys," he said to the media. "But I'm really not, man. I don't mean to kill your buzz."

Before his team took the floor, Phil Jackson told his coaching staff that he wanted to win the game in the worst way, and that he hoped Michael would put on a good show. He meant all this. He wanted to beat Collins, and he wanted to defeat the player he loved just to show he still had his coaching chops. But he did not want any pieces of Jordan's legend scattered on the arena floor.

The Wizards, riding their five-game winning streak, believed they could win, especially as they would be facing an undermanned Lakers squad. With O'Neal out, Bryant would need to carry virtually all the Lakers' offense and hold down Richard Hamilton, too. The Wizards dominated early, with Hamilton scoring 12 points in the first quarter, mostly on pull-up jumpers in and around the lane, where his quickness seemed to bother Bryant, who irritably shoulder-bumped Hamilton after one score, making him stumble. They had been rivals during their high school days in Pennsylvania, where Bryant always had won their confrontations, his Lower Merion High School team knocking out Hamilton's Coatesville Area High squad from the state high school tournament in 1995 and 1996. But the most memorable moment in their schoolboy duels had come in a 1995 regular season game, when Bryant hit a three-pointer from just over the midcourt line at the buzzer, to beat Coatesville by a point, an outcome that Bryant never had let Hamilton forget. Now at 23, they seemed in the grips of a fierce territorial struggle. Although each was 6' 7", Bryant enjoyed the physical advantage, considerably stronger and more durable as the game wore on. He shoulder-bumped the thinner man again, and one could see the reason for Tex Winter's concerns about Bryant: Once Bryant became preoccupied with a matchup, it threatened his ability to see the rest of a game.

Meanwhile, Jordan had a quietly efficient first half against Rick Fox and Lakers reserve Devean George, scoring 11 and combining with Hamilton's bursts to give the Wizards a 13-point lead. At the start of the second half, the Wizards seemed on the verge of putting the game away. The Lakers turned thuggish. L.A.'s Mark Madsen whacked Hamilton with an open hand, bloodying his mouth, on a Hamilton drive to the hoop. Soon, nowhere close to the ball, Bryant had struck Chris Whitney with an elbow to the head. More elbows flew, whistles blew, two flagrant fouls on the Lakers were assessed, and a parade of Wizards stepped to the free-throw line to stretch the lead. Hamilton next hit a jumper and Washington led by 20, the Wizards about to push the Lakers into a ravine.

And then Kobe Bryant lifted off.

It was something to behold. He took the game over in every way that a player can seize a contest. He scored inside and outside. He passed, rebounded, played choking defense, screamed at teammates, glared at his opponents, nodded to himself during time-outs as if to say his team would find a way. What he did immediately was drive to the hoop hard, flying past Hamilton. With his worried foes forced to double- and triple-team him, he then passed the ball outside to open shooters, and the Lakers quickly cut the lead to 12. At the moment when the Wizards began paying more attention to his teammates, he started firing, scoring 12 points in the third quarter, which ended with the Lakers leading by three—a 23-point turnaround in 10 minutes.

Single-handedly, Bryant cut the heart out of the Wizards' offense. Whenever Hamilton drove to the basket or around screens, Bryant bumped him, knocking him around with his forearms, shoulders and

legs, limiting him to five points in the game's final three quarters, denying him even the chance to pass inside to the Wizards' big men and Jordan. For good measure, and because he had an acute case of on-court
nastiness, Bryant gave Hamilton an elbow to the head, much like the
one he gave Whitney, having by then bent Hamilton to his will.

Through it all, the eye hardly noticed Jordan, who scored 21 points
and played decently, though not spectacularly. He tired as the game
moved along, his 41 minutes leaving him noticeably slowed in the second half. Nowhere to be seen on this night was the Jordan who shut
down Latrell Sprewell in their last game at Madison Square Garden and
who held Vince Carter pointless in the second half at Toronto. Nowhere
was the man who scored in the 40s. Those images faded in Los Angeles,
replaced by the picture of a tentative Jordan finally trying to guard the
league's young prince. For 46 of the game's 48 minutes, the older player
and the younger version of himself had carefully avoided each other.
But then came a screen, a defensive switch and, suddenly, Jordan found
himself facing a stationary Bryant alone on the court's left wing.

The crowd roared, having waited all night for this. The moment
had the feel of a short, dazzling prizefight, with the young man the
aggressor. Never had the old predator looked so much like prey. Bryant
stared him down, took a short hard dribble to his left that had Jordan
moving unsteadily backward, then lifted like a phantom and connected on a 22-foot jumper.

The moment answered any last questions about their relative abilities. The younger man had the weapons now.

Lakers 103, Wizards 94.

Bryant strolled away with his career's third triple-double—leading
all scorers with 23 points, to go along with 11 rebounds and a personal
best of 15 assists.

Jordan struggled to explain what happened. "I felt everyone was
expecting me to take over the game," he said. "I couldn't get the ball . . ."

He noted Hamilton's problems—"I think [the Lakers] took Rip out [of
the game]"—and complimented Bryant: "Defensively, he stepped it up
on Rip, and Rip certainly didn't get anything going [in the second half].
This is definitely a lesson for us. . . . We folded under their pressure."

He talked, a bit wistfully, about Jackson's role in the evening: "You
know his team is going to play solid defense. It was kind of difficult. . . .
You can imagine what other teams felt like going against us [in
Chicago]."

In the hallway, Collins noted that he'd like to get Jordan's minutes down to 36 or 37, but that he couldn't tonight because "we were leaking oil."

Tex Winter thought that Jordan appeared tired in the game. "He looked worn down," he observed. "I think Phil [Jackson] is right when he says it's hard for Michael when he's going past thirty-five minutes. How long did he go? Forty-one? That's a lot. *Risky.*"

The Wizards' second-half collapse deeply worried the coaches. A few feared that Hamilton's lack of strength, even frailty, had been exposed by Bryant, and that opponents thereafter would routinely try to bully him. Jordan rode Hamilton the next day at practice in Sacramento, telling him he better muscle up and hit the weights. The next night, in a lopsided loss at Sacramento, with the Kings banging Hamilton every time he drove or came around a screen, he hit only 3 of 14 shots in the first three quarters. By then, even Hamilton realized he had to build up his body, telling the coaches that he would begin regularly lifting weights with Jordan and a few other team members early in the morning.

But the coaches' greatest concern revolved around Jordan. Privately discussing his performance against the Lakers, the Wizards coaches had become newly concerned about Jordan's mobility and health. Running gingerly, he hit only a third of his shots for a quiet 16 points in Sacramento, then floundered for most of an evening in Phoenix, again having hit only a third of his shots, when the Wizards called time-out with 5.6 seconds left, trailing by a point.

The Wizards would not have been in the game at all but for Tyrone Nesby, who scored 18 points and had ten rebounds, having a spectacular night, likely the best all-around game of his career, blocking two shots, coming up with a key loose ball and tipping in an errant Jordan shot in the final 20 seconds that kept the Wizards close. Hamilton had rebounded from his recent poundings to score 29. The disappointment until that moment had been Jordan, who looked shackled, visibly laboring. Just the same, everyone in the arena knew where the ball was going. A talented young Suns defender named Shawn Marion had hawked him the entire game, daring him to drive, living in his jersey, it seemed. Now Collins designed a play to isolate Jordan against Marion on the right wing. Inexplicably, as soon as the ball touched Jordan's hands, Marion began backing up, tentative for the first time all night. Jordan took a hard step toward the basket, stopped, pump-faked Marion into the air and hit a game-winning 16-foot jumper. He wheeled, pumped his fist and yelled toward the Suns: *"That's what they pay me for. That's what they pay me for."*

It was the 28th time in his career that he had hit a winning shot in the final 10 seconds of a game. The brief celebration in the locker room was raucous. The team hurried to the airport and boarded their plane. While in the air, Jordan remarked that he felt a bit of stiffness in his right leg. By the time he awakened in Washington the next morning, his right knee was swelling badly.

His knee steadily worsened. He sat out another practice, this one on his 39th birthday, February 17. He stepped up his icing and electrical stimulation treatments. The bruise that his knee suffered when he collided with Etan Thomas in the last game before the All-Star break had hastened the buildup of the tendinitis-triggered fluid in the knee, aggravating an existing and chronic problem. His biggest mistake came in pushing the knee after the collision, a knee already worn down by too many minutes. Alternately favoring it to compensate for his pain and driving hard on it, he left the knee vulnerable to more serious injury. By the time he arrived at MCI on President's Day, February 18, surgery on the knee was only nine days away.

Seeing his pain, Grover raised the possibility of skipping a game, as did Collins and trainer Steve Stricker. Jordan said no. But, in a rare admission that betrayed his pain, he told Nesby and several other teammates before a game against Houston that his knee was hurting, that they had a chance to step up and show what they had.

He started and missed his first three shots over 6' 4" Houston guard Cuttino Mobley. He didn't hit a shot until about eight minutes remained in the first half—a gimpy-looking 15-foot fallaway—moving like a sea captain with a wooden peg for a right leg. He couldn't get back often on defense, unable to cut off a fast-breaking Steve Francis in the third quarter, Jordan fouling him, wincing, Francis looking back at him with concern. Jordan nodded at him: *I'm okay.*

He could still pass, so he found a way to assist on 11 baskets. Hamilton had 21 points, but none when it counted most. Jordan could score only 11 points, and the Wizards lost by 13, with Collins allowing Jordan to log 36 minutes and play until the final 1:34, after which Jordan dragged his right leg off the court and immediately went into the trainers' room to lie on a table.

Having run out of reassuring words, Collins told the media he would advise Jordan to take a game off and rest the knee. Jordan minimized the problem—"It's a little bit of tendinitis"—while saying he would not travel with the team for its next game, two nights later, in Detroit. He would stay in Washington, getting the knee treated and ready for a home game, the next night, against New Jersey.

Nesby would start in Jordan's place against the Pistons. During the next day at practice, just before the team flew to Detroit, Hamilton spoke excitedly about the chance to prove that the team could win without the star. "It's definitely going to be motivating . . ." he said. "Nez can get himself going; he doesn't need anybody else to get him going."

The team flew to Detroit and lost by seven, in a game close down the stretch. With his big chance, Nesby played strong defense but could only manage four points. Hubert Davis came off the bench to score 19, and Hamilton had 22. "I think if a couple shots went down, we could have won," Hamilton said the next night, back at MCI. "We had some things to prove, and I think we proved we can fight like a team and be competitive. We're not no supporting cast for anybody. We got a lot of talented young guys. We had a chance to win if a couple of those shots fell."

But they hadn't, and now they were mired in another bad run, which made it all the more essential, Jordan thought, that he play that night against New Jersey. A worried Collins asked him how he felt.

"I'm fine, Douggie," Jordan said, politely but curtly.

He was half of himself. The Nets outscored the Wizards in fast-break points, 27–0. Jason Kidd had 30 points, and Jordan struggled to score 16, while committing four turnovers. He spent some of the game icing the knee, then returned, going from stiff to stiffer. Even with his woes and Hamilton unable to find his touch, the game stayed competitive into the final four minutes, with the Wizards hanging around, down by nine. With his teammates having isolated most of the left side of the floor for him, Jordan had the ball, trying to post up a resistant Kidd, who knocked the ball away. Jordan retrieved it and doggedly, laboriously set up in the post again. Then he spun toward the lane and, with Kidd right alongside him, pump-faked. It was the move that usually so tormented the Nets. But Kidd did not bite, remaining on the floor, waiting. When Jordan went up on his bad knee, Kidd soared above him. To shoot would have meant having the jumper swatted away. With no other choice, Jordan passed blindly in the direction of a teammate no longer there. The ball was intercepted and turned into a dunk at the other end. Game over.

"I don't think it's going to be a lingering problem," he said afterward of his knee.

It was not what he told friends privately. Hurts like hell sometimes, really hurts, he told them. But he lost patience if they argued against him playing. He'd snap: When hadn't he played through *anything?* He'd fall back on his mantra. "No one knows me like me," he insisted. As he came closer to a physical breakdown, he was in disciplined denial.

Now, with questions and alarm spreading among coaches and reporters, he delivered a game so scintillating as to make observers wonder why they ever had doubted him. At MCI, on Saturday, February 23, he scored a point a minute in a two-point loss to Miami, after which his believers—on the team and in the media—exchanged chuckles and congratulated one another on their faith and wisdom: *See? How can anything be wrong with somebody who can play so well? Nobody who scores 37 can be hurting too badly.*

But those 37 points had meant another hard 37 minutes on the floor. He hurt so badly that he limped down the aisle of the team plane that night, flying to Miami for a game there the next night, in another back-to-back. Trainers treated his knee in the plane's rear lounge—ice to reduce the swelling, electrical stimulation to prompt blood flow— but neither offered relief. He could hardly walk on the right leg. Grover and the team trainers knew he couldn't run.

The plane flew along the Eastern seaboard. Those around him talked softly. Jordan fell uncharacteristically silent. No profane teasing of anybody. No soliloquies about the best basketball programs next to his alma mater, North Carolina. There was no talk. Instead of venturing up front for a card game, he stayed in the lounge with Grover, Koehler and bodyguard Wooten, people who knew his moods and the limits of his patience for chatter. Somebody came back to say hi, took a look at his vacant expression and decided against it. The plane hummed, players slept. Jordan stretched out his bad leg and closed his eyes.

There is no meaningful difference, medically speaking, between towering pride and hubris. Having ignored his high-priced experts' advice for months, he finally had pushed too hard. Part of his right knee's cartilage had torn, an injury resulting in part from three decades of his on-court fury, but dramatically hastened by his determination since the season's start to push exceedingly hard on inflamed knees riddled with tendinitis and vulnerable to breakdown if subjected to undue stresses. In pushing and in alternately favoring one leg over the other, he had dramatically raised the odds of catastrophe.

The next night, hardly able to move, he listened as Collins urged him not to suit up. He found himself slumped behind a crude makeshift partition in the visitors' locker room of the American Airlines Arena, having his right knee drained again, listening as the stranger doing it—the Miami Heat team physician Harlan Selesnick—advised him against playing, too.

He played, getting beaten by obscure players who had worn his shoes as children. All the while the knee swelled. He yelled at officials more than he had all season, berating referee Ron Garretson over noncalls—traveling violations missed, a thrown elbow undetected: *"You didn't see that?"* Dragging the right leg like it had a steel ball on it, he took himself out of a close game for good with six minutes left. No one around him could deny any longer that something was terribly wrong. No one yet knew how wrong, or that 90 minutes of arthroscopic surgery awaited him, three days later. But something in the leg had given out, and he could go no more.

The Wizards lost. Hardly anybody noticed. Afterward, the locker room had the feel of a morgue. Jordan managed to smile, briefly. His eyes glimmered with the force of an epiphany. Something strange happened in the same moment, something that hadn't happened all season. He glanced my way, as if expecting a question. I simply asked what he said to himself now. "I'm getting old," he answered. "It's a sign that, obviously, things are coming to a closure . . ."

People faintly gasped, thinking they could read his meaning. A few reporters talked of his end. But when had they ever really known him? Three days later, the surgery complete on his knee's torn lateral meniscus, word leaked that Jordan hoped to rehab his knee within a month. Closure never had met Michael Jordan. He still needed a game.

8

Collapse—and the End
of the New Jacks

WHAT I REMEMBER BEST ABOUT THE NEXT FEW DAYS IS THAT no one in the locker room sounded busted up about what had happened. None of the young players offered the familiar bromide about the difficulty of filling the star's shoes. "It's a new time," one Wizards official said. "They're a new breed. You know what the attitude is? *Everybody gets his.*"

It was the old school's take on what seemed to be the new school's instinct for opportunism. The New Jacks muttered that they wished Jordan a swift recovery but that they had confidence in their abilities to win without him and looked forward to proving it.

This seemed a perfectly ingenuous response to me, in a sports world where feigning shock and humility is the order of things. All season, the New Jacks had heard their team characterized as garbage aside from its star—a one-man show in which they would be humiliated if ever without him, an assumption that their coach had done little to discourage. Now at last they had an extended chance to demonstrate otherwise. Jordan's absence meant more playing time for many of them, and more on-court freedom for everyone—more chances to fast-break, run, shoot, play *their* kind of game, a young man's game, without having to wait on their elder star to jog downcourt, take the ball and expect everyone else to run the offense through him.

Like the coaches, they heard the official announcement about Jordan back in Washington, not knowing what the arthroscopic surgery might reveal about his knee or when Jordan might play again. That his playing future lay in doubt shook none of them. As usual, Richard Hamilton's words reflected the group's attitude, his candor flavored with just enough diplomacy to be passable. While praising his fallen teammate as a "warrior" and casually allowing as to how it would be "great" if Jordan came back for the following season, Hamilton made clear that the young represented the future no matter what happened to Jordan. "I mean, we expected him to play *this* year . . ." Hamilton said. "But, you know, we're a young team. So we know M.J. is not going to be playing here for the next five years. . . . We know that, in order for us to grow, this is the team to grow right now."

I'm going to be back, Jordan told a few of them in the locker room, on the eve of the surgery.

None of them said anything to that.

I'm going to be back, he repeated.

Okay, said Hamilton. We know you will. Wanna get you back.

Hamilton wished him luck. Lue did, too.

Everybody was subdued, thought one witness. Not subdued as in uncomfortable, just that there didn't seem much to say.

Everybody wished him luck a last time.

I'm coming back, no matter how we're doing. No matter if we make the playoffs or not.

The next day, Wednesday, February 27, doctors put Jordan under a general anesthetic, and the Wizards' physician, Stephen Haas, repaired Jordan's torn cartilage. It was a simple procedure, but doctors forecasted it would take Jordan three to six weeks to return to the court. John Hefferon thought three weeks sounded overly optimistic—"very challenging," he tactfully put it—for a 39-year-old, believing Jordan required at least four weeks before playing again and that, even afterward, his rehab would need to be ongoing and his playing minutes carefully monitored, as never before. "If you push too fast [during rehabilitation] and inflame the joint, you need to back off or you'll have problems . . ." Hefferon said. "The pushing is where you run into the challenge of Michael's desires. Michael will probably want the minimum of [rehab] time. . . . Michael wants to get back to make it to the playoffs. He'll want to push—as always."

But Jordan could do nothing for now, the start of his rehab at least a few days away. Tyrone Nesby would start in his place, and Courtney Alexander would see a marked increase in playing time, suddenly out

of the gulag and receiving a last look, with the Wizards needing someone to make up for at least some of Jordan's lost points. "It's good to see
Courtney get a chance, because he can run, he can shoot and he can
score," Tyronn Lue said. "He has talent. . . . Rip knows that. I know
that. All of us do. It's tough to prove yourself in this game without getting time to play and playing the way you're used to and comfortable
with. That's sometimes hard for a lot of guys. Confidence is really
important for all of us."

Ty Lue had a unique position among the New Jacks. His intensity—his
dives on the floor and his hunger for getting into an opponent's body
—had made him a pet of Jordan's. Still, Lue had frustrations with Jordan and Collins's methodically slow-paced style of play, which made it
difficult for him as a point guard, he thought, to exhibit his speed and
improvisational strengths. At only six feet, with no prospect of ever
being able simply to shoot over bigger guards, and never having carved
himself a reputation as a pure, spot-up, feet-planted, long-distance
shooter, he was at his best moving in the open court. This he had done
as a high school star in Kansas City and later at the University of
Nebraska, where his reputation as a scorer, a passer and a tenacious
defender had made him a first-round draft choice in 1998.

For his first three years in the NBA, he played sparingly for the Lakers. Jackson wanted a point guard to find an open spot in his Triangle
offense and stroke open jumpers. The Triangle never meshed with Lue's
style. For Lue, L.A. amounted to career interruptus.

His entire Los Angeles stint may have been disastrous but for the
publicity he received during the last NBA Finals, when he hounded and
nearly fought Allen Iverson. He looked at once like a ballplayer and a
dervish of a tough middleweight.

Doug Collins loved such a player.

Jordan had yet to commit himself to a comeback, which meant that
much was in flux, including Collins's coaching strategies. At 24, Lue
did not want to give up any more years to an offense that did not suit
him. He signed in no small part with the Wizards because those closest
to him thought they understood from Collins that the team's offense,
regardless of Jordan's presence, would be basically up-tempo. Had Lue
believed anything else, he likely would have tested more of the NBA
marketplace, in search of a compatible suitor.

Feeling comfortable after his discussions with Collins, Lue signed with Washington. He had begun training camp ahead of Chris Whitney on the depth chart, only soon to discover that Collins and Jordan's offense called for little running, and far more of the methodical, set-up offense that so limited him in Los Angeles. With Jordan on the floor, the Wizards offense looked in many moments like a variation, or amalgam, of several offenses—the old North Carolina motion offense, the Chicago Triangle and, lastly, when whim struck, a simple scheme in which Jordan attempted to isolate a side of the floor for himself, to work one-on-one against, hopefully, a hapless defender. Collins did not favor references to the Wizards' use of any elements of the Triangle (for one thing, the word conjured images of Jackson and Winter), preferring to talk of his own offense's quick cuts, screens and passing. But his offense always relied on Jordan, and Jordan, for the first time in his career, was running the Jordan Offense, a melding of strategies and personal improvisation. It was as if Jordan had taken pieces of all the battle plans he liked best over the years, reserving for himself the option of discarding all of them at a moment's notice if he thought he could score in isolation.

Lue found himself usually being asked, after he passed to Jordan inside, to find a spot on the outside and be ready to shoot a long jumper, should Jordan pass the ball out. For a point guard in those moments, the only meaningful difference between the Chicago/L.A. Triangle and the Washington offense was that the Wizards' offense called for Jordan to be an ad hoc point. Everything—sometimes a point forward of sorts operating low in the post—and for a traditional point guard like Lue to slide along the outside and wait. It represented, in Lue's case, no difference. The arrangement still forced Lue in those moments to slow down, wait for a star and stay put on the perimeter. Not long after the team's arrival in Wilmington, Whitney moved ahead of him, demonstrating more aptitude and patience for the Wizards' offense, and a better three-point shot.

For all Jordan's affection toward Lue, the star thought that Lue often looked tentative and out of position on the floor. There had been a particularly bad scene early in the season, when Lue, trying his best to follow Jordan's wishes to slide along on the outside and await a pass, had moved to a corner, where he stood open, waiting. A Wizards shot from the other side missed, producing a long rebound out toward the top of the key, where Lue normally would have been. The rebound led to a fast-break basket for the opposition. Friends of Lue could see a livid Jordan in his face. *Why weren't you at the top of the key?*

Lue felt himself thinking too much on the court, not relying on his best weapons, his instincts and superior quickness. Sometimes Collins shouted so many instructions at him as he dribbled up the court that the Wizards would be slow to execute their offense. Finally, a Wizards official, concerned for Lue and convinced that Collins's micromanagement of the games had become counterproductive, urged Lue to stop giving so much of his attention to Collins. "You don't have to *look* at him," the official said to Lue. "You don't have to slow down, you don't have to turn your head his way. You can listen if you want, but don't look. You don't have to listen to everything Michael is yelling out there either. You're trying to please too many people."

Lue listened but said nothing.

"You just have to *play*, Ty. If you think you gotta make Doug, Michael and everybody else happy every minute, you'll be too wound up to play. That's what's happening."

Lue nodded. But through the midpoint of the season, he had yet to look comfortable in the offense.

Sometimes a player like Hamilton hinted at his comrades' frustrations with the offense, talking wistfully of a game or two from the previous season when the young guys had won big while running all night, segueing into a remark about how it would be great to run. A popular presence among his peers, Hamilton could make the dream come alive; he had an evangelist's fervor when it came to the subject of running. Lue and the other New Jacks loved the talk, as one loves any pleasurable fantasy.

The New Jacks always had had to rub up against the resistance of Jordan and Collins. Before Jordan's injury, Collins and Jordan privately and publicly discouraged talk of the team adopting an up-tempo style. "Enjoy this slow motion game we're playing, okay?" Collins told reporters.

Jordan agreed. "We can't run with this team," he'd regularly say of opponents.

But, with Jordan having gone down, the shackles were taken off the young players. Fans suddenly saw the young players fast-breaking routinely, with Hamilton often out in front of the pack. "I'm sure it's more fun to watch," he said one night in the locker room.

He pointed out that with Jordan out on the floor, sometimes "you kind of defer to him and get him the ball, and the defense can stack up against us. Now [without him], we're getting easy baskets. . . . We're pushing the ball and running, but we're not turning the ball over . . ."

Hamilton had strained his groin again—a slight pull, he thought—and, though it hurt, he was determined to tape it tighter and play through it, determined to lead, aware and proud that opponents were focusing on him now. On the night of Jordan's surgery, he scored 31 points in a loss at home to powerful Portland. Two nights later in Chicago, Hamilton strapped his groin and carried them again, scoring 30, only to see the Wizards lose by nine. It was the Wizards' seventh straight defeat, their ninth loss in 10 games since coming back from the All-Star break, and their second since Jordan had gone down. Popeye Jones, reading the question on the minds of the media, said, "We don't want you guys writing and saying that these guys in here are nothing without Mike."

Jones and Hamilton knew that skepticism would be the new theme. Their record had dropped to 27–30, with the team no longer looking like a certainty to make the playoffs. Worse, Hamilton was stricken with a stomach virus that would cause him to miss the next game, in Washington, two afternoons later. The Wizards had no choice but to turn for offense to the largely forgotten Courtney Alexander, fresh out of exile and still showing rust.

No second-year player on the Wizards—or for that matter, in the entire league—had fallen farther or faster than Alexander over the last three months. Collins had sliced his playing time, and Alexander had missed 13 games with a sprained ankle. He had met with Collins several times, asking how he might earn more playing time.

Work, said Collins. *Earn it with your play.*

But it was hard, Alexander pointed out, to earn anything without the opportunity to play. And without playing time, his conditioning, subpar even before his injury, became worse. Now he was being thrust onto the court, ready or not. His burden would be complicated by having to start against Orlando, which meant that Alexander would be asked to guard Tracy McGrady, who had a quicker first step to the basket than any man of his size in the NBA and a reputation for quickly devouring undersized defenders like Alexander. Their matchup sounded about as fair as putting a bunny in front of a cheetah.

On Sunday, Alexander got off to a poor start, hitting only one of his first six shots, which ordinarily, as Christian Laettner pointed out, would have earned him a spot on the bench, perhaps for the remainder of the game. But, with Jordan out and Hamilton sick, Collins had nowhere else to turn.

By the second half, McGrady looked like All-World, scoring 15 points in the third quarter, draining jumpers, spinning and throwing down a tomahawk dunk. But Alexander was suddenly playing brilliantly, too, and one could see at last everything about him that had made the scouts so excited. He hit long jumpers off the dribble against McGrady—hit them moving in either direction, hit them while jumping straight up, hit them while falling away and falling down. He backed McGrady down toward the post, then shot a fallaway over him. He had a tremendous vertical leap, so that even at only 6'5"—giving away four inches in height and perhaps another inch or two in reach to the long-armed McGrady—he sometimes soared over him in shooting his jumper.

On the offensive end, he looked like a future All-Star. It was the other end of his game that haunted his future. For all his physical gifts, he had not proven that he could play defense worth a whit. McGrady was doing anything he wanted. In the fourth quarter, each young player scored at will against the other. Alexander hit hanging jumpers with McGrady all over him, including a 14-footer to tie the game with 47 seconds left in regulation.

Alexander grabbed his trunks and bent, taking deep breaths. Now it seemed his run had to end, for he hadn't seen this kind of playing time for a year. In overtime, a distracted McGrady lost sight of him for an instant, and Alexander hit an open jumper from the top of the key to give the Wizards the lead. It was a day for all underdogs. Saving his best for the end, Nesby scored on a short bank shot, hit a huge outside jumper and made a steal. The Wizards won by five. Alexander led all scorers with 32 points and, just as amazingly, had played 50 minutes.

He kept the media waiting, as long as Jordan would have. It was his special day, and he would let people know it, after many months of being overlooked by the media and coaches alike. Sometimes a reporter mumbled to him and he simply hmmmmed. He did not smile, he did not frown, he just wore his impassive look, part of the reason why a Wizards official long before had dubbed him "The Sphinx." Dressing slowly, placing a diamond stud in each ear, he paused before putting on his shirt, allowing everybody to wait some more and glimpse his tattoo, which consisted of Chinese characters on his left shoulder and triceps.

"Mandarin?" somebody asked him.

"Power and truth," he murmured, though it wasn't clear whether this meant the tattoo or some vindication he felt.

"Power and truth?"

"You all need to wait for me to get ready," he said softly, bringing a finger to his lips as if asking for respectful silence, then and only then resuming to put on his shirt.

Hence, the Sphinx.

Finally ready, he said that he had seized the day's opportunity. "I'm an up-and-coming player in this league," he declared.

Sometimes his teammates sniped about what they regarded as Alexander's pomposity and affectations. His perceived aloofness had made it difficult for some to feel sorry when Collins demoted him. But among the New Jacks, they were with him to a man on this day, happy to see another young player step up and show that the team could win without Jordan. Even a few of the veterans expressed pleasure, with Christian Laettner saying that a pure shooter like Alexander needed time at the start of a game to shoot and get into a rhythm. "If he's getting yanked all the time, it's tough for him to find that rhythm," Laettner added. "He has to play. . . . I've tried to help when it's been tough for him. I just say to him, 'This is bull. Hang in there.'"

Everyone wondered how long this good feeling for Alexander would last. Collins had only about 15 seconds to enjoy the victory before somebody asked him if Alexander was out of his doghouse.

Collins's face reddened. "Excuse me—*whose* doghouse? We don't have a doghouse. . . . I take offense to that. I don't put guys in doghouses."

But, all around Collins, players thought that Alexander finally had received a long overdue chance. Two nights later at MCI, the Wizards blew out the Bulls. Hamilton, who looked drawn but found a way to play, reentered the starting lineup, taking Alexander's spot and scoring 15. Coming off the bench, Alexander hit 9 of 11 shots and led the Wizards with 26 points. While not close to Alexander off the court, Hamilton viewed Alexander as a young player with whom his own future might be inextricably linked. "Courtney's *always* played hard," Hamilton said. "Now people are seein' what the real Courtney Alexander is all about. We have *a lot* of character in this locker room."

An excited reporter sliced in: What did *Michael* say to you guys when he came in the locker room after the game?

Hamilton shrugged, managing to look simultaneously poised, polite and a touch bored. It was a fabulous feat. "I didn't hear what he said."

Casually and without edge, several other players allowed as to how they hadn't heard what Jordan said. He came to the arena but didn't sit on the team bench, as rehabbing players at MCI were generally expected to do. Sometimes he watched a game on the locker room's big-screen TV, alone with his entourage. He issued quick congratulations to the team at the game's end and spoke briefly with Collins, departing hurriedly, leaving behind a locker room far more festive in his absence. All music was louder, the laughter more raucous, like the sounds of a classroom where the regular teacher had stepped out indefinitely and no substitute could be found.

The distance between Jordan and the young players grew during his time on the injured list. Alexander spoke about the star with a stiff formality, often referring not to "Michael" or "Mike" or "M.J." but to "Michael Jordan." Amid the lingering Tonto–Lone Ranger references to Jordan and Hamilton, Alexander was creating his own duo, linking himself not with the idol but with Hamilton. His words reflected Hamilton's message: the future depended on the young. "A lot of people said this would be myself and Rip's team, you know, in some years . . ." Alexander said, noting that "Rip's a scorer; I'm a scorer." He nodded at someone who said the fans seemed to like the running and high-flying. "Sure," he said, "because it's exciting and it's the future. We all hoped for that style, Rip and myself, and you see now what happens when we get a chance to execute it."

The New Jacks had won two in a row without the idol, climbing to 29–30, very much in playoff contention with 23 games to play, aglow with self-fulfillment. Then potent Detroit came into MCI—led by scoring machine Jerry Stackhouse and shot blocker extraordinaire Ben Wallace—and Hamilton and Alexander combined for a respectable 44 points. But, on the other end of the court, Stackhouse abused each of them, the duo's defensive liabilities exposed under a light becoming hotter with Jordan gone.

"You want it, you got it," a Wizards official said of the attention that the duo chased. Hamilton still looked overmatched against a muscular player like Stackhouse who could bull him inside. And now, as often as not, a confrontation with any capable scorer revealed the blemishes of Alexander's game, negating its beauty and all those points. His stretches of lethargy and lapses in judgment cost his team as frequently as his athleticism lifted them. With the game tied in the final seconds, Detroit worked the ball to Jon Barry, who had been left alone in the left corner by a momentarily confused Alexander and hit the game-winning three-pointer at the buzzer.

It was the start of a five-game losing streak.

They went to Orlando, where McGrady, getting payback, scorched

Alexander and scored 50, as the Magic won by three points. Road and home losses to Boston dropped the team five games under the .500 mark. Some of the coaches wondered whether the young players were so enamored of running that it had become like a drug. Chaos infected them at a game's critical stages—turnovers on the rise, players' shooting percentages plummeting in the second half. Hamilton was being forced to face what Jordan saw: Neither of them could regularly win at this stage of their careers without the other. Kwame Brown and Brendan Haywood still had not materialized, and defense remained a problem. Aside from Nesby and Lue, the New Jacks didn't have anyone who could reliably defend scorers. There was always a defensive hole in a forward or guard matchup, which begged for a healthy Jordan to fill it.

A defeat to the lowly Clippers, in Los Angeles, completed their five-game skid, leaving the Wizards with 14 losses in its 17 games since the All-Star break, the worst record among all the NBA's serious playoff contenders over that stretch. The team was on its second Western swing in four weeks, a six-game trip, and Collins hoped that Jordan might join them at some point on the road, not to play but simply to provide a morale boost. Two weeks had passed since his surgery. Once in a while, a reporter asked Collins, *Where is he?* And Collins would admit that he hadn't heard from Jordan that day, that he didn't know when he might next speak to him, that he didn't even know Jordan's whereabouts much of the time. Jordan did not routinely check in with Collins or anyone else. He was above that.

While he wished Jordan were around more, Collins didn't want him rushing on to a court. His own mistakes in dealing with injuries as a player convinced him that a premature return ran the risk of setting back the knee's rehab and damaging Jordan's chances of playing the following season. If the team completely fell out of the playoff picture in the week or two ahead, Collins resolved to advise Jordan to sit out the remainder of the season.

Then the Wizards fortunes turned. Following the loss to the Clippers, the team surprisingly won two of their next three road games. In Seattle, Lue had his best night of the season, scoring 26 points, setting his feet and hitting the long three-pointers supposedly out of his range. After losing the next night in Portland, the team flew to Oakland and beat Golden State. Improbably, they found themselves in the same position as at the beginning of their Western swing—five games under

.500 and still in the race. In the 12 games missed by Jordan since his surgery, the team had gone 4–8, not good, but not disastrous either. The New Jacks had not set the league afire, but they had hung on, and the team still had life with 15 games to play.

Yet the huge news in Oakland came before the game, during Collins's scrum session. Even measured against his frequently jittery demeanor, Collins looked and sounded uncomfortable. Something was up. Did he have any news about Jordan? someone asked. That tuning fork of a head shook ever so slightly. His voice rose, not angrily, not at all unpleasantly, just uneasily enough for one to hear the tension in it. The voice had a flutter. "I talked to Michael today," he said, and that information alone had people leaning forward. "He says he's feeling better and, uhh, he was, uh, actually he'd gone to Chicago. He and Juanita had gone to Chicago, so he sounded good, you know. We talked for about five minutes. He said, uh, he was working out a couple times a day, trying, you know, to pick up the workouts. And [he said] his knee felt pretty good, so that's basically all I know."

The key word in that last sentence was "basically." When a coach says, "That's basically all I know," you can be confident that he hasn't told you all he knows, basically or otherwise.

Basically is one of those words that gives all coaches, like politicians, the license to fudge and sometimes lie altogether. The media knows this, which is why no coach in the modern age should use the word "basically." It is like saying, Look at me, I am dissembling now.

I said that I just hoped to ask him, basically, a little question.

By then the rest of the media had pounced. Someone asked if he knew whether Jordan would be joining the team before the road trip's end.

"No, no," Collins said.

You don't *know* or you don't *think* he's going to do it?

Collins looked above the heads, licked his lips, talked very fast. He was not made for this. "I don't know, I don't know. I mean, he could show up anytime, you know. It just depends on how he's feeling. He might say, Jump on a plane, let's go. But as of right now, I don't know. . . . He says his knee feels a hundred percent better than it did before the surgery, so those are all positive things."

Collins declared that, when it came to the issue of Jordan playing, he would do whatever Michael wished. "I think what I would do is sit down with him and say, 'Okay, how do you want to play? Do you want to play the second quarters and the fourth quarters? Do you want to go back to playing at the start?' I think that's *his* call. And whatever he wants to do, I'll try to blend the team around that."

Still, Collins emphasized, "He wouldn't play without practicing, *he wouldn't do that.* I would expect him, before he played, to try to get in two or three practices with us. . . . I would be *shocked* if he tried to play without practicing. . . . I still think he needs to test his knee a little bit, to see how it's going to hold up."

"Two or three practices?" an amazed Wizards official said later of Collins's hope. "*Two or three?* I'd say to Doug, 'Prepare to be shocked.' Michael will land somewhere, shoot some balls and say, I'm in. Doug would have to say, You're not in."

He was in.

That evening in Chicago, the boss secretly boarded a plane. When the Wizards arrived in Denver that night from Oakland, several of them noticed Tim Grover and George Koehler at the team hotel. Simultaneously, everyone on the team knew who was resting somewhere in a suite.

"He'll just practice," Collins assured team personnel the next morning.

Jordan came to practice, shot some balls and jogged around.

"He wants to play," Collins told people.

The game came the following evening, Wednesday, March 20. It was exactly three weeks to the day since his surgery, or at the quick end of what Wizards physician Stephen Haas had told him was medically sensible for a rehab. To John Hefferon, three weeks remained "very challenging," which was to say, a roll of the dice.

You're not ready. Think of the risk, Michael: Some around the Wizards' locker room dreamt of saying it to him. Others in the organization went a step further, telling colleagues they'd confront him if they thought it might stop him. On the other hand, they knew their warnings might have just the opposite effect, stoking his fury, pushing him to do the very thing they most worried about. So, in the end, after all that hand-wringing, they leaned toward saying nothing. They knew they were enablers, and that gave them pause, but the alternative might be to infuriate Jordan, and who wanted to deal with that shit storm? They were portraits of self-conflict. One man heard himself saying, unreally, to the star, "Fantastic to have you back. We need you out there."

Jordan agreed. His knee might heal more soundly if he had more time off, but his spirit would atrophy. His mood had darkened in his time away, rehabilitation having been a reminder of his athletic mortality. On the cusp of middle-age, he was not so different from other men, after all. "I gotta be out there; I go nuts sitting; I don't have a lot of time," he said, in response to a friend who asked, *Why do you go on the court with these pains? What's the point?*

The point was . . . The point was he had to have it, and he would have it. He played, taking on the new role of a reserve asked to come off the bench midway through the first quarter. Running gingerly, he went 2–9 in 16 minutes against Denver, scoring seven points. Hamilton scored 30 and Alexander added 16. Nesby mauled the hapless Nuggets and pulled down eight rebounds. Washington won by 32, and Collins rediscovered the party line. After the game, he expressed shock—absolute *shock*—that anyone might suggest Jordan had put himself at risk: "Michael isn't going to come back too early and set himself back just because he wants to finish out the season."

They flew to Utah to face the Jazz the following evening. Just 22 days after surgery, Jordan would be playing in games on successive nights. Before the game, he sat in the visitors' locker room in black bicycle shorts and shower sandals, receiving stim treatment on his right knee and unconsciously fidgeting with the ice bag affixed to his left knee. A kid brought him coffee. He sipped it, staring through everybody, surveying a game tape of Utah. It was quiet. Tim Grover sat close by in a pin-striped suit, next to Koehler and Larry Wooten. Everything was the way he liked it; everything was as it always had been. He studied Utah on the screen. Jordan checked the tiny pads on his right knee. Nothing had changed.

An hour later, he rode a stationary bicycle in the tunnel of the Delta Center for the game's opening six minutes, keeping the knee loose. At a time-out, he coolly got off the bike and checked into the game with 5:11 left in the first quarter. Walking over to his favorite foil on the planet Earth, Bryon Russell, he smiled, chuckled and gave him a little elbow to the stomach, tossing in a shoulder bump for good measure. *I'm back. Hi.* Russell just nodded.

Jordan had not played on this floor for four years, not since he had hit The Shot over Russell to win the '98 championship. Now it was as if Jordan immediately wanted to remind Russell of that moment. In just seconds, he had the ball at the top of the key, staring down Russell, going one-on-one, dribbling between his legs, lunging forward, pulling back, then rising. Not fooled, Russell had a hand in his face, almost blocking the shot. The 20-footer didn't even touch the rim, hitting the right side of the backboard.

Russell grinned.

Jordan soon came looking for payback. By then the task of guarding him had fallen to a tall, thin Russian import named Andrei Kirilenko, a 6'9" rookie who had size and youth on his side but not enough guile. Moving a tad stiffly but quickly, Jordan hit a fallaway over him. But the most pleasurable Jordan moment came with about 1:50 remaining in the first half. He pump-faked, got the gullible young Kirilenko in the air, flew by him on bad knee and all, passed to Kwame Brown and then received a return pass from Brown while darting toward the hoop. With Kirilenko two steps behind him, he leaped and dunked.

His torn meniscus had been worked on just 23 days earlier.

He hit four of eight shots in 12 first-half minutes. But he had nothing left in the second half, missing all four shots he took and beginning to drag the bad leg. The team looked similarly exhausted, showing the effects of a nine-day road trip. Hamilton was having an awful night, going 2–11, and Nesby was 3–12. Utah drew away.

After four years of waiting, Bryon Russell found a tiny measure of revenge, hitting a three-pointer over Jordan with 2:55 left to give Utah an 11-point lead, then pressuring him so tightly that Jordan dribbled the ball off his foot. It rolled away too quickly for him to recover it. He watched it, wearing a look of pure puzzlement. Russell retrieved it and fed ahead to Karl Malone, whose score put the game out of reach. In the next minute, Jordan was sitting on the baseline. He had played only 22 minutes, but already he seemed to be favoring the knee.

By then, the dangers were obvious. Afterward, Collins steadfastly insisted he looked physically sound, if rusty. Jordan told the press the knee felt good. The team, he pointed out, had gone 3–3 on the road trip, still in the Eastern Conference race at 32–37.

He mentioned that it was great to return to Utah, gloating a little, prodded by the media to gloat a little more, saying with a chuckle that he didn't talk with Russell about The Shot because "I don't think he wants to remember things like that."

The media laughed.

Over the years, the evening's Jordanmania simply added to Karl Malone's irritation. Although Utah had won, Malone had had a history of losing with a grudge, and Michael Jordan had a history of rubbing in Utah's playoff losses. It was a combination made for ill will. Malone was asked what it had been like to play against Jordan that night: "When I retire, I'll say what I really want to say," Malone curtly answered.

Good-bye to bitter Utah. With everybody around him insisting he looked and felt great, Jordan walked slowly toward the team bus.

"How's the knee?" someone asked him.

"None of your concern," Jordan answered, which was the precise moment when, for some people, it again became a concern.

For a week, Tim Grover had gently urged Jordan to consider all the options and think through the consequences. Better to err on the side of *too much* recovery time, said Grover, who suggested to Jordan that nothing less than his career might be at stake. A knee that blew up or tore a second time might be a knee without the capacity to heal completely again, Grover thought, assuming it had healed *this time*—which no one, in truth, could be sure about. The knee still needed strengthening. Jordan was tired of hearing about it. "Just get me ready," Jordan said to Grover and the Wizards' trainers.

Grover had yielded to the inevitable, though a couple of the doubters still believed they could rein Jordan in. Now and then, someone around the team convinced himself that he had found just the right line for changing Jordan's mind. "I think I might say to him that you don't want to see the Hope diamond forever marred just for a couple of lousy games in March," said a member of the Wizards' staff. "And that, goddamn, who gives a shit about games in March when your stage has always been the playoffs?"

But a playoff spot still looked possible, a point that Jordan, an inveterate debater, seized upon for advantage, arguing that the team's position necessitated that he play. The man contemplating the Hope diamond metaphor began worrying about a possible backlash if he opened his mouth: Jordan had a long memory, he knew. A man who uttered a perceived slight could go from acquaintance to pariah overnight. Everyone remembered that, during Jordan's rehab of his broken foot, Jerry Krause forever had earned his contempt by urging that Jordan stay away from the court for the season. No one around the Wizards wanted to be the next Krause. Even while missing more practices, Jordan resolved to play. The team trailed in the playoff race by 3 ½ games and, with only 13 games left, the Wizards were running out of days to make up ground. Charlotte and Indiana were ahead of them, and Toronto looked positioned to make a run.

But Toronto had problems, with Vince Carter having gone out with a knee injury. Jordan left for a day to attend a family funeral in the Chicago area, rejoining the team for a Sunday game in Toronto. "All you motherfuckers needed me back," he happily teased some team-mates, after getting off the team bus and walking into the visitors' locker room in the Air Canada Centre.

This was a winnable game, Jordan told people. They had to have it.

Sitting on the bench at the game's start, he watched Hamilton dunk and the Wizards sprint out to an 8–0 lead. But the young Wizards quickly squandered the advantage. Jordan entered a tie game with about four and a half minutes left in the first quarter, bulling 6' 7" Mo Peterson down low, trying to get position for his fallaway. His shot was off. He missed 9 of his first 13 field-goal attempts, agitated by the play around him, yelling at Kwame Brown to get in the right place, barking at Hamilton in the third quarter about his defense against Toronto's fast breaks: "You gotta get back, you gotta *get back* . . ."

He was bitching at the refs, particularly Phil Robinson, complaining about being fouled and not getting any calls. In another era, when Jordan reigned above all others, NBA refs made him the beneficiary of almost every borderline call. But, in his twilight, the old favoritism had given way to a near evenhandedness late in a game. He was on his own now. The rest of the league might treat him like a sacred cow, but refs generally made him earn his keep. If he was bumped slightly on a shot, or stripped of the ball on a murky play by a pair of brutes, so be it.

Looking tired at the start of the fourth quarter, he said to Collins, in a voice loud enough to carry to the media table, "Do you want me out top?"

This meant he *wanted* to be out top, out at the top of the key, from where he could set up the offense and wouldn't have to expend as much energy.

Collins nodded.

Jordan drove and missed a four-footer in the lane.

Collins buried his head in his hands.

It was that kind of game, maddening and thrilling. The Wizards had blown their early lead, and gone on a run, and now Toronto had lost all of its 13-point lead. The Wizards seized the advantage. Collins went for the kill. In the last three minutes, he abandoned all restraint and ran virtually all the offense through Jordan, who hit two jumpers, and the Wizards led by three points with under a minute to play. Toronto scored, Jordan missed another jumper, and, with a half minute left, the

Wizards one-point lead hinged on stopping Toronto a last time. When Jordan rebounded an errant shot, victory seemed ensured. But, in the same instant, Toronto's rugged Jerome Williams and Antonio Davis swatted at the ball and his arms. In the next second, the ball dropped from Jordan's hands to the floor.

No moment said more about the changing status of Michael Jordan. The refs blew no whistle. The ball was free. Antonio Davis snatched it and, in one motion, jumped, stretched his arms and scored on a layup with 15 seconds left, giving Toronto the lead. An irate Jordan, stricken in the same instant by a back spasm, writhed in pain and screamed at Phil Robinson that he had been fouled, berating the official as Robinson turned his back. A shout from the Wizards bench finally brought him back to the game at hand. The Wizards needed to set up a play. Jordan trudged to the bench, clutching his lower back.

The trainer and a couple of players asked him if he was all right. He waved them off. Of course he was all right; of course he was staying in the game. Fuck that. I'm fine. He was already thinking of how they would win. He did not need to say, *I want the ball*. Hamilton had 21 points, and Jordan had both a fragile knee and a shot that had been erratic all afternoon, but there was no question where the ball was going. Collins told everyone else to clear out a portion of the floor, to give him room.

He was guarded in those last seconds by the 6'9" Williams, one of the league's toughest defensive players, who forced him farther away from the basket than Jordan wanted to be—not around the free-throw line, from where he typically shot in the final seconds, but at least two feet beyond it. Jordan faked a shot and waited for Williams to leap. Williams stayed on the ground, waiting.

When Jordan jumped, Williams leaped with him, waiting for the older, shorter man at the apogee, his right arm elongated. Jordan had no choice but to put extra arc on the ball to get it over Williams's hand. Its flight remains on the mind's eye: the exquisite rotation, its finely measured distance to the hoop, the improbable realized, again. The ball went in. Simultaneously, Jordan's teammates on the bench leaped deliriously.

In the next instant, the ball spun out.

The Wizards disconsolately shuffled off the court. Their slide continued. Jordan rushed to scream at Phil Robinson, finally coaxed away by team members, head down, right leg dragging, ominously so.

He had made 6 of 17 shots, and scored 14 points in 23 minutes.

Afterward, he said the referees had swallowed their whistles in not calling a foul on the controversial ball strip. He pursed his lips hard. "I hope this game doesn't come back to haunt us when you're talking about the playoffs," he murmured. "Still, we got twelve games left."

At 32–38, they would need a stunning surge to make the playoffs. Jordan found Collins and told him not to lose faith, that they were going to find a way to win the next 10 straight.

In the days ahead, he reclaimed the locker room turf from Hamilton and the rest of the New Jacks. He let them know it was his team, not in a confrontation, or by waving his putative title as once and future chief basketball executive. He simply did what he had always done everywhere, imposing the force of his personality over teammates, sending barbs their way, needling their play, making certain all understood that their games had deficiencies. He turned up the heat now. He made cracks about Hamilton giving away too much defensively and being pushed around, and remarked that Alexander still didn't look very interested in grabbing a rebound or shooting anything other than a jump shot.

Even with all his scoring, Alexander had become seen by the coaches and Jordan as the antithesis of the tough player, a bad sign for his future in Washington. His powerful 6'5" body belied the softness of his play, some thought. He seldom drove hard to the basket or threw his body between the path of a ball handler and the basket. Hamilton's big numbers and camaraderie made him a leader of the New Jacks, but the coaches and Jordan still questioned Hamilton's commitment to getting stronger. His defense had improved a bit, but his lack of strength still plagued him, with a couple of the coaches still talking about a moment in Portland when Hamilton had grabbed a loose ball near the scorer's table, only to have Scottie Pippen yank the ball so hard from his hands that Hamilton went flying.

The New Jacks seemed especially on guard now that Jordan had returned. Lue felt Jordan getting tougher and more demanding. Kwame Brown looked more miserable than ever, his anger seeping out, particularly over what several of the young players regarded as the team's double standard in all things related to Jordan. It was an exasperated Brown who first broached the matter when asked about how he'd managed to miss a dunk in a game. "Hey," he said softly. "Even M.J. misses dunks. But no one says anything about that." His words hung there, awkwardly. He covered quickly. "But Michael's earned that."

Still, Brown's deference toward Jordan was fading. If prodded, he acknowledged his harsh treatment at the hands of several veterans, including Jordan, early in the season. He hung exclusively with the New Jacks now, spending much of his free time playing Xbox and watching his videos, a man-child doing a man-child's things. Trying to explain what had gone wrong with his prized draft pick, Jordan talked about how high school kids came to the league with psyches not yet developed. He went so far as to suggest that, for the sake of his development, Brown might have been better off playing college ball. By then, Brown's confidence was shredded. At 20, he was already, psychologically, a rehab project.

Collins sounded regretful, wishing he could start all over again with Brown. "I've probably done a very poor job," he said one night. "I saw a young guy with this tremendous skill level and potential, and maybe I wanted too much from him, too soon. . . . I think he's overwhelmed. I want to restore him; I want him to start feeling good about himself again. . . . But he's gotta learn how to play. I talked to him the other day and said, 'Kwame, I apologize to you if, in any way, I've made this tougher for you, or I expected too much too soon.' I've never coached a player out of high school. I didn't do a very good job."

But Collins wasn't sure what he would do next. In the end, he thought, the kid would rise or fall alone. "Kwame needs to find another gear," he added. "That can't come from me."

The coach and Jordan didn't sound buoyed by much about their team, and some young Wizards had difficulty taking their minds off the question of how Jordan viewed them. Players sought to be careful in what they said about him. Sometimes surrogates talked for them. "Right now it's especially weird to play with a guy who you think of as your boss," said an agent for one player. "Because guys are already thinking about next season. They gotta keep one eye out for [Jordan]. They wonder, Can you shoot much? Or does shooting get you in trouble if he wants the ball a lot? That's a hard thing to play through, because it means guys are thinking too much out there. Can you run, or do you have to slow it down and wait for him? Can you have any fun around him? They don't know. These guys have to learn to play with Michael, and everybody understands that—it's his team. But he's gotta play with them, too. No offense to Michael—I know Michael's busting his ass on the court—but he doesn't talk to 'em enough for them to have any idea what they're allowed to do."

The agent could read the future. The shadow boss had his own plan for the future, and not all of the New Jacks would have a place in it.

Over the next week, anytime you saw Jordan off the court at MCI, he seemed to have something on his knees—wires, electrical stim pads, ice bags. Two days after the Toronto game, he received 45 minutes of stim treatment on the right knee, readying himself to play Denver.

That night, a journeyman named Voshon Lenard—whom he'd routinely thumped when Lenard played for Miami and the Bulls gave Miami an annual series of whippings—blocked his fallaway jumper late in the first quarter. Not merely blocked it, but got his hand on top of the ball and so stuffed him that the force of Lenard's hand pushing down on the ball from above sent Jordan tumbling. *Jordan on his knees.* Camera shutters clicked. It was no small embarrassment, and Lenard's trash-talking only angered him more. But he had nothing with which to answer on this night. Hamilton and Whitney had 22 apiece, and Nesby shut down everyone he was asked to guard, as the Wizards won by 16. Jordan had only nine points in 20 minutes, and afterward the scrum mostly wanted to know about the Lenard block. Jordan tried smiling. He said he felt good.

But club officials were skeptical. Then the most public face among all the team's officials made a mistake. On a TV show, Doug Collins let it slip that he would be surprised if Jordan played the following season.

Collins's remark triggered a behind-the-scenes furor in the Wizards' front office, which had season tickets to sell, plus preseason games to arenas in small cities whose offers would be considerably less if word spread that Michael Jordan might not be playing the next season. The Wizards brass instructed the coach never to say anything like that again.

Cast in the role of basketball's Homer Simpson, Collins had to go out before cameras and say that his comments had been misunderstood. Baying reporters pressed him to explain his comment. All he needed to say was that he'd been guilty of a poor choice of words, that the truth was Jordan wanted to return for another season but that nothing was certain. Instead, Collins opted for defiance and denial. "I don't know what the big news is . . ." he said. "I don't think anything was said that nobody already didn't know. . . . *What did I say?* Did anybody hear it?"

A reporter answered, "You said you'd be surprised if he played next year."

Doh. This is not what Collins wanted to hear. His claim seemed to be that he had not said what he said. He had a new take on what he said. "I said that Michael will make that decision."

Someone chuckled derisively.

A few people wanted to know if Jordan had taken him to the woodshed. "Did Michael talk to you about what you said?"

Collins flared. He inhaled. His head did its little shake. Stress did nasty things to him. "Guys, that's done. *Done.* Okay? We're *done.* . . . I know Michael wants to play next year. . . . To start running with this at this particular time, I think, is a disservice to our team."

"Does your gut tell you that he will play?"

Collins looked as though his head might lift off. *"Now, you just, come on now—"*

"Any more questions?" the Wizards p.r. man asked, bringing it to a merciful end.

Collins walked away, muttering forlornly, "I don't need this."

Then Jordan sauntered before the cameras, cool, commanding, the anti-Collins. Grinning, he assured everyone that no decision had been made about his future, defending Collins the way a boss comes to the aid of a mistake-prone underling. "I'm not mad at him," Jordan said. "That's his *observation.*"

Actually, Collins had been more right than wrong: Jordan was a long ways from committing to another season, uncertain of how his knees might hold up. Privately, Jordan reserved his irritation for the Wizards' top executives. The thought that Susan O'Malley and other Pollin subordinates might be conveying the impression to arena operators in preseason cities, or to Washington ticket buyers, that his return was a virtual certainty angered Jordan. If he did not come back for another season, he did not want people making money off his name. The executives' dismay with Collins's statement merely confirmed Jordan's sense that people were profiting from the idea that Michael Jordan would continue to be in a Wizards uniform. His indignation heightened, he saw the incident as just one more example of O'Malley's crass exploitation of the Jordan name.

Turning a basketball profit for the first time in many years, Abe Pollin gave public thanks to Jordan while carefully avoiding any reference to occasional tensions with his star, who had spent a part of the winter talking like an executive again, noting his interest in considering possible trades.

For a long while, since the beginning of Jordan's comeback and the relinquishing of his executive title, the Wizards had pretended that

Wes Unseld, the team's general manager, was in charge of basketball operations. But those close to Jordan, and Jordan himself, increasingly dropped the pretense that anyone other than Jordan was in control. Collins regularly told the press that Jordan would be running the franchise once he left the court. In February, Jordan had alluded to his own decisive role in all of the Wizards' basketball decisions, using the royal *we* in discussing his designs. "I think there are some holes we need to continue to improve on, so we will entertain deals," he said, privately exploring what could be done to obtain Charles Oakley from Chicago.

Nearing the league's trade deadline, he had changed his mind, declaring that he thought it wise that the team not make any trades that might disturb the chemistry of the team. With Jerry Krause declining to let Oakley go, Jordan preferred that the organization stand pat and not push any trade buttons.

Abe Pollin quietly endured all of Jordan's comments about trade possibilities. Never in the face of Collins's assertions or Jordan's presumption did Pollin correct the impression that Jordan's future as club president was anything less than certain. I saw the owner briefly during this period, our paths crossing for a few seconds at MCI. Pollin walked briskly. I asked for his opinion on "Michael's leadership of things." Not stopping or looking over, appearing a tad tense and annoyed at having his peace interrupted, he mumbled, "Sensational, sensational. Michael's leadership is sensational."

Not as long as Jordan wore a uniform and the money flowed did Pollin hint at any problem. Later, when things publicly came apart between the two of them, his lush praise of Jordan seemed like rank hypocrisy to many Jordan allies. But I always viewed Pollin's behavior as instinct, basic business, a function of his proximity to all that money. When I think of Pollin from this period, I have this image of a smiling crocodile, waiting.

Jordan's two sons, Jeffrey and Marcus, flew to Washington, to spend the weekend with him. He had three days after the Denver game to rest his knee, and the presence of his sons relaxed him. On the morning of a Friday night game against Milwaukee at MCI, he watched Jeffrey and Marcus play a pickup game with the sons of assistant general manager Rod Higgins in the Wizards' practice gym, and Wizards personnel who watched said a delighted Jordan laughed and clapped his hands, happy in a way they'd seldom seen. Collins, who had left the arena, came back to find Jordan still watching his sons—a good sign, the coach decided. He told his wife that Jordan looked energized.

The struggling man had one great burst left in him for the season. With a black circulation-support sleeve around his knee, and his pain and stiffness having slackened, he ran better that night than at any time since before the surgery. Trying to save wear on the bad knee, Collins had acceded to Jordan's wish to play him more as a point guard on the perimeter, from where he could afford to move less, alternating between passing and bursting around screens set by Jahidi White and Popeye Jones. At the end of the Wizards' nine-point victory, he had 34 points in 26 minutes, shining in front of his children, who, like his skeptics, sometimes told him he was old.

"It's always good to see your kids," he said afterward. "Even though they call you old. . . . I just felt good all day. I came into the game pretty loose."

With only 10 games left, he told people that he wanted to be up to 40 minutes a night for the season's final week. Grover, Collins and anybody who had his ear continued to stress *caution*. It was a word that, especially in triumphant moods, Jordan found particularly distasteful.

But his knee was fickle now. It might be okay on a Friday, only to leave him miserable on a Sunday. Two days after confounding Milwaukee, he had nothing against Dallas in an Easter afternoon affair, being held scoreless during the first half by 6'5" Adrian Griffin, whom he tried posting up down low but who had a hand in his face on his half-dozen errant jumpers. He didn't have a field goal through three quarters, finishing with a mere 10 points, and only Hamilton's 23 kept the game close against Dallas's triumvirate of stars—Dirk Nowitzki, Steve Nash and Michael Finley. Nesby hindered Finley, and Lue managed to keep Nash under reasonable control. A typical performance from a healthy Jordan would have meant a certain win, but Jordan, as Collins said later, had a knee at only 50 percent by then.

Even so, he played the entire fourth quarter. The Wizards' loss made everything more painful. Once off the floor and in the tunnel, he began dragging the right leg again, his knee swelling. But he would not admit it, choosing to focus instead on mistakes in the game, seeming to blame Collins for not using him more as a point guard out on the perimeter, where, Jordan thought, he might have saved some of his energy. He spoke of Collins as if he were an unproven coach who needed to prove his mettle. It was not a flattering side of Jordan, and this was a rare instance when he showed the side in public. "He's gonna have to earn his coaching ring to minimize my minutes and keep me in the focus of what's happening," he said. "In the Milwaukee game, [I thought] I could utilize myself a little better playing point guard. [That didn't happen] as much today. And he may have used me up a little bit."

The coach had his own spin on what was happening, praising Jordan for playing through pain. In hopes of inspiring a banged-up squad that had difficulty scoring points, Collins began citing Jordan as the model of the indomitable warrior. "Is he healthy?" Collins asked rhetorically. "The answer is no. Is he gonna compete? The answer is yes. And I think he's a tremendous example for the rest of our guys. . . . When you look across the locker room and see M.J. playing, you're sort of thinking, It's the time of year that I've gotta strap it on and play, too."

Strap it on was a favorite Collins phrase. The players had begun to use it, too. Everybody had to strap it on.

Only one player would not be able to strap it on much longer. Jordan had gone to talk to trainer Steve Stricker. He had a small problem, he said to somebody. The small problem involved not being able to flex his right knee totally. "I think it's going to be stiff after playing so many minutes," Jordan said matter-of-factly.

Delusion for many people can be an eternal state, can be so deep and complete that they are blissfully numb to it. But for hurting athletes in denial of their physical problems, delusion has limits and endings. The end now was approaching for Jordan. The following morning, April Fool's Day, his knee swelled anew. Surgery mended the cartilage, but no 39-year-old knee in the midst of rehab was made for this pounding. Over the next 36 hours, it filled with fluid and so stiffened that, shortly before the Wizards took the MCI floor to play the Lakers, Collins told Jordan he did not want him to play.

Jordan said he wanted to try. In a mark of his desperation, he went out on the floor looking to the world like a man wearing panty hose on his right leg—dark, tight, blue panty hose that a man as aggressively virile as Jordan never would have stood for wearing except for the hope that it might provide his knee with protection and relief. He looked liked the tallest man ever to play Peter Pan. Those who had told him about the synthetic legging—a "therapeutic circulation stocking," a trainer dubbed it—touted its ability to alleviate swelling by keeping the knee warm and enhancing blood flow in the area, the same theory by which electrical stimulation sometimes helped. Not everyone was so sure. Steve Stricker voiced uncertainty about whether it could help, but if Jordan wanted to try the legging, Stricker added, it couldn't hurt.

At the start of the game, Jordan rode the stationary bike in the tunnel, then took the court with about three minutes left in the first quarter, by which time the Lakers were already up by 10 points, the slaughter underway. Kobe Bryant and Shaquille O'Neal did whatever they wished. The Wizards committed a turnover, and the Lakers were fast-breaking, with Bryant racing to the hoop. Jordan was in a position to try contesting him but didn't, Bryant dunking, Jordan slowly turning and starting back up the court.

He was beaten on defense by a journeyman named Brian Shaw. Bryant left him flat-footed on a drive, a moment that a pained Jackson later mentioned to friends. Jordan took a seat on the bench with three minutes left in the second quarter.

Collins told him at halftime that he shouldn't return to the game unless the Wizards staged a dramatic comeback. Jordan was surprisingly docile.

"When Michael doesn't fight you, you know he's hurt," Collins said later.

He had a career-low of two points.

He said little to his teammates. With the Wizards on the way to losing by 20, he spent most of the second half on the end of the bench, two seats away from his closest teammate, mumbling over his shoulder to George Koehler, and otherwise alone with his thoughts.

Jackson said afterward that he looked like a shadow of himself.

Bryant added, "He might not have been moving like Michael wanted to move, but he wanted it as much. Nobody wants it more than Michael."

It was exactly that wanting—his salvation so often—that had been his undoing. He had, as John Hefferon observed, a 39-year-old's knees but a 25-year-old's dreams. In the locker room, he declared that he had "no pain" and felt "good." In the next moment, however, he seemed to be bracing the world for a possibly unsatisfactory ending to the season, his sorrow palpable when he spoke about the frustration of having to play hobbled against Bryant and Shaquille O'Neal—his tone a kind of faint plea: Please don't compare this version of himself against the younger stars. "It's tough . . . when you're going against the best and you don't have the same"—he paused for an instant, searching for a synonym, not wanting to use the word "knee," "body" or "youth," finally settling upon a word—"*equipment,* to go against them." His voice trailed off.

In that last week before his season's end, if only for a moment, he pulled up the shade on a mystery. He talked candidly about his tendinitis and related knee problems for the first time, grimly offering a theory about the origin of his troubles. His explanation eerily echoed the words and warnings of Tim Grover, six months earlier. The problem began, he said, with his broken ribs, and the favoring of his hurting left knee. "I came back without that period of building myself up, and from there it started: the flaring of the knee, the tendinitis. And parts of the body start to break down. *And you start compensating, and other things happen.*"

Now that those other things had happened, he could not be whole, or even close to what he had been. Even when healthy, he felt age altering him, and wondered how to say this without sounding self-pitying. The comparisons with Kobe Bryant cheated him, he thought, but he knew that people always would compare him to young princes.

The softness of his voice made clear how unfair he regarded this. Not only wasn't he the same, but his Bulls comrades were all gone. "I don't look over and see Pippen or Rodman," he said. "This is a different time."

Because it was so different, no one in the scrum followed up with a question about Pippen, Rodman or the old Bulls. Reporters wanted to know about his knee before he flew to Milwaukee, where the team would play the next night. "Are you feeling okay?" somebody asked.

"Fine," he said, his secret safe for another 12 hours.

When Jordan awakened the next morning, Wednesday, April 3, with his knee ballooning in a Milwaukee hotel room, his season ended. He phoned Collins and, in the athlete's vernacular—talking about his body as if it were a thing apart from the rest of him—he told the coach that he was "gonna shut it down, let the thing heal." He voiced his desire to play the following season, to take six or eight weeks off to rid the knee of its inflammation, then slowly rehab.

He didn't tell Collins much more. He didn't let him know when he would be flying out of Milwaukee, or where he would be headed. He didn't gather his teammates to break the news personally. He simply packed.

Collins met him in the hotel lobby. Jordan said good-bye and walked out.

He had teammates but very few intimates. In the end, he told virtually no one what had happened, most of the Wizards not learning the news until they prepared to board a 5 p.m. bus headed for their game at Milwaukee's Bradley Arena.

Only then did Lue, Nesby and the rest of the team hear from others that Jordan's season was finished. By then he had left for the airport with aides, a flight to Washington ready, his future a mist. "I think Michael realizes he pushed the envelope by coming back too quickly," declared a somber Collins.

Late that afternoon, Lue, shrugging forlornly, said he had known nothing. "I didn't know it was that bad," he murmured, asking for more information, as much in the dark as fans inside the Milwaukee arena, wondering aloud whether Jordan was already out of the city. Seldom was the divide between Jordan and others more evident.

Players kept asking, *Where is he exactly?* No one had answers. Trying to make sense of what had happened, few reporters even watched the game, in which Alexander scored 22 and the New Jacks fell short again. At halftime, Collins told somebody that the team looked discombobulated. Everybody is wondering where he is and what's happened, Collins explained.

At the airport, Jordan got on a private plane with Tim Grover, two bodyguards and the rest of his small crew. No one spoke to him for most of the flight. He stared out a window. Soon, he reached that place where all aging athletes eventually land, a solitary place where uncertainty makes everything quiet. That is a small death, and some athletes make an easier peace with it than others. "I think Michael needs to be alone for a while," Collins said.

With Jordan's season finished, the Wizards' playoff hopes succumbed, and something changed in Collins. His hazel eyes stopped flashing irritably at questions about Jordan's health. He began searching for ways to explain why the comeback had imploded.

By the regular season's final week, he confessed that his younger players' struggles early in the year "probably seduced me" into playing Jordan too many minutes, admitting with regret that Jordan had controlled their relationship.

"Michael has such a dominant personality," he said softly, "that he tells you he's feeling good, and you want to believe it even when he's not. There are games when I played him forty-one minutes when I probably should have played him thirty-five. But I kept saying to myself, 'There's no back-to-back. He doesn't have to practice tomorrow.' That [approach] took its toll, no question."

And then came the most surprising disclosure, one that seemingly nullified everything Collins had been saying for six months. "That knee wasn't right all season long," he said. "He probably hurt it in the summer."

He thought about the future, wondering what Jordan's attitude about his playing time might be if he came back for another season. His minutes would have to be cut, Collins said. "And the thing about it is, if it means he gets mad at me, then I'm gonna have to do it anyway, because"—Collins paused for a split second, looked up in the air and said it—"he won't do it on his own."

He never had, he never could. His appetites prevented that. Collins knew it, too.

Three days later, Collins said he still didn't know where Jordan was, that he hadn't heard from him since Jordan walked out of that Milwaukee hotel lobby.

Four more days passed. Jordan flew into Washington for an event with highly regarded high school basketball players participating in an all-star game that Jordan and Nike sponsored at MCI—the Jordan Capital Classic. Each star received a pair of Jordan's latest shoes, which came in a small, gray metallic Bond-like suitcase (it looked charmingly suitable for carrying toxic substances and a tasteful semiautomatic with silencer) and would soon be going on sale to the public for about $200.

Jordan congratulated a big kid named Amare Stoudemire, soon to be the first-round pick of the Phoenix Suns, wishing him luck and adding that he hoped he liked the shoes. Stoudemire's pair had come in red and white. If Stoudemire and other young stars enjoyed the shoes and one day signed with Nike, Jordan's clout with the shoe company would be enhanced whenever his retirement came. The trip was built around his promotional activities. While in town, he planned to talk with Collins and and watch some games.

He saw Collins that afternoon at MCI. A full week had passed since Jordan had left him in that hotel lobby. Jordan gave him about a half hour, and later that afternoon, Collins said he thought that Jordan would be watching the Wizards' game that evening against Philadelphia, assuring reporters that Jordan "gets fired up about [Wizards] games. . . . He sits back and agonizes, trust me."

Collins remained as loyal and feisty as ever, protecting Jordan against all questions that he regarded as unflattering, especially those raising the question of a double standard. Asked why a rehabbing but ambulatory Jordan did not sit on the team bench with other sidelined Wizards at MCI, per the team's custom, Collins insisted that this could *never* happen, that, given the attention he attracted, Jordan couldn't be expected to sit anywhere close to the public—"Michael can't go to Starbucks."

Collins likened the thought of Jordan sitting on the team bench to a scene, many years earlier, when Jordan, he said, exited a vehicle near the Chicago area, only to encounter about a hundred spectators who immediately descended upon the car, "stripping it down."

Was he saying Jordan would be mobbed and stripped on the team bench?

"You just can't do that," Collins insisted.

That evening, after spending the first half with the Nike-shoe-wearing high school stars, Jordan took a seat on the Wizards bench for the remainder of the game. Jordan hadn't forewarned Collins, who was left again to explain how he could know so little about what Jordan ever was planning to do. Jordan accorded him all the respect of an underling.

Jordan took a seat on the end of the bench, two seats down from Laettner, dapper as ever in a black suit and gold tie, wearing a credential around his neck, chewing gum, laughing, yelling at referee Leroy Richardson, thoroughly enjoying himself.

Fans did not strip him. The atmosphere was, if anything, laid-back. A seat remained open between Laettner and Jordan, and when Alexander came out of the game, he paused, not taking the seat, allowing Jahidi White to fill it. Jordan joked a little with White, covering his mouth with his gold tie to stifle a laugh, looking up at the action and exhorting Etan Thomas, who was pulling down 15 rebounds, scoring 14 points and having a superb game on a night when the Wizards easily beat the Sixers.

At a time-out, Jordan gently slapped Kwame Brown on the chest with his credential, as if to say, Wake up. At another time-out, he delivered an impromptu lecture on pump-faking to Hamilton, who, on his way to a game-high 21 points, listened expressionlessly.

He would not travel with them, but at least he cheered from that last seat on the bench during the final three games at home. On the second Sunday in April, attired in a gold-checkered sports jacket, mustard pants and mustard shirt (he was, in all things, from head to toes, a mustard lover, the precise shade being French's mustard), he smiled, genially hassled refs and watched the Wizards lose to Indiana. At the end of the game, he shook a hand or two and started walking off, headed toward the tunnel leading to the hallway and locker room. Susan O'Malley stood in the tunnel, alongside a wall. As he got close to the tunnel, Jordan lowered his head and looked at the cement floor, bounding past the short woman, never acknowledging her. Nor she him.

In the last days of the season, to be on the road anywhere with the Jordan-less Wizards was to be reminded of what it must have been like, almost every night, with Abe Pollin's unglamorous teams of the '80s and '90s. In Charlotte, there were 8,000 empty seats one evening—one of only three non-sellouts among the Wizards' 41 road dates, all occurring with Jordan out—and anyone could have bought an upper-tier seat off a desperate scalper for five dollars. As a writer whose sole responsibility it was to write about one man, I found myself reduced for a few days to contemplating the phantasm in his absence—like writing about Howard Hughes while tracking his company's trucks.

The Wizards lost a close game to a good Charlotte team that night, and Hamilton scored 22, all of which had a familiar ring. But, on a nice note, with the season winding toward the end and the New Jacks leading the way at home, they won two of their next three, beating Memphis and Philadelphia. Alexander had a big steal late against Memphis, and Hamilton played well enough through his bad groin to score a game-high of 21 against the Sixers, after which they flew up to Philadelphia for a game on the last Friday of the Wizards' season.

They would be officially eliminated from the playoffs that evening. The players seemed accepting of the reality coming, with Nesby and others already making their workout plans for the off-season and looking forward to their summers, like kids getting out of school. "I'm going to blow out my hair on the last day," he said to Lue of his cornrows. "Gonna blow my stuff out." Nez seemed happy; they all seemed happy in the locker room in Philadelphia, Rip talking to a reporter and displaying the tattoo on his chest—FOR THE LOVE OF THE GAME, which had a heart alongside it. Some guys were good-naturedly teasing Lue over the team photo, which he had missed, leaving the Wizards to superimpose his body and head on the picture.

"They brushed you in," said somebody, who pulled out a copy of the photo.

"It's messed up," Lue said. It was. His body and head looked askew and scorched in the photo. Nesby was softly chuckling.

Lue moaned, "I look like a burn victim."

Everybody laughed hard, Lue especially. They enjoyed hanging with one another, and seldom had the locker room ever seemed livelier than during that last week. But it would be over in just a few days, and then the worry would begin for some about their futures, especially those without contracts for the following season.

Just a couple of days earlier, Collins had told Nesby that "hopefully" he would be playing on the team the following season, that Nez had had "as big a turnaround as anyone on the team," a remark the coach repeated to the media. Nez's hopes soared. "I'm tryin' to finish up the year strong," he said. "And I'll be keepin' my body strong over the summer, workin' out. All I'll be doing in Vegas is workin' out and restin' at my home—workin' out and restin'."

Jordan had spoken to him briefly, just two nights before. "He said, 'Keep your energy up,'" Nez recalled. "That's the only time I've talked to him since he left Milwaukee. . . . He didn't talk about the contract. I'm waitin' till we finish up to start thinkin' real hard about it."

He had done everything right since Leonard Hamilton kicked him off that bench, a season earlier. He had worked hard for seven months and, as Collins said privately to coaches, played his ass off. Now Collins said publicly that he hoped to get Nez back. His words offered no clue about Jordan's thoughts. But Collins's support could only help.

"Gonna play every minute hard now, no matter if the games count for us or not," Nez said. "What are you gonna do now, man?" He meant me.

I wasn't sure I understood. "What do you mean?"

"You gonna do summer basketball games somewhere, man?"

"I don't think so, Nez."

And then I said something I'd sworn I'd never say to a player, because as a journalist concerned about preserving my objectivity, I'd tried to keep a subtle distance between myself and my subjects. But I told Nez I hoped he made it back. I meant it. You come to care about certain players, as you would about kids down your block. They are not übermen but merely young guys with huge dreams, upon whom the window usually shuts quickly. At 26, the odds were 50–50 at best for Nez, after which, no matter what happened, he probably had two-thirds of a life still to lead.

"See you next season, man," he said, grinning.

The Wizards were mathematically laid to rest in the next couple of hours. Most questions afterward turned to the players' futures. Some-body asked Hamilton about Jordan. "He said he's thinkin' he's gonna come back," Hamilton said hunching his shoulders in a neutral gesture meant to mean, Maybe.

He saw a friend across the locker room and waved. He was back home, a half-hour or so from his hometown of Coatesville. Many of his friends had come to the game, people whose faces alone reminded Hamilton of his success as a schoolboy player, of all the talk in those days about his vast potential. "I like being around home," he said. He put on his platinum medallion chain with the block *CV* for Coatesville and waved to another friend, thinking of the New Jacks and their futures. "We know that Michael's not gonna play for the next five, six years. We know that we're the future of the team. So if Michael comes back, that's great. But we don't depend on him like everybody thinks we depend on him. In order for us to turn around this organization, it's gonna be us."

Just his tone now—direct and firm—said everything about the way he regarded himself in the Jordan orbit. He was finished being the star's sidekick. Their relationship had become badly strained. Hamilton had stood up to Jordan, back in Washington, not in any shouting match but during some bantering in the locker room, the same turf that Jor-dan had taken back a few weeks earlier. Jordan had needled him once too often about defensive lapses, and, smiling, Hamilton had finally replied that his defense was getting better and that, besides, he was *running* just fine, that all the *young guys* were running now that they were *allowed* to run. Oh, yeah? Jordan said, sarcastically. Hamilton wasn't backing down from him any longer. We're scoring and we're running now, Hamilton said. Each man seemed careful not to cross a line, a wit-ness thought. But tension charged the space between them, and the digs and searing of egos went on for a considerable while.

What had being with Jordan meant to him? someone cheerfully asked now. Hamilton thought it over. "Michael taught, and that's always good," Hamilton said. People waited for elaboration. He left it at that.

In the aftermath of the season, Collins and other coaches told the Wizards brass that the team could not improve with its roster, triggering uncomfortable questions: How could they set out rebuilding a team around a man just three months shy of 40 at the beginning of the next NBA season, a player likely to be around for only another year? What would happen when his departure necessarily meant the team must retool? How much longer were the New Jacks willing to be the chorus for the Michael Show?

No one had answers to the questions, though some things were certain. Courtney Alexander was gone. He had never proven himself to be tough or versatile enough for Collins and Jordan. In a kiss of death delivered in the season's final week, a sympathetic-sounding Collins praised Alexander's recent games, before adding that Alexander's play revealed he found it "tough" to match up against bigger guys playing the small-forward position.

Collins wanted someone capable of defending small forwards, a banger like Nesby but a player who could provide points, too. Jordan, he thought, had been forced to guard far too many small forwards during the season, rugged young players like Ron Artest who outweighed him, pounded him, wore him down. He wanted Jordan playing guard exclusively for the rest of his days. And he wanted him playing fewer minutes, perhaps not even starting any longer, just coming off the bench as a superb sixth man to lead the second team and be on the floor for stretch drives in the fourth quarter. But the plan depended on finding that new player. To acquire a real small forward—the *Three* spot, in basketball parlance—was an imperative. That person, the coaches concluded, certainly wasn't Alexander, too small at 6'5" and not a strong enough defender against formidable guards his own size. Within weeks, Alexander was jettisoned. He became the reclamation project of New Orleans, which, in exchange, gave the Wizards a late first-round draft pick.

While Alexander had disappointed, others had risen in Collins's estimation. The young power forward Etan Thomas had shown great potential late in the season as a rebounder and shot blocker. Tyronn Lue had steadily improved as a backup point guard, especially in his outside shooting. He had hit 42 percent from behind the three-point line, a higher percentage than even the renowned three-point shooter Chris Whitney, whose starting job at point guard seemed in jeopardy, with the coaches wanting an upgrade at the position. Popeye Jones had proven himself one of the best rebounders in the league, landing in the top 10 of a most arcane but meaningful statistic—rebounds per minute. Collins loved Jones, wanting to re-sign him, if possible.

But above all else, he told his assistant coaches, they needed to add someone to play the Three. He had ideas on a possible Three, he said. If they landed a versatile performer who could play at the Three and at the shooting-guard position, perhaps someone like Detroit's Jerry Stackhouse, and complemented him with a highly talented point guard, they would be a solid playoff contender, he predicted. During his Detroit days, while in his capacity as the Pistons' coach and general manager in 1998, Collins actually had traded for Stackhouse, high on him as someone who could do everything—drive hard to the basket, shoot jumpers and play bruising defense when motivated. Stackhouse could change the dynamic of a team, thought Collins. He might be the *difference*.

The coach projected optimism, trying to sell everyone on the idea that the team had just concluded a *good* season. *Plus-18,* he kept saying, meaning that the Wizards had won 18 more games over their 19–63 mark of a season earlier. Even our record, 37–45, is misleading, he insisted, arguing it only told half the story. "Look at our injuries," he told people. Jordan missed 22 games, Hamilton 19, Laettner 25 (most of those with his broken leg), Alexander 26 (Collins forgot to mention that he had benched Alexander in half of those)—and, at different times, Lue, Hubert Davis, Haywood and White had been out for significant stretches. Without the injuries, particularly Jordan's, "we would have been a playoff team," Collins declared, pointing out that their second-half tailspin came only when Jordan's physical problems seized him, after which the team went 11–24.

But, in fact, the team had barely kept its head above water even with Jordan on the floor, winning only half of the 60 games he played, and going 27–26 in games he started before his surgery. The team always had needed a healthy Hamilton and his 20 points per game. With Hamilton and Jordan both playing well, the Wizards had thrived in stretches, especially as Hamilton modestly improved his defense. If, as Collins observed, they signed a star who could play the small-forward position a good portion of a game, they might see dramatic improvement.

That judgment had immediate implications for the roster.

Tyrone Nesby would not be offered a new contract. The more the Wizards executives looked at their current player-payroll numbers, and pondered the likely financial demands of a highly regarded free agent or two, the more their interest dimmed in Nesby. Collins had said many glowing things about Nesby, but coaches said glowing things about many players. Coaches' sentiments could not be trusted. Coaches could not be trusted for a variety of reasons, not the least of which was that coaches were seldom their clubs' money men. Attitudes quickly changed when coaches saw the bean counters' ledgers and had to make choices.

That quickly, Nesby went from an annual league salary of $3.2 million to zero.

No other NBA team would sign him to a regular season contract. Tyrone Nesby's window had closed at age 26.

That left only one major disposal job. Michael Jordan no longer believed he needed Richard Hamilton, who, in standing up to him, had become expendable. No one in the organization argued otherwise. All along, most of the coaches had been ambivalent about Hamilton. Some thought he might never build his body. "You still have to chain him to the weight room," one official groaned.

There were issues of morale, too, tensions exacerbated by Hamilton's impression that Jordan's stature still meant that others had to fight sometimes just to show their skills and get recognition. Two club officials had not forgotten when a frustrated Hamilton, coming back from his groin injury, had gone to Collins and complained about not feeling like an integral part of the offense.

Collins answered: "Rip, you have a coach who's gonna run every play for you and Michael . . ."

But *every play for you and Michael* never freed Hamilton from worry. The officials were convinced that Hamilton could no longer abide playing in Jordan's shadow, that the bad feelings between the two men could only get worse. Hamilton became trade bait. Jordan suggested acquiring the same player that Collins had in mind. In early September, in a six-player deal with Detroit, the Wizards dealt Hamilton away for Jerry Stackhouse.

Jordan had no comment about the deal, declining to talk about anything that summer, not having made up his mind about whether to play again. "What are his options?" said one Wizards official. "What else is he going to do? Go back to that office?"

It was the right set of questions.

9

One More Gamble

WITHOUT A GAME THAT SUMMER, HE GRAVITATED TOWARD OLD pleasures. He had found what he needed in Pit 21 in the Mohegan Sun casino, on the eve of his season. Now, with the games over, he spent part of his time in Monaco and Las Vegas, doing the predictable. There was always a Pit 21 somewhere out there, always a pile of blue chips waiting. Twenty years of breathless gambles played out in the din of arenas had left him with fewer interests than raging appetites, in love with adrenaline rushes that necessarily put a strain on real life to measure up. It hadn't, it couldn't. Not even blackjack combined with frequent golf rounds could sate his competitive needs. He turned to the only thing that would help. In June, he resumed light workouts, uncertain about the soundness of his knee, not yet having committed himself to anything. No one knew, including Michael Jordan at midlife, where all this was going, or for how much longer. He always gave the impression he craved even this. The uncertainty. Some exquisite doubt. He was in love with risk.

A year earlier, having had his preparation interrupted by his broken ribs, Jordan's rush to make up for lost training weeks ruined his season. This time around, Grover persuaded a chastened Jordan to take his rehab slowly—to strengthen the knee, build his workouts in prudent increments and point toward being ready not for the start of the meaningless NBA preseason but for the opening of the regular season, nearly three weeks later, on October 30. Even then, Grover thought, the goal would be to peak at some point well into the season, requiring that Jordan permit a rationing of his playing minutes as he steadily built his body—a concept met with enthusiasm by Collins, who hoped that Jordan would agree to being a reserve at the season's start, the goal to spare his body the rigors of a starter's duties while giving Collins the option of playing him for most, if not all, of a typical fourth quarter, with a game on the line. The coach's vision reflected that of skeptics, in and out of the organization, who did not see Jordan finishing the season unless he consented to a drastic cutting of his playing time.

The most sanguine of the observers was also the one most honest around Jordan. While accepting of the uncertainties in training a 39-year-old athlete, Grover felt confident that he could gird Jordan for a full season, so long as his boss (or client—as Grover seemed to be evolving from underling to someone with his own stature in NBA circles) adhered to a cautious training schedule. Grover's optimism equaled his pessimism of a season earlier, when Jordan disregarded his advice after suffering the broken ribs. Grover did not delude his clients. If he felt that Jordan had a chance to stay intact throughout the season, then Jordan had a shot to play a full year.

Durability was not the same thing, however, as speed or loft. Regardless of his knee, no one in the organization believed that, yet another year older, he would be a better player, the history of aging athletes' performances suggesting, if anything, that he would be slightly diminished from a season earlier, the intervening months claiming just a little more of his skills and endurance. The slide in his performance would become particularly more noticeable in the second halves of games now, when fatigue gripped him. If he preferred not to fast-break during the previous season, he would like it even less in a new season. Teammates would be under increasing pressure to get him the ball at certain places on the floor, so he would not need to run around and fight to get free. He would be inclined to steal a little rest on defense occasionally, and smart teams, like Detroit and Boston, would see it, burn him and subtly allude to how they had been keen to his need for a breather. He would have greater difficulty soaring over foes, making drives to the hoop an ever rarer occurrence.

He still drove the lane sometimes, only to find its aperture ever shrinking. Age had taken something ineffable from his first step on a dribble, something too small and fine for the eye to see when he warmed up against an invisible defender before a game, but an erosion happening all the while. On the edge of 40, his body was inexorably losing muscle mass, particularly of the fast-twitch variety, costing him a good half step, at least. If he returned, the effects would be all too obvious from the first days: Young unpolished defenders who couldn't have stayed within a step of him once would cut him off in the lane, reducing his slashing drives to about one or two in a typical game, and his dunks roughly to one a week, leaving him with no choice but increasingly to shoot either fallaways in the post or pull-up jumpers around screens.

Like an aging Hollywood leading man who acknowledges the inevitable and segues from being an action hero to a venerable character actor, Jordan already had become a niche player—cast in that least flamboyant of basketball roles, the jump shooter. There was no markedly diminished stature in this: He would forever have top billing on a marquee. Only there would be no opportunities left to be swashbuckling and dunk down the throats of seven-footers. There would be far fewer chances to be heroic, for being a jump shooter is a finicky thing. Once in a while his touch would be very good, even great. But on most nights, it would be just so-so, and on a few nights very bad—which mirrored a mortal's life and is the way it goes for even highly skilled jump shooters. There would be the pedestrian cant to describe it—*good numbers,* solid output, valued performance and pride, to go along with a certain All-Star selection for a cherished legend. Certainly, he would not embarrass himself if he came back. Even working under his new limitations, he would remain one of the best 20 to 25 players in the league, someone capable of abusing a highly touted youngster once in a while and holding his own against all but the game's greatest. He just would be nothing close to the player remembered.

His improvisational skills, the source of his ascendancy, were gone, as well as a part of his endurance. His fires burnt out quickly now. He would be used up after a half, if not careful. He needed to plot carefully on a court from here on out, and husband his energies for just the right moments in a game, those five or six minutes when he would try for a run of pull-up jumpers, a blitzkrieg of 10, 15 points to ice a contest or humiliate some smart-ass kid. If he came back, he would need to live for those few moments. He would need to be content in being dominant for a brief run, or maybe for only a couple of possessions—to palm the ball, wave it in front of a foe's face, pull it back and forth like a yo-yo, the fans ooohing and laughing, their anticipation as sweet as the thing itself, the memory of which would be gilded by their imaginations, Jordan finally rising, hitting the jumper, the crowd exploding. He would need to believe those moments were still out there for him.

No one could be certain how hard the changes might be on him or his legacy. The old pictures of him in the mind's eye already had begun blurring with the fresher images of Bryant leaping over him in Los Angeles. The reason was simple: People tended to remember best what they saw last.

This was not at all fair, it was not at all scholarly or sensible, it was just human, and understood therefore by anyone who couldn't get out of his head an image of Willie Mays stumbling after fly balls in Shea Stadium, or Ali, in a dump of a makeshift fight site in the Bahamas, being pounded on the ropes as a ridiculous cowbell sounded his finish. Unpleasant endings are the norm, not the exception, for gods who hang around near 40. The basketball people who loved Jordan the most had had questions from the comeback's beginning about what effect the extra years might have on his reputation and happiness.

No one in the Wizards organization cared more about him, or his historical impact, than John Bach, the assistant coach who had served in the same capacity for eight years in Chicago, and during the first three of the Bulls championships. If one thing concerned the young Jordan, Bach remembered, it was that he might be exposed to embarrassment at some distant date, when he aged and slowed. He knew of the humiliations suffered by Julius Erving, who had been tormented on-court in his twilight by both Jordan and Larry Bird, the latter of whom was nothing less than cruel, mocking Erving throughout one long night, talking to him while taking him apart, providing the older star with a running update of their respective scoring totals—"That's 38 to 6"—so goading Erving that the beaten and infuriated legend turned on Bird and started throwing punches.

But taunters usually paid a price. Jordan saw what happened to Bird late in his career, when the Celtics god began getting shredded by players he had once decimated and ridiculed, like Scottie Pippen, who got payback, taunting Bird while scoring at will against him, a not inconsiderable humiliation. The incident raised the question of whether Bird had left himself vulnerable at the end, perhaps retiring too late. The moment had deeply affected Jordan, who, never wanting anyone to get payback at his expense, said to Bach, *You gotta let me know if you ever see me slipping like that.*

Bach stayed with Chicago beyond the Collins firing, celebrating with Jordan and Jackson during the first of the Bulls championships in

1991, and was there, in 1993, when after title number three, Jordan retired, contemplating an escape from Chicago to try his hand at baseball. Bach was happy for him. He viewed the best players as modern gunfighters and knew how much it meant to Jordan to retire as the greatest gunfighter ever. Bach told him how pleased he was that Michael would be getting out of the sport on top; that he could still painfully remember an old Joe Louis being pounded between the ropes by Rocky Marciano, and Joe DiMaggio limping after fly balls, and a corpulent Babe Ruth flailing for a barnstorming semipro team in a game that Bach had watched as a child, in New York.

"Not going to happen to you, Michael," he remembered saying, and then, just in case Jordan might ever have second thoughts about his future, Bach let him know about the psychic cost of comebacks he'd seen; how desire at some point dwarfed a player's skill; how he thought that aging returnees, like Louis, found it impossible simply to deal with the expectations surrounding their returns; that the pressure upon them appeared to have been crippling. It was both a sports story and a homily, a small warning; for Bach, a selfless coach, loved the player. Jordan nodded at the tales, thanked Bach for his guidance and wished him luck.

Jordan came back a season and a half later, as brilliant as before his departure. But, seven years later, his second comeback raised vexing questions. From its start, Bach could see what was in it for others to reap. Pollin and the Wizards organization would prosper, as would the NBA and a couple of television networks. But what would Jordan be getting out of it? Bach asked himself. He wasn't at all sure. Finally, after speaking to Jordan, he felt assured that Jordan's gains would come from the simple conviction that he was doing what he wanted.

Bach had been among those during the first season who hoped that Jordan would be careful not to overextend himself, believing that heavy playing time after three years away posed a risk to many parts of his body—his back, his Achilles, his knees. Now with the uncertainty of the right knee's rehab, Bach again had to confront the concerns that Jordan expressed to him in the mid-'90s.

In the end, Bach felt no need to warn him about anything. The Jordan situation in 2002, he concluded, was much different from that of the Pippen-Bird nastiness that had so worried the young Jordan, in the early '90s. The older Jordan had weighed all the risks to his reputation and decided that he wanted another season more than he did a guarantee that everything would be okay. He fully understands the risks,

Bach thought. If he fails, at least he'll be doing what he wants. He's like a proud gunfighter, Bach told people. He can't get away from it.

Bach admired him for that. As close as they were during the season, he didn't really know Jordan away from basketball, and wouldn't have presumed to say he understood all aspects of Jordan's life, or even Jordan. But he believed that you could admire and love different parts of people. He cherished Jordan the competitor, particularly the competitor's willingness to bear serious risks for nothing more than a last chance to play a game they both loved. "I just don't want him to have disappointments at the end of this," Bach said.

Jordan had suffered disappointments in life, but losing never had been at the top of the list. As much as anyone could remember, he'd sobbed but once over a defeat, and that had come only after losing as a young man, in a bitter Game Seven, to his hated nemesis, the Detroit Pistons. Even then, he recovered quickly, and would best Detroit within a year. Jordan seldom flogged himself over defeats. What he did stew over were missed opportunities, still looking back wistfully on those three years he missed after Jackson left the Bulls. Count the 1994 season where he starred as the tallest right fielder to hit .200 in the low minors, and that made four full seasons he had given away. Not playing was much tougher on him than playing and losing.

To live now with the idea that he might miss another season in which he could have competed was too much. To go out knowing that some people's final memory of him would be that last limp across a Milwaukee hotel lobby was unthinkable. He felt reasonably confident, so long as his right knee was sound. After all, he asked people around him, what had his numbers been during the past season when he largely suffered with tendinitis? He could answer his own question; he was a savant when it came to his statistics or anyone else's. His numbers had been generally good: 22.9 points a game, with respectable averages of 5.7 rebounds and 5.2 assists.

But his 41.6 percent field goal percentage for the season was the lowest of his career, far below his 50 percent lifetime average, his percentage often plummeting when he tired in the second half of games. Even when reasonably healthy, he missed more than ever, with his team-high in turnovers indicating he handled the ball too much. If he were to play again, Collins wanted to bring him into the game no sooner than eight minutes after its start, then allow him to play out most of the two halves. His plan would depend on Jordan's assent, however, and Wizards officials understood that for Collins to sell it, Jordan had to believe that he would still be directing the team, particularly on offense, in a game's critical minutes. Any media questions that suggested a diminished role for Jordan only heightened the chance of irking Jordan and complicating Collins's challenge. He aimed for fealty to the boss: "Michael's gonna decide what he's gonna do next year." He waited until he talked privately with Jordan in the summer, before indicating that Jordan seemed in support of having his minutes trimmed.

Jordan, still rehabbing and training at a cautious pace, gave a tentative blessing to Collins's idea. Shortly later, about two weeks before the start of training camp, Jordan told Collins and the Wizards that he would be playing another season.

"Michael and I have discussed his role," Collins said at the start of training camp, noting that the two had decided that Jordan should not play more than 30 minutes in a game. "The critical thing is to keep his minutes down . . ."

Collins cited the lesson to be learned from his past mistakes. "We let it get away from us last year," he told reporters. "We got off to a horrible start and we played him too much. We can't break him down early."

Jordan didn't openly disagree, but he put Collins and everyone else on notice: "I'm not going to play insignificant minutes." If he played well in training camp, he expected to have an opportunity to be a starter by the opening regular season game. Collins's plan already had been scaled back.

In Wilmington, Jordan came out for the first practice, and Collins could see, just by the way he stiffly jogged, that Jordan wasn't even at 20 percent. Stunned, Collins said privately to his assistants, "He can't play this year. There's no way . . ."

Collins kept watching the hobbled Jordan. *He's gimpin'*, the coach told people. *He has no lift. He's having difficulty even running. This is it. He can't play.*

Except that Jordan was set on playing. In time, he would make sure that he was no longer the league's most famous sixth man, but a starter again with most of the offense in his hands. Here his needs and ambition threatened to conflict with the team's interest: The central question about the comeback's second year should never have been whether Jordan ought to have played another season—after all, who among the media or fans has the moral claim to ask that an athlete or anyone else not do what has been his life's work—but whether in aggressively pushing to remain the team's centerpiece he showed a disregard for his team's best interests and his teammates' futures. For all his public assurances that he had returned to complement younger stars, Jordan's patience with this experiment quickly waned. He pointed out that defenses trained their attentions on him. He told the media that not only did he expect to be playing in the postseason but that he saw the bolstered Wizards competing for the Eastern Conference championship, just a series away from the NBA Finals—a vision that, as he saw it, made it all the more critical that his playing time be steadily increased.

Collins pleaded with Jordan to take it easy. Jordan agreed, participating in just a few workouts during the twice-daily sessions at the nine-day training camp. "We've got to build him," Collins said to the media, "and we think we have enough guys on this team that we don't have to break him down."

The organization had acquired a mix of new scorers and able defenders. Collins now had 23-year-old Larry Hughes, already in his fourth season in the NBA, drafted out of the University of St. Louis in his freshman year, after which his saga had been the increasingly familiar tale of expected stardom unrealized. He had struggled in his early professional years—first, in Philadelphia, where he failed as a 19-year-old point guard for the Sixers; and next at Golden State, where his big-scoring nights gave way to difficulties, a benching and stardom for someone else, a potent rookie named Gilbert Arenas.

As so often happened with the Wizards, the team would be receiving someone else's discarded goods, except that, in Hughes's case, there seemed to be reason for hope. If not a natural point guard, and neither a great ball-handler nor passer, Hughes was a pure and prolific scorer, capable of hitting all kinds of shots—long jumpers, driving dunks, post-up fallaways, pull-up J's, and at his best in a running, freewheeling, pressuring game, the very up-tempo style that Collins had been preaching since the start of camp. There would be risks. Hughes was capable of abysmal and glittering performances in the same week. But, for all his ups and downs, he had youth and vast potential on his side, a sleek, powerfully built 6' 5" disciple of self-belief who believed, as all the good ones do, that he could score on anybody ("You can't back down in this league; you gotta attack everyone, and I think I can.") and whose size, it was thought, gave him a better chance of defending burly point guards than the smaller Lue or Whitney.

Then there was the 6' 7" Bryon Russell, three months from his 32nd birthday as camp began, essentially cut loose in the off-season by the Utah Jazz, which chose not to re-sign him, a decision that left him alternately indifferent and caustic about the Jazz franchise. He seemed the antithesis of a Larry Hughes, somebody who had built a career off no reputation. He'd arrived in Utah as an unglamorous kid and a lightly regarded 1993 second-round pick out of Long Beach State, the kind of draft slot from which players usually hang around training camps for a couple of weeks, hoard their modest bonus money, get cut and slink off to a lesser league. Russell stayed the next nine years, to become a longtime starter in a lineup that included future Hall of Famers Malone and Stockton, part of a hard-luck team that never won a championship largely because Michael Jordan said no.

Those wondering how Russell would respond to playing with Jordan needn't have worried. Russell had the archetypal veteran's acceptance of how things work. If still bitter in moments about The Shot, he could put aside his feelings in exchange for the veteran's desire to pick up a steady paycheck in a career that likely did not have much time left. Collins and Jordan saw Russell as someone who could defend both small forwards and shooting guards. He would be a solid Three, sparing Jordan from having to play the position. If healthy, and not wasted by age, he had the capacity to average about 10 or 12 points a game.

So the Three looked filled, and if Russell ever faltered at the position, then the year's star acquisition, Jerry Stackhouse, would move into it. Even if Russell performed well, Stackhouse needed to be ready to switch positions. He would begin the year as a starter at shooting guard, understanding that when Jordan returned to the starting lineup, he would need to make room for the legend by vacating his preferred position and moving to small forward, there to be matched against bigger defenders. It would not be the ideal place on the court for him, but wanting to demonstrate his selflessness around his new teammates and coach, Stackhouse said he would gladly do anything asked.

Throughout training camp, the man nicknamed Stack projected cooperation and enthusiasm, an auspicious sign. About to turn 28 and possessing an option at season's end to walk away from the final two years of a contract that would pay him $15 million during that span, he had enormous financial motivation to play well, likely looking at his last shot to prove himself worthy of star status in the league—already having been dealt away not by one but by two teams. Trades carried a stigma, no matter how often general managers insisted other-

wise. Fabulous players frequently opted for free agency, and sometimes teams' financial challenges dictated player swaps. But players
deemed great by their coaches and front office seldom found themselves traded, for the simple reason that greatness was the scarcest
commodity in the NBA, like anywhere else. The two Stackhouse trades
indicated that he had not proven to be indispensable to his former
teams, neither a reliable winner nor a successful leader. Privately, Jordan said that teams, unless expecting a player to leave via free agency
or feeling financially squeezed, never traded a great star, nearly always
found a way to hold on to what they most treasured. To be traded
meant a team believed it had improved its chances to win by getting
rid of a player.

Seven years earlier, as the third overall pick of the NBA draft, Stackhouse had left the University of North Carolina as a sophomore and
headed to Philadelphia, with supporters talking about him as a future
star to rival Jordan. But neither his persona nor game ever had come
close to matching his fellow North Carolinian. While distinguishing
himself as a scorer with the Sixers, he found himself in a battle with a
younger teammate for control of the offense and the heart of Sixers
coach Larry Brown, lasting only two and a half seasons in Philadelphia
before losing out in basketball's version of a cockfight to fellow back-
court star Allen Iverson.

Shipped to Detroit, he became a two-time All-Star and thrived there
for his first three years, his climb highlighted by his 29.8 points a game
in the 2000–2001 season, when he was runner-up to Iverson for the
league scoring title. He finally won an intrasquad battle, his play having pushed out a rival Detroit superstar, the oft-injured Grant Hill, who
landed in Orlando. But toward the end of that same year, he began
experiencing strains with his Detroit coach, Rick Carlisle, who questioned Stackhouse's defense, wanting him to shore up that end of his
play.

In the season before his acquisition by the Wizards, Stackhouse had
seen his defense improve but his scoring average fall by more than
eight points a game, down to just above 21 points. For another season,
a highly talented Detroit team had failed to advance deep into the
playoffs. Rumors spread of Detroit's continued dissatisfaction with
Stackhouse's defense and commitment.

Being traded away for the younger Richard Hamilton amounted to
an unmistakable rebuff. The image of him as a player destined for
greatness was gone. Still a star, but a lesser one, Stackhouse needed to

demonstrate his worth in the shadow of Jordan, who, even if coming off the bench, would hold sway over the offense. Stackhouse aimed for grace and diplomacy whenever the subject of Jordan's clout arose. "Michael Jordan, with everything he's accomplished, he's Batman," Stackhouse told reporters. "I don't concede to many people. To nobody, really. But in this case, I will."

Still, he added, it was a good situation, because *he* would have the opportunity to "set the tone" as a starter while Jordan sat on the bench in a game's opening minutes. In the weeks ahead, he staked out his turf with increasing forcefulness, making clear that neither of them had indicated to the other who would lead or follow when together on the floor—no assertions of control, no concessions. "Nah, nothing was said," Stackhouse amiably declared. "You don't have to tell a scorer [Stackhouse] to score. I think we understand that whenever I have an opportunity, I'll take it."

At training camp, the two moved carefully around each other. With Hamilton gone, Jordan was finished suggesting that he would play a supporting role to anybody. There would be nothing like his wry, self-effacing references of the previous season, no more dubbing himself "Tonto" to anybody else's towering masked man. As Collins and Stackhouse regularly talked about the legend coming off the bench and aiding the team's new starters, Jordan increasingly discussed how the newcomers, particularly Stackhouse, could serve to assist *him.* "Stack can complement me . . ." he told reporters after a practice, engagingly offering a rationale. "I'm going to take some of the weight off him because of my whole reputation. But he's going to take the weight off me later down the road. Once I expose him as a threat, it makes me so much better. When we play together, he and I are going to have to work hand-in-hand [in] attacking."

Their dance was nothing unusual in American sports. A half-century earlier, Joe DiMaggio's Arctic cool, in the face of Mickey Mantle's arrival, famously signaled that gods don't like the possibility of their worshipers ogling false idols. There is always a bit of tension in the joining of two stars that only homage from the younger athlete can undo. Gods look for fealty from the newcomer first, and dispense blessings and kudos later. Jordan waited before talking much about Stackhouse.

Some in the Washington media and the national press already had begun likening the duo's potential to the league's most successful combinations in history, but Collins wanted to reserve judgment. He knew that the results of mixing two stars never could be predicted with reliability; that, while the results were sometimes spectacular, sometimes they were not; sometimes they could be catastrophic or, almost equally bad, just fizzle. And there always existed the possibility of the duo succumbing to injury. Jordan had loosened up during the first few days at camp, moving better, but still not great. The Orlando Magic had had a highly touted duo, too, in Tracy McGrady and Grant Hill. But now, plagued by a chronically injured ankle, Hill looked finished in the NBA, the Orlando duo dead. You never knew about duos, Collins cautioned people.

As Jordan ran a little better with each day, Collins continued projecting his new authority, especially over Jordan. In Wilmington, he insisted that it wouldn't matter how much Jordan lobbied for more playing time, that he would hold Jordan's minutes down in the interest of protecting his knees. The media's skepticism was huge. Collins, grasping for a motoring analogy, said he would be putting a "governor" on Jordan.

A reporter asked, But who's the governor?

Collins vowed steadfastness, but, as the days passed, Jordan slowly ratcheted up the pressure on him. He began saying how good he felt, emphasizing that he would be playing significant minutes. His increased role would eventually test whether he and Stackhouse could coexist.

Both men had a huge stake in making the partnership work. In his role as de facto head of basketball personnel, pending his anticipated official return as club president, Jordan had personally approved the trade that brought Stackhouse to Washington. For his part, Stackhouse needed to prove he could meld with a team, that he was more than a showman capable only of amassing glittering statistics. He offered to take occasional cues from Jordan: "When he comes in, then I have to see when to defer and play off him."

Stackhouse accorded him public praise and, in return, Jordan extended pointers, sharing information about the little things that he had tried using to his advantage against Stackhouse over the years, particularly Stack's habit of driving almost exclusively to his right. He urged him to think of going left more often, and Stackhouse thanked him, even mentioning the moment to the media later. Beyond such short, polite exchanges, however, they forged no link with each other.

Though raised in the same state, and bred among many of the same attitudes and passions, the two athletes could scarcely have been more different in their personal styles. Jordan was privately assertive, the lead wolf accustomed to having the first bite and last. Stackhouse was quieter, so quiet that some teammates regarded him as aloof. Their public personas were the polar opposites of their private personalities. While Jordan avoided nearly all requests for community appearances, Stackhouse was available to attend virtually any function the Wizards' public relations department had in mind. When the department asked if he might be interested in attending a Read to Achieve program in a Maryland suburb, Stackhouse's response was immediate and enthusiastic, the rare athlete who did not need to be pestered into making a community commitment.

Circumstance had bred public interest into Stackhouse. Personal loss had driven him to establish a foundation bent on promoting awareness and raising government funds to attack diabetes: Two older sisters had died of the disease, and both his parents were afflicted by it. Becoming a passionate advocate only heightened his skills with language; he spoke in full paragraphs, often eloquently so. Whether appearing before congressmen to lobby for more funding or casually lounging among reporters pressing him about basketball, he gave people time, answering questions courteously and thoroughly.

But Stackhouse's mien belied a competitive fierceness and a temper. Disagreements in the past with teammates had not always ended well. Skilled with his fists, he had pummeled two of them over the years, including Christian Laettner, when they were teammates in Detroit and had an argument during a card game. He could be placid for weeks, even months, then snap in an instant if he felt insulted or disrespected.

Stackhouse was not a guy to mess with, or rib too hard or often— and Jordan wouldn't. The tough jibes that Jordan had occasionally inflicted on Hamilton and Alexander wouldn't be coming Stackhouse's way; there would be no snickering lines about how a pair of Air Jordans might help Stack grab a rebound, unless Jordan wanted to risk a brawl with a man of the same size reputed to be considerably tougher and to whom he would be giving away 11 years.

They would enjoy a détente throughout the season, though this did not mean that Jordan would resist looking for a game in which to best Stackhouse. They had competed fiercely against each other since those days in the mid-'90s when Stackhouse had bested him in their private summertime one-on-one game, and Jordan had answered by scoring 46 against him in their opening NBA matchup of the following season. Jordan's first season as a Wizard had only heightened their competitiveness, with Stackhouse generally getting the best of Jordan in their brief one-on-one encounters, something that neither man had forgotten. "I felt I had some good moments against Michael last year," Stackhouse permitted himself to say.

Their history, and Jordan's eternal compulsion to find someone to beat, guaranteed that Jordan would find a way to match up with him in Wilmington. He had sat out most of the practices during training camp, but one evening, he declared he would play in an intrasquad game that took on unusual importance when the two stars found themselves on rival squads.

Stackhouse's squad enjoyed a healthy lead into the final quarter, when Jordan's team went on a late run. Jordan hit several shots, the game tightening, Stackhouse's team complaining about the officiating, the trash-talking rising, Jordan doing most of it. The outcome hinged on a shot in the final seconds. Jordan dribbled, drove and, surprisingly, passed.

The moment reminded onlookers of a game early in his first comeback when, having already scored 55 points against the Knicks in Madison Square Garden, he rose in the climactic moment and, drawing the defense to him, passed to a little-regarded Bulls center, Bill Wennington, who hit a short winning shot. Now, with Stackhouse and a teammate smothering him, Jordan whipped the ball outside to 29-year-old journeyman Horacio Llamas, a 6' 11" center soon to be cut by the Wizards. Llamas sank a long jumper, and Jordan and his squad won.

Horacio Llamas: The new Bill Wennington. Jordan loved it, exulting, woofing. A disgusted Stackhouse rushed off the court, muttering, furiously pushing through the gymnasium's double doors in what sounded like a crash—BAM. It was not a harbinger of harmony, but neither was it, or any other incident that season, poisonous to relations between the two stars. Like the rest of their preseason together, the intrasquad game merely signaled the obvious: They were at once rivals and teammates, just as Hamilton and Jordan had been. The new duo made the same respectable effort to make their coupling work, but each man carried expectations and a style that hopelessly conflicted with the other's, dooming any chance of success.

While mulling over how Stackhouse's role in the Jordan saga seemed indistinguishable from Hamilton's, I thought about not a sports parallel but, being an American boomer, remembered an old television series from my childhood. It was called *Bewitched,* a show about a pretty American witch named Samantha Stephens. She lived with her bedazzled ad-man-husband Darrin, played by a likable actor named Dick York, who left the series at some point, replaced as Darrin by another likable actor named Dick Sargent.

The producers of the show, of course, wanted no one to think too hard about the fact that the first Darrin had gone away. If the producers had their wish, no one would think that Darrin number one ever had been replaced at all.

What the Wizards wanted you to believe, on the other hand, was that Jerry Stackhouse's situation was altogether *different* from Richard Hamilton's; that one had nothing to do with the other in the Jordan story; that they were entirely different kinds of players and characters. This was a fun bit of make-believe. Like TV's change in the Darrins, the Wizards just substituted a new player for the same role. Jerry Stackhouse was the replacement Darrin. It was not a glamorous part.

Adhering to his careful training schedule, Jordan played in only the last three of eight preseason games, logging no more than 23 minutes in any of them. His rust and lack of timing plagued him. He shot only 5–14 for 14 points against Detroit, which used Hamilton to guard him for a few minutes, a matchup highlighted by a mano a mano moment when a dribbling Jordan isolated Hamilton and tried bulling him down low on the right side of the basket, finally turning and rising, only to miss a jumper that caromed off the side of the backboard, as Hamilton got a hand in his face. An exultant Hamilton happily hopped, then started flying the other way, flying the way he was seldom encouraged to fly when sharing the floor with Jordan. The Pistons turned the Jordan miss into a fast-break layup, on their way to a 20-point rout. Things did not improve for Jordan in Boston, on the night of the final preseason game, when he shot 5–13. The Wizards' loss meant two defeats in the three Jordan preseason games, which compared unfavorably to the team's 4–2 record without him.

The new Wizards already had shown difficulties in playing with him. Collins privately worried about Larry Hughes's ability to fit in. With Jordan off the floor, the team galloped and Hughes frequently shined, at his best racing down the court on fast breaks and pulling up for jumpers, or driving to the hoop for short bankers and dunks. But Jordan's presence in a game meant the style of play changed, the team generally locked in the setup offense that Jordan preferred, leaving Hughes with few opportunities to exhibit his talents. He struggled in his role as a point guard, not nearly as adept a passer as more conventional point guards.

Collins loved to talk about synergy—a state where, in the coach's applied definition of the term, his team's performance would be greater than the sum of his players' individual talents. Actually, the Wizards were the antithesis of synergy. If anything, the key Wizards appeared diminished when playing together, like their energy was sucked out by a giant chunk of basketball kryptonite. Stackhouse looked at his best the greater his distance from Jordan, a trend that would persist throughout the season, especially when Jordan began games on the bench during the first month. Stackhouse had 36 points in the preseason loss to Boston, most of them with Jordan uninvolved, a judgment that Stackhouse did nothing to discourage, observing afterward to reporters that he and Jordan were "still learning [about] each other."

In a foreboding note at the end of training camp and the preseason games, Hughes said the team had not clicked. He tried his best to put a positive spin on the dilemma, telling reporters that the team had so much physical prowess that it likely could "get by on talent alone until we get on the same page together." He saw their talent prevailing over any difficulties: "If we do things halfway right, . . . we'll win games."

While supportive, Stackhouse did not sound nearly so confident. Quickly, he observed that he and Jordan had "contrasting" styles, as Stackhouse diplomatically put it, *contrasting* being a polite synonym in most moments for *conflicting*. He viewed himself, said Stack, as more of an "attack guy," while Jordan was a "set-up player." Sometimes Jordan and Collins wanted motion and schemes, while Stackhouse, believing he saw an opening to the basket, wanted "to go," he said, "to put the pressure on guys, take them off the dribble and beat 'em, or get out on the floor and attack the basket, because that's always been my strength."

Even Jordan acknowledged that his radical overhaul of the team presented new problems. A large crew of unfamiliar athletes had been brought together and asked to learn each other's playing preferences and idiosyncrasies in a few weeks. The Wizards had six new players, and three new starters—so many new permutations to consider that sometimes Jordan lost count of personnel numbers. "We've got seven, eight new players we have to adjust to," he said, forecasting that there would be periodic struggles with chemistry. Still, he said, he wasn't worried; it was early, he said. Never did he back down from his prediction that the Wizards would travel deep into the playoffs.

His confidence had the expected effect, especially on his media friends. A few of his more devout disciples, in an impressive display of fidelity, publicly prognosticated in their columns and broadcasts that the loosely cobbled team would make it to the Eastern Conference finals. It was proof, if nothing else, of Jordan's undiminished power to inspire and delude. Even as the season's disappointments would build, these believers would not abandon him, insisting until the last weeks that the turnaround might come.

It couldn't—not with a team so haphazardly constructed. As it fractured and players became uncertain about what they were allowed to do on the court, Jordan and his teammates would reprise the previous season's failure, with one meaningful difference. This time, people, including his own teammates, began losing patience with all that he had wrought—with the coach he chose, the offense he dictated, his heavy-handed treatment of young players, the insults, the presumption, his manifest self-absorption. And that is when simple failure became a disaster gathering momentum, like a flood washing out everything in its path.

This time, there would be no knee to blame. With Jordan finally having listened to reason and carefully abided by their advice, Tim Grover and Steve Stricker had him healthy and ready for a marathon season. He would play in all 82 regular season games—the first 15 as a reserve, and the last 67 as a starter. Unlike the first year, there would be no peaks or valleys for the Wizards, no real reason for intense excitement or despair, only a flatline mediocrity befitting a team in the NBA's second tier.

Like the rest of the league's chronic disappointments, the Wizards organization, with the assistance of the media, would hype the team's possibility of making the playoffs, though in a league where even losing clubs sometimes reached the postseason, a reasonable pair of questions seemed to be: Who should care? And what glory was to be found in limping into the playoffs and being bounced in an early round? The media's gushing now about a playoff possibility derived merely from Jordan's insistence that, given that the Wizards had made the playoffs only once in the previous 15 seasons, any playoff appearance would be proof that he and his crew had turned the franchise around. In truth, it would mean next to nothing. But if a sports superstar, with a legion of supportive media, pushes an idea long and hard enough, it becomes the standard. A mere playoff appearance therefore would constitute success in Washington.

But even this would not happen. The team would be 6–9 when, cast in the role of Savior, he reentered the starting lineup, after which the Wizards would compile a record of 31–36 with him as its front man. His return to the starting lineup improved the team's fortunes not at all. The Wizards' final record would be 37–45, identical to the first season of his comeback. From the time Jordan reclaimed his starting position to the season's end, the team never ascended higher than one game above the .500 mark, and was there for less than a week.

It is best to digest those numbers before contemplating anything more about that last season. To know the numbers is to realize that, in practical terms, the Wizards' chance of being a meaningful contender in the conference race ended early; that, thereafter, the season was a slow good-bye, as Jordan tried coming to grips with the end of his playing days while plotting his next move. The games had less meaning during that final season. What had more meaning was watching him try to accept what was happening to him—the losing, the betrayal of the storybook ending, the slow waning of the media's fascination with him as younger athletes like Kobe Bryant began seizing ever more attention, the blow to his image resulting from a lawsuit involving a former mistress whose silence he had sought to buy, his loss in the fans' balloting for a starter's position in the All-Star Game, the public backlash to his on-camera rages about teammates, his incredulity over having sparked so much alienation on a team and within an organization and, lastly, his befuddlement over how he had incurred the ire of Pollin, whose disaffection came, in a remarkable coincidence, with the drying up of the Jordan revenue stream.

The days would end for him as they had for Ruth and other assured gods—badly—climaxed by the owner's move against him, as sure and stealthy as a mob hit. The final season would be a study in how an athlete awakens to the understanding that, all along, there was an end to Shangri-la; that, from the beginning, it had been tied to how much money he could make others; that when the money stopped, so did the slavish deference. It would be a look at how segments of fans lose their rapt fascination for an athletic idol who, for all his successes, never built a lasting connection in the culture beyond his cultish idolaters. It would reveal what happens when that culture, like a small child, begins tiring of the exalted action hero. The year would hold a mirror up to him and, ultimately, us.

10

"They are probably the most fragile team I've ever been around . . ."

AT THE START OF THE NEW SEASON, INTEREST IN JORDAN AND the Wizards slackened among the Washington-area fan base. Sales of Wizards season tickets fell, according to a *Washington Post* report, from roughly 14,000 seats during the first season of his comeback to about 12,000 seats in his second. Twenty-four hours before the team's first home game against Boston, 1,200 tickets remained unsold, a Wizards publicist blaming the lagging sales on the game's Halloween date.

The Wizards' box office was not helped by what happened to the team on the season's opening night on October 30 in Toronto, where the Wizards lost 74–68, shooting a dreadful 30 percent, and tying a franchise-low for field goals. Coming off the bench in the first quarter, Jordan looked sluggish, hitting only 4 of 14 shots for eight points in 25 minutes. He had more difficulty than ever driving to the hoop, his first 12 shot attempts consisting solely of jumpers.

But it was his 13th attempt, with 3:30 left in a game not out of reach, which drew the most attention. Dribbling out in front of the pack, seemingly on his way to a breakaway dunk, he became conscious of a Toronto defender slightly behind him, guard Alvin Williams. He rose, but he had lifted skittishly and too soon, too low. Triggering memories of his All-Star embarrassment in Philadelphia, he badly missed the dunk, throwing the ball off the back rim, complaining to a ref that he had been brushed from behind. But nobody could see this, and no gift would be bestowed upon him on a night when he went scoreless in the second half, missing all six of his shot attempts. Stackhouse, whose 19 points belied his own struggles, later tossed up an air ball.

None of the Wizards stars played well. With Jordan on the court, Hughes looked tentative. Stackhouse seemed to be searching for space away from Jordan in which to operate. "We started to press a little bit . . ." Stackhouse told reporters. "We got tight with plays."

Jordan declared the game "pretty ugly." He brushed aside his missed dunk ("I exploded pretty good. Just wished I finished it . . ."), then dismissed any suggestion that his playing time would remain fixed for the foreseeable future at between 25 and 30 minutes a game, as Collins insisted. "No, that's just a starting point," Jordan declared, putting Collins on notice.

The 1,200 unsold tickets for the home opener remained on sale the next morning. A greater portent of trouble could be seen inside and around MCI that night. In pricier season ticket sections, large patches of empty seats signaled that well-heeled and corporate ticket holders thought they had something more exhilarating to do than attend a Wizards–Celtics game featuring Jordan. Outside the arena, ticket scalpers faced another tough night. At the beginning of Jordan's comeback, their business had been great—ordinary people happily paying $300 to $400 for a pair of floor seats, ready to shell out anything to see Jordan. It was what ticket sellers had dreamed about: big bucks every night, Jordan driving street sales up, up and out of sight—to be followed by obscene profits when the expected playoffs came.

But demand had been steadily slowing since the first season's midway point, a scalper pointed out. It was about the time when fans began showing up with extra tickets—a single ticket here, a pair of tickets there—tickets unused because excitement was ebbing. Most of the scalpers' tickets came from people with company season seats on or close to the floor, businessmen who arrived at the game with an extra ticket or two because they couldn't find enough colleagues who wanted to take in another Wizards game. "Look around the floor," the scalper said. "You'll see a lot of empty seats here and there—ones, twos. Not everyone's coming anymore."

It was like going back to the same popular Broadway play. As a few months passed and demand slackened at the same pace as a culture's fascination with the show, business went from pantingly hot to simply brisk, and from there slipped to merely very good. And there it would stay—solidly respectable—for a long while, because most people had bought their tickets long before—with season tickets now constituting more than 60 percent of all MCI seats in the Jordan era, and most of the remaining individual tickets purchased weeks in advance of games, a fact that generated a false sense of rabid interest. By midway into the first season, an eyeball assessment suggested that 10 to 20 percent of seats on the floor level went unoccupied on an ordinary night.

This hardly could have been more inevitable. After all, it was not a *team* that the new ticketholders had come to see but a man and his show, and having seen the spectacle a few times, they had no reason to hurry back. A Jordan game remained an *event*, but the event did not create the fervor that attached to fans' embrace of the area's football Redskins, or that partisans in any city felt toward a franchise with a hold on the city's passions—say, the old Bulls with the young Jordan. The Washington show was devoid of a deeply caring fan base, reflective of a cultish appeal, the same Jordanphiles and basketball addicts showing up, night after night, as the empties grew from ones and twos to threes and fours in places.

Even with those unfilled seats, the Wizards had announced the same sellout attendance figure every night during that first Jordan season: 20,674.

It was 20,674, whether you could see 100 empties, 500 empties or 2,000. It was always 20,674.

It was a powerful number, but seldom a real number. Something had changed, something hidden by 20,674, something steadily more noticeable in those empty seats on the floor, in the ones and twos. It explained why my 12-year-old son, holding a scalped ticket, could watch Michael Jordan from about ten rows off the floor for $20, with another empty, if purchased, $100 seat alongside him. The thrill of the high rollers and corporate set was wearing off.

By the start of the second season, at least a third of the arena was unoccupied at tipoff for the home opener. Even after all the fans had taken their seats, a solid 20 percent of the arena remained empty. The Wizards would again lead the league in home attendance, as affluent patrons bought most of the good and pricey season seats. But fewer of them were actually showing up.

It was merely more evidence that they were selling an act, not a team. As fans' fascination with the spectacle cooled, so, too, did their interest wane in Jordan the aging player—a reality evident in the tepid support for him in All-Star balloting. But nothing spoke louder about the absence of a connection than the growing number of empty seats around MCI—in many cases the seats of season ticket holders who had shelled out hundreds and, in some cases, thousands of dollars only to become blasé and turn elsewhere.

For Abe Pollin and Susan O'Malley, this meant needing—as in the pre-Jordan days—to find ways to sell tickets. Under O'Malley's authority, the Wizards marketing department, seizing upon the expectation that 2002–2003 would be Jordan's final season, soon unveiled the "Final Flight Plan"—an offer of tickets for six games, the purchase of which would guarantee the buyer free tickets to what was to be Jordan's final regular season home game, in April. Later, as the Wizards began gearing up to sell tickets for a future team not to include Jordan, the marketing department would extend the offer of free tickets for Jordan's last home game to anyone willing to purchase a package of tickets to games for the Jordanless Wizards, in the 2003–2004 season.

Privately, Jordan continued to express amazement at what O'Malley would do to make money off his name. That Pollin never countermanded O'Malley ensured that whatever the owner did for him would not be enough.

What Pollin gave him was nothing more or less than the praise the owner periodically showered upon other star players. Occasionally, after a victory at home, Pollin popped into the locker room to congratulate Jordan and his teammates. Jordan would usually still be in his uniform, sweaty, not yet having showered, anxious to get moving. Preceding Pollin, serving as the owner's advance man, Wes Unseld would arrive in the locker room, telling Jordan, Collins and others, "Mr. Pollin wants to come in and say hi." Always in public, and usually in private, Unseld referred to the owner as "Mr. Pollin." Jordan called him "Abe." It reflected the difference between a longtime executive who viewed himself as an employee and a star who regarded himself as an aspiring titan doing business with an established baron.

And here would come not merely Pollin but Pollin's small entourage toward Jordan, complete strangers in some cases who, as witnesses remembered, would stare at Jordan, almost wordlessly, as Pollin said to him and others, "I'm so proud of my team."

The gawking went on long enough, thought one witness, that it felt like the strangers were looking over Jordan the way excited visitors to a horse farm once admired Secretariat, happy and proud of themselves for having made it to this place where they could be up this close to a sight this spectacular—Michael Jordan in front of his locker. Jordan had told people that he didn't do the "show pony thing" for people, not for anyone, but when Pollin and his entourage appeared, he courteously gave them a few minutes, shaking hands, making small talk. It said much about his feelings toward the Pollin visits, however, that word of them leaked, particularly through those in the locker room who did not care for Pollin, believing his presence at Jordan's locker was an exercise in ego.

Momentarily finished with Jordan, the owner sought out coaches and other players. "I'm so proud of my team," he repeated. The line did not go over well in the locker room. It smacked of a rich man's paternalism to some of the inhabitants, rich themselves. Their reaction bespoke a reality: The players did not think of themselves as part of an *owner's* team, nor did they see Pollin as their leader or patriarch. Pollin was *just* an owner. It was *their* team, thought several players and at least one official inside. *They,* not he, did the running and sweating. He had little to do with their daily fight, and so they wished he would stop referring to the Wizards as *my team,* as if he had the most claim to it.

At the very least, the irritated official thought, Pollin should drop the *my* and substitute *our.* It was his organization, but it was *their team* and *their* locker room, *their* territory. They would have preferred that Pollin stay out of it, most of the time. He owned it, he owned everything inside the arena, but it was their sanctuary, and respect for their turf and privacy in the first few minutes after a game was due them. They needed time to relax, to come down from the war on the court, to congratulate or console one another. You *do not* come inside the players' and coaches' sanctuary, the official insisted, so why was it that Pollin did not understand this?

For an outsider, the attitude could be difficult to understand. Pollin owned the club, and so why should he not at least be welcomed inside a locker room whose stalls, uniforms, big-screen TV, medicines, trainers, clubhouse attendants, players and coaches his money had paid for? Why should he not gush about a team he owned and helped to build? But Pollin was the type of owner whom several players and the Wizards officials did not particularly care for. They loved winners, and he was not one. He was neither a money man deeply involved in the day-to-day details of making them better and happier, nor a money man who completely stayed out of the picture and left the team to be run by executives experienced in basketball.

Instead, Pollin fell between those two types, a man who did not invest as heavily as other NBA owners in his team but who wanted to be closely identified with it. A few players much liked what they had heard of Dallas's Mark Cuban, who, besides tapping into his fortune to pay huge salaries, heavily invested in new facilities and perks for his players. Absent a Mark Cuban, the disgruntled Wizards official said he would not have minded working for someone like Chicago's Jerry Reinsdorf, who was regarded as someone who largely kept his distance from the Bulls' basketball operations during the team's glory days. Reinsdorf owned the Chicago White Sox, too, and there existed a deep feeling in Chicago that he was far more passionate about the White Sox than the Bulls, that he would have exchanged nearly all his Bulls championships for just one World Series title. People who worked in basketball did not mind such an attitude. They much preferred a businessman who stayed out of their way and did not need anyone's reflected glory, over someone like Pollin, who seemed to them to talk of *my team* too much.

Pollin built the team, such as it was, from next to nothing. His organization was not thought to be a great NBA franchise, it was not thought to be even a very good franchise, but Pollin saw it as solid, and improving all the time. "So proud," he'd say to Jordan and the rest of his players. One night, as Pollin walked back to Jordan's locker, ready to schmooze a little longer, he found it empty. Jordan had grabbed his clothes and headed for the showers—not rudely, thought the observing official, but only because it seemed that Pollin and his entourage had finished with him for the evening. Pollin was unbothered, ecstatic over his team's win. "Michael was great, *great*," he told somebody. It was a reference to the on-court performance of Michael Jordan, the player.

Even with his skills declining, no player could possibly have loved more the simple act of getting ready to compete. Anyone wishing to prepare for any professional task in life would have been well advised to watch Jordan during warm-ups. Most players gabbed like kids and desultorily shot jumpers. Jordan had rituals that no distraction could penetrate, his free-throw practice looking just as it would in the game: He bounced the ball twice on the floor, aligned its seams, threw it underhand about a foot straight up in the air with enough reverse spin that you could see the seams twirling, caught it, jiggled it slightly, bent his knees, looked down, raised his head, then lifted his arms slowly and shot, always with perfect rotation, the ball's seams in symmetry—never a knuckleball.

If a teammate's practice shot caromed weirdly and headed toward him, he merely raised his own basketball and coolly ponged it. Then he resumed his shooting. He did it in a practiced solitude, no matter that thousands stared and the world around him seemed unable to be still. A couple of teammates roughhoused close by. The miniature blimp hovered 20 feet over his head. Cheryl Miller, the former basketball star and now a television commentator, yelled his name from the baseline, trying to get his attention. He gave no sign of perceiving anything but the rim. Bounce, bounce, spin, catch, bend, shoot. He did it 12 times. Then he lifted his head, blinked, heard Miller's shout, smiled, walked over to her and exchanged kisses on the cheeks.

On this night of the Wizards' home opener, he had listened to the anthem and taken a seat on the bench, his new ritual. Stepping onto the floor about six minutes into the game, he had a big night, scoring 21 points in 21 minutes, while Stackhouse added 22 points and 10 assists. The Wizards annihilated Boston and won by 45, the worst loss in Celtics franchise history, and predictably, the media and nearly everyone else made too much of it. The Celtics had come into the game woefully tired, their two stars, Paul Pierce and Antoine Walker, having logged 40 and 42 minutes, respectively, in a game just the night before.

Just the same, Jordan looked smooth and efficient, showing no signs of knee problems, his greatest cause for irritation coming late in the third quarter, when the Celtics dispatched a 6' 1" rookie named J. R. Bremer to try guarding him while Pierce stuck to defending Stackhouse. Did this suggest that the Celtics thought the Wizards had a new primary threat in Stackhouse, that Jordan had become number two?

As if to punish his foes' impudence, Jordan immediately hit two jumpers over the undersized Bremer. Afterward, the Wizards' leading scorer joked about the apparent new order to things. "You can't disrespect the Godfather like that," a grinning Stackhouse said of the Celtics' decision to place Bremer on Jordan.

Everybody smiled on this night. Bryon Russell had played sensational defense, helping to shut down the weary Pierce, limiting him to 16 points, on 3–16 shooting. The Wizards dominated every rebounding statistic, and overwhelmed the Celtics in fast-break points. Collins never had sounded more impressed. "That's as good as I've ever had a team play," he said, attributing much of the success to the Wizards' rarely employed running game. "[Before the game] I told the guys: We got to run the floor. . . . I didn't want to get in a half-court game [with Boston] . . ."

Players wanted to celebrate, whispering into cell phones, making plans. Lue hurried out, speeding off in his silver Mercedes. In a hallway, Jordan aides waited for the boss. George Koehler muttered into a phone, "Yeah, yeah, we'll see you there or at Café Milano. No, no. He feels *good*."

And Jordan did. No stim treatment. No shuffle. He was reasonably happy: His teammates had looked good. It was only the second game of the year, but never would the team's mood be as bright again that season. He talked with pleasure about Kwame Brown, who had played the best games of his career on back-to-back nights. Having pulled down a stunning 18 rebounds and blocked five shots just the night before in Toronto, Brown hit 8 of 12 shots, scored 20 points and blocked six shots against Boston, playing every bit like a first pick in the NBA draft might be projected to perform at some point in his second season. "I think [Brown] is relieved, I'm relieved, everybody is relieved . . ." Jordan said, then delivered a warning. "The thing he's gonna have to deal with is it's expected every night. So you gotta be ready to do it *every single night . . .*" Coming on a little heavy, Jordan ratcheted back, concluding on a cheerier note. "If we can get that consistent play from him, he's infectious to everybody. Everybody feeds off things like that."

Aside from Jordan and Stackhouse, no Wizard received as much attention as Brown, who received questions aimed at trying to discover how he had emerged from his hellhole. At 20 now, he wasn't the same kid who had amiably, if hesitantly, answered reporters' questions a season earlier. The ridicule and doubts had chipped away at him, leaving an edge. "I'm a year older . . ." Brown icily said to a reporter. "I bet you weren't the best at your job in your first year."

The same people kept making the same mistakes around him. Even after two games in which Brown had put up All-Star numbers, a smiling Collins called him "stubborn." "Kwame—and I say this with great affection—he's stubborn now . . ." Collins said. "In all seriousness, there's a stubborn streak in him that is good from the standpoint of—" Collins paused, floundering already, uncertain where he was going with this on Kwame's big night. Good from the standpoint of *what?* "You know, the last year, he fought a lot of things . . ."

It was Collins's way of building bridges.

But, even as Wizards officials privately talked of Brown arriving at training camp overweight and out of shape, Brown had demonstrated improvement. Then his play began sliding again, first slowly, then with a rush that left Jordan and Wizards officials more frustrated than ever. Only two weeks after the Boston game, he sunk to a two-point, three-rebound performance against Utah, and Collins had to yank him after 21 minutes.

He already had his own NBA playing history: big games early, followed by a fall that could not be broken. A school of thought had formed that perhaps he had an innate problem with endurance that extended beyond his lack of conditioning. His motivation, or lack of it, still baffled coaches. Although he showed flashes of *something,* running the court and rebounding better than a year earlier, he didn't seem to be adding any new dimension to his play—no offensive moves, especially.

The awful feeling began taking hold again that perhaps Jordan and the brass had blown the number one pick in the draft; that, if Kwame didn't improve relatively soon, the pressure would mount to get rid of him in exchange for whatever the market would bear for a high-risk project player. Maybe, coaches told one another, he could still become the next Jermaine O'Neal. But it seemed just as likely at that moment that they had deluded themselves, a year and a half earlier; that what they had here was a callow kid short on desire and talent. Not a bad kid. Just a kid. A man-child overrated and pushed too soon. And so, in the NBA's mind-set, maybe a lemon.

What made the pain worse was the knowledge that, in romancing Brown, Jordan and his staff had passed on an opportunity to pursue other young players already in the league, notably Elton Brand and All-Star Shareef Abdur-Rahim. The Wizards' basketball executives and scouts—all handpicked or approved by Jordan—had looked at other ballyhooed high school players about Brown's age but they had overlooked more experienced talent, particularly Spain's nimble, long-armed, seven-foot Pau Gasol, the 21-year-old forward who would become the NBA's Rookie of the Year. Jordan had been smitten by Brown.

The top man, his brass and the scouting staff settled on either examining the new rage—American high school players—or, in 2002, opting for the safest picks—well-known college stars from big-name schools. They were players whom any group of weekend Fantasy League executives could have picked, the kind of selections that freed a scouting staff, and the top man himself, from having to beat the bushes in search of a gem from a small school. For all of Jordan's mocking of Jerry Krause, at least Crumbs had traveled and probed enough to consider a little-known kid out of Central Arkansas, Scottie Pippen.

The choices of Jordan's crew prior to the last of his comeback seasons reflected a new caution. Burned by their experience with Kwame Brown, the unofficial top man and his staff drafted likable, earnest players who had virtually no chance for greatness on a professional level, only a serviceable reliability at best. Each was a major college star whose skills simply did not translate well enough to the pro game to make them superb NBA players. Even after overcoming injuries, Jared Jeffries, a thin but agile 6'11" forward drafted out of Indiana after his sophomore year, would neither look strong nor quick enough to stand out among the league's best players. Hardworking Juan Dixon, an All-American shooting guard on an NCAA championship team at Maryland (located nearby, which ensured he would be a popular selection) did everything winningly at the college level, but nothing well enough for the NBA—neither skilled enough as a ball handler to play point guard nor quick enough generally to free himself for jumpers or drives. Renowned for his steals in college, he often found himself beaten off the dribble in the pros. The latest two draft choices of the Jordan crew would do nothing to improve the team's prospects.

Jordan had skillfully presided over one major task during his executive days, unloading those fat contracts of underproducing Wizards veterans. Otherwise, his record as the Wizards' official and unofficial leader was characterized by missteps, and a preference for favoring friends over fresh faces. The pattern extended into his front office, for which he had hired two of his longtime friends, Rod Higgins and Fred Whitfield. Higgins had played with Jordan in Chicago, later to be an assistant coach and an official in the Golden State front office. Whitfield had no prior NBA experience, a longtime Jordan buddy who had worked at Nike, negotiating deals with NBA players looking for endorsement contracts with the shoe company. Higgins served as the Wizards' assistant manager, and Whitfield as the director of player personnel, charged with, among other things, understanding the salary cap and closely advising Jordan whenever it came to such matters as how best to unload fat contracts.

The two subordinates were adequate, simply not great, like the rest of Jordan's basketball operation, which had nothing to show for an abundance of player signings and transactions. The culture of cronyism extended to the hiring of Collins and even the acquisition of a player in 2002. Jordan wanted the Wizards to sign his longtime friend and old teammate Charles Oakley, who, in early 2002, had made clear he would not be signing again with the Bulls. Oakley would turn 39 in the first half of the new season, a 6'9" power forward whose production and playing time had steeply declined during the previous year. But Jordan had fond memories of his off-court days with Oakley, and how Oak had served as his on-court bodyguard. The Wizards signed Oakley.

The move illustrated the cross-purposes at which top Wizards officials worked. Collins did not have plans to play Oakley often. With the organization having decided against re-signing Popeye Jones, Collins preferred to take a chance on younger frontline players like Brown, Haywood and Etan Thomas, having concluded that, at nearly 39, Oakley could not endure heavy playing time. In lieu of giving Oakley many minutes, Collins flattered him, praising his work as a tutor for Brown. It was a human relations strategy destined to blow up, for a simmering Oakley had come to Washington to play. Collins went to him at the start of the season and tried to assuage his irritation. "Oak, I don't know when your number is going to be called, but you always gotta be ready for me," Collins said. "That's why you're here. And I want you to be a player. You're not here just to be a cheerleader. You're going to play."

"A guy who has been great for Kwame is Charles Oakley," a smiling Collins told the press, after not playing Oakley at all in the home opener. "I told Oak, 'You can do more for that guy than I ever could.'"

Oakley projected an agreeable calm early, aiding new assistant coach, Patrick Ewing, in working with the team's young big men. But with time, he became increasingly perturbed. He tried remaining publicly positive while sending a notice. "I think I can help the team, and I didn't come here to sit," Oakley said. "And I don't think they brought me here to sit. I'm ready. I'm a ready veteran who's gonna do anything to help. Sometimes you ask yourself . . ." His words trailed off.

Jordan had lured him, only now he had no real place for him. It was a reflection of sloppy planning everywhere. The off-season jettisoning of veterans Jones, Chris Whitney and Hubert Davis had left a critical vacuum in veteran leadership that would go unfilled.

Things got worse. The new combinations of pieces did not fit. Jordan didn't think his teammates passed him the ball enough, particularly their new point guard, Larry Hughes. And Jordan believed he himself wasn't receiving enough playing time. He wanted the problems remedied. Remedied meant immediately. He decided to pay Collins a visit.

He'd experienced a rough first 10 days by the time he reached Collins's office. He had discovered the difficulty of functioning as a reserve, of coming off the bench cold when everyone expected him to be hot, complaining about needing time to get loose, the reserve's lament. He went 5–14 for only 10 points, in a loss at Minnesota, where Stackhouse had a productive 25 points and the Wizards blew a nine-point lead during a fourth quarter in which they shot only *nine* percent.

It grew tougher the next night for him, though not for the team, which won back at home against abysmal Cleveland, with Stackhouse playing spectacularly, scoring 35 points. Hurtling toward the hoop and knocking foes around, the new Wizards star made bank shots, scoops and dunks against a variety of Cleveland defenders, and when the defenders played off him, leery about being beaten inside, he hit a series of jumpers. He made 9 of 16 shots, had three steals and looked like the prospective megastar again.

Meanwhile, Jordan went scoreless through three quarters.

Along the way, a pair of Cleveland defenders, like pickpockets, stole the ball off his dribble, so coolly that for an instant it seemed Jordan didn't know what had happened. He finished with six points on only 2–6 shooting, the numbers of a suffering benchwarmer. Afterward, virtually all the talk was of Stackhouse. Adrian Dantley, a former NBA star who served as an analyst on Wizards telecasts, excitedly said, "They won the game *without Mike.* Mike was really not a factor. . . . Stack is going to walk away with a lot of MVP games. *He's the Man."*

Collins sounded equally enamored of Stackhouse: "He's *fearless.* That's why I've always loved Jerry Stackhouse. He will attack the rim, he will put his body in there, he'll get knocked down. . . . He gives us a tone that we desperately need."

Trying to spread a little love, Collins segued eventually to Jordan, praising his "great passes. He kept us organized. . . . And that frees Jerry up to do what he does . . ."

Suddenly, Collins saw Jordan as a "quarterback," a distributor of the ball. As in the days when he tried to get Jordan to stop holding the ball by telling his other players that they had to pass more, his spiel sounded designed to plant and reinforce suggestions. "Michael can be a facilitator for us with his brilliance. . . ." he said. "A basketball genius. . . . And what I would like him to do, without having to handle the ball that much off the dribble, is to be able to get the ball in spots where he can be the quarterback."

Jordan was subdued. Somebody asked him what it felt like to be a "facilitator."

"When the time comes, or it presents itself, and Doug asks me, then

I'll step my offense up," he said slowly, his baritone deeper than ever. "But right now, we got good rhythm with Jerry and the way he's playin', and we'll feed off that."

"Last question, guys," the Wizards p.r. guy said.

"No more," Jordan said.

On the evening of their next game, he entered Collins's office and told him what he didn't like.

Collins accepted the blame for not getting the ball to him enough. He assured Jordan that he would make sure his teammates did a better job of feeding him down in the post, from where he could shoot his fallaways.

Playing against a Laker team missing the injured Shaquille O'Neal, Jordan had a fine game, hitting 9 of 14 shots for 25 points in a season-high 30 minutes. But others were the big stars—particularly Kobe Bryant, who had 27, and Stackhouse, who had 29, including the most important hoop of the evening. A three-pointer by the Lakers' Robert Horry had given the Lakers a one-point advantage with 2.9 seconds left, when the Wizards called time-out to set up an out-of-bounds play.

Collins called for Stackhouse to take the last shot.

The ball wouldn't be placed in Jordan's hands at all. Nobody along the bench, not even the old Chicago people like Bach and Oakley, could ever remember that happening. Jordan, who would be guarded by Bryant, would serve as a decoy.

Collins diagrammed the play. Stackhouse would inbound the ball along the left sideline to Russell, who would immediately toss it back to Stackhouse, setting just enough of a screen against Stackhouse's defender that Stack could hopefully break for the rim along the left side and get a layup, dunk or a short bank shot.

Two-point-nine seconds, Collins told everybody, was plenty of time to get to the rim and either score or get fouled. Jordan would stand in the lane just before the ball was inbounded, then dart toward his right, hopefully luring Bryant and clearing out the left side for Stackhouse.

Jordan said nothing.

The moment encapsulated both the coach's and his new star's chief strengths—Collins's aptitude for drawing up a quick play, and Stackhouse's gift for bursting to a basket and beating somebody one-on-one.

Everything worked. Stackhouse fed the ball to Russell and received a return pass while Russell set the slightest of screens on the Lakers' Devean George, who received no defensive help. Stackhouse dunked at the buzzer for the victory. MCI exploded. Kobe Bryant was furious. Jordan was quiet. His teammates pounded Stackhouse's shoulders.

Almost immediately, the focus turned from the win to questions about how it was that Stackhouse received the ball at the end of the game.

Was the last play really designed for Stackhouse? somebody asked Collins.

"Yes . . ."

Why not go to Michael?

"I mean, I got two great players," Collins reasonably answered. "I shouldn't have to make excuses when we win."

Stackhouse sounded relaxed. "This is the kind of thing that could catapult us to some really good things . . ." He complimented Collins on isolating the court for him. "Doug drew up a good play to kind of get everybody to go to the other side of the court, and I had an opportunity to get free."

Jordan had his own view of the play. "Doug drew it up, and it worked perfectly, in terms of me being the decoy and everybody focusing on me."

He wanted people to remember the indispensability of his aura on that last play. "I'm going to take more [of the opponent's] attention. . . . If you look—everybody is looking at me, as if I'm an option. . . . [It] was easy to get an easy layup."

The next night, in Cleveland, the Wizards won by 14, improving their record to 4–3, and Stackhouse led all scorers with 27 while gathering a team-high nine rebounds. The game climaxed a great opening run for Stackhouse, whom the NBA selected as the Eastern Conference's Player of the Week. No one could have known that his best days of the season were already behind him.

As Jordan's minutes steadily increased and he inched closer to taking back what he wanted, both he and Stackhouse were plagued by bouts of erratic play, wild swings during a string of losses in which each player would score in the high 20s on some nights and in single-digits on others. Stackhouse suddenly could not make a jumper. "There's a lot happening," he muttered. "A lot of new adjustments to make."

Jordan said nothing critical about Stackhouse's performances, and that alone made their relationship different from Jordan's dealings with other players. He continued losing confidence in Larry Hughes, finally going to the new point guard and telling him that he had to do a better job of getting him the ball. If he didn't get him the ball enough, he would be on the bench.

With the team's three offensive threats struggling, the club made no headway in the Eastern Conference playoff race. Jordan had simultaneously run out of patience with his playing status and the team's performance. After Hughes had only two points and Stackhouse went 4–19 with only nine points in a loss at Memphis, Jordan told the media that it might be time for him to play considerably more.

Collins publicly surrendered. "I've tried to keep my eye on [Jordan's minutes]," he said. "But I don't think Michael wants me to keep my eye on that. Michael feels he is strong enough to do these things. All the eyes are on me about the minutes, but I have to trust him. It's his body, and he knows what he can and cannot do."

On Thanksgiving Day, Jordan announced that the season would be his last as a player, finding the precise words that he thought would free everyone from worrying about his body, declaring he had *no future* as a player. He would play out the season, he told reporters, and return to Wizards management. "I think we have the right [players] in place," Jordan said. "They will continue with their education when I go back upstairs."

The team lost its fifth in a row the next night in Indiana, sinking to 6–9. Afterward, Jordan told Collins that his role as a reserve had ended, that he wanted to be returned to the starting lineup immediately. He became the starting shooting guard the following night at home against Philadelphia, taking the place of Jerry Stackhouse, who, in turn, took the small-forward position of Bryon Russell.

Stackhouse had a luminous evening, scoring a season-high 38 points. Jordan added 16 points, hitting 8–20 shots in a season-high 37 minutes. To look at the scoring lines of the Wizards' two stars—a combined 54 points from the duo—suggested a big night for Washington, especially since Juan Dixon had come off the bench to score an unexpected 18.

But the Wizards had only four fast-break points to Philadelphia's 23. In their two games before Jordan's return as a starter, they had averaged more than 15 fast-break points, with the team frequently piling up fast-break points in the high teens and low 20s. That statistic meant nothing now: the team did not run with Jordan on the floor. If Jordan wanted to slow down, Stackhouse and others complied.

Such deference made for cordial relations between the two stars, but it also made for two games within a game, two styles of disjointed play, the way an All-Star Game feels. The individual statistics of the two stars were glittering, but the whole was less than the sum of the parts. Philadelphia's 19-point advantage in fast-break points meant the visitors enjoyed a one-point lead with less than 10 seconds to play. Then Jordan blocked an Allen Iverson shot. Washington had the ball. The Wizards called time-out with 5.4 seconds left.

Collins diagrammed another last-second inbounds play. The coach ordered that the ball go to an isolated Jordan around the top of the key. Jordan, who would be guarded by Aaron McKie, would either drive to the basket or shoot a pull-up jumper. If Philly double-teamed him, he would pass outside to Stackhouse.

The play looked stymied from the beginning. Jordan drove from the top of the key down the left side, hoping at least to be fouled, only to be cut off and double-teamed by the Sixers' Keith Van Horn. Down to three seconds now. Jordan went up in the air, with Van Horn so high above him that a block was certain if he tried to shoot. He attempted a pass to Russell underneath the basket. The ball was tipped, Van Horn reaching for it as the horn ended the game. The Wizards had lost six straight, to fall to 6–10. They scored 94 points, their two stars having combined to shoot better than 50 percent, and they were still losers. The game, serving as a microcosm of the season, bore lessons. All-Stars do not make teams. Gods do not necessarily fare well when coupled with aspiring gods.

Walking off the court, Jordan mumbled disgustedly to himself. Later, he told his teammates, *You cannot NOT get a shot in that situation.*

No one uttered that he was the one who did not get off the shot.

"We made a lot of dumb mistakes," Jordan said to the scrum.

It was a display of pique to be oft repeated. He had entered the starting lineup with the team three games under .500, the same spot in which it found itself, 10 evenings later, in early December. Then came the first of his many memorable insults that season. After a blowout loss at home to Portland, a team graced by Scottie Pippen, Jordan found himself being prodded by questions that he interpreted as suggesting that Pippen finally had bested him. His pride kicked in. "His horses were ready," Jordan said, in dismissive distillation, "and my mules were sick."

Almost always in his adult life, he had restrained himself when the cameras rolled. His composure broke more often now, an anger growing in direct proportion to the pressure mounting on both the professional and personal fronts. In late October, he had filed a lawsuit in Cook County, Illinois, against his former mistress Karla Knafel, alleging she was trying to extort $5 million from him—$5 million being the exact sum that, according to Knafel, Jordan owed her as part of an oral agreement, in the early '90s, that had called for her not to publicly reveal their sexual relationship or to file a paternity suit against him, as she was pregnant at the time with a child that turned out not to be Jordan's. In his suit, Jordan acknowledged paying Knafel $250,000 to keep quiet about their affair. A famous man, with an image to protect, had worried about a secret, and tried buying somebody off. Now he asked that she be prohibited from seeking any more money from him.

Jordan declined comment about his lawsuit, other than to say one day during the preseason, "That's private. That's totally private."

No one in the media asked him about the subject for a month. Then Knafel filed a countersuit against him in late November, asking the Cook County court for enforcement of the alleged oral agreement, including the $5 million payment. The odds of Knafel legally prevailing were slim. Even if she could prove that Jordan made such a promise (it would be her word against his), Jordan's attorney might point to several court decisions outside of Illinois that had declared such hush-money agreements unenforceable, and powerfully argue that Illinois courts should follow the same path.

But Knafel's countersuit presented a public relations mess for Jordan. Her suit offered details of their relationship from its origins, in the spring of 1989. Allegedly, NBA referee Eddie F. Rush met Knafel on an evening when she performed as a singer in an Indianapolis hotel, and that same night introduced her over the telephone to Jordan, raising the question of the nature of the relationship between a league ref and the NBA's most famous player, particularly whether the ref was doing some friendly pimping for the player that might leave his objectivity about Jordan forever compromised. Otherwise, the alleged details sounded unremarkable, as NBA affairs go. The star and the aspiring singer saw each other infrequently over the next two years, perhaps together on no more than six occasions, according to sources close to Knafel. But their relationship continued even after he married. In Phoenix, they dined together, had sex and went go-carting, according to her story, which included accounts of how she occasionally accompanied him in public—once to a commercial shoot.

Casual seemed the best characterization of their affair. Knafel had no expectations that he would be monogamous, as she wasn't. But that hardly was relevant to the impact that her suit and story might have on Jordan's stature. Knafel's attorneys had a photo of their client and Jordan together on a bed—a picture taken, they claimed, in a Phoenix hotel room. Everything that the Jordan attorneys and publicists had hoped to keep private was breaking publicly, including information that the two sides supposedly engaged in settlement talks that had broken off.

It was about the time that pundits—his defenders and detractors—began assigning dueling adjectives like "great" and "disillusioning" to Jordan, when neither of those words really fit. If he were a literary character, he wouldn't have been a god but more like John Updike's former basketball star and aging dreamer Rabbit Angstrom—glib, kind of charming, always believing it will happen for him, looking for the next gamble, and gripped by a wanderlust he hadn't yet come to terms with. The disdain for Jordan's extramarital mischief in particular always missed the point. He never displayed a sordid character in the relative sense of that term (how many Americans engage in adultery, after all?), but simply an ordinary character—ordinary in his cravings, ordinary in his failings, ordinary like many American males who have belittled their work associates, or sniped from the shadows at the big boss running the operation, or manipulated underlings, or had affairs, or neglected the people closest to them, or left wives and children at long stretches to gamble and golf. Ordinary.

However, from the beginning, ordinary would never do, not for a commercial god whose image and words would sell an estimated $2 billion worth of goods during his career. You needed an image transcendent for that, something mythic, and his partners had seen that this happened. It was a certainty that, at some point, a portion of the media would scrutinize the image—which is what made the Karla Knafel episode potentially so dangerous to his image and marketing appeal, and much of why he had tried to buy her silence in the first place. So what once had been simply ordinary now sounded cynical and manipulative, raising further questions about him.

In Wizards country, it was taboo to ask about Knafel. Two days after the filing of Knafel's countersuit, a television camera crew came to MCI after a practice on November 21, approaching Jordan for a comment about Knafel's move. As usual, Jordan wore something from his Jordan Brand wardrobe for the cameras—on this day, a Carolina–blue and white letterman's jacket with a big *J* on it, and his tall Carolina blue fez-like hat.

Jordan decided against talking, hurriedly striding down an MCI hallway alongside a woman from the Wizards' p.r. department, the camera crew following, filming.

A man from the crew asked him, "Any comment at all? On the lawsuit?"

"Nothing," interjected the p.r. woman.

The TV man repeated his question.

Jordan angrily tried shooing him away: "Come on, dude. Come on, man. Come on now. My goodness. Why don't you come here every day? Don't just come here yesterday or today. Come here every day. Then I give you respect."

It was instinct now for much of sports media to back off or downplay sensitive stories involving Jordan, or risk becoming a pariah. His publicist already had told me that I would not be receiving any more one-on-one sit-down interviews with Jordan (though no other print journalist in the country received one either). By the winter of Jordan's second season, I was regarded as a troublemaker, a reality that his publicist made no effort to hide. I'd already written about his sway over Doug Collins. I'd revealed that he called Kwame Brown a faggot. I'd reported on his belittling of teammates, and the roots of his failed relationship with Richard Hamilton. I'd written about his gambling night in Uncasville, Connecticut, and the closed practices in violation of league rules. And he knew I would eventually be writing about the Knafel matter, as I'd been asking people about it. In short, I'd seriously gotten myself on his bad side. If journalists wanted to know the risk of being in such a place, they needed only to look at what had happened years earlier to no less august a publication than *Sports Illustrated*.

After he retired from basketball for the first time, and went off to hit about .200 for the Double-A Birmingham Barons in the Chicago White Sox organization, *Sports Illustrated* ran an article positing that he and the White Sox were embarrassing baseball. It would be part of just one out of 52 cover stories that the magazine ran on Jordan by 2003, the vast majority of which were flattering, a few even worshipful. But anybody wanting to know what Jordan expected from the media needed only to watch the respected *Sports Illustrated* writer Jack McCallum approach him after a game, during the second comeback season.

McCallum, whom Jordan liked and who'd had nothing to do with the baseball article, hoped for a personal interview to be woven into a prospective story about Jordan's 40th birthday, in February 2003. He broached the idea to Jordan alongside a wall leading out of the locker room.

"Yeah, my girl told me about it," Jordan said, glancing up at the ceiling. "I don't think it's gonna happen."

You're not going to talk to me, McCallum said.

"I talked to you," Jordan said, looking down at him and rubbing the top of McCallum's head. What clasping elbows and shoulders had become for Bill Clinton, rubbing heads was for Jordan. "I talked to you. I still love you. I still love you; I just don't love your magazine."

McCallum allowed as to how this had been going on a long time.

Now Jordan smiled through pursed lips. There would be no story for *Sports Illustrated*. He looked at McCallum and then turned his head toward a writer along the wall whose presence had come to irk him, glancing at me for a couple of seconds. He looked back at McCallum, then quickly eyed me again, raising his voice slightly. "I carry grudges."

I can't say I was surprised.

What surprised me, however, was something a *Washington Post* colleague said to me, a few months earlier: "I hear Mike Wilbon isn't talking to you. It's in a magazine. It says he won't talk to you."

Michael Wilbon is a sports columnist at the *Post,* as well as an acquaintance and admirer of Jordan. David Falk happily described him, with tape recorders running, as "our buddy."

The colleague showed me the line in the magazine that said Mike Wilbon was not speaking to me. It was along the lines of this: Sources say Wilbon won't talk to Leahy.

I decided to let the thing blow over. But something happened at the end of the first comeback season that seemed destined to make things nastier. An article appeared in *City Paper,* the alternative Washington weekly, which contrasted a story I'd written about Jordan to Wilbon's years of columns about Jordan.

A section of the article was certain to leave bad feelings. The reviewer began by quoting portions of Wilbon's columns about Jordan, including this Wilbon passage about the start of the 2001–2002 season's training camp: "There was one important thing you could feel on the practice court even after Jordan left the court: energy. Make that two things: energy and hope."

Then the reviewer put Wilbon on the horns of a dilemma, by basically asking what his much-touted relationship with Jordan had delivered for his readers. What had Wilbon gotten for all his presumed connections within the NBA and the Jordan camp? Why did he so seldom seem to turn up anything revealing about Jordan? Why had he not uncovered and/or written about any of the matters that appeared in my story?

In brushing aside the criticism, Wilbon told the *City Paper* that he disagreed with much that I'd written about Jordan. Fair enough. I kept quiet, not wanting a public spat with a *Post* colleague. Less than a year later, during a *Post* online chat with readers, Wilbon publicly said that he didn't care to read anything I wrote on the subject of professional basketball (this meant Jordan, as I'd never written about any NBA subject other than Jordan). The dustup felt like something from junior high, but it was out there now. I felt free to reply.

All along, I thought that Wilbon's treatment of Jordan highlighted the basic danger in getting too cozy with a subject. Many sportswriters believe they have something special merely because they have a *relationship* with an athlete, and therefore access. That access lends a certain cachet; they can tell their friends and colleagues that they have the athlete's private cell-phone number and can get him on the phone when big stories break. But what sportswriters in that situation never tell their readers is that their access lasts only as long as their cooperation does, that at the moment the latter is called into question by the athlete, their access wanes or ends altogether. If the journalist ceases to be malleable or ever writes anything deeply critical about his athlete, their relationship dies.

That wasn't going to happen here: Wilbon always could be relied upon to provide the steadfast Jordan defense and generally trumpet the latest wave of Jordan optimism. Embracing Jordan's vision during the last comeback season, Wilbon predicted that the Wizards would reach the finals of the Eastern Conference playoffs. He would keep that cell-phone number.

But what did such conditional access yield for him? Such a sportswriter relied on Jordan to be his chief source about Jordan. That arrangement could only favor the star, who now had a conduit for whatever message he wanted to deliver to the Wizards, the league and the public. If things ever were to get bad for Jordan with Pollin (and things would, of course), then he could get on the phone with Wilbon and deliver a rebuttal. It was as if, in that moment, the athlete had his own column.

And that is when sports columnizing about a figure like Jordan becomes celebrity journalism, an exercise in giving the deified celebrity-athlete a forum to say whatever he wishes, and making it sound noble. The arrangement has been around as long as the sportswriting profession. It was the way of many sportswriters during the first half of the 20th century, and Hedda Hopper, too. It was part of the basic compact between sports businesses and sportswriters. It is why, historically, sportswriting has given us but half stories about too many celebrated athletes, until long after the athletes' departures from the games and sometimes from life. Joe DiMaggio was a half-story during his career. Babe Ruth, too. And Marciano, Louis and Mantle. The problem with being so cozy to a Jordan is that the basic compact is always in place. And it is a short fall from being a sportswriter to an adjunct publicist.

So I found myself alone in Washington in writing about such things as hush money and Jordan calling Kwame Brown a faggot. It was like being a castaway.

Amid the bright hopes for the Jordan-Stackhouse coupling, the Wizards went 8–7 in December, which brought their record at the close of the calendar year to 14–17. The most painful loss in that span came at home, the day after Christmas, when the team faced Detroit, the occasion marking Richard Hamilton's return to MCI. Jordan already had taken a veiled swipe at Hamilton, talking about how the Wizards finally had found someone capable of guarding a strong guard like Kobe Bryant, that the team had suffered in that same matchup a season earlier. "Last year, in L.A., when [Bryant] got that [intensity], he took over the game," Jordan said. "We made it a point that it wouldn't happen this year. We got someone who, I think, can definitely challenge him, and that's Stack and B-Russell."

Hamilton and Jordan matched up against each other for a part of the game, with Hamilton winning their personal and statistical battle, scoring 22 to Jordan's 17 and outplaying him through key stretches of the second half. Ben Wallace, another ex-Wizard who had found success in Detroit, blocked a Jordan shot in a critical moment. The Wizards led at the end of three quarters, then unraveled in the game's final minutes. Jordan had four turnovers in the fourth quarter alone. The last two were the most costly. First, he had the ball slapped away by Pistons defender Michael Curry, unable to retrieve it in time to shoot before the shot clock expired. Then with 15 seconds left in the game, trailing by three and battling Curry's tight defense, he dribbled the ball off Curry's foot. Lue dived for it and somehow got it back to Jordan, who was promptly stripped again, the theft leading to a Pistons dunk, wrapping up the game.

"We went dead in the water," Collins said. "And when our team does that, I can't bring them out of it. I can't do it."

Hamilton whooped going off the court, ecstatic in the visitors' locker room. He looked as though the Pistons had won a Game Seven. Someone asked him how he felt when Jordan lost the ball during the Wizards' final possession. "Oh, *happy*," Hamilton said. "You know, happy. I couldn't feel anything better than that. M.C. [Michael Curry] played great defense on him. He turned the ball over, and we pulled it out."

Did he feel vindicated?

He rubbed a towel slowly over his FOR THE LOVE OF THE GAME chest tattoo, as if burnishing it. "Uhhh, I can't really call it *revenge*. I just say, Man, we're one up on them. I know they're over there heartbroken." He allowed himself a little smile. "I've been in that locker room before. And I'm just happy to be in *this* locker room right now."

Who got the better end of the deal in the Stack-Hamilton trade? someone else asked. Was he happy being in Detroit?

He deftly ignored the first question, answered the second. "Oh, I'm happy [with Detroit], man. I mean, I definitely feel *welcome*. It's good to feel appreciated for what you do."

Is that how you felt in Washington?

He rubbed his towel against his tattoo for a few seconds more, just thinking. He answered slowly. "Like I said, it's good to feel *appreciated*. I feel welcome [in Detroit]. And that's all a player asks—to feel welcome."

He never had looked happier inside MCI. He asked about former teammates, like Tyrone Nesby, who had gone off to Europe to play. He hugged old friends. His big night against his old team had been a jettisoned player's dream. He allowed as how the Pistons' system was more suited to him. "There's opportunity to develop *me*," he said. "By myself. You know what I mean? I can—what's that word I'm looking for—just do me. Everybody is looking at me to step up and make things happen. . . . And the coach has been great . . ."

He had another thought. He put his shirt on over his tattoo, buttoned it, looked around, wondered how he wanted to put this. "Them trading me, you know, it was kind of funny, because when I first got here [in Washington], it was like, Man, [I knew that even] if I go ahead and blow up [play well], they might trade me. I ain't got no hard feelings about [the Wizards]. I'm in a winning situation *now*, you know."

He would be in the playoffs that year and, increasingly, it looked as if the Wizards might not be again. Hamilton now took his own swipe. "[The Wizards] have the greatest player ever to play the game," he said, smiling. "When I played with him, I always felt we had an opportunity to win. I don't know what their problem is now. That's something *they* have to figure out—it's not *our* problem."

About 75 feet away, and 20 minutes later, the man whose problem it was stood before microphones. "We had no offensive rhythm," Jordan said. He wouldn't compliment the player in the other locker room whom he had shipped away. "He felt he had something to prove," he said of Hamilton. "So he came out and forced the issue. . . . I think we did a pretty good hold on him. . . . And in the second half, I don't think he made that big of an impact."

"I think the trade was a good thing," Hamilton concluded, smiling.

On that same night, the Wizards began slowly coming apart. Jerry Stackhouse had become upset at Doug Collins's demand for more passes and plays in their half-court offense, particularly during the last minutes of the game. He'd led the team in scoring with 24 points, but the team had lost, and he felt he had hardly touched the ball when it counted most. He believed he wasn't getting nearly enough opportunities to run or attack the rim. Worse, he thought, Collins's strategy had deprived him of the chance to exploit physical mismatches against smaller, slower defenders, like his former Pistons teammate Jon Barry. "I should be wearing out his ass, but I can't do it if I don't have the ball," Stackhouse said. "[Collins says], 'Pass the ball, pass the ball.' But we're not playing instinctively."

In the next game, a home win over Atlanta, Stackhouse shot 21 times and had 29 points, at his best in the final minutes.

Is this what you wanted tonight? someone asked him afterward. Having the ball more down the stretch?

"Yes," he said tersely.

Player relations threatened to become a bigger problem for Collins. As usual, Larry Hughes had started that night at point guard, but Collins sat him down in favor of Ty Lue with the game on the line. In a setup offense, Lue did a better job than Hughes of distributing the ball, thought some of the coaches, who realized, besides, that Jordan increasingly preferred having Lue on the floor in critical situations. Collins worried about Hughes's reaction if he continued being lifted from games in key moments. Given Stackhouse's public peevishness, it already had been a hard week; Collins didn't need any more dissenters. His stress seemed to be mounting. "You always run the risk [as a coach]," Collins said, "of [thinking], 'I hope Larry's okay.' I'm so ultrasensitive to these guys' feelings . . . I'll tell you, as a coach, one thing you find out in losing [is], You better walk on eggshells, because guys just get so sensitive."

The next 10 days should have been the most pleasurable of the season for Collins. The team had its only notable run all year, winning five games in a row, and Jordan scored 41 points—the 117th 40-point game of his career, and his first of his season—during a valiant 53-minute performance in a double-overtime victory at home over Indiana. For the first time in his comeback, he found his range from behind the three-point line, hitting three of four bombs, to go along with 12 rebounds. It was the high point of a stretch in which Jordan won Eastern Conference Player of the Week honors.

Even with 61 points between Jordan and Stackhouse on their home floor, however, the team had struggled to beat Indiana. They would have lost but for the 23 points of Hughes, who had shot 19 times, a fat number reflective of Hughes's need to shine, too. Hughes was quite open about his aspirations: He wanted nothing less than to be regarded as among the top 15 players in the league. His whole life, he thought, had been pointing toward this moment—a measure of stardom, big money ($4.9 million that season), a chance to join the league's elite and an opportunity to help his family. In large part, he had left St. Louis University after his freshman year because his younger brother had recently undergone a heart transplant, and his family had no health insurance. He would do whatever was necessary, he said, to take care of his family.

He had an up-tempo style at odds with Jordan's walk-it-up-and-set-down-low preference. Time was running out on Hughes's point-guard days. Just as the coaches thought about slashing his playing minutes, however, he would have a big night, and keep his position. A week after Indiana, he had 16 points and 11 rebounds in a loss against his old Golden State teammates, and 22 points and eight assists during the following week in a win over Orlando. He couldn't be successfully melded into the Jordan team, but, with all his gifts, he couldn't be spurned yet either, the coaches told one another.

The team was a prisoner of all its offensive talent. But the refs could roll only one ball onto the court. Nothing was going to change: Jordan remained exasperated with Hughes, and Stackhouse was increasingly dissatisfied as Jordan assumed greater control over the style of the offense. Collins's quandary was impossible to resolve. How could the coach satisfy the demands of such indulged stars—one an aging god,

the other a 28-year-old new to the team and presumably in his prime—
each of whom had spent nearly all his career accustomed to having an
offense built around his demands?

Stackhouse badly wanted to run, but by then, Collins had come to
believe, despite his early season enthusiasm for fast breaks, that he did
not have the players, particularly a sterling point guard, to run effectively. Besides, with Jordan scoring in big numbers again, the team
didn't *need* to run, thought Collins, who could point to Jordan's 32
points in a 15-point victory over Orlando as proof of the setup game's
effectiveness.

But, with the Wizards, even good produced bad: So reliable was Jordan's shot in stretches that running became ever rarer, making it difficult for the team to shift gears when the idol tired and his shot
betrayed him. Often when the Wizards had a clear opportunity to fast-
break, Collins's booming voice rang out with a play, halting everyone.

Though he wouldn't yet publicly say it, Stackhouse thought the
coaches were catering to Jordan. His mood had grown darker. A Wizards official thought he saw a major blunder in the works. He pointed
out that Stackhouse could run, Hughes could run, Lue could run,
Kwame could run. Early in the year, before Jordan reentered the starting lineup, they frequently ran with effectiveness. Why *not* run? he
asked. "Setting up, with five players on five," said the official, "is the
hardest way to score a lot of the time. But Doug always has thought he
had Michael and the strategy to beat you. Michael liked that. And for
Doug it was like, Give me the chalk and I can *always* find a shot for
Michael or Stack."

Openly displaying his skepticism to Collins's approach, Charles
Oakley weighed in. "Doug calls plays ninety, ninety-five percent of the
time," said Oakley. "It's good to have a system. But when we play those
teams in the West that like to run, it's hard to run plays on them every
night. I know you want to show you're Coach of the Year, but sometimes you gotta run."

With potential fast breaks cut off, the young players looked over
their shoulders and waited for Jordan. Arriving downcourt, he often
bore fruit, another fadeaway jumper whistling the net. But the depen-
dency on him came at a cost to several players' spirits and the team's
versatility. Privately, Collins had lost confidence, said the official, in
the team's young big men, including Brendan Haywood, so that as the
season moved into its second half, the team's options narrowed further
still. Now, besides having little inclination to run, there was virtually

no plan for an inside game with a center or power forward. The limits of the Wizards' game plan meant that whenever Jordan went cold in the stretch, the team could generally be fitted for a coffin. It would not matter then that Collins screamed for ball movement, or called out instructions. The set plays ended with low-percentage perimeter shots, a disproportionate number cast by Jordan and Stackhouse, the latter of whom was becoming rankled that he couldn't just grab the ball and *go*.

Nonetheless, Collins preached confidence, at least in front of the team. In mid-January, he told his players that they had a realistic shot of seizing home-court advantage in the opening round of the playoffs.

By then, dissatisfaction verging on dissension gripped the club. The scene at a time-out during a January game was illustrative of a .500 team sliding toward ruin. With the Wizards trailing and Collins fuming about people not listening, the players began grumbling among themselves about not taking advantage of fast-break opportunities, the strife bursting into the open. One person on the bench listened incredulously, thinking, *It's coming apart.* Players sniped at one another, some directly, others behind their teammates' backs:

"Wake up, Kwame."

"We gotta run. Had fuckin' numbers there, three-on-one there."

"Fuckin' Stack gonna take *another* shot?" (This was mumbled. No one would have likely said this to Stackhouse's face.)

"Coulda gone got a dunk. We had numbers."

"Attack the fuckin' rim."

"Be quiet."

"Everybody's standin'—why are we standin'?"

An exasperated Jordan shut them up, barking: *"Settle down. Pass the ball. Slow it down."*

For several seconds, the man who always had a play to run had no play. He just looked at all of them. The players hardly noticed, filling the silence by resuming their muttering and bitching at one another. Collins finally interrupted, resuming his diagramming, staring hard at Kwame, as if to say—thought the observer in the huddle—*Pay attention.* Collins had a play: Michael off a screen.

Now that's a fuckin' surprise, thought the observer.

None of the players said anything. Collins shouted: *We can do this.* Silence.

They were the most sensitive, the most fragile team he'd ever been around, he privately told people.

He had so much, and he had nothing.

11

The Backlash

GOLDANG, CHIEF, DOUG COLLINS SAID TO ME ONE NIGHT, WALKING away after a scrum session.

He never could get over what he thought the media put Michael Jordan through.

Goldang, he repeated. What some of you guys *do* to him. Goldang, Chief. You guys are just *doing it* to him.

His scorn revealed Collins at his most contentious and admirable: No coach could be more loyal to a player than Collins was to Jordan. But his protectiveness would not stem the curiosity. Nothing would be easy for Jordan from this point until the end—the end being not the end of his career, but the end of all his days. The toughest times lay ahead.

It is a burden just *being* a sports idol at midlife. Fans and the media want their gods, at least in spirit, to be young and happy forever, which is not a certainty for gods any more than it is for the rest of us. We want their lives to be enduring tales of success and contentment—if for no other reason than to assure us that we did not waste our time revering the wrong people. There are tests. If a god fails to project grace on the brink of retirement or thereafter, he is diminished. If he blows all his money, succumbs to crack or molests the baby-sitter, he crashes altogether. If he sounds too wistful over the prospect of soon having no games to play, we are a trifle embarrassed for him and us. An athletic hero bears expectations that do not ease on retirement's doorstep but follow him to the grave. And, on the doorstep of 40 and moving toward his end as a player, Michael Jordan had begun experiencing them.

For two decades, it had been enough that he won, and looked stylish in doing so. But as he approached the end of his playing days, all the games become secondary to the public's desire to see him demonstrate how to let go. It suddenly seemed to be the ultimate test of his growth.

We want an idol to show us how to make the passage to the next thing, to demonstrate that he is not dying (and neither will we be when our time comes). We'd like to hear that he can already see on to the other side, that it's okay over there, the rims are soft and giving, and there are businesses to run and people to help. If he manages the transition right, he reveals the ease of a middle-aged man at peace with all he has achieved and discovered about himself. If he doesn't, there is the whiff of arrested development to him.

We especially don't want a god looking as though losing will leave him despondent at 40, that he is so desperate to win he'll mock and harass greenhorn teammates not much more than half his age. We want him to put his athletic interests second to those of the next wave of dreamers, the ones in kindergarten when he began playing in the league. To behave otherwise makes him look callow, like his riches have brought him everything except perspective. In the end, we don't want a god looking too needy too late. Michael Jordan had come to look needy, at a cost to his image.

It hurt him in America in ways that could be felt only empirically, and in other ways as clear as the returns of fans' All-Star ballots. One needed only to turn on Washington talk radio to sense the disappointment when he referred to his teammates as mules.

People argued on radio and Internet chats: Had his ego runneth over? Was he more scold than mentor? Was he holding up the development of young players to sustain his on-court position?

This last question—the suggestion that he consciously impeded young players—was ludicrous, merely another reflection of his new image problems. His future as an executive largely depended on the young players' development, and so not only did the shadow boss care about them, he had become preoccupied, even agitated, over the inability of some of the players to make real progress. But the shadow boss was also the proud star, and the conflict between those two personas augured disaster. From the season's start, the star in him had difficulties accepting any role other than that of supreme showman, making clear his irritation with not getting enough shots as Stackhouse starred at the season's beginning and became the offense's number one threat.

By mid-season, the needs of the player Jordan hopelessly conflicted with the demands of de facto executive Jordan. With most of the offense readjusted by then to abide by his wishes and account for his new limitations, Jordan flourished for a time while others declined. Stackhouse was no longer Stackhouse, just as Hamilton had been diminished. The Wizards looked as mediocre as ever. Jordan the star talked about the defense "focusing on me," proud to the point of vain, even as Jordan the *boss* fretted about losses and Stackhouse's periodic struggles with his shot. That the needs of the star overwhelmed the plans of the executive ensured that one player on the team would thrive while his high-profile teammates felt themselves floundering.

He was not the model of middle-aged performer that fans generally cherish. George Foreman, winking and laughing during his training, en route to knocking out a young man named Michael Moorer to regain the world's heavyweight championship at 45, had just the right mix of humor, resolve, self-deprecation and comfort with his belly to win over the young and graying alike. Foreman seemed cool enough to embrace what was happening to him. He talked candidly, chuckling, about young fighters that, hopefully, he'd never need to face, *Ohhhhh nooooooo*. He sounded like equal parts fighter and pool hustler—Minnesota Fats laced with gloves. The public anointed Foreman as lovable.

By contrast, Jordan's intensity had the odd effect of adding to the perception that he needed the mantle of greatness more than a grown man should. In January and February, he sporadically played his best ball all season, scoring 40 points or more in each of three games. But even those performances, set against his teammates' deepening woes and the Wizards' struggles, could not stem the desertion of fans voting for his rivals in the All-Star balloting.

A new view of Jordan had taken hold: He clung too hard. He would never let go. Increasingly, observers and even old friends, like former Bulls assistant coach Tex Winter, wondered whether he would be able to stay retired at the season's end. He had the loyalty of his large cult but not of the country. In the online All-Star balloting that determined the game's starting players, he had lost his early lead for good at the guard position to both Tracy McGrady and Allen Iverson.

Even Vince Carter—who had been injured and would play only about half the season—had far more All-Star votes than the legend, enough to win himself a starting forward position. Jordan had the points; Carter had the support.

A reasonable question seemed to be what effect, if any, the Karla Knafel episode—with its details of sex on the sly and his hush money payment to her—had on the All-Star balloting. The answer was, Probably none. While outsiders to basketball may have been troubled by Jordan's behavior, All-Star balloters tend to be unmoved by scandals, disproportionately represented by the happily and monomaniacally sports-crazed, the kind of crowd whose definition of a social wrong is a televised game preempted by a State of the Union address. They are people who evince little interest in controversies unrelated to the games themselves. A year later, with Kobe Bryant under indictment for rape, the Lakers star would still lead all Western Conference guards in All-Star votes, further evidence that personal scandals count for nothing with diehards.

Among these fans, Jordan simply lost a hold on imaginations, the same reason why Nike and Gatorade had no more use for intense, year-round television ad campaigns bearing his image. (Gatorade had a TV campaign featuring an ad with a mythical young Jordan playing against the 40-year-old Jordan, but it had only a brief run as a game-day item.) His endorsement power had declined markedly. In the early '90s, his Super Bowl commercials for Nike and McDonald's had been big hits with network audiences. After the 2003 Super Bowl, *USA Today*'s "Ad-Meter," a measure of the appeal of TV commercials with viewers, reported that Jordan's ads for Gatorade and Hane's had failed to make even the top 20. It was simply another indication of his declining appeal.

Meanwhile, the ardor of millions of former loyalists faded. Fans have wandering eyes and cheating hearts, too. Many of them ran off with Bryant, McGrady and Iverson, who, in addition to siphoning these older fans, were already the new idols of the playgrounds and streets—guaranteeing each of the trio a larger, more intense American cult following than Jordan. Fans who fell in the 18-to-30-year-old demographic overwhelmingly gravitated to the wunderkinds, giving them a natural advantage in the All-Star balloting.

Measured against the old Michaelmania, Jordan was suddenly a lesser god. He had failed to make the starting All-Star team, as chosen by the fans, for the first time in all his years of eligibility. What did it mean that Michael Jordan—the greatest and most famous player in NBA history—could not win a popularity vote during his final season in the league? No one on the TV networks with NBA contracts touched the subject. To listen to the TV commentators was to believe Michael Jordan remained as popular with fans as ever.

But already, speculation resounded as to what All-Star starter might be pressured into giving his spot to Jordan. Maybe Vince Carter could be punked into facing reality.

This had not yet happened; this did not look likely to happen. Early in the mess, Carter signaled he would not be giving up his spot to anyone *ever*.

Jordan would need to play as a reserve.

Meanwhile, as Jordan turned 40 in February, the Wizards muddled along toward nowhere. The team was Jordan's alone now. A hobbled Jerry Stackhouse missed several games, leaving Jordan to shoot the ball as often as he wished, 30 times or more. He was on his way to another first—his 43 points at home against New Jersey making him the first 40-year-old in league history to have a 40-point game.

But his team was two games under the .500 mark and seemingly stuck there, its dissension becoming ever harder to conceal from the media and Abe Pollin. Injured and increasingly frustrated with the offense and Doug Collins, Jerry Stackhouse was miserable. This was ominous. An agitated Stackhouse was Vesuvius ready to erupt.

Short of a torn knee cartilage or a broken bone, no injury is worse for a basketball player than a severely pulled groin. It is ruinous to his mobility. An otherwise fit athlete can often play through a hamstring pull, but an injured groin has him in a vise, producing an agony predictable in an area so close to the abdomen, inner thighs and genitals. "I have a groin," Stackhouse said dispiritedly, employing the players' shorthand to describe his troubles. He had badly pulled his left groin in early January, and it was getting no better.

No one could reasonably doubt Stackhouse's guts through that stretch. He played brilliantly through much of it, no more so than when he scored 33 points against the Phoenix Suns and made a game-saving block on the Suns' 6'10" power forward, Scott Williams.

But after a long night in Madison Square Garden—a 6-for-15, 22-point, 42-minute performance that helped the Wizards win by five over the Knicks—he could hardly walk, clutching his hips for support as he shuffled off. He would miss the next four contests, coming back to play in the following six games though the groin had yet to heal fully, then going down again, agony creasing his face throughout a losing effort in Milwaukee, when he managed only five points.

He would be unable to play for 18 days. Collins urged him to ride a stationary bike and do whatever else he safely could, to keep his legs and wind strong while the groin rehabbed. *You're so important to us—I need you to be ready when you're healed,* Collins told him.

Hurting, Stackhouse became irritated at what he regarded as Collins's nagging. Convinced he had given the team all his effort even when in terrible pain, he resented what he regarded as a veiled questioning of his commitment.

Finally, early in February, with ill feelings already convulsing the team, Collins pressed him once too often. The two found themselves on the practice court of MCI, when Stackhouse thought Collins had suggested to him that he wasn't working hard enough in his workout.

Stackhouse snapped.

It took but an instant. He was placid in one moment and screaming and cursing Collins in the next.

Heads wheeled. People in the closed gym had a look at a Stackhouse not previously seen that season, the volatile Stackhouse they'd heard about, the one who had thumped two teammates and whose fury could be frightening when ignited.

Collins, thought a witness, looked frozen. Stackhouse was still howling. Collins tried muttering something about only wanting to *help* Stack. Jordan looked on from the other side of the gym. Other players and assistant coaches stared, slack-jawed.

Someone took a step toward the two, just in case Stackhouse grabbed for the coach. He didn't. Stackhouse trudged with his bad groin to the other side of the gym, slowly calming. The incident was over.

If other players' outbursts were to become messy little storms, Stackhouse's was a typhoon, threatening to lay waste to everything: The team would not have a chance of winning regularly without him focused and motivated. Moreover, his rage loomed as a huge public relations embarrassment if word leaked about it. The day after his blowup, with his teammates under strict orders not to speak of the incident to the media, Stackhouse apologized to the squad at a closed practice.

Collins said, Thank you.

Jordan said, Let's practice.

The matter seemed over, though one official believed a mistake was made in not seriously disciplining Stackhouse: The wrong kind of precedent, he thought, had been established. Players might think they could vent their disgust at a variety of Collins's decisions.

Christian Laettner, who played little during the season's early games, already had complained behind locker-room doors about young players getting so much playing time at the expense of veterans. Kwame Brown sounded increasingly frustrated. Had Collins opened the door onto a mutinous mood?

Some players had too much at stake financially to complain for long. Recognizing his chance to opt out of the remaining two years of his contract at season's end, Stackhouse wanted to play impressively enough to attract a big offer on the NBA open market or receive a contract extension with Washington that would improve on the $6.4 million he was making in 2002–2003. In the aftermath of his blowup, Stackhouse publicly remained a supportive face. But his frustrations festered, particularly as he struggled to come back from his injury and reassert himself in an offense now dominated by Jordan. His chances for driving to the hoop had dwindled, he thought, and, being in and out of the lineup, he was struggling to find his shooting touch at the very time when he needed to excite league executives.

Even when his groin felt slightly better and he found himself playing, his shot opportunities and productivity dropped. Exasperated, he met privately with Collins, who again recounted part of a closed-door conversation for reporters: "I said [to Stackhouse], 'Jerry, you just play. Let me do the fretting. You just play. Be aggressive. And everything is gonna be just fine.'"

On that same night, Collins did not hesitate portraying himself as the leader of players lacking emotional toughness, trotting out a line he had used privately, now an invitation for the media to consider whether he labored under a handicap. "This is probably the most fragile team, confidence-wise, I've ever been around," he now said publicly. "I don't know [why]."

Jordan had no bonds with teammates strong enough that he could intercede and make peace. Besides, he had his own problems. His inconsistency made every game an adventure. On a good Jordan night, the Wizards could beat the best teams in the conference; then they could turn around and be humiliated in the same week by the NBA's worst. At home, in January, the Wizards faced a badly undermanned Toronto team, missing Vince Carter among others, which needed to play with three players recently signed to 10-day contracts, all fresh out of a branch of basketball's minors, the NBA-owned National Basketball Developmental League. The Wizards were a laughably heavy favorite, the most popular pregame question centering on the expected margin of the Washington victory.

One of the evening's standouts was 6'9" forward, 23-year-old Damone Brown, two years out of Syracuse University, who had just arrived the night before from the Charleston Lowgators of the developmental league to be told that, as his opening assignment, he would be spending much of the game guarding Michael Jordan. Welcome.

The coaches had only this bit of advice for him: Don't go for Jordan's pump fake.

Brown played so well against Jordan that the Toronto coaches kept him in the game for 32 minutes. His size and the constancy of his hand in Jordan's face seemed to bother the star as the game wore on. By the fourth quarter, Brown was as strong as ever, and Jordan, who was logging 41 minutes midway through a mid-season of too many long nights, appeared tired, hitting only about a third of his shots for a glossy but subpar 22 points.

With two minutes left, Brown blew by Jordan for a layup and the game was over, Toronto winning by nine. There were Damone Browns all over the country now, guys you'd see up in the NBA for a year, or a month, or 10 days, and then never see again, headed to Europe, or back to the developmental league, or to a playground. They were floating all over, and that one of them had just stepped into MCI and done a number on Jordan meant that the line between the aging god and scads of players could not be any thinner, that *nothing* was a guarantee when it came to an old legend's play. A Damone Brown meant anything was possible.

The Wizards locker room had difficulty believing that a team with three guys on 10-days had beaten them. "How can that happen, is what you should damn ask yourself," Oakley muttered.

Jordan was so upset that, for the only time that season, he rushed out of the locker room without talking to the media. The last of the illusions about his physical capabilities had begun peeling away. His play would be beset by unpredictability for the remainder of the season, subject to his body's fatigue. He could still score 40, but it was just as likely in a game that he would be limited to fewer than 15, as happened when he was held to just 11 points during his last game in Chicago, the culmination of three miserable performances as a Wizard there.

Washington lost, and fell the following night at MCI, blowing a 15-point halftime lead against Minnesota. Collins was irate. "We just went dead in the water for whatever reason," he said. "I can't tell you [why]. . . . We came out sleepwalking [in the third quarter]. It was like somebody drugged us at halftime. . . . I told our guys, 'I can take losing—but not like that.' *That is not right.*"

Jordan's assessment was short and dour. "In the second half, we looked like a [NBA draft] lottery team."

The team's record had dropped to 21–23. Someone asked about his level of concern. That he felt the need to say what he murmured next portended trouble: "I don't think we want to start separating and pointing fingers."

He couldn't find his shot in New Jersey or Milwaukee, but then, back in Washington, his touch on all varieties of jumpers returned against the New Orleans Hornets, Courtney Alexander's new team. Like Richard Hamilton, Alexander didn't hesitate telling people that while he had no ill feelings toward his old club, he appreciated having been traded by the Wizards. ("It's a much better situation for me now. I'm under a great organization that cares about me. Got a great coach [Paul Silas] who does nothing but motivate players. . . . It's definitely a professional kind of atmosphere.")

Alexander matched up with Jordan for a few minutes, and Jordan did whatever he wanted against him. On an evening when the Wizards trailed most of the way, a determined Jordan was abusing every New Orleans defender sent to shackle him. For a long while, 6'1", 203-pound David Wesley had the task, a mismatch that afforded Jordan not merely the opportunity to jump over the shorter man but also bull him down in the post, where Wesley gave away about 20 pounds. That strength discrepancy counted far more late in Jordan's career than a five-inch reach advantage. Even a shorter man could sometimes match his leap now, but much lighter foes seldom had an answer when he started bumping their bodies. He could knock a smaller man just enough off-balance and backward—two inches or so of room was all he needed, a margin too small to make an impression on officials, but a Grand Canyon for a shooter like Jordan—to leave the victim slow to react when he lifted, creating space for his fallaway jumper. This he did, over and over, against Wesley.

He had an encyclopedic knowledge of virtually every player's vulnerabilities. It made him, on-court, nothing less than the dean of his craft, a fact embraced late by bedazzled observers who had felt the need for two decades to compare him reflexively to Julius Erving, David Thompson and other soaring black icons.

Regarded as nothing less than the apotheosis of natural talent in his prime, he had been seldom viewed as the consummate student in those days. Like Larry Bird and Cal Ripken Jr., he inhabited a world in which parts of him were undervalued, obscured by the prevailing racial stereotypes of his time. As two white stars heralded for their work ethic and wisdom, Bird and Ripken always had possessed far more physical talent than the media ascribed to them. (Bird's ballhandling and agility in body-bumping traffic were preternatural; Ripken revolutionized the shortstop position by proving a large man, 6' 4" and 220 pounds, could play it nimbly enough to win two Gold Gloves while being strong enough to hit more than 400 home runs.)

On the other hand, Jordan had gifts of acuity that others simply didn't possess, able to sense where nine other people would be on a court at any instant, where someone in space would be flying next and how much time remained on a shot clock. It was why he so seldom looked surprised on a court; why, almost never in a career during which he took well over 100 last-second shots, did he shoot too late or too early. Never had anyone ever labored harder to understand how to succeed in his profession. It was why, at that moment, Jordan could bump David Wesley closer to the basket and, with the shot clock at two seconds, calmly rise, fade back and bury another jumper.

MCI erupted. The Wizards had mounted a fourth-quarter comeback, drawing close. Jordan hit another fallaway, and most of the 20,000 in the arena stood now, their howls frenzied. New Orleans wanted a time-out. Jordan pumped a fist. He was over 40 points now. Bedlam.

The din did not die through the time-out. Reporters languidly swiveled heads and quelled yawns, looking around, checking out the crowd and action. It is what reporters typically do during mid-season, trying to fight off the monotony of four games in a week. Meanwhile, they could view the business of Abe Pollin's arena proceeding with cool efficiency, the message boards presenting the names of corporate advertisers: "US Airways . . . Intelligent Decisions . . . Pepco Energy Services . . . Giant Food . . ."

More corporate names, more dollars.

Advertisements invited people to spend their money. Then came more advertisements for *everything* Jordan:

Did you know that with the Wizards' "Final Flight Plan," you could get six games plus free tickets for Michael Jordan's last home game ever?

Did you know you could take advantage of the "Jordan Jersey Package": Four tickets in the upper deck and a replica Jordan jersey for $76 for an upcoming game against Cleveland?

To spend two seasons following a professional team is to understand that, in every moment, the game exists to pry away fans' dollars. That's it; that's the deal. The next thing to understand is that ball teams, like casinos, need you *not to mind* having your money pried away. It is not that you don't know the prying is happening. It's that you know and that you have decided there is some feeling that comes over you in the arena that makes it all right that your money has been lifted in the form of that C-note for the seats, the twenty for parking, the fifty on drinks and munchies.

I'd always wondered what could draw people, night after night, to what is after all just a game. But in a world marred by so much imperfection and loss, on frigid winter days when the sun died too early and a man felt the chill of his life's regrets, it was nice sometimes just to drive to the arena with the defroster on and contemplate the possibility of seeing Michael Jordan perform brilliantly, to imagine fallaway jumpers rippling nets, again and again. There is a benefit to being reminded that we are not so hardhearted that we cannot be moved like small children, that there remains room in our lives for something as mysterious as magic. That is why we always have had sports, loved sports. And there are winners there, unambiguous winners. It can be uplifting, when, in truth, not much else is.

When the fans screamed as they screamed that night, they signaled their happiness with the delirium, which the reasonable among them understood could not be described and would not last. Whatever pleasant sensation they had likely would be gone by the time they left the arena and found their cars. But they had it for this instant. And then Jordan came out of the time-out and hit another jumper and a couple of his teammates hit shots and now the din in the arena sounded like a wail, a plea, as it always does when the home team struggles in a tight game.

There is something achingly prayerful about it—I don't mean anything religious—but prayerful just the same, the screamers wanting something to lift them for a few seconds, to remind them that obstacles are not always insurmountable. People pray with their shouts. And if, afterward, they don't precisely know what they felt or why, they remember vaguely this stirring, and that keeps them coming back to the games and to a Jordan, which perhaps is something worth having your money pried away for, every once in a while.

They were a raucous crowd on this night. Jordan scored 45, Bryon Russell hit a couple of threes in the final quarter, and the Wizards went on a 13–0 run late and beat New Orleans by five. Just the same, few fans or observers were deluded afterward: The game didn't mark a turn-around. The team didn't look better, the only difference between this night and the Wizards' many losses being that Jordan was unusually hot and, with Stackhouse out, had license to shoot as often as he wished. If he had scored his average as a starter, in the low 20s, the Wizards would have lost by 15. So, as a measure of the two teams' relative abilities, the score could not have been more misleading; the game was an aberration. No other Wizard had more than 13 points, and the team's paltry four fast-break points meant its players had walked the ball up the court virtually the entire game, waiting on Jordan to jog downcourt and set up in the low blocks. He did not have teammates so much as designated feeders now, and those who did not feed played fewer minutes. While a personal triumph for Jordan, the night offered scant encouragement.

He played a season-high 44 minutes, including the entire second half. Afterward, Collins was asked: *Did Michael tell you he could go the whole second half?*

Collins did not even pretend on this night to make such decisions. "I didn't ask him; I wasn't going to take him out," he answered, and the media room busted up, even Collins laughing. "I was not going to get *that wrath.*"

Jordan looked happy, too, telling everybody, "My offense ignited everything, energy-wise."

He slapped the hands of a few friends and walked off, on his way to the All-Star Game in a few days, at which point the team would be only a game below .500, with Jordan telling teammates that he fully expected to be in the playoffs, *that it was gonna happen,* that they'd have made it the year before if he hadn't hurt his knee, *it's gonna happen.*

Collins told people that Jordan looked frisky. "Frisky" was Collins-speak for healthy and deeply focused, an indication that Jordan had gone deeper than ever into his tube, insulating himself from the last distractions, leaving Frederick Sperling to deal with Karla Knafel, against whom he'd be pitted in a Chicago court hearing in six weeks.

He wanted only to enjoy himself at the All-Star Game in Atlanta, get a little rest and reach the playoffs. Nothing and no one could be allowed to get in the way of that. He'd heard about a brewing fuss over whether Vince Carter or another All-Star starter should give up a starting spot to him, and said to people: Please no controversies, no headaches. And, while he knew he would be honored at the game, he didn't want his final appearance as an All-Star to feel like a funeral either, he told people. He wasn't a guy for eulogies. *Fuck a funeral,* he told somebody. *They do that for you and you never play well. I don't need that. I don't want that.*

He preferred something respectful but upbeat, a message that he wanted conveyed to David Stern. Light on the solemnity, please. He did not need a downer; it would harm his energy. He still wanted to kick some ass while in Atlanta, because he counted on playing.

There is no greater exercise in corporate self-love than an NBA All-Star weekend. Every league event is designed to tout the product and trumpet the sterling character of the All-Stars. Nearly all the players, it is pointed out, have a favorite charity. A few emphasize the importance of reading to children. The league distributes publicity sheets in case media attendees forget. Sports commentators working for the networks demonstrate an uncanny instinct for self-preservation, by not straying from the spirit of the publicity sheets. Over the years, they have been particularly supportive by not mentioning any of the following: charges for drug possession, gun possession, domestic battery and sexual assault, along with nightclub scuffles, civil suits or hush-money payments made to conceal extramarital affairs—anything, in short, that might raise a question about a star or the product. The commentators sunnily emphasize the positive.

When it came to Jordan, there would be no reference to the Karla Knafel matter. Other negatives would be ignored as well. Television would not be discussing the All-Star vote, particularly Jordan's finish behind both Allen Iverson and Tracy McGrady at the starting guard positions. Instead, television helped to create a controversy, casting Eastern Conference starting forward Vince Carter as a villain, his sin being his unwillingness to give up his starting spot to Jordan. TNT commentator Bill Walton, pushing the idea that Carter had a *duty* to step aside, reported details of the Eastern team nudging Carter to do what Walton characterized as "the right thing."

According to Walton, the Eastern Conference coach, Isiah Thomas, turned to Carter in front of the East squad and said, "Vince, it's on you. What's it gonna be?"

Carter answered simply, "You're looking at the wrong guy."

Giving up a starter's spot wouldn't be unprecedented. In the '70s, Doug Collins once generously stepped aside so that aging Celtics legend John Havlicek could start on the East team. But no one could remember an instance when pressure had been mounted to drive a player out of an All-Star starting honor. Jordan, who said he felt badly for Carter, always had the power to make the hassling cease. At anytime, he could have emphatically declared that he wanted no more pressure applied against Carter, that if the controversy continued, he might simply pull out of the game altogether. His careful expressions of sympathy for Carter, without condemnation of the strong-arm tactics, ensured only that the pressure would persist.

Carter was no counterfeit All-Star. He had been voted as a starter to three consecutive East teams by then, and though injuries had kept him out for stretches, he would average more than 20 points a game that season, a worthy number roughly matching Jordan's production. Certainly, no one argued that Carter was unfit to be an All-Star starter. People on the East team and in the television booth simply wanted Jordan to get the nod in his last All-Star Game, believing the league and its players owed him this, ready to do whatever was necessary to coerce Carter into surrendering. "The players in that locker room should not let Michael Jordan say no," Walton told TNT's viewers. "This is a critically important chance for the world to say thank you for giving us so many thrills."

What went carefully ignored, of course, was that the world already had shown a preference for other players, according to the fans' vote. But television kept pressing its case. Now, back on the air, a shrill Bill Walton fumed: "Michael Jordan does not want to make Vince Carter look bad. Michael no longer has to worry about that. Vince has taken care of that all by himself."

The heat finally became too much for Carter. On the night of the game, minutes before the stars took the floor, some East players hinted they might boycott the affair unless Carter stepped aside for Jordan. Carter surrendered and spoke briefly with Jordan, who would later say, "Obviously, it was a last-minute decision with Vince. I felt he had taken a beating when he shouldn't have. . . . I could have easily come off the bench. I would have been proud to do that. . . . I didn't want him to take any more of a beating, so that's why I stepped in and took his spot."

"He deserves it," Carter calmly told reporters afterward.

But, as time passed, Carter had difficulty hiding his resentment. He had been browbeaten into giving up something he wanted to do right down to the last moments. Before next seeing Jordan, he would be asked how memorable it would be to play against the legend for a last time. *Not very,* said a shake of his head. "I had *my* memorable moment at the All-Star Game," he said curtly. "*That* I remember."

For believers in the theory that one can anger the fates and court a jinx, there seemed to be much bad karma throughout that All-Star evening. Jordan got off to a miserable start, missing his first seven shots and blowing another dunk attempt. He was on his way to missing 18 of 27 shots on a night when Mariah Carey serenaded him at halftime. His East team led by one point with 15 seconds left. Then his old Phoenix foil, Shawn Marion, blocked his shot, and Jordan fouled Kobe Bryant, who made one of two free throws to tie the game. After Jordan badly missed a shot at the buzzer, the game went into overtime, during which he had his best moment, giving the East a two-point lead on a gorgeously arched 15-foot baseline fallaway over Marion with only 4.8 seconds left.

For a moment, he seemed destined to leave the All-Star competition a winner. Perhaps his 20 points, his apparent game-winning jumper and all the nostalgia in the building would be enough to land him the game's MVP award. Then, as if in proof of the evening's curse, he watched as his East teammate Jermaine O'Neal clumsily fouled Bryant as Kobe awkwardly tossed up a desperation three-point attempt. Bryant made two of three free throws to tie the game again. For the second time, the East diagrammed a buzzer-beating shot for Jordan, who was stuffed once more by Marion, the fourth blocked Jordan shot of the evening.

Tired, having played too much already, he took a seat on the bench for the entire second overtime, which was dominated by the winning West and game MVP Kevin Garnett. Then his last All-Star Game ended, another milestone behind him, just part of a February in which he turned 40 and celebrated with a party whose guests included Jay-Z and Donald Trump. It was a reminder that his life had been unlike any other athlete's in the second half of the 20th century, or as yet in the new millennium. He did not much care for reflection about birthdays, resisting the idea that anything had changed. "I don't feel like forty," he said at 40 years and four days. "I feel *good*. . . . My effort is always gonna be young. My desire to win is always gonna be young. . . . My body may say forty, but those other things are gonna be young always."

More than ever, he sought to project youth, a bearing that was, among other things, good business. For an aging athlete trying to remain viable as an endorser and sporting apparel marketer, it was helpful to maintain the look of someone atop the ever-shifting cultural wave, to look forever young while winning, too. Jordan's ride on the wave had been the longest of all time in sports. Most of the old stars around him had enjoyed only brief rides before falling forever, with new stars emerging all the time to take the fallen's place. In Washington, lounging in the visitors' locker room, was a fresh young luminary. Phoenix's All-Star point guard, 25-year-old Stephon Marbury, wearing not one but two diamond earrings, stood before a thicket of microphones, basking in the praise of questioners who basically wanted to know what it felt like to have climbed so high—to be, in short, him.

Although generally viewed as a flashy player falling well short of greatness, Marbury still had an opportunity at endorsement contracts for a few seasons more. Generally, a player's prime years passed quickly. As if to serve as living proof of this reality, leaning against a wall at that moment in a brown sports jacket and cream shirt, one of Marbury's teammates, a relatively young man whose best times were already behind him, waited for a brief audience with Michael Jordan.

He'd missed the game that night with an injury. At 31, Anfernee "Penny" Hardaway played shooting guard for Phoenix, on the dark side of his career now, entering that stage where he could reasonably expect to be shipped around the league for his remaining years, serving as a role player. He had been regarded once as a future NBA great, someone who might even one day acquire the title as the league's best guard. It never happened.

For years the press had anointed challengers and possible successors to Jordan, only to see them, one by one, fade away. In the king's early years, long before Hardaway played his first NBA game, Portland's Clyde Drexler had been viewed as someone who might seize the crown. But Jordan had thoroughly beaten Drexler and his team in an NBA Finals, then taunted and outplayed Drexler during practices for the 1992 Olympic team, making clear who would always be the alpha dog between them.

Later, a young swingman out of Duke came along, to be drafted by Detroit. Grant Hill fit the profile of the promotable star that Madison Avenue loves best: a prodigious talent graced by looks, humility, an absence of off-court troubles, and a seeming disinterest in controversial social causes. The combination made him as perfect as Jordan. But Hill suffered an ankle injury that became chronic and now his career was in a spiral. Hill's days as a star had ended.

The long column of Jordan's failed successors stretched for years now, and the sight of Penny Hardaway, alone in the MCI hallway, reminded one how quickly a failed challenger in the NBA went from demigod to also-ran. In the mid-'90s, the 6'7" Hardaway was a super-star guard for Orlando, a teammate of Shaquille O'Neal, a fixture as an Eastern Conference All-Star and a growing commercial personality. He had his own high-profile Nike campaign, in which his miniature TV alter ego "Little Penny" partied with him poolside, sharing the life of an ascendant NBA idol. He starred with O'Neal and Nick Nolte in the film *Blue Chips,* where he played a young basketball superstar. For one season, he became Jordan's heir apparent. During the 1995 Eastern Conference finals, he held his own against an out-of-shape Jordan, who had recently returned from baseball. Hardaway actually outplayed the king down the stretch, as Orlando knocked off the Bulls.

Then Jordan got in basketball shape to smite everyone again. Now, eight years after Hardaway's most glorious professional moment, few young basketball fans even knew his name. Injuries and age had taken his greatness, stripped him both of his greatness and his "Little Penny" campaign, and led him to a secondary role in Phoenix. Phoenix would ship him at year's end. He was on the downside.

Having dispatched an attendant to carry a message to the Wizards' locker room, he hoped for at least a little time with Jordan. He waited patiently for about 10 minutes, his back not moving from that cement wall.

Tim Grover appeared. *"Penny,"* he shouted, smiling, and shook Hardaway's hand.

In that moment, Grover was less Jordan's personal trainer than one of his gatekeepers, there in the hallway to find out what the visiting player wanted. He looked like a chief of staff, natty in a gray suit, wear-ing a Jordan-like silver earring in his left ear, still pumping Hardaway's hand. "Can I do anything for you?" Grover asked.

"Just would like to see Michael, say hi," Hardaway said.

Grover nodded. "Well, he's back there getting treatment and getting ready. Let me go back there, Penny, and see what he has to do. Then I'll come out and bring you to him, okay? Stay here and I'll be back."

"Thanks," Hardaway said.

Grover walked back down the hallway, into the Wizards' locker room. Hardaway did not move from the wall. Another five, 10 minutes passed. Grover reappeared, bearing a pair of autographed Air Jordans for Hardaway, who accepted them with a small nod, mumbling thanks. Grover went off again. Hardaway remained affixed to the wall, holding the Air Jordans like a consolation game show prize.

After a few more minutes, Grover at last escorted Hardaway back to the locker room, where Jordan waited. Hardaway paid his respects. Jordan granted many of these audiences, especially to players like Hardaway who remained part of the Nike roster of endorsers. The lucky would be ushered into the Wizards private training room, off the main locker room, for a few minutes with him. Whether young stars or aging players on the slide, nearly all left smiling, most carrying a pair of autographed shoes, part of their bounty for being in the Nike/Jordan Brand fraternity or for simply paying homage.

If Jordan no longer had the same pull on young fans and shoe buyers as he once enjoyed, he still had a pipeline to players for Nike, determined to be as valuable now for the company as during the peak of his appeal in the '90s. There never had been a time since Nike began skyrocketing in the mid-'80s when, at least in the public's view, Jordan was not the athlete most identifiable with Nike—the Jumpman, the leading endorser in sports marketing history, amen.

Nearly as competitive in business as in sports, he did not want that perception changing, proudly pumping up Nike and Nike athletes in other sports when their names arose in non-basketball conversations. A young superstar with a global following like Tiger Woods might be Nike's present and future when it came to igniting the excitement of young fans, but Jordan would remain the man for Nike well beyond his retirement as a player, if he could manage it. After all, when had he *not* been Nike's man?

He made a fortune for the Chicago Bulls, but he had made far more for Nike, his impact most keenly felt, competitively speaking, in the first decade after the company signed him. It was impossible for most analysts to imagine a scenario under which Nike could ever have won its shoe battles in the '80s and early '90s without him. Whoever had

Jordan had the prize, and his presence had enabled Nike to make billions of dollars, swiftly overtaking Reebok and putting Adidas at a further competitive disadvantage. In turn, he had made more than $150 million from Nike alone by 2000, with Forbes.com and other analysts calculating that he received in excess of $35 million from Nike and his other endorsements in his last year before coming out of retirement to accept the Wizards' presidency. Over his career, he had earned more than $420 million by selling his image, and would take home another estimated $34 million in endorsements in 2003.

The money meant much to him. A businessman generally needed to stockpile big sums if he ever hoped to be a major or majority owner of an NBA franchise. But Jordan also wanted to be recognized as a successful businessman, no more willing to be a mere show-pony for Nike than he had been to serve in that capacity for Abe Pollin. To that end he wanted to continue building the Jordan Brand and to distinguish himself as a savvy man capable of generating Nike business even when not on television screens. It was much of the reason for his Jordan Capital Classic high school all-star game, and just that day, he had seen tangible evidence of the Jordan Classic's business benefits. He was greeted by Phoenix's rookie sensation, Amare Stoudemire, the kid who had played in the Capital Classic just a season ago and received a free pair of his new Air Jordans in the special silver suitcase. Stoudemire now was a Nike man, wearing Nike and Jordan Brand gear right down to his sweatshirt with the Jumpman logo. "I asked Michael to give me the key to success," Stoudemire said, "and he told me I got it already."

Stoudemire signed, sealed and delivered by Nike.

Business.

Jordan's pipeline extended all over the country. He had his summer basketball camps, and he had his pickup games, and over the years he had made contact with the best high school players on the planet, including LeBron James, still in high school and insisting that he was as yet uncommitted about endorsement deals, though even officials of Adidas had their doubts. Jordan had his ear, and Nike had the dollars. A privately held view within Adidas was that the negotiating competition for James would merely have the effect of driving James's price up. In the end, James signed with Nike for $90 million.

Outside of Nike, the best shoe executives in charge of recruiting athletes, like Adidas's Sonny Vaccaro (who formerly served in same scouting role for Nike), understood they were at a huge disadvantage when

Jordan played a part in the wooing game. What no one knew was how long Jordan's allure with other players might extend beyond his retirement as a player. For now at least, his appeal remained formidable. A meeting with Jordan was like a papal audience: A cherished moment for the young star; a meet-and-greet for Jordan.

That networking, and the athlete signings for Nike that the idol had assisted with his Jordan Capital Classic, enhanced his reputation as a man who could stoke business. The meet-and-greets were a common part of his post-game routines now. He developed new player relationships, and maintained old ones with longtime players he regarded as loyal. Penny Hardaway fell into this category. Although Hardaway's star had dimmed, Jordan liked him. They chatted for a few minutes, until it was time for Jordan to talk to the media and for Hardaway to stroll to his team bus, soon to depart for the airport.

Jordan stepped through a door, wading into cameras. Grover said good-bye to Hardaway, who walked back down the long hallway, a receding figure holding a pair of shoes. He passed about a dozen people, not one of whom gave him a second look. The moment spoke to the fragility of most men's dreams, and to the tenacity of Michael Jordan's.

After the All-Star break, the Wizards slowly collapsed, losing 20 of their remaining 33 games. There was no dramatic cause for what happened—no last-second loss that broke spirits, no crushing injury, no mutineer lighting the match. The explanation was simple: From the beginning, the team was a beautiful edifice with a shoddy foundation. The pieces didn't go together, not Jordan and Stackhouse, not Jordan and Hughes, not Jordan and the young runners. Collins had failed to reach Stackhouse, hopelessly alienated Kwame Brown, and lost the support of veterans like Charles Oakley. Haphazardly arranged from the outset by Jordan and his managerial crew, the different parts of the structure had been cracking for months, until the collapse gathered a speed in the final weeks that no longer could be hidden. Jordan had built the Wizards' edifice in his image, and now as it began buckling, he and Collins increasingly blamed those stuck inside it.

The first four games after the All-Star break were on the road, and the Wizards lost three of them. Jordan flew from Atlanta to Sacramento, where the team fell by 18 points and Jordan made only 5 of 19 field-goal attempts, sitting in the fourth quarter with the team trailing by 25. He shot 8–24, 3–12 and 8–23 in the next three games, respectively (a victory over the Clippers in Los Angeles, followed by losses in Utah and New Orleans), meaning that he had shot a horrific 31 percent over the four games, with his 78 shots, and 54 misses, more than twice those of any teammate.

His free shooting hand did not go unnoticed by teammates. Brown was taken out of the game in Utah after missing a couple of shots that Collins regarded as out of his range. "You wouldn't take out M.J. for taking those shots," Brown snapped at the incredulous coach, who seethed over what he regarded as another instance of Brown's insubordination. But Brown had said it, giving voice to a common lament on the bench—that there were two standards on the team: one for Jordan (and sometimes Stackhouse, depending on his performance), and another for everyone else. "You wouldn't take out M.J. *or Stack* for taking those shots," Brown went on.

Brown's comment further opened the door onto a steadily flagging respect for Collins. Meanwhile, Jordan was further separating himself from the team, even in triumph. The Wizards went home and, on February 21, in a victory over New Jersey, he scored 43 points in 43 minutes—suddenly just as hot as he had been frigid, only two nights earlier. It was the 119th 40-plus-point game of his career, and his last. He hit 18 of 30 shots against a variety of New Jersey defenders, and scored nearly half of his team's 89 points, while the rest of the starters took only 26 shots between them.

He did virtually everything a player can do. He pulled down 10 rebounds. He knocked a ball away and dived in a headlong attempt to secure a turnover. After the game, he happily agreed to do a brief television interview, during which the on-air reporter, alluding to Stackhouse's measly 11 points and the scant shots from all starters besides Jordan, simultaneously posed a question and offered a brief commentary: "Can you score 40 every night? You're gonna have to get Jerry and some of these guys *involved*."

Jordan made clear he would go it alone, if necessary. He was not Tonto; he was not anybody's nursemaid or running companion any longer. "I only have twenty-eight games left in my career," he said, "and I'll do whatever I have to do to get to the playoffs."

Facing the media scrum later, he issued grim warnings that would make their way to his teammates. Alluding to how he had dived for that loose ball, he indicated he wanted players to follow his example for tough play—or else. "[The dive for the ball] set the tone in terms of how bad I wanted to win this game," he said. "If they can't see that, if they can't see my love for the game, then obviously they don't need to be in uniform. And they don't need to be on this team."

The NBA trading deadline was just passing, and Jordan expressed scorn for those of his teammates who had privately worried about being dealt away (Kwame Brown's name had been among those bandied in trade rumors), particularly at a time, he suggested, when the team's mediocre record and their own play justified their worries. "If you're worried about a trade, then obviously you don't feel you've been playing great," he declared.

An agent for one Wizards player said later, "The message he sent that night was crude. And the timing sucked. Here they'd *won* and he's *talking to reporters* about maybe some time getting rid of players? People start wondering if they're going to have jobs there come summer. Are they gonna go unsigned? Traded? You go from being excited about a win to uneasy about your future. That was sure to piss some of them off."

Jordan left with Grover and the rest of his retinue, which had changed hardly at all during the two seasons but for the occasional presence of his old friend Oakley and Patrick Ewing. No young player had made it in, and few young players were any longer interested. He had spent much of the previous summer in Chicago working out with Bobby Simmons, who had won back a roster spot after being exiled to the developmental league for a while. Simmons regarded him as a mentor, perhaps the closest among the young players to having an off-court friendship with Jordan. But at 22 now, and well into his second season, Simmons had not shown anything on the court that offered hopes of greatness. He remained hardworking and loyal, and Jordan continued to offer encouragement, but that would be as far as their relationship went.

Still, he enjoyed having teammates and Wizards personnel around him once in a while. He required them for the same reason he'd always needed part-time companions—to serve as card players, comrades, foils and faithful listeners as he talked about everything from music to an insider's stories about the league and what he had learned, whom he thought he had figured out. He could sound very young in those moments on the plane, alternately affable and brash, thought a listener, who was struck by Jordan's love of stories that suggested he had outsmarted people and systems, transcending these limits just as easily as he had once surpassed physical ceilings. The star told people about his philosophy on dealing with referees, how he sought to charm the older officials and *shape* the young ones.

He studied refs, especially the older ones, he said—having made it a point to know the ones with quick tempers, the ones whose stubbornness increased if you challenged them, the ones who responded favorably to a little praise, the ones tough on a road club or, conversely, good for a home team. He said he thought several good refs seemed slightly and unconsciously to favor home teams, and mentioned a name, Joe Forte, a highly respected official who never, in the eyes of other observers, had evinced a tendency to be tougher on either road or home teams. But Jordan thought he had detected something that made Forte's presence a good thing for home teams, which, Jordan added, a smart player could use to his advantage. If you were talking to refs, you needed to know *how* to talk to them for maximum benefit. Never scream, never embarrass them, if you can help it, he advised. Talk conversationally, tease them, gently lecture them and do it discreetly, so they do not feel exposed in front of a crowd or television audience. *You get the most that way.* He mentioned a game in which he had complained to referee Gary Benson, another capable official, about a Wizard being held by an Indiana player.

Benson had not given ground, shaking his head, answering him: *Who's grabbing whom, Michael?*

Jordan calmly shot back, hoping at the very least to make Benson think twice the next time: "Gary, that's the *easy* way out."

Benson answered: "No, that's the *honest* way out."

Jordan had not succeeded in getting his teammate the call, but he thought the moment instructive as a way to give yourself the best chance of shaping an official's future behavior. He liked the idea of using his savvy to craft a subtle advantage over people, and enjoyed as much sharing the stories of his prowess.

But you needed listeners for that, and so it was necessary, as the second season wore down, that he had teammates around occasionally, and a variety of Wizards personnel. In these last months, he acted younger, needling teammates more, requiring the occasional games and banter even as he pulled back from the players in other moments.

Few occasions were exempt from the possibility that he might feel the need to compete. When a visiting Dean Smith walked with him through the Washington locker room one night, Jordan stopped, pivoted, pointed at Christian Laettner like he was throwing out a jab and loudly recalled how the North Carolina basketball team had recently whipped Laettner's alma mater, Duke. Jordan turned to Smith, his long finger still pointing at Laettner. His voice boomed: "Coach, ask him what happened in the game. Ask him *what happened. It shut him up.* It shut him up *good.*" His voice was unusually high-pitched, like an adolescent's. Smith's presence seemed to have transformed him. He was like a grown man who, around a parental figure, had reverted to his teenage self. It was a Jordan you seldom saw in even a quasi-private setting. "Coach, *look:* It shut him up *real good.*"

Smith was smiling in amusement, like a patriarch who had been through this before. Then Jordan wheeled on rookie guard Juan Dixon, an NCAA champion just a year earlier at Maryland, which had also fallen that week to North Carolina. "He's *reeeeeal* quiet, too," Jordan happily yelled. *"Shut him up good, too, Coach."*

He and Smith strolled over to his locker, and the player and his former coach sat on folding chairs opposite each other. Smith asked him about his mother, and Jordan said she was well, and they chatted a few more minutes about mutual friends and more family members—the general talk of men who love each other but, separated by generations, have little in common other than their reverence for each other. This was quite enough. Smith would do anything for the younger man, and vice versa. Jordan had been fortunate at many stages in his life, but never more so than when he had entered the world of Dean Smith, where he had been changed forever. As a freshman, he had hit an open jumper to win an NCAA championship for North Carolina—The Shot, Jordan called it, the *real* shot—and overnight, his life and persona were altered forever. Even his name, he thought, seemed to change—from Mike Jordan to Michael Jordan. And that would have been enough to make some players drunk on self-adoration, except that Dean Smith had told him what parts of his game still needed improvement if he wanted to be a truly great player. The day after the championship victory, Mike Jordan could be found in the North Carolina gymnasium, working on his shot.

Dean Smith had prodded all that out of him, though Smith also served as a quiet model for the proposition that there was a world beyond sports in which a complete man needed to be engaged, that there was an obligation to something beyond scores and trophies. He had fought racial segregation in the early '60s and lobbied now against the death penalty. He assisted the poor and worked for better schools; he had contacts ranging from powerful politicians to desperate people on death row. Regardless of an observer's politics, it was hard to dispute the notion that Smith was as decent as men come, and several people close to Michael Jordan wondered how the star's life may have been different had he experienced a few more years around Dean Smith, who had coached him, after all, for only three seasons, a much shorter period than either Phil Jackson or Doug Collins.

Jordan mumbled something about big games coming up, and the two bowed their heads toward each other, whispering, Smith doing most of the talking.

Jordan softly responded, "Right, right, yes, Coach," a title he reserved for Smith. "Yes, Coach. Right."

And then they were done. The two stood, Jordan sticking out his hand, his adolescent tone of 15 minutes earlier giving way to his middle-aged baritone. He shook his old coach's hand and said, "It's always good to see you, my friend."

He took a step toward the door with Smith, looking over his shoulder. He saw Laettner and grinned. "We shut 'em *all up,* Coach."

Laettner smirked. From a chair, Juan Dixon just looked up, open-mouthed, staring respectfully back and forth between Jordan and the departing Smith, appearing uncertain what to do next. Jordan smiled at him. Jordan liked Dixon, a good, if streaky, shooter and a thin self-invented kid, whose steeliness in basketball and life, as the son of intravenous drug users who had died of AIDS during his Baltimore youth, defied doubt. His right arm sported a tattoo: "ONLY THE STRONG SURVIVE." Work on your ballhandling and point-guard skills, Jordan had suggested to him, and Dixon labored to get better.

Dixon was his kind of player, like Tyronn Lue, for whom he continued to demonstrate in public an affection he seldom displayed around the other youngsters. Lue was what he wanted in players, even if sometimes he had a dig for him, too. He'd drape an arm around Lue's shoulder after a good hustle play, reaching down, with his six-inch advantage in height, and rubbing the top of Lue's head, his hand lingering there. "I listened; I learned more about how to play with Michael this year, because sometimes before it was hard," said Lue, who felt himself at last understanding where Jordan wanted him positioned on the floor.

Lue and Dixon persevered, a quality that Jordan long had insisted upon in anyone who wanted to win his lasting respect. When Lue missed several games because of a separated shoulder suffered in diving for a loose ball, Jordan uncharacteristically talked at length about how much a single player's absence meant, declaring, "That T-Lue injury *really* hurt us." And no play by a teammate all season seemed to excite him more than when Lue dived to the floor and secured a loose ball late during a one-point overtime win in Boston, Jordan yelling happily and clapping on the court, exclaiming afterward: "Our guys were diving on the floor for loose balls today . . ."

But, in fact, it was generally just one or two guys, which had come to infuriate him. He had a will to match his artistry, and strings of championships as a result. But never had he learned tact in his work, nor had anyone ever insisted that he acquire some. Greatness had spawned entitlement: He could lash teammates because he was Jordan. His productivity gave him eternal license. His rants of February became his ripostes of March. He likened himself to a parent whose children didn't listen.

He had viewed the young Wizards most perceptively at the start of his comeback, when he stepped onto the court as a man in his late 30s and recognized just how far the early twentysomething players, and his teenage prodigy, needed to progress simply to make the franchise respectable, and just how much patience would be necessary. He displayed his most sensitivity during the first season's earliest days, and perhaps no more so than at the first preseason game, when they had been thrashed in Detroit. It was the night when, with the team looking badly outclassed at halftime, he had gently encouraged them in the hallway just outside the locker room before they retook the floor for the second half. He had complimented Brendan Haywood on a dunk, and told the others that they were all doing fine, that they just needed to concentrate and play hard. *Let's go, we can do this. Okay, guys.*

He sounded so much *older* in those early days, older and more enlightened, more worldly and supportive. The approach represented the best Jordan, but it lasted only weeks into the start of that first season, before it began dying. "I think he was rougher at the end [of the first comeback season]," Lue observed. "In the beginning, he was a lot more lenient because he didn't know what to expect." His attitude changed, thought Lue, down the stretch of that first season, "when he thought we had the potential to make the playoffs."

All along, he had needed an appearance in the playoffs to be satisfied. With the team's prospects gloomier by the day now, his rants about his failing teammates began. He sounded increasingly *young*— young and indulged, young and self-pitying, lashing out in a manner certain to trigger headlines and a public backlash.

With the defeats mounting, and his remaining games down to 20, his anger spilled out following his final appearance as a player in Madison Square Garden—a one-point loss in a Sunday matinee to the Knicks that dropped the team three games under .500. Jordan had played brilliantly—scoring 39 points in an indomitable effort that left him with a cut chin when he dived to the floor for another loose ball. But his effort was overshadowed by his postgame reaction. He excoriated a group of unnamed twentysomething teammates for lack of effort: "It's very disappointing when a forty-year-old man has more desire than twenty-five, twenty-six, twenty-three-year-old people. He's diving for loose balls, he's busting his chin—and it's not reciprocated by other players on the team."

The focus of the following day's stories changed in that instant. Had Jordan remained silent, the theme would have been his stalwart finale in New York, on a day when no other Wizard scored more than 13 points, and Stackhouse made only one field goal all afternoon. But the media became riveted by the image of a bullying Jordan turning on his team. Following a crushing 26-point loss in Phoenix, he disclosed to the press what he had angrily told his teammates at halftime: that, if they just gave him the word, he could go home and golf while they continued exhibiting so little will and skill. "If you want to play hard basketball, we'll play hard basketball," he told them. "If you guys want to take it off, I could be playing golf somewhere . . ."

He made clear to them that he had other options. "I'm not wasting my breath. . . . I can do other things with it. I can have a nice cigar."

He showed the side of himself that had belittled teammates dating back to his pre-championship days in Chicago, where he enjoyed the prerogative of a royal to flay any unworthy commoner, once declaring that his Bulls teammate Horace Grant shouldn't be permitted to eat on the team plane as he hadn't played well enough to deserve an in-flight meal, and demonstrating his disdain for an ill Grant before another game by telling him to take a fucking aspirin and play. His tirades now mirrored perfectly the habits ingrained during his Bulls days, contrasting unpleasantly with his long-standing insistence that he had returned to the court to give the younger Wizards the benefit of his knowledge and on-court leadership. He looked far less like their mentor than a temperamental raja.

Between the New York and Phoenix games, the team had come home. One evening, I found myself standing in front of him in another press scrum, wondering whether he worried about the possible damage his blasts might have on team morale. I finally asked: "Is there a risk of alienating teammates over the long run with such public criticism of them?"

He looked at me, long and unflinching. No matter how enduring his grudges against particular journalists and publications, he never was rude with cameras on, and seldom declined to answer a question. He blinked and pursed his lips, and his eyes narrowed in thought.

Exposure and pain were good things, he reasoned aloud. "The truth *hurts*," he said, staring hard. "Sometimes you just got to say the things that may hurt. . . . You have to look in the mirror and say, Maybe he's right. . . . That's why we say we have the freedom of speech, [because] sometimes we take a pause and listen and maybe evaluate. Now at the end of the day, you may say that was a crock of shit, but at least you took the time to understand."

Crock of shit: He spoke like that only when testy and in the mood to argue.

So I asked: "But publicly [criticize them] rather than privately?"

"Sure. Frustrations aren't always maintained privately; we play publicly," he answered, and went on in this vein, and it was in that moment that one could see how Jordan always had used to his advantage this arrangement between professional athletes and the sporting media. He understood the symbiosis at work. He knew that the media would only be too happy to report his words about team-mates screwing up, that generations of reporters had been accus-tomed to having underperforming players fed to them. Most reporters had come to expect it, as part of the compact. In sports, par-ticularly for superstars, such attacks were generally seen as the pre-rogative of greatness.

He wouldn't stop now. Staring into a thicket of cameras and recorders on another occasion, he ridiculed his teammates as a group, rhetorically asking how they could think of being content, given their basketball histories: "It's not like they've done anything." Aside from himself, the only one in the group who had won an NBA champi-onship, he noted, was Tyronn Lue, during his Laker days. One winning teammate then became zero, somehow. Thinking about Lue's champi-onship ring, he added, "And he was only a reserve." Message: Jordan was the only winner.

At least publicly, the youngest player on the team understood how best to deal with Jordan's criticisms. Kwame Brown said largely prudent things to the media about the boss: "Anyone can learn from Michael" if that "player listens." But, privately, Brown continued to reel under Jordan's and Collins's lashings. There were games in which he would be yanked, vaudevillian-like, after a missed shot or two. Despairing anew, he began to seek counsel from other teammates, notably Stackhouse, who could provide solace but little else, suffering beneath the weight of his own disappointments. Brown had nowhere to turn.

Brown was not blameless—his intensity remained sporadic, and his conditioning needed vast improvement—but few other 20-year-olds in any line of work suffered under such persistent public and private critiques from their superiors. So it was that, one morning, he endured another insult. From 15 feet or so, during a closed-door practice session, Jordan threw a missile of a chest-pass at him. The ball thudded against the surprised Brown's hands and fell to the floor. Jordan snapped, in what sounded like a final verdict to one observer: "Bad motherfuckin' hands."

Jordan had brought him close to tears the season before, but no longer. Brown stared back stonily, the estrangement complete.

Veterans generally had an easier time coping with the boss. In the wake of Jordan's New York outburst, 32-year-old Bryon Russell smiled. "He could have been talking about me also," he said. "And if he says something [critical of teammates], who's gonna say anything about it?"

Russell muffled a chuckle, understanding the media well, not about to feed the beast, not about to express surprise at anything, full of sly wisdom about the way things worked, about who was where in the pecking order. He had fit in nicely with the team, even if his play had not lived up to expectations. He had quickly become one of the most popular Wizards, occupying Tyrone Nesby's old locker, from where he'd banter with veterans like Oakley and Laettner, and the younger players, too. He tried to click with everyone, even becoming a part of Jordan's informal Breakfast Club, lifting weights early in the morning with his past and present antagonist.

No, it wasn't weird playing with Jordan, Russell said. He still *knew,* he said—that Jordan had pushed off on him just before hitting the winning basket in the '98 Finals, and that always rustled between them, he thought. "But it's no big deal for me," he said. He went back and forth as to whether he would be immortalized as the fallen defender over whom Jordan made the shot, or whether he should even care. "Maybe *this year* is what people will remember most about him," he said, this sounding like a faint hope.

But Jordan never let him forget about '98, he added, smiling crookedly, exuding the stoicism of a veteran who prided himself on being able to endure any taunt.

"I own you," Jordan sometimes said to him before they matched up in practice scrimmages.

"Okay, let's get it on," Russell routinely responded.

He was a survivor. He still exchanged trash talk with Jordan, because if the Man wanted it, he would give it back to him.

No player on the Wizards that season was more misunderstood. Visiting media tended to see him as rough and a tad bitter, but B-Russell was probably the most congenial of all the Wizards, and certainly the most generous with people who could do his career no favor. Without ever talking about it on the road, he regularly gave $100 to young locker-room attendants just for bringing him a box of popcorn or a sports drink or whatever other small thing he might need, interested in them in a way that most players weren't.

He could be kind without losing his steeliness, without forgetting how tough it had been to get to this place. At this advanced stage of his career, he was a bubble player who knew he could not afford to back down to anything or anyone. One night, against his old Utah team, new Jazz guard Matt Harpring had hit him with an elbow, and not knowing whether it was intentional or not, Russell had swiftly told him that if he did it again, he'd *whip his ass*. Russell did not view his threat as an act of malevolence, simply a survivor's response: He could not allow himself to be pushed around. A survivor in the league had to stay tough, be a good teammate and use his savvy, and this he had tried to do—in games, on practice courts and in the locker room. If Jordan wanted to bait him during a scrimmage, he would answer the call. Married and a father of three, Russell stayed tough. "He could have been talking about me," he repeated carefully of Jordan's outbursts, still grinning. "Who's gonna tell him he can't?"

Russell's rhetorical question represented the typical player's caution in deflecting Jordan's criticisms. But, privately, the irritations of some players grew, often with matters that had nothing to do with Jordan's statements. Several players had tired of Jordan holding the locker room closed after the game for well beyond the 10-minute limit permitted under league rules, while he took his time shedding his uniform, showering and beginning the process of receiving treatment for his knees. If the media wanted to talk to them, the players needed to wait until at last Jordan said it was okay for the doors to be opened. His indifference to their desires, and his flouting of another NBA rule that the organization and league chose not to enforce in his case, struck several players as simply more evidence of how Jordan was regularly coddled; that though he wanted players to abide by standards, he exempted himself when convenient.

The matter of doors opening late would not have mattered on a winning team. It was the kind of thing that second-tier teams bickered over, a symptom of much graver problems, particularly an offense that, in the judgment of players, had thwarted their talents. The slow-moving offense, Stackhouse believed, catered to Jordan. Out of respect and the need to sustain club morale, nobody on the team talked about it. Then they picked up newspapers and turned on televisions to learn that Jordan had skewered them, again. The team's tensions became more difficult to conceal. In a bit of interesting timing, Abe Pollin came to speak to his team, at a morning practice, on March 11.

It was an unexpected visit, and it occurred less than 48 hours after Jordan had criticized his teammates in New York. The owner noted his pride in the players, mentioned his hope of making the playoffs and wished everyone well. Pollin was getting a look at a team seized by dissension.

And that is when the danger of Jordan's New York eruption revealed itself. The very criticism that Jordan hoped would spur his teammates had actually raised questions about morale and, in turn, about his fitness as a leader. No one else could have done such an effective job of undermining his future in the organization, especially as the players, at least publicly, had remained obediently quiet. He alone had opened a window onto the Wizards' turmoil. Jordan had exposed Jordan.

He never had faced such a dilemma in his Bulls days, enjoying the power then to lacerate teammates, as it was always understood that he was coming back to play and bring riches to the owners the following season: Midas could do what he wished. Now, with his playing days and ticket-selling clout nearing an end, his leverage was running out. Someone else was in control of his fate, and no one could be sure what Abe Pollin felt as he said good-bye to the players that morning. At the very least, just a month before the season's end, Jordan had supplied Pollin with a pretext for his dismissal: Morale was low; a managerial change might be in the interests of all.

Collins wasn't helping Jordan's position. The coach said that he didn't understand his team: that the players were so sensitive and unpredictable, that he never knew what he would be getting from them on one night to the next, that he didn't know if he'd *ever* know.

The problem with exuding doom is that it tends to attract doom. Players hear about it. The nervous and resentful become more nervous and resentful. There is something self-fulfilling about fatalism. Seldom had a star and a coach so jeopardized their futures with so few words.

Collins's pressures mounted. By then, Jordan had told Collins that he still expected to make the playoffs and, in late February, shared his belief with the press, raising the stakes: "I think we're gonna make the playoffs. . . . I've never had doubts we would make the playoffs."

Collins knew he had problems. The fit of the team wasn't right, he told people. They had too many shooting guards—too many Twos—and not enough people at the Three, the small-forward position. Stackhouse was playing hard at the Three but he was better at the Two, where he had thrived until Jordan became a starter and Stack had to move to the Three. B-Russell had played hard at the Three, but Russell couldn't supply the offense of the league's premier Threes, strictly a backup man now. So they had no bona fide Three, and were overloaded with Twos—no different from last season.

These realizations were coming late—too late, really—at the same time that morale problems were coming to a head. Collins freely admitted to having made mistakes with players, though, on balance, he thought he'd gone easier on people this time around, after his failures in Chicago and Detroit. Sensitive to the perception that he was, as he put it, "a ballbuster," he had sought to be less strident in Washington, and to avoid becoming consumed by the job. He learned much, he thought, from his time in Chicago and Detroit, where he regularly came into his office too early, stayed too late and then rushed home to find a TV and watch all the basketball he could. Sometimes, having seen upcoming opponents on the tube, he wouldn't be able to sleep at all, lying in bed and replaying in his mind everything about the foes, wondering how he would stop them, his mind not shutting off. He couldn't get away from basketball, and it had fried him, he thought.

His basketball obsession had ended, his friends hoped. He had tried, he thought, to do everything right since coming to the Wizards, honoring a deal that he struck with his wife about his nights at home. He didn't watch any TV basketball, unless there was a game involving his son's Duke team or an NBA foe whom the Wizards would be playing the very next night. Predictably, after watching a league game, he sometimes wouldn't be able to sleep all night. So he wasn't entirely cured, though everyone hoped his promise to his wife meant there were far fewer of those nights.

The comeback's start had seemed so promising: a relaxed Collins talked of a new approach. He had tried being more accepting and steady in the face of difficulties. When the team struggled midway through the second season, he sought to be inspirational, loosely quoting the inventor Thomas Edison on the subject of perseverance: "Many of life's failures are people who did not realize how close to success they were when they gave up."

He grafted his own moral onto Edison's success, viewing him, tellingly, as a resolute workaholic whose evening habits bore a striking resemblance to those of a driven basketball coach: "*a guy who used to sleep two hours a night, a guy who had many failures but never gave up.* That's what I told our guys. To face failure: that's one thing. Giving up is something else. And you're closer than you think. You just gotta keep fighting."

His close friend Alvin Gentry, once an assistant under him in Detroit, and for a while the head coach of the Clippers, had felt sympathy for him in their days together, believing that Collins had no releases, that his basketball team was akin to a great love, that it was like a child that Collins felt he had to care for in every moment. His friend had been able to think of little else, said Gentry, who believed that Collins had learned from his excesses and would better manage his third coaching chance. Other friends said privately that he better have learned, because head coaches seldom received a fourth chance in the NBA without having won and demonstrated cool.

Collins tried his best, but he could not resist the tides of his nature. He became irritable with media and even those close to him, snapping disdainfully one morning at an assistant coach who was trying to make a point about strategy: "You've had too much coffee."

He was not great at listening to suggestions from peers, so it came as a surprise to no one that he had trouble dealing with any dissenting player whose last name was not Jordan. His relationship with Christian Laettner, a moody man himself, had been up and down, particularly when Laettner expressed dissatisfaction early in the season at seemingly being passed over for playing time in favor of younger, unproven players. But no player, aside from Stackhouse, had been more explosively defiant than Kwame Brown, who said he felt himself playing scared again, like the previous season. Collins's public statements about him had heightened the youngster's anxieties. Even Collins's rare praise of his efforts usually sounded like partial criticisms: "Kwame was great—until he got tired. I told [Kwame], 'Go in there and get on a bike . . . so I can play you at the end of a game.'"

After Brown had snapped at him in Utah for being benched, the player apologized. But their fragile truce lasted only five weeks. When Collins pulled him from a game in Phoenix with a critical comment, Brown blurted, "Fuck you . . ."

Collins seemed shaken. Afterward, Jordan told the team that such misconduct would not be tolerated: "You do not treat our coach that way."

Brown apologized for the Phoenix incident, too, but nothing in his relationship with Collins really changed, he said later. He privately told people that he had given respect to Collins that had not been returned. For Collins, the process of mending relationships had ended; he was focused on winning. The days for reversing the team's slide were running out. After going back and forth about it, Collins decided to replace Hughes for good in the starting lineup with Lue, though the change would be coming late, with more than 80 percent of the season over. The coaches had concluded that Hughes wasn't the right point guard for the Wizards' setup offense, not very adept at distributing the ball, especially to Jordan, who was peeved about it.

Collins continued to insist that only he made coaching calls. But if Jordan demanded the benching of a youngster slow to accept reality, like Hughes, so be it. Hughes knew how to score, Jordan said, but he hadn't shown the ability to get him the ball often enough or where he wanted it. Jordan's demand didn't necessarily reflect ego, thought one team official; it was somewhere between ego and commitment to team, like most issues involving Jordan. He wanted to win and he wanted his points.

So Hughes would be benched. The coaches waited, according to one witness, until just before a game in Portland to tell him, fearful that otherwise the change would leave the young player distraught and worthless as a reserve. Hughes quietly listened to the news of his demotion, then sat out the very next game with an injury, in Seattle.

No personnel change or juggling of the lineup made any meaningful difference. The team couldn't reach the .500 mark in February or March, the possibility growing that the Wizards might fail to make the playoffs.

By then, a season and a half in Washington had left its marks on Collins. His gray crew cut looked sparser; the deep crease under his right eye deeper still. He vented: "The players have to *hurt* when they don't win, just like the coaches do. We have to hurt together."

His face shook ever so slightly as he spoke. "This is one of those wins you really remember with your team," he said, after triumphing at home over New Jersey, "because we've had a lot of ups and downs. . . . I've never been more proud of them. . . . I was very emotional. I became a grandpa yesterday." It seemed, for an instant, he was close to tears. His voice trembled. His baby grandson, he said, "got his first win tonight."

It was Collins, all of him, in about 30 seconds—his pride, joy, anxieties, hurt, his demand that others hurt, his emotions naked and spilling, the very impulses that led associates to worry about him, just as people had worried in Chicago and Detroit.

He was more mercurial than ever. He could be very kind, as when, before a game, he praised the job done by the then struggling young Denver coach, Jeff Bzdelik, and defended the beleaguered coach of the losing Toronto Raptors, Lenny Wilkens. But too often he walked through flames of his own making. When an out-of-town reporter wondered aloud one night whether Jordan's presence might be a "double-edged sword," asking whether the star's criticisms might be harming young players' confidence, Collins flared at her: "How do you know that?"

"I don't. I'm just asking you."

"You just said that about Michael. You said that is what he is like."

The reporter sighed, plunged ahead: "Can it be a double-edged sword?"

"I don't think . . . it can ever be a negative."

"Unless you're not strong enough to handle it," the reporter said softly.

Collins fired back. "Whose weakness is that? . . . To be successful on this level, you can't be weak."

The questions signaled a new wave of scrutiny. Two weeks later, someone else asked Collins if players had become afraid of the legend. Collins snickered, "How would I know that? You'd have to ask them." He added, "It doesn't scare me." He looked around and, with a broadening smile on his face, began laughing loudly, a touch mockingly, looking back at the offending reporter and then at the rest of the press corps, as if to say, GET A LOAD OF THIS GUY, WHAT A QUESTION, studying the faces, in the way of a man trying to get a read on a room.

The coach proved his fealty to Jordan at every turn. But never did Jordan send a message of unqualified admiration for Collins. Few scenes so reflected Collins's status in Jordan's eyes as a practice on the morning of a late March game in Los Angeles—the last time Jordan would be competing against Phil Jackson.

Wizards players and coaches lingered around a basket, idly chatting and bouncing balls while Jordan held court with reporters. He was asked about Jackson, about whom, in the late '90s, Jordan had said he "loved." It seemed, now as then, such a strong word for a man with no history of lavishing affection on people in the basketball world. Jordan took his time answering. "The thing I remember greatly about Phil," he said, "is that he challenged me. He was never intimidated by me. When most coaches could easily be intimidated by me, he came in and if I played bad, he told me I played bad. If he felt I needed to improve in areas, he told me I needed to improve in those areas. I respected him for doing that. I wanted a coach who could always tell me what my weaknesses were . . . because it would only help me be a better basketball player. This is what Coach Smith did for me. This is what Phil Jackson did for me."

Doug Collins stood only 30 feet away, in Jordan's line of sight. The omission of his name said much, and in the end too much. He had given Jordan his friendship, deference and loyalty for years. But there are limits to what deference can get you. Maybe men cannot love those who need their love too much. Jordan appreciated Collins, who had given him whatever he wanted, whenever he wanted it—given Jordan everything except a reason to revere him.

While Collins fretted and Pollin contemplated his star's diatribes, Jordan's attorney, Frederick Sperling, prepared to deal with the problem posed by Karla Knafel. On a foggy March morning, he headed toward the commodious Chicago courtroom of Cook County Circuit Judge Richard A. Siebel, who had begun his day by presiding over hearings in the civil cases of *IEP, Inc. v. Williams and Crab Street v. Mid-City National Bank*. Most of the matters in Siebel's courtroom involved unglamorous litigants and their business disputes, which meant that the three rows of comfortable spectator benches on each side of the courtroom's center aisle were generally free of reporters or anyone else. This seemed just fine for Richard Siebel, a quick-witted, good-humored man with a wry smile that signaled he had heard every legal ruse ever advanced by connivers, so, Please, we'll all be out of here sooner if you spare me any nonsense.

Solemnity seemed an extravagance. The court clerk wore a tie with a sketch of a golf ball on it. Siebel peered over horn-rims and tried to move the morning's motions along: "What do you want to do? . . . Just give me a date. . . . You got it. . . . We're just talking a couple of minutes on the phone. . . . Let's get it done. . . ."

They came, they went.

At 10:00 a.m. on Thursday, March 20, 2003, the spectator section of the courtroom was still empty. At 10:45, a man and a woman entered the courtroom, two sketch artists who had arrived early for the main event. Then at 11:22, the doors flew open—bam, bam—and, in a few moments, Siebel's quiet courtroom was packed for the 11:30 hearing. Karla Knafel arrived in shades, sporting streaked blond hair, a long black sweater over black hip-huggers, and a white blouse unbuttoned at the midriff. Male reporters selflessly took time-out from scribbling notes to observe that she had a spectacular body.

Alongside Knafel sat her lead attorney Michael Hannafan—60ish, tall, lean, gray-haired, ruddy-complected, wearing a gray pinstriped suit and fiddling with his light horn-rims. He had index cards on the table in front of him. In red ink, he had written on one, in large capital letters, EXTORTION ARGUMENT—and just beneath these words, in blue ink, he had jotted, PHONY.

At the other counsel's table sat Sperling, adjusting dark horn-rims, compact in his own gray pinstripes, already with his game face on, looking around, taking a swipe at his dark hair, now and then hunching his shoulders, his head involuntarily jutting to the right, a tic of sorts, like that of an athlete poised for battle. He stood to whisper to a colleague, which was the moment Hannafan chose to call out to him from across the aisle, *"Fred, Fred."*

Sperling took a few steps toward Hannafan, who said brightly, "Fred, I want to introduce you to Karla Knafel. Karla, I'd like you to meet Frederick Sperling."

Knafel, remaining seated, smiled, extended her hand toward Sperling and said, "Hello."

Sperling froze, as if a lethal contagion might be on Knafel's palm. He stayed planted about five feet away, declining the handshake. "Good morning," he said, and turned away.

Titters in the courtroom.

Sperling took his seat.

The man with the golf ball tie called out: "Jordan versus Knafel."

What Sperling wanted from Siebel by the hearing's end was a dismissal of Knafel's $5 million counterclaim against Jordan, and a judgment in favor of Jordan's claim, which would bar Knafel from attempting to make Jordan pay any part of that $5 million. On the other hand, Hannafan wanted his client's counterclaim to be moved in time to a trial, which, if he got it, would permit him to depose Jordan about his admitted affair with Knafel and why he had paid her $250,000 for her silence already. The prospect of a deposition and trial would be Hannafan's best chance of getting something for his client, agreed most legal analysts, who envisioned a possible scenario: a worried Jordan, wishing to avoid the embarrassment that would accompany the release of a deposition transcript and trial coverage, agreeing to a settlement that paid Knafel a substantial sum.

A consensus view was that an out-of-court settlement would be the only winning outcome for the Knafel team, given that analysts found it virtually impossible to imagine the circumstances under which a judge or a jury would believe that a genuine contract existed between Knafel and Jordan. None of the classic elements of a contract appeared to exist. What was Knafel giving Jordan aside from her promise not to expose him to the public? New York courts did not enforce such hush-money contracts, so why would it be reasonable for Illinois to do otherwise? Wouldn't enforcement open the door to tacit extortion of public figures engaged in embarrassing private behavior? Moreover, in a he-said/she-said case, how could Knafel prove to the satisfaction of a court that Jordan had orally promised her the $5 million?

Knafel's past suggested that a jury might not find her an altogether sympathetic figure, her love of sports figures having sometimes embroiled her in difficulties. She had a two-year-old daughter with Portland Trail Blazers forward Dale Davis, whom she had successfully sued for child support. She had an 11-year-old child with a former minor league pitcher in the Chicago White Sox organization, that pregnancy occurring during her sexual activity with Jordan, who had paid for her hospital bill during the delivery and sent her flowers, believing that the child might be his until tests proved otherwise.

Jordan's $250,000 payment to her had been conditioned in part on her agreement that she would not file a paternity suit against him. Any trial now held out the possibility of embarrassing her, too, but she was not the one with a public image to protect. She was a small-town Midwestern girl, living in an Indianapolis suburb, doing hair. She had sung in a band off and on, hoping to put a CD of her songs together.

On that day, Hannafan would allow reporters to meet her briefly at his Chicago office. At 39, Knafel was a composed and pleasant woman, smiling and solicitous and all-American perky-voiced in that way of affable hairstylists, happily telling thirsty reporters they could find "pop" in the office refrigerator.

Later she would stand in front of microphones to say she was "saddened and shocked when Michael [claimed] that I've tried to extort him into paying the amount he owes me under our contract. I've honored our contract for the past several years by remaining publicly silent about our love affair while he, apparently, had no intention of keeping his promise to me."

She said she looked forward to presenting her case to a Chicago jury. "I sincerely hope that this unfortunate episode can be resolved fairly in court—or *out of court,* excuse me."

Hannafan stressed this point, too: They hoped to settle out of court.

If the case actually went to a jury trial, the odds of the Knafel team prevailing with a Chicago jury seemed roughly akin to that of a small college basketball team knocking off the old Bulls. The Knafel team had to pin its hopes on Jordan's recognition that grave embarrassment awaited him if Hannafan ever got him on a witness stand or into a deposition.

But no settlement talks would be necessary if Siebel dismissed Knafel's claim. Fred Sperling wanted to send Knafel and Hannafan home as immediate losers. If he got his wish, he could telephone Jordan and break the good news before the star began a Western road trip.

He stood, faced Siebel, squared his shoulders and spread his feet slightly, like a wrestler. "Our position is this is extortion under Illinois law," he said.

Sperling argued that, even if an oral agreement between Knafel and Jordan had been entered into, that it was unenforceable because it violated public policy, just as a murder-for-hire contract would be unenforceable.

In his seat, Hannafan chuckled. "Murder?" he muttered.

Sperling continued pressing the extortion point: "*No one* would gratuitously offer to pay $5 million for silence unless he believed such payment was *necessary . . .*"

Hannafan now had his turn. He revealed that it would be a day filled with basketball metaphors, responding that Sperling had cast up an "air ball," asserting that Sperling's claim of extortion was baseless: that Knafel never had threatened Jordan with exposure, that Jordan had made an offer of five million in exchange for her promise to keep their affair confidential, and that she had agreed and now wanted him to abide by the terms of their deal.

Hannafan presented the court and media audience with a look at the affair and Jordan's effort to keep it quiet—all matters that he would expound upon at trial, if given the opportunity. "They'd had unprotected sex in Phoenix in November of 1990 . . ." he said. "She had a basis for believing [she was pregnant by him]."

Hannafan argued that the married Jordan became concerned about the damage that an affair and Knafel's pregnancy might have on his image, the star fully understanding at the time that Knafel's child might or might not be his. "Mr. Jordan is not a dumb person . . ." Hannafan went on. "He'd been around the league for seven years, and he figured he wasn't her only partner. . . . He was concerned that Karla might be forced to file a paternity suit. . . . He wanted to protect his image. He wanted to keep it from the public and from his family. . . . [Jordan] entered into an agreement. . . . He didn't care *whose* baby it was. He cared only about [the] tarnishing [of] his public image. . . . He [had] millions of dollars in endorsements and millions to come. . . . [So] he hedged his bets. Everybody knows Mr. Jordan is a gambling man, and he took a gamble. If the child turned out to be his, he got the bargain of the century."

Hannafan concluded nimbly by focusing on the $250,000 payment. "[Jordan's attorneys] are admitting that even that payment *obligated* her to keep their affair silent."

Sperling swiftly rose and asked for a dismissal of the Knafel claim.

Siebel interrupted Sperling: "This is what troubles me: You're saying there was *no* agreement, but that if there *was* an agreement, it was unenforceable."

That is when it became clear that the Jordan team wouldn't get what it wanted. They wouldn't be walking out of here with a dismissal of Knafel's claim. The suit would stay alive for a while longer, so the story would stay in the news. By June, the Knafel side would lose, its counterclaim dismissed. But they weren't going home as losers on this day. The newspaper headlines, at least in Chicago the next morning, would include Knafel's allegations and how she was going forward with her claim. The bad p.r. would persist.

Sperling's shoulder hunched. Skillfully, he tried a final time: Whatever agreement might have been entered into between Jordan and Knafel, he argued, was "violative of public policy." New York courts, among others, did not enforce such agreements, he reminded Siebel. "Illinois courts should do no less," he concluded.

Siebel smiled: It was over for today. There would be no decision. He scheduled another hearing. Sperling would need to wait another two and a half months to get the dismissal he wanted. He wouldn't be able to call Jordan in the West that afternoon with great news. Siebel looked at a new sheaf of papers, moving on.

Hannafan had cause to be only temporarily delighted. The day's hearing had ended, but the ill will hadn't. Afterward, attorneys from the two sides hotly disagreed with each other over a procedural matter. Mike Hannafan thought that someone from the Sperling team had acted menacingly around Hannafan's son Blake, also an attorney on the case. Hannafan raced over.

"Don't you do that, don't you do that," Hannafan yelled at the guy.

In turn, Sperling rushed up to Hannafan, going eye-to-eye. It was better than 99 percent of NBA stare-downs. Hannafan puffed his chest out, yelling at Sperling to back up: "Don't touch me. I mean it. Don't touch me."

"You *glare*," Sperling shot back. "You stare me down all you want, Mike."

"Get out of my space," Hannafan boomed.

"Fine. I'll get out of your space." Sperling took a step back.

Through it all, Karla Knafel looked on impassively. There was much weirdness to that morning, none greater than the sensation that Michael Jordan seemed to have nothing to do with this courtroom or the day's event, so deftly had he distanced himself from the controversy. It was exactly the effect the Jordan team had hoped for.

By the time Frederick Sperling left Richard Siebel's courtroom, and Michael Jordan stepped on a plane for his final Western road trip, the Wizards had only 15 games left in the season. They would lose 10 of them. Jordan looked exhausted by the late stages of games now. During the four weeks prior to this final stretch, he had run himself into the ground. On February 23, he played 51 of 53 minutes during an overtime loss at home to Dallas, during which he and Stackhouse each scored 30 points and the Wizards led early, 21–4. He insisted he felt neither discouraged nor tired afterward, moving on to play 41 minutes during a win in Indiana, 49 minutes in an exhilarating overtime victory at MCI over Houston, and 43 minutes in another home spanking of Chicago. Jordan averaged nearly 27 points during the four games, but he also had played an average of 46 minutes a night, and neither he nor the team would be as effective again for the remainder of the season.

They lost four of their next five games, including the stinger in New York. He looked not only angry but spent afterward, his 39 points having come in 43 minutes, matching the time he had spent on the court less than 48 hours earlier, in a loss to Milwaukee.

His tank was emptying now. The season had another 38 days to go, but he had scored 30 points in a game for the last time in his career. Stackhouse would take over as the team's leading scorer for the next four games, averaging 30 points while the team went 2–2. Jordan continued to play more than anyone else on the team, averaging 42 minutes a game—including a team-high 50 minutes in an overtime loss at home to Detroit. But his second half production had plummeted. While still proficient, he was no longer the player of even a month earlier. His anger escalated. He repeated his demand that his teammates start playing tougher. They squandered leads, he said. It was the team's "M.O.," he declared.

In Los Angeles, thinking back on their Bulls days together, his old assistant coach Tex Winter thought he saw a thread running from the star's beginning to end. "I think the [Wizards] are better for having had him," Winter said. "But I think he expects too much from teammates. . . . No doubt, an awful lot of the players that he's played with in the past, at least in their own minds, believe he alienated them; they've resented the treatment they've received."

Winter wondered: Did he make the humiliated better? At what cost?

Horace Grant, he thought, never had entirely forgiven Jordan.

And the others? In Chicago? In Washington?

Winter wasn't sure.

In the end, he didn't think the humiliations had been good for morale. He worried that a new generation of superstars now emulated Jordan's criticism of lesser teammates. "They feel they have that *prerogative*," he said, and referred specifically to Kobe Bryant. "I don't think it's necessarily good."

His 13 years with Jordan meant that Winter had coached him longer than anyone else. But, in all that time, Winter never thought he understood him, mystified over why a man so beloved so often played the part of a tormentor. "For some reason, Michael gets a satisfaction out of humiliating people," he said. "I think it might be part of his competitive nature. I think he competes even there . . . [in] personal relationships."

Jordan's last appearance in L.A. meant that Phil Jackson would need to field questions about their friendship, questions that always played to the popular belief that he enjoyed the kinds of bonds with players that most coaches didn't. In fact, he didn't have close relationships with quite a few of his players, past and present, some of whom, like Tyronn Lue, had had no real relationship with him at all. He could be hard and distant with people who did not help him win and, in that way, was not so different from scores of old-school coaches. If there was any difference between them, it was that he had an unshakable confidence, a measure of serenity and a certainty about his goals. And, in Chicago, he'd had Michael Jordan. Nearly anywhere the Lakers found themselves, Jackson heard a similar question: What did you learn from Jordan?

Almost without his listeners knowing it, Jackson turned the question around and told his audience what Jordan had learned from *him*. Zen Master or not, Jackson was not without a sumo-sized ego. "He had to *share* the ball," Jackson said one night, "and he had to incorporate his great individual game to a team game. Even into the last game of that [first Bulls'] championship—the one against the Lakers at the Forum—I had to encourage Michael: *'Penetrate, pitch to Paxson, he's gonna be wide open. . . .* Show them you can pass the ball and move ahead. Just middle penetration and easy dishes.' What Michael really learned is how to play in the system . . ."

It sometimes seemed that Jackson did not want history to miss the turning points in the career of Phil Jackson. If somebody asked him to guess at what conversation between the two of them had mattered most, Jackson answered immediately: "I think it was when I first told him what I was going to run as an offense. I said, 'We're going to run [the Triangle]. It's not a motion offense like you had [at North Carolina]. It's more of an overload system; it's a *triangle*.' He said, 'You mean that equal-opportunity system that Tex Winter espouses?' And I said, '*Yeah,* I think more guys have to be involved with the basketball . . .' And he thought about it, and we went on and won."

Jackson proudly talked about it, attaching a meaning to the story that would have been guaranteed to offend Jordan had the same kind of self-serving tale come from Jerry Krause. But the difference for Jordan was that Jackson had been right: the Triangle Offense which Jackson had implemented despite Jordan's grousing had been a winner; *pitch to Paxson* had been the right call; and Jordan never would have won so many rings without the Bulls' system.

Los Angeles also meant a last dance with Kobe Bryant, increasingly cast as his heir apparent. But heirs had disappeared before. Jordan resisted questions about the matter, though Bryant and the other ballyhooed young star, Tracy McGrady, seemed not to be going away, only looming larger. An anointing was in the works, even among several of his teammates. A couple of times, they asked him: Who's the Man, who's better—Bryant or McGrady?

He did not give them an answer. An answer, it seemed, might be to open the door onto the legitimacy of a successor, and he had shown no inclination to go there.

He vacillated, understandably so, between the roles of mentor and rival for Bryant. When Jackson arrived in Los Angeles to assume command in 1999, the coach had solicited Jordan's help in persuading Bryant about the worthiness of the Triangle, and explaining what adjustments the new offense would require from a guard accustomed to handling and shooting the ball so often. Jordan told Bryant that he knew from experience that the Triangle could be frustrating because it demanded more passing and movement than dribbling and scoring. There's not a lot of room for individual showmanship in such an offense, Jordan told him. But the offense is a winner.

Tensions steadily grew between Bryant and Jackson. Shaquille O'Neal had his own problems with Bryant, suggesting the younger star sometimes placed his own interests above those of the team. One Lakers official believed that Bryant could not enjoy his success, that it was never enough, the official revealing how melancholy Bryant had looked in the locker room after winning his first championship as a Laker, in a series where O'Neal, not Bryant, had been chosen as the MVP. Jordan had spoken to the wunderkind about viewing basketball as a career in which accolades would come with time. You're young, it will happen, Jordan assured him.

Both Jackson and Bryant, whose relationship with each other would become increasingly strained, expressed gratitude for his guidance. Yet the young star could not forever be thanking and deferring to the legend. Some assertiveness inevitably had to seep into their relationship, too, a subtle declaration by the presumptive heir that his time had arrived, which had been part of the point when Bryant jokingly advised Jordan to stay upstairs and not flirt with the idea of a comeback.

Since then, their dance around each other had been respectful, punctuated by phone calls during which Jordan gave him the benefit of his counsel on matters ranging from basketball to business.

However, each regularly heard questions about their relative abilities—who was better now, who was better in their primes. Jordan generally avoided measuring himself against any rising player, drawing comparisons only with a group or a duo, as if the young would need to tag-team his legacy to stand any chance. "I know it can't be the '94, the

'93 Michael Jordan against those guys . . ." he said, his brown eyes fix-ing hard on his questioners. "See, it wouldn't be a fair comparison. The realistic look is that they're not going to face me in my prime, and I'm not gonna face them in theirs."

But, in late February, Jordan had casually talked about Bryant with a television reporter he liked, standing along the same wall where he had spurned *Sports Illustrated*'s Jack McCallum a few weeks earlier. Everyone else would need to eavesdrop. At that point, Bryant had scored 30 points or more in eight consecutive games, a spectacular run to rival the young Jordan's, and he wanted to talk about Bryant's evolution as both a player and business force. He knew Bryant already had begun search-ing for a lucrative new shoe endorsement contract and suggested that Bryant's run of big games in recent weeks would serve him well, so long as he and his advisers had a plan. "You gotta come up with a marketing strategy . . ." he said, then citing advantages that Bryant had in the new millennium over the young Jordan of the '80s. "The game is a lot more advertised now [on television], . . . which is *good* for him."

He was Jordan the analyst in that moment, a role he enjoyed, but inevitably the discussion on Bryant moved to the matter of compar-isons about their marketing prowess. "I wouldn't put him on the same level as me," he said. It sounded only a touch boastful, much more a casually voiced observation about the reality of their relative fame. Still, it was Jordan gently expressing superiority where he could still find it. "But where he's a lot like myself is the way he separates him-self," he added, a remark that seemed a nod to Bryant's burgeoning stardom, Bryant no longer "Bryant" as often as *Kobe,* in the same fash-ion that Mike Jordan had become Michael Jordan and, then simply, *Michael*. But Kobe, he pointed out, enjoyed the kind of supporting bas-ketball cast that he hadn't possessed. Given that advantage, and Kobe's youth, he didn't see any reason why the kid couldn't match his six championships. "At twenty-five," he said, and stopped himself. "*Shit,* at *twenty-four,* he's got three championships already." It amazed him. He hadn't won his first until 28. "Three at *twenty-four.*"

So he had gotten through another Kobe discussion without his pride running over, a very good thing, because sometimes it was hard. On other nights, he was hit with questions bent on finding out whether he thought the younger man had as much raw athletic skill as he did in his prime. "What would a twenty-four-year-old Michael Jor-dan do with a twenty-four-year-old Kobe Bryant?" he asked rhetori-cally, repeating a question that I'd just posed to him. "No one knows."

Is it fair to say *you* don't know?

"That *I* don't know what would *happen?*" he asked softly. His eyes narrowed, not so much that they showed irritation, but enough that you could see their intensity, like when he was on a court draped over a foe. His voice turned deeper, slower for emphasis. "I would know. I definitely would know." And then he said it: "I think I'd have a *goooood* chance of taking care of business."

The crowd around him laughed. Maybe the laughter went on too long. "But we'll never know," he added.

For better or worse, their last game against each other, played in Los Angeles, wouldn't be forgotten; last games never are. Especially in Jordan's case, nobody wanted to see a beating. Nobody wanted even a moment that could call to mind Larry Bird abusing an old Dr. J, or Larry Holmes thrashing Ali.

Jackson was blunt, insisting he had solid strategic reasons for avoiding the Jordan-Bryant matchup: "We don't want [Bryant] to get in a head-to-head duel [with Jordan]. We don't have anyone else with the athleticism right now to guard *Stackhouse*. Michael is a great athlete, but at least we can maybe hang in there with him. Our ability to guard Stackhouse is limited. We have to keep Kobe on Stackhouse, and Kobe has gotta focus on what he's got *in front of him*. I'm sure there's gonna be a point in the game when the two of them [Jordan and Bryant] are going against each other. But we need to focus on Stackhouse."

This was not entirely a spiel designed to downplay a confrontation. In truth, the Lakers coaches felt more concerned that night about the younger Stackhouse, who, if he got hot, could have a 35-point game easily, they thought. Jordan seemed more manageable at this late stage of the season, more tired. The Lakers' locker room blackboard was covered with scrawl about the need to shut down Stackhouse, with references to Wizards' plays that Washington's point guards would shout out or signal, the blackboard complete with a glossary of what the Wizards' play-calls meant:

Fist Open/Close = Stack P/R.

This meant that when the Washington point guard opened and closed his fist quickly, the Wizards' play would be designed for Stackhouse to come off a screen on a high pick-and-roll and get the ball—free either to shoot or to pass the ball to an open teammate.

Zipper = Iso for Stack.

Either the shout of "Zipper" or the motion of a zipper being opened meant that the Wizards would be isolating a portion of the court for Stackhouse, who would try to beat a defender one-on-one.

The Wizards understood that the Lakers knew these plays. All NBA teams, especially late in the season, know their opponents' offenses and basic play-calls. They know their opponents know theirs. They don't give a damn. The attitude becomes, *If you can stop us, you win that possession. We think we can score on you even if you know where the ball is going.*

This alone makes basketball radically different from either football or baseball, neither of which can operate without opponents contemplating the possibility of deception—surprise draw plays, disguised changeups. Losing players in those sports often tell viewers, We were *fooled*. Because basketball players so often know exactly what is coming at them, excuses by the beaten are seldom respected. The game is a virile and personal test—much more about punking and being punked. It was no wonder that Bryant would be kept off Jordan most of the game, and vice versa.

The Lakers' emphasis would be on shutting down Stackhouse, and allowing Jordan whatever points he could get while working against Lakers defenders Rick Fox, Robert Horry and possibly Devean George. Phil Jackson would not risk the possibility of his young superstar losing his head. He had a clear vision of things, as always, and an ego and will that guaranteed people would do what he said.

It was a beautiful game—beautiful because everything about it seemed so exquisitely timed. Jordan hit his first four shots and, late in the first quarter, stole a pass intended for Bryant, dribbling the length of the floor for a two-handed dunk. The crowd was in a frenzy, and Jordan on his way to a hellacious 13-point quarter.

But Old soon yielded to Young. Bryant, whom Jackson had urged to be aggressive, hit a three-pointer, and another, and another. He ended the first quarter with 19 points, and had another 15 points in the next three minutes. It was like watching a mudslide. The Wizards were buried by halftime.

Bryant had 42 points by then, cruising to 55. Afterward, the Lakers talked respectfully of Jordan's dunk and his 23 points. Bryant sidestepped suggestions of a torch being passed, or of becoming the next Jordan. "I want to be like Kobe," he said simply.

Down a hallway, someone asked Jordan whether he'd handed over his crown.

"Is he *better* than you?" somebody else shouted.

Subdued, Jordan kept things short: "It's easy for people to say, 'Well,

the torch is in his hand.' He definitely has a share of the torch. But
there are a lot of other guys who I think will have to carry that. . . .
Obviously, it's tough for one guy to try to carry that."

Wrapping up, he murmured to someone: "Phil still around?"

He wanted to see Phil, he said.

Ten games left now. The six-game Western road trip ended in Denver,
which is the worst place to conclude any basketball trip. Legs are tired
from the games, and the Denver altitude quickly saps what energy is
left, especially from aging bodies. For the Wizards, Denver was a grave-
yard. As in Los Angeles, Jordan hit four jumpers in a row to start the
game. Then he shot 5–19 the rest of the way. In the second half, he was
3–9, Stackhouse 1–10 and starting point guard Lue 0–5—a combined
4–24 for the trio—and Washington lost by 16. At 34–39, with nine
games left, the team's record was its worst all season. Amazingly, the
Wizards were still in the playoff race, only a half game back of Milwaukee and two games behind Orlando.

Then came a defeat at home to lethal Sacramento, followed by a
flight to Atlanta for a winnable game against the struggling Hawks,
who quickly surprised the Wizards by scoring on six of their first seven
possessions. *We are not ready to play,* an infuriated Collins told others on
the bench.

Jordan fought fiercely, as if the postseason hinged on the outcome,
which it might have. He had 22 points, 14 rebounds, seven assists and
several flashes of healthy anger. In the fourth quarter, stepping to the
free-throw line to shoot a pair of foul shots, he found his path impudently blocked by young Atlanta guard Jason Terry, who was treating
him like a journeyman up from the developmental league. Furious, Jordan shoved the upstart, promptly punking him. The act seemed to lift
his teammates. The Wizards chipped away at a seven-point deficit and
tied the game late. Jordan had an opportunity to win it with a jumper
in the final seconds, the kind of shot he usually buried. His 15-footer
was wide to the right, and the tied game seemed headed to overtime
until the refs said that, actually, six-tenths of a second should be put
back on the game clock for Atlanta.

In basketball, six-tenths of a second doesn't afford time for so much
as a pump fake. Six-tenths of a second usually means an inbounds pass
close to the basket, a catch and a simultaneous shot. The Hawks didn't
even lob the ball toward the hoop, lofting it crosscourt about 12 feet

from the basket along the right baseline in the direction of Shareef Abdur-Rahim, the same Abdur-Rahim whom the Wizards had considered trying to obtain in exchange for the Kwame Brown draft pick. Abdur-Rahim nudged Jordan to get room, caught the ball with one hand and, in the same motion, flung it toward the basket, while awkwardly falling away. It looked like one of those gag shots in a game of H-O-R-S-E. It had no chance of going in, and so, of course, it bounced around and went in.

The Wizards had lost four straight games, plummeting to 34–41, falling two and a half games back of Milwaukee, with only seven to play, four of which would be on the road. Only their presence in the dreadful Eastern Conference left them with any chance at all. "There's just a little light at the end of the tunnel," Jordan said somberly. "But there is light. . . . That's the way we have to look at it."

Two more losses and Jordan could probably begin contemplating a summer refurbishing of his old office looking out on the 7th Street parking lot. The team had to have a victory in Boston, on the first Sunday in April, to have any reasonable shot of staying alive. Jordan looked to protect any slight edge he had over any Boston player. Talking on the record to a visiting reporter about his longtime Celtics friend Antoine Walker, he laughingly boasted: "I told [Walker] we were going to beat them every time we played them."

Jordan paused, mulling over the possible impact of his words, having second thoughts. "Don't write that. It might give him too much energy."

The reporter didn't. His media favorites would be compliant to the end.

Jordan played gritty ball in Boston: 25 points, 13 rebounds. Antoine Walker got off to a horrid shooting start, and a comradely Jordan provided his friend with statistical updates: *You're oh-for-seven . . . Oh-for-eight . . .* Walker hit only 3 of 16 shots for seven points—his misery making the difference. Paul Pierce starred with 36 points, but down the stretch, Jordan hit a pair of big jumpers and Lue dived to the floor to snatch a loose ball, an exultant Jordan rubbing his head. The Wizards clawed out a one-point overtime win, to remain in contention. They flew to Cleveland, where they won again, closing to within a game and a half of Milwaukee, with five games to play. Carrying the team on a night when Stackhouse went 5–17, Jordan had 26 points and 10 rebounds, the 200th game of his career in which he had amassed double-digit totals in points and rebounds.

The victory and his double-double milestone would have been the story lines of the evening but for the news out of Chicago: Jerry Krause had resigned the Bulls' presidency, citing "minor" health problems. Whether voluntary or not after five straight 50-loss seasons in Chicago, Krause's departure left the club's top executive position open. Two former Bulls players—assistant general manager B. J. Armstrong and Bulls broadcaster John Paxson—immediately became top candidates. But the most intriguing subject for much of the Chicago media was the possibility that the prince in exile might return, their city ablaze with questions about whether Bulls ownership had interest in hiring Jordan.

From Cleveland, Jordan doused the speculation, affirming his satisfaction in Washington, suggesting he had no interest in chasing a job elsewhere. "Why worry about Chicago?" he cracked, a remark that most observers interpreted as a disavowal of interest in the Bulls' vacancy, as well as another jibe at his old team's woes, an apparent signal that his Bulls days were forever behind him.

They weren't necessarily behind him. They especially weren't behind him if Jerry Reinsdorf picked up a phone. Michael Jordan was still very open to listening to Bulls officials, particularly if Abe Pollin didn't give him what he wanted, notably meaningful control over basketball operations and assurances of cooperation from Susan O'Malley.

The media's broadly framed questions in Cleveland had afforded wiggle room to Jordan, who had a politician's skill for dispensing vaguely worded denials. My thoughts wandered back to our meeting in his office, more than two years earlier, when he dreamt aloud of what it would be like to return to Chicago, atop the organization he loved. "A great fit," he had said wistfully.

Such dreams do not die easily. The next night, April 9, back in Washington, I asked him to clarify his position about Chicago, posing a question meant to leave no wiggle room: If Jerry Reinsdorf offered you the Bulls' presidency, are you absolutely ruling out the possibility that you would accept it?

"I figured you'd ask that," he said brusquely. He took a breath. "Obviously, my focus is to go back upstairs [to the Wizards' presidency]. Hopefully . . . it works out that way. But if it doesn't, then, obviously, I have options. Not just Chicago. But other options as well. So, for me, ideally, it's to keep this thing rolling, to keep this team moving in the right direction. That's what I truly want to happen. And Chicago is a second order, a second thought—as well as any other opportunity."

He had not ruled out Chicago, after all. He made clear that if Pollin did not give him a satisfactory deal, he had "options." This meant a possible position, as he saw it, not only in Chicago but also in the NBA's new Charlotte franchise. In the instant that his voice floated into microphones, the atmosphere around him changed. He was no longer an employee expressing an unwavering commitment to his organization, but a contract player giving voice to his professional alternatives. He was a free agent. His words reflected a player's mind-set, only he was soon to be an ex-player, coming off two losing seasons that had fallen short of everyone's expectations in the organization. Everything around him had changed, but he acted as though he enjoyed the same leverage as during his championship days.

Something was put into motion by his words that he wouldn't be able to stop thereafter, a sense that he was less than entirely faithful to Abe Pollin's organization. His old box office magic had given him license to say whatever he wished once, freeing him ever since from having to learn anything about the danger of certain words. He still had a *young* superstar's presumption, which no one close to him had ever helped him see might be a danger when the superstar's magic waned.

He was irritable that evening for several reasons, none more painful than what had just happened on the court. His team had lost to Boston in its biggest game of the season, a contest decided by a three-point shot from Celtics rookie guard J. R. Bremer with 19 seconds left. The team stood now at 36–42, a hopelessly second-division club. One more victory each for Milwaukee and Orlando—or a single Wizards defeat— would mean the end of the team's playoff hopes. Trying to provide solace, a bubbly reporter complimented him on his play and asked whether he might come back for one more season.

"Are you sick?" Jordan snapped at him.

The media chuckled, a tad uncomfortably. It was not a Jordan they usually saw. But the season had been unlike any other in his life. His career was down to four games, and his days in the Wizards organization down to precisely four weeks. He could see nothing coming.

12

The Romance Ends

THEY FLEW TO MIAMI, WHERE THE DEATHWATCH BEGAN. DEATH-
watches are part of sports theater. Nearly always the dramatic elements
are the same. The dying team's mood turns confessional. The players
plaintively disclose where and how the team was stricken, promising to
learn from the experience and play better for the coach; for there is
nearly always an afterlife in sports, a resurrection in the form of the following season. But, the scene in Miami was not that kind of deathwatch. This was the deathwatch-from-hell scenario—the kind with
bickering family members sniping at one another from the shadows
before the corpse is even cold.

The NBA calls it "elimination" when a team falls for good. This was
more a liquidation—the life of Michael Jordan's playing career down to
a few April nights, the atmosphere funereal, the bitterness around the
team palpable, especially among players who had dreamt aloud of traveling deep into the playoffs with Jordan and Stackhouse. Most of the
sufferers privately blamed one or more associates for their fate—several
of the players believing their coach bungled the job, with the coach in
turn seething over their disdain for him.

Observers reasonably wondered how badly multimillionaires about
to head off on summer vacations could feel about a basketball season.
But there are two large groups of players in the NBA—those accustomed to winning, and those who never have won and never have
starred—and no one in either of these groups lives well with losing on
a team that has a star cast as a savior. Some Wizards felt duped for hav-

ing signed on. In Miami and elsewhere, the duped started floating their resentments as that last week wore on and they sensed they had nothing to lose. Anyone in management who now wanted to take on Jordan or Collins would have the cover of tacit player support.

The boss for the moment sank deep into his folding chair in the cramped visitors' locker room of Miami's American Airlines Arena, his eyes familiarly hidden behind his shades with the charcoal lenses. On this, the last night that one of his teams would ever be alive for a play-off spot, Michael Jordan took refuge behind his pair of big silver headphones. Their volume had been turned up high, the voice of Stevie Wonder leaking out of them.

The sight of Jordan with his headphones on had the intended effect: It kept people away—the media, certainly, but his coach and most of his teammates, too, who knew not to approach him before a game unless a matter couldn't wait. Now and then, feeling a stare or sensing footsteps getting closer, he adjusted the headphones tighter over his ears, getting deeper into his cocoon. He said nothing to anyone for 20 minutes. Mostly, he watched videotape of the evening's opponent, the Heat, another failed NBA team. Now and then, he turned his head from the screen and just stared through people, the media, his teammates, his coach—his expression blankly meditative.

Across from him, Miami reporters mingled among players they didn't necessarily know in front of lockers, discreetly asking one another for names: There was Larry Hughes, sitting in a locker alongside Kwame Brown, who plopped into a chair next to Tyronn Lue, who was just down from Charles Oakley and Bryon Russell, who sat across from, in order, Jerry Stackhouse, Juan Dixon, Brendan Haywood and Bobby Simmons. Jordan, who had the locker closest to the television, sat next to no one.

He commandeered two lockers. In the locker next to his own, he conspicuously hung his gray herringbone suit jacket, as usual reserving the adjacent locker for a possible guest or a member of his entourage.

His remove from nearly everyone else was complete by then. His eyes scanned the television. One of his few companions, Charles Oakley, came by to say hi, pointing at a young Miami player, 6'10" Malik Allen, who was dunking on the screen. Jordan lifted one side of his headphones off an ear, mumbling approval of the kid's move: "He's quick. That's some young Patrick Ewing shit."

He pulled the headphones back down, returning to Stevie Wonder. Oakley moved on, and Jordan glanced back at the screen, before another voice jerked his attention away. "I want some popcorn," Kwame Brown was saying from his own folding chair across the locker room, talking to no one, talking to air, riveted on some teammates who already had popcorn. *"Popcorn,"* said Kwame, the way people say *Eureka.*

Doug Collins was suddenly standing over him. Fifteen feet away, Jordan lifted his head, glanced at the pair and looked away. Collins bent over and whispered something to Brown, who from that folding chair did not look up to meet the coach's gaze, just stared straight ahead, as if in a self-induced trance. Collins bent a little more, as if determined to make eye contact. It was a contest of wills now. As Collins whispered, Brown stared into a little slice of nothingness that he had fixed his eyes on, nodding, nodding, nodding, nodding without really acknowledging the coach, and it was then that even a first-time visitor could have seen just how dysfunctional this team had become.

The coach had lost the confidence of at least half of the Wizards by then. Now with the season entering its last weekend, emboldened players increasingly said what they felt. Never before had Stackhouse been so publicly blunt, trotting out the thoughts and phrases that until then he had reserved for private. That morning at shootaround, he said he hoped the Wizards would be running more next year, playing to the strengths of the younger players, following what he called "the Michael Jordan farewell tour." He said this casually, without edge: He knew better than any other Wizard how best to walk the public relations tightrope when addressing questions about Jordan. "We're a young, athletic team, you know, and this year we really played a little more of a slow-down pace," he said amiably. "I think having Michael in the lineup had a lot to do with that. Next year we come in [running more] definitely, because I feel that's the strongest suit of my game, getting in the open court and getting to the basket."

Savvy and seasoned, he had the unusual ability of at once speaking respectfully about Jordan—"The greatest player of all time, and he played in all eighty-two games this year, which says a lot about him"— while gently declaring that their styles were "contrasting" and "did not always fit." Smiling, he summarized the season, noting that it had been built around doing "everything we can to cater" to Jordan. He made this sound pleasant and benign. While an explosive personality in private, he had a public future, if he wanted it, as a charming diplomat.

The team would belong to Stackhouse next season, assuming he still found himself in Washington. He had decided to wait Jordan out.

"I'm twenty-eight," he said. "I got, hopefully, a lot more time." He was philosophical about his part in the failed duo. "I guess we gave up some things for each other," he said softly. "But the mix of us didn't work out . . . We never have had a problem with it, but we just had our own ways."

Stackhouse's use of the past tense indicated that the Wizards were finished for 2003. He already had begun looking past the final week of the Jordan veneration, focused on a new season, wanting the re-prioritization to begin even before the end of the Jordan farewell tour. "Michael can give the fans a last glimpse of greatness," he said. " But I think our focus has to be toward next year and trying to get our young guys involved in getting as much playing time as they can. . . . We need to be thinking of that time *right now.*"

Toward that end, he did not want to play that evening. He told Collins that his right knee was hurting him—a flareup of tendinitis, he thought—and that, unable to jump with any effectiveness, he wanted to heed his body's message and not risk the possibility of a serious injury. Collins did not protest. Now Stackhouse only needed to break the news to Jordan, who, not having moved from his folding chair, was hoping to extend the team's hopes beyond that night.

At 6:55 p.m., with the game a little more than an hour away, Stack-house walked over to Jordan wearing a plastic blue brace that ran from his right knee down to his instep. It looked like a catcher's shin guard, with buckles that one could do and undo in an instant. Stackhouse gently tapped on it and said, "Hey, Mike." He had to repeat this, just to penetrate those silver headphones—Jordan still had Stevie Wonder streaming into his ears: *"Mike."*

Jordan looked up from his folding chair, squinting, and slid one side of his headphones off, slack-jawed, his face a question mark.

"Talked to Doug," Stackhouse began. "You know, I tried. Tried running. But it's bothering me when I push off on it. Just can't push off on it any good."

There was a pause. Jordan did not speak immediately.

He faced the game tape on the television monitor. "Yeah?"

Stackhouse nodded quickly. "Feels a little weak. I plant and can't do it. It hurts when I go up."

Jordan cocked his head to regard Stackhouse. "Yeah," he said vaguely.

Stackhouse paused, as if waiting for something more. The silence lengthened, uncomfortably. Stackhouse resumed talking about his knee. Jordan languidly nodded, glancing at the television, murmuring, "Yeah." It was in the gaps between their words that the truth revealed itself: A stiff courtesy prevailed between them. They shared an alma mater, but really nothing else. They were not antagonists, but they were not close either, merely two polite and powerful partners who never had made a personal connection, in large part because they wanted the same thing and only the titan between them could have it. But now the titan was on his way out. It was awkward. "I wanted to be out there," Stackhouse went on. "I—"

Jordan interrupted, gently, and looked at him, still holding up one side of his headphones. "Uh, you rest it," he said. He looked back at the television. "See tomorrow how it feels."

"Wish I could be out there."

Now Jordan wanted to wrap up. "Rest it. It's about long-term value, not short for you—right?" Stackhouse didn't say anything to this. Jordan went on: "See tomorrow. Long-term value. All right then." He was already repositioning his headphones, lowering his head, back in his cocoon.

"Thanks, Mike."

Stackhouse walked away, unbuckling and removing the blue brace.

Everyone playing was in uniform now except Jordan, who remained on that folding chair in his herringbone trousers, not having so much as unknotted his blue tie—waiting, as was his way, for the media and strangers to leave, when he could at last have sanctuary. He beckoned to somebody, who brought him coffee.

Down to an hour now. An hour before the last game to have any competitive meaning in his career. Life went on around him, life for people with no endings approaching. Kwame Brown had found a bag of popcorn, snacking contentedly. In a bathroom, Bryon Russell, who had given a hundred bucks to another clubhouse attendant, drank from a water bottle and happily munched on his own popcorn. Doug Collins stood over a urinal, tilted his head back and told B-Russell that, with Stackhouse out of action, he would be playing extra minutes. Russell's reaction was restrained and telling—a curt okay. The days of players conveying any enthusiasm for Collins's orders were over. Now most Wizards tended to affirm his instructions with monosyllabic grunts, giving him their cooperation but no affection. The deathwatch was on everyone's mind, which guaranteed that contempt for Collins would only build.

A few players listened skeptically to reporters talking about the possibility of Orlando and Milwaukee losing all their remaining games. "Keep hope alive," an encouraging Baltimore reporter said to Russell, whose chuckle said he knew better.

Jordan, who had not moved for 40 minutes, leaned far back in his chair then. He seemed to have closed his eyes, though you never could be sure what those eyes were doing behind the charcoal lenses: He could see out, but you couldn't see in. Amazingly then, someone dared to speak to him, and more amazingly, he answered. His head jerked and flew up. He lifted off his headphones to grin at Greg Stoda, a journalist who had covered him during his high school days in Wilmington and now wrote for the *Palm Beach Post*.

"How you doin'?" he muttered at Stoda.

They'd seen each other that morning, falling into a conversation about golf and the Masters tournament, which was approaching its midway point. Stoda shared some news now: Tiger Woods was trailing badly in round two.

At the morning shootaround, Jordan had accepted Stoda's invitation to a bet on the Masters. "Tiger will win," Jordan had said. "And I'll give you the field."

They'd bet $50, a paltry sum, but it didn't matter, not to a man who so loved any kind of action—a shooting game against a teammate for a few hundred, low or high stakes poker, or a bet with a journalist who didn't want to go more than fifty. Just to have anything riding on a game—something that would come back to him as winnings: Was there anything sweeter?

"You need my address so you can send me the money," Stoda jibed, grinning.

Jordan chuckled. "I'm not worried about it. . . . My boy's gonna come back. I'll give him a call if I gotta."

He smiled, picturing this. The little bet served as a reminder of all the action out there, the good life ahead. "You'll be paying me," Jordan cheerfully said.

Stoda was the best part of his evening. But Stoda had moved on, and other things in the locker room could not be made any more pleasant. In a corner, Jerry Stackhouse casually mentioned to a group of reporters that he had had to "sacrifice" for Jordan, politely adding that Jordan had had to sacrifice for him; that, in the end, something hadn't worked; that the Wizards would need to run next year. Charles Oakley muttered that he had been underutilized. It was open season on Collins's strategy and coaching style. Jordan acknowledged none of the tensions, warding them off with Stevie Wonder. Finally, at 7:15, emerging from his cocoon, he began lacing his white shoes with the blue piping and sparkling silver eyelets. He stood and removed his headphones. Not coincidentally, it was time for all strangers to go.

They played the game, but not before a surprise. Miami's coach Pat Riley retired Jordan's 23, vowing the number never would be worn again by a Heat player, presiding over the hanging of an arena banner festooned with a Jordan jersey in half Bulls red and half Wizards blue, a move that, among other things, drew attention to the fact that Abe Pollin had not ordered any similar honor at MCI. Alongside the Wizards' bench, as Riley spoke, Jordan looked underwhelmed. Congenitally suspicious, wondering by the end of the ceremony whether Riley had bestowed the honor to leave him psychologically softened, Jordan decided to attack the young Miami team early. Thirty-six seconds into the game, he badly missed his first shot, a driving layup almost swatted away by a pair of soaring youths—lithe Mercurys to his hefty Zeus—who forced him to arc his shot so clumsily high that it thudded off the backboard without even hitting the rim.

This was not part of the script: Twenty thousand Floridians groaned; a couple of thousand flashbulbs went wasted. But then Jordan mesmerized them, at least for a half. He spent most of it guarded by a lean, Gumby-supple 23-year-old 6'7" rookie out of LaSalle named Rasual Butler, who, not yet in kindergarten when Jordan began his NBA career, now could routinely outleap and outrun the older man, just not outthink him. Jordan abused him. It was Bobby Fischer against the chess champion of the Fort Lauderdale YMCA: There were too many moves and gambits for the kid to process. Jordan made Butler look silly a few times, no more so than when, Meadowlark Lemon–like, he extended his arm with the ball on the end of it beyond Butler's head and pulled it back, to the ooooohs of 20,000, just before blowing by the entranced kid for a layup.

He schooled the foe in a game that never stopped trying to expose the aging. That alone made basketball far different from other major American sports. In baseball particularly, the autumn shadows lengthen slowly over the graying idol. He stands in the late afternoon's gloaming, the perfect symbol of his unharried twilight. There are no shadows in basketball. If baseball is pastoral at its heart, basketball is street-tough. Every day to the last day, older players are tested—the weaker to be preyed upon. Jordan not only had survived but preyed himself in many moments, making what he had done, at least as an individual player at 40, remarkable—a feat obscured in those last few months by all his problems, self-generated and otherwise, with teammates and Pollin. He was streaky, he tired more quickly, but he could still punish greenhorns.

It was happening again. He employed his jab-step, and an alarmed-looking Rasual Butler backed up, which was the moment when Jordan rose for an open shot. Now the scoring jumpers came like a flood, eight in total, and after each he ran backward in his familiar canter. If his name had been not Jordan but Michael Jones, his on-court productivity at middle-age would have been deemed miraculous. But he was competing against not merely a defender but the ghost of his younger self. He ended the half with 23 points, with the Floridians marveling over his fallaways but longing for a high-altitude dunk.

It would be his last great half.

He was tired. All the 40-plus-minute nights had worn him down: He admitted to being weary sometimes now. For the first time, he admitted that his right knee sometimes felt "tired"—not injured, not terribly sore, just incapable of delivering bursts in some moments, mysteriously quitting on him when he played on it too long.

He scored only two more points on this night, those coming on free throws, missing all eight of his second-half field-goal attempts. Still, the Wizards won narrowly. There was excitement: The deathwatch might be on hold for at least a night; a reprieve was possible. Milwaukee had won, but Orlando was locked in a close game with the formidable Pacers in Indianapolis. The Wizards' locker room remained closed as Jordan, Collins and the rest of the Wizards waited out the returns from Indiana. Then word floated out that Orlando had increased its lead to 11 points with about four minutes to play. Collins appeared in the hallway to say it didn't look good. He talked for a few minutes, then went back inside behind the closed door.

At 10:40 p.m., Orlando led by 13 points with 47 seconds to play. On the television screen inside the Wizards' locker room, Tracy McGrady exited the game to hugs from his celebrating Orlando teammates. Jordan just stared. At 10:42, the game ended, and Collins turned to Jordan. "I'm very disappointed we didn't get there, Michael," the coach said. "You know how much I wanted you to get there."

Everyone around them waited for Jordan to speak. But he was someplace else, just as he had been three hours earlier, on that folding chair.

He said nothing, or nothing that anyone around could quite make out. He mumbled something inaudible, which to someone close sounded like nothing so much as resignation. Then he went off to change. And that is the way it ended; that is the way these things generally end.

Twenty minutes later, having rushed in and out of a steamy shower, he emerged in his gray suit, with sweat running in rivulets alongside his left eye and down his cheek, to face the media. It had been about two and a half years since he sat in his Washington office on a dreary winter afternoon, looking like a prisoner, and began flirting with an idea. Two years since he looked out his window and, patting his paunch, said that having power did not compare to playing. Two years since his eyes scanned some panhandlers in the snow, and he talked of what the "insanity" would be like if he could take on Vince Carter and Kobe Bryant. It seemed like 15 minutes ago. It had all passed quickly, he said.

Now that quiet office back in Washington seemed to be waiting for him again. There wasn't much else to say, but Jordan found a few things. He praised Larry Hughes for playing with a bad ankle and casually noted that Stackhouse had sat out the game. ("Yeah, Stack not playing—that hurt.")

And, even now, he looked for a goal, wanting to claim a bit of success before he stepped out of his uniform, intent on demonstrating his team's improvement: He wanted to end the season, he said, with more victories than the Wizards' 37 wins of the previous season. That would require only one win in the team's remaining three games, a reasonable expectation given that two of them were at home.

But that wouldn't happen either. And Doug Collins's anger was about to spill over.

The schedule called for the eliminated team to play a game at home the next night. Washington led Atlanta by a point in the final 10 seconds. Jason Terry, the young Hawks guard who had blocked Jordan's path in Atlanta and got shoved for his insolence, missed an outside jumper, but Jordan had left his man, Ira Newble, who seized the opportunity to rush to the boards, grab the rebound and dunk.

Now trailing by a point, the Wizards still had a chance to win in the final seconds. During a time-out, Collins diagrammed a play for Jordan, who would get the ball in isolation at the top of the key, and do what he wanted.

Jordan and Newble stood alongside each other before play resumed. Jordan smiled and said to him, *You know it's coming to me. And I'm puttin' it up.*

Newble nodded. "I know. But I'm gonna do my thing, too."

Jordan dribbled the ball near the top of the key, darted and rose. Newble had a hand in his face.

"I didn't feel I was comfortable shootin' the ball," Jordan said of his miss at the buzzer.

Atlanta 101, Washington 100.

The night frayed Collins a little more. He'd barked at Brown again, exasperated by what he regarded as the kid's lack of concentration. It had been perhaps the most embarrassing night in two seasons for the prodigy, who shot 2–13, missed two dunks and conspicuously failed to dive for a couple of loose balls.

Brown tried to put the best light on his lingering tensions with Collins, calmly talking about the state of their relationship since the night he had blown up at the coach in Phoenix: "I mean, there haven't been any outrageous conversations [between us]. We speak. It's been respectful. . . . And that's about it. It's not like we're playin', yukkin' it up. But, you know, we don't have to. I have to respect him as a coach, and he has to respect me as a young man and a player."

Had their relationship improved since Phoenix?

Brown shrugged. He didn't want trouble, but he didn't want to lie either. "I can't say it's better or worse," he answered. "It's just about the same."

Jordan looked on edge during his last morning media session at MCI. A woman asked whether any of his family members would be attending his final home game that evening, and he snorted at her: "Now that's a dumb question . . ."

It was a dumb question for reasons that reporters could only guess at. He heard his voice, read the faces, looked back down at the woman and finally added that, yes, his family would be coming—his kids, wife, a sibling, maybe his mom.

He was not himself—certainly not as we were accustomed to seeing him, neither smooth nor in command. He faltered in talking about his record as an executive and leader of the Wizards, vacillating between admitting that the team hadn't fared well during his three and a half years at the helm and defending his performance by insisting that the young players were "learning." He reemphasized his intention to take back the club presidency. His language suggested this was a virtual certainty. "I still have some solid work to do, once I go back upstairs, in terms of trying to find the right mesh . . ." he said. "We still haven't gotten to that point yet, and I will have to assume some of that responsibility. I think it has been moving in a positive direction."

His season had included challenges that had nothing to do with playing basketball, of course. I tried asking him how his love of a game had helped him cope with the pressures of business and life off the court, including, as I tried gently putting it, "the court proceeding in Chicago."

It was the first time since November that anyone, even cryptically, had asked him about the effects of the Knafel matter.

I had not finished asking the question when he cut me off, something he hadn't done until that moment in the entire two years of the comeback, shaking his head, talking over me. He wanted only questions, he said, "pertaining to the game tonight."

It was a reminder of the arrangement that always had been at work here. Someone mentioned that when things concluded that evening, there would be no more games left for him in Washington. No more games: the phrase hung there. How did he wish to leave?

He looked grimly at the questioner. It was not a question he would have preferred ending on. He offered that he preferred leaving quietly, with no big ceremony. "I'm not dead; I'm still alive," he explained, and, with that, started moving, as if to prove his point.

His old office was just a couple of stories above him, close enough that, if given the word, he could start moving some things back inside it that day. But, as he had made clear to people more than once, he had *options*. He had talked about Chicago, and perhaps that was a possibility. If Jerry Reinsdorf was interested in him and Pollin didn't offer him the right deal, all that would be required for Chicago to land him was Reinsdorf's willingness to wait until July 1, when Jordan's playing contract with the Wizards would expire and Reinsdorf would be free to officially negotiate with him, under league rules.

News came out of Chicago about an hour later. John Paxson had been hired as executive vice president in Chicago, becoming the Bulls' chief basketball executive. No Bulls official had ever contacted Jordan, or sent anonymous word through the media, to suggest that the Bulls would be interested in talking to Jordan when his Wizards contract ran out. Swiftly, word leaked that, like the Wizards' top brass, the Bulls management had doubts that Jordan's work habits as an executive ever measured up to those of Jordan the player.

Jerry Reinsdorf had done everything to keep him once, paying him $30 million for the 1996–1997 season alone, and raising his salary by 10 percent to $33 million for his final Bulls season, in 1998. The Bulls' franchise was a colossus, basketball's version of the old Yankees, and Jordan the sport's Ruth. Along the way, after Jordan's first retirement, Reinsdorf had shown his gratitude in the way team owners commonly and cost-efficiently do, building a shrine to the god that would double as a popular tourist attraction, erecting the famous statue of Jordan outside the entrance to the Bulls' offices and the United Center, its engraved words proclaiming that Michael Jordan was the best there ever was, the best there ever will be.

As a player.

Which had nothing to do with the way the owner and star privately regarded each other, a common theme running through Jordan's professional life.

Tensions had cropped up between Jordan and Reinsdorf in the star's final two Bulls seasons over the issue of Jordan's salary. Having made, depending on how an observer wanted to read the numbers, an average of roughly $3 million in the years following his first comeback through the end of the 1995–1996 season and the team's fourth championship, Jordan had been, if anything, a bargain for Reinsdorf, who knew it, readily agreeing that Jordan's salary would be significantly increased for the 1996–1997 season. The question was, How much? After negotiations with Jordan and David Falk, Reinsdorf agreed to pay $30 million for the season. It was as if Falk and Jordan had skipped going from Earth to Mars and leaped all the way to Pluto. Thirty million dollars for seven months of ball.

Good feelings radiated from the Jordan side. But, as Jordan later remembered, Reinsdorf shook his hand, alluded to that 30 million coming out of his coffers, and said, *I might live to regret this.*

Later, Reinsdorf could not remember having made the remark, though he did not deny making it. If anything, people close to him thought, he probably said something exactly like it, but jokingly, a touch worriedly, self-mockingly, all the things that many people feel when they shell out huge dollars on something carrying an element of risk.

Jordan was profoundly offended, however. He believed he had done everything in his power to make the Bulls a champion, in the process leading the franchise to riches. He shared his hurt over Reinsdorf's private statement with *The New Yorker* and repeated the account for at least one other publication. He had his $30 million for the year, but he did not easily forgive a display of disrespect, a category of offense that he broadly defined.

The owner and star resolved their differences, but their relationship never would be close, a professional courtesy characterizing their relations, Jordan viewing Reinsdorf as another well-heeled man with whom he did business. That perception of their relationship seemed to run both ways. "Your client," Reinsdorf would sometimes say of Jordan during discussions with David Falk.

So there was respect, but respect across a chasm. At the moment Jordan stopped filling Reinsdorf's coffers, his appeal ended for the Bulls owner. That reality went a considerable way toward explaining why Jordan had arrived in Washington. It accounted for why, in his Wizards executive office in December 2000, Jordan had said, in referring to the Bulls organization, "I don't know why I'm not here," the *here* meaning Chicago. He didn't understand why Reinsdorf or someone else from the organization had not called to ask him, even vaguely, whether he might want to come back, why Reinsdorf had never said, We want you.

He couldn't make sense of the indifference. Now, in his silence, Reinsdorf indicated a second time that the organization did not want him for a position of leadership. The Bulls' decision had consequences extending beyond Chicago. After Jordan's talk of having "options" if Pollin's offer did not satisfy him, the news out of Chicago made him look like rejected goods, further undermining his leverage in Washington. For the first time in his business life, he found himself on defense, a position he never had played off a court, and one that he could not possibly master in the time he had left.

His standing deteriorated in Washington as news leaked of teammates' resentments, particularly the young players' disgust with what they regarded as his flagrant displays of disrespect for them. Among the leaks was an old criticism: His presence had retarded the growth of teammates. Jordan flared in talking about it. "Me being in the locker room is gonna make people afraid to step forward and play the game that they've been playing for years? It's an easy cop-out [to say] that

just because I've been down here we haven't been assertive and successful. I think I've been *beggin'* for guys to step forward . . ."

Then he sent a warning shot his detractors' way: "When I go back
upstairs, hopefully there won't be *any* excuses. If that is one, they're
never gonna use it [again]."

His lashings exceeded some threshold now. His words sounded like
a threat. Something broke in his young teammates. They would pay
him no more homage, extending him few of the courtesies that would
be given even to the average retiring player. Someone in the locker
room mentioned the possibility of everybody chipping in to buy Jordan a good-bye gift.

The young players expressed no interest. The matter was dropped.

The New York Times reported that Jordan's teammates hadn't wanted
to buy him a present. Still left to be learned was the dynamic of that
discussion—who said what, and what bitterness was vented toward Jordan, if any. During the weeks ahead, in learning details of that discussion, I was struck by what hadn't been said by the young players; how
they carefully made certain that nothing they did or said could be
traced back to them.

I found myself talking to people who had natural conflicts of interest. Anyone from that point forward who claimed to know what happened during the gift discussion was necessarily an interested
participant in one of those encounters, or closely associated with a participant.

Actually, it was less a discussion than a spontaneous exchange
among players. Someone simply said: We getting a present for M.J.?

Silence for a long moment.

There was no expression of open contempt for Jordan. Players were
careful. Who knew who among them might be an informant? Whenever the subject of Jordan arose among a large group of players, the
young were careful to keep their comments to a minimum. Their candor came only around a trusted teammate, or when somebody dared to
say something, and a chorus would mutter in agreement.

In a group this large, there were risks. No young player in the locker
room said much. Jordan's summer workout partner, Bobby Simmons,
loyal to Jordan to the end, seemed to indicate with a murmur and head
nod that, Sure, he'd contribute toward getting Michael a gift.

Simmons seemed alone. No one else offered enthusiasm for the
idea. The responses of the other players were most interesting for their
nonresponsiveness, thought someone with knowledge of what hap-

pened. It was as if, the person said, the players wanted deniability for what was happening around them, worried that Jordan might punish them if he ever learned they were part of this cabal.

Kwame Brown simply mumbled and looked away, as did Larry Hughes. Each of their responses to the gift question seemed to be a *no,* but an observer couldn't be certain—each of them having been just cryptic enough to give himself deniability. It was thought that Lue's mumble indicated he genuinely could go either way; Jordan had been kind to him in moments, and so he would be agreeable either to giving a group gift to M.J. or not, depending on what the others wanted to do. But he wasn't going to push anybody.

More teammates delivered nonresponsive responses. More silence, more looks away, which seemed to represent a muted *no* chorus.

Not one of them spoke on behalf of getting Jordan a gift.

Not one, on the other hand, voiced his scorn.

Not one of them openly said no to a gift.

Their collective silence saying it for them.

And the gift proposal died.

And they preserved their deniability.

Everyone would be safe.

And Jordan would get nothing.

It was warm and sunny at five o'clock on Monday, April 14, a portent of summer and vacations coming. Arriving in his silver Mercedes and a retro orange Denver Broncos jersey with John Elway's number seven, Kwame Brown smiled and waved at fans lined two-deep, his car cruising into the Wizards' garage and down the ramp. Minutes later, a Mercedes convertible arrived, this bearing Doug Collins, who paused from sunning himself to deliver a quick, military-like salute to the fans as his car shot by.

By contrast, darkness had settled over the Wizards' locker room, with the grousing ratcheted up. The young guys were privately disgusted with Collins's volatility, and the older players had jumped ship because they believed that Collins had favored the young players. Now it was Charles Oakley's turn. He spoke with microphones in front of his face, no longer making any effort to hide his disenchantment with Collins. "I thought we could have made the playoffs *easy* in the East," he said. "It should've been no problem. But, you know, [Collins] wanted to play the young guys early. . . . I don't know if they understand the game. . . . We did a lot of experiments this year. If I knew a lot [of what would happen], I wouldn't have signed here."

Oakley had come to conclude that the Collins offense had chipped away at the morale of the team. "That's how we've been playing *all year*," he said. "We run a set offense. I think coaches get into: 'This guy can't do this thing; this guy can't do that. So let's slow it down.' You gotta believe in *everybody* on the court."

Oakley offered to talk more in the days ahead. He was just getting started.

The media, the Wizards p.r. staff and the rest of the NBA churned out a mound of Jordan trivia. Jordan had scored 40 points or more eight times as a Wizard, including his 51-point game, in 2001. His 32,200-plus career points (he would end with 32,292) were more than the entire active rosters of seven NBA teams. Nike had made 18 versions of Air Jordan shoes. Jordan would complete his career in first place all-time in career per-game scoring average, less than a tenth of a point ahead of Wilt Chamberlain. He had averaged 31.5 points per game in his years with the Bulls, and would average 21.2 points in his two seasons with the Wizards. That evening's game against the Knicks would be the 82nd consecutive home sellout for a Wizards regular season home game, two years' worth of sellouts.

And the Wizards began the night six games under .500.

For all the hype about the game, you could still see empty seats. The crowd was subdued at the start. Perhaps sunny springtime had sedated everybody. The game had an exhibition feel, with the Wizards playing their third straight home game in the franchise's old Washington Bullets uniforms, which looked good, actually, with red stripes that made the players look like tall candy canes and temporarily distracted you from the Wizards' miseries. Donald Rumsfeld came out before the start to give Jordan a flag flown over the Pentagon on the first anniversary of September 11, and then the teams played a game, which the Knicks basically controlled throughout, though no one on either of the non-contending teams, aside from Jordan, seemed to care much.

He got off to a quick start, then slowed. As nearly always, he took more shots than anyone else on the floor, 22, and had the most misses, 13. He played aggressively, badly wanting victory number 38, so he could at least make his case that the team had marginally improved. The crowd hardly seemed to pay attention to the game, as if absorbed by the end coming and the question of what the Wizards management would do to honor Jordan.

Even into the final week, Pollin and Susan O'Malley had continued offering tickets to the idol's last home game to desperate, ticketless fans willing to buy ticket packages for the following season. Far more time had gone into formulating the ticket plan than in planning a tribute to Jordan. Pollin had approved card stunts to be conducted in the stands during time-outs—nothing memorable or costly, in keeping with his style. On command, a few hundred fans seated on one side of the court held up cards, the mass of paper revealing messages: "DC LOVES MJ" and "DC LOVES 23."

Jordan stared down at the floor during time-outs, not once looking at the stunts. Every few minutes, there was a new carnival act, the same thing the Wizards organization put on virtually every night. There was the Parachute Drop, where tiny toy parachutes floated down with little souvenirs, and a tug-of-war basketball shooting contest between two fans, and more card stunts.

It was a tacky night that added to the malaise of the place. Pollin hardly spoke to minority owner Ted Leonsis, who had angered him with comments critical of MCI's treatment of Leonsis's Washington Capitals. The Jordan managerial crew kept its distance from Pollin. All around, the vibe was terrible.

When Shandon Anderson stripped Jordan with about two minutes to play and scored on a layup, the Wizards' defeat was certain. Collins removed Jordan for the final time at MCI, and the crowd cheered. On the night, he scored 21 points on 41 percent shooting, fairly representative numbers for the season. Most of the game's numbers looked reflective of the two years, especially this one: The Wizards had had only two fast-break points to their opponents' 13. They had walked the ball up the court for a season with Jordan and Stackhouse, and neither the strategy, nor the coupling, delivered them a single additional victory. Nothing was strikingly different, except for the postgame ceremony coming.

Pollin joined Jordan on the floor. Conspicuously absent was any microphone around the two men. They just stood there for a while, the public address announcer babbling away, some feedback distorting his words. Jordan glanced down at the floor and shuffled his feet as if he might be late for a dinner reservation.

Peculiarity characterized the star and owner's last awkward public minutes together. The public address announcer spoke virtually as long about Pollin and his wife, Irene, as about Jordan, noting in detail the Pollins' contribution of computers to area schools in Jordan's name, and heralding their "commitment to the environment," an unusually prolonged encomium for a couple not leaving the scene.

The man who was departing from Washington, but did not know it yet, displayed his famously imperious streak, having earlier decided he did not want to speak to the fans. His distance from them was never clearer. He was the visitant who had touched down, and now the one walking off with a wave. The smaller man next to him smiled, holding a secret between his pursed lips like a sour candy.

If Abe Pollin had any lingering questions about the Wizards' disunity, Collins confirmed them in the next half hour. By the time he reached the podium at his last Washington press conference, gaunt and enraged, Collins was an open wound. Pollin allies would say later that the owner had flirted with firing Collins late in the season, backing off only to give himself a last chance to review the coach's performance. This night ended the review. By the time he finished, the coach's remarks overshadowed Jordan's Washington good-bye and illuminated everything wrong. It was Collins in all his stubborn self-righteousness, setting himself afire.

The session began normally enough. Collins tried explaining the team's shortcomings, characterizing his team as below average, becoming more candid with each sentence. He simmered: "We lost our edge about two weeks ago. . . . Michael can't carry a *subpar* team into the playoffs at forty. . . . We had too many people playing the same style. And we were overloaded at the Two guard and [didn't have] enough people playing small forward."

Asked if he would have changed anything, he took his first shot of the evening, without mentioning Larry Hughes by name. "I would've started T-Lue at point guard."

There was a pause. He moved off Lue and Hughes. Then he lit the match.

It came abruptly, with no segue, no one asking him a question related to the subject: "I've had guys in that locker room curse at me this year, show no respect. And Michael stepped in immediately and [said], 'Don't treat our coach that way.'"

His voice shook. His tuning-fork quiver came over him. The media assemblage sat stunned.

Collins went on, saying the offending players' disrespect "was insidious," that the problem had begun with one player and then snowballed. He paused and took a breath, knowing that his Chicago and Detroit experiences would be on people's minds. "I've got to be careful. I've got a reputation as a ball-busting guy. So anytime there's a little flare-up, it's *me* again. Sometimes, you need to look at the players." He suggested a purge of the roster was possible. "This won't happen next year; trust me. . . . Somewhere along the line, we've allowed players to disrespect [coaches]. . . . Anytime a player disrespects a coach, everybody thinks it's all right."

His public pain said nothing so much as this: He had lost the team. He had lost it while abiding by Jordan's wishes. He continued indicting unnamed players. He did it for all the crazy reasons that people do these things: to strike back, to justify what had happened, to offer an explanation for the Wizards' failure to improve a whit. He had presided over a team, once touted to go deep into the playoffs, that would conclude the season eight games under .500.

His harangue wasn't impulsive. Later, a Wizards colleague would say to him: "Doug, are you sure that what you said about the players was the best thing?" Collins solemnly nodded, assuring the man he had thought about it beforehand, that he knew what he was doing.

It was a manipulative and self-serving rant, sealing his fate. He had unwittingly exposed the worst of the Jordan regime's problems. Now, in the face of his miscalculation, the players, sensing his new vulnerability, took him on. "Obviously, he feels someone disrespected him," Brendan Haywood said. "And if he feels that disrespected, maybe he should have called them [the names of the players] out to you all instead of just doing it like this, no names, like it's *all* the guys, because that's not fair."

Added Bryon Russell: "I haven't disrespected him—not yet."

Jordan finally appeared. Anticipating the large media throng that had come to see Jordan at his final home game, the Wizards had moved this last Washington postgame press conference into the team's practice gym, to accommodate the overflow of reporters. Everyone had expected a session dominated by requests for Jordan to reflect on his last playing days. Instead, the room immediately wanted his response to Collins's blowup. What did it say about the team's morale, and the relations between his handpicked coach and players?

Jordan did not deny the problems. "We had situations where [Collins] felt like he was disrespected," he said somberly. "And I felt like, you know, I had to step up and say, 'That's not going to be han-

dled [like that], as long as I'm here.' If [Collins] felt like there were situations like that, then those situations will be dealt with over the
course of the summer. . . . That's not the kind of peace or harmony you
want in your organization. It's definitely a concern."

But he would have preferred for Collins to keep his mouth shut
about the dissension. Could there have been any greater nightmare
than the disclosure of the divisions on the night of his final home
appearance, at a time when Pollin was scrutinizing him and his leadership of the organization? "Now is *this* the correct forum for [Collins to
have talked about the matter], or the correct time?" he continued.
"*Doug* felt that it was. Obviously, these are things that you have to deal
with. But I'd rather for them not to be out [in public] for everybody's
opinion. . . . Those things I like to deal [with] internally."

The Collins eruption dominated the media's stories. Two nights
later, on April 16, the final game in Jordan's career would be beset by
reports about a team unraveling, presided over by a coach who had lost
the support of his players and a star too distant to end the feuding.

In Philadelphia, Jordan did not want to answer any more questions on the subject, letting Collins know that he favored canceling
the morning shootaround and media session, going off with friends
to play golf at a local course. That evening, resentful players resumed
talking to the press. In the visitors' locker room, Charles Oakley
anointed himself spokesman for Kwame Brown, commonly regarded
as Collins's target when the coach lashed out at an unnamed Wizard
supposedly responsible for sparking a season's worth of problems. The
players knew that Stackhouse had erupted at Collins long before
Brown's explosion, and were tired of what they regarded as Collins's
attempts to find scapegoats. "If a number of [morale] problems had
been corrected from the *beginning*," Oakley said, "it wouldn't have
lasted a whole eighty-two games. . . . Doug *felt* something. [But] if
you don't strengthen out the issue, then it's going to be a disease,
like when that disease spread in China and Toronto. I think Doug
should've taken responsibility right there and then. . . . I'm gonna
say it."

Now and then, Brown grinned and said: "Get 'em, Oak."

At 39, playing in his final game, Oakley reemphasized that he
regretted his Washington experience. "If I knew all this would happen,
I never would have signed here. . . . I didn't want to go out this way. I
didn't want to see Michael go out like this. It's just a bad time. . . .
When you got Michael and Jerry Stackhouse and you don't make the

playoffs, something's wrong, and you gotta make changes." He thought about the implications of his words. "I don't know where," he added.

"Get 'em, Oak," Brown repeated from a distance, chuckling.

When somebody tried asking Brown a question about Collins or Jordan, Oakley interrupted.

"I'm his spokesman," Oakley said. "He said I'm his spokesman."

Brown giggled, nodded.

But, finally, Brown stepped into the scrum, talking about his cursing of Collins in Phoenix. "I got frustrated. I said something disrespectful to him, and I went, like a man, and apologized to him the next day. I said to him, 'I was wrong. That's not me.' Anybody who could meet me for two minutes would know I'm not like that. . . . It's just crazy how—" He stopped himself, shook his head. "I'm just a little upset that [Collins] mentioned it at the end of the year, trying to make me look—" He stopped himself again. "I don't even want to get into it. . . . I just think the timing [of Collins's statement] didn't make sense. Why would he say that at the *end* of the season? I thought it was *over*."

Bryon Russell had become more acidic as the hours passed. "I don't even pay attention to what was said [by Collins]. It's easy to point the fingers now. That's what's so sad about the whole thing . . ."

Oakley leaned toward him. "What they askin' you about?"

Russell chuckled, bitingly. "They're asking, 'What do you think about what he said?'"

Oakley groaned.

Russell laughed. "Fuck what he said."

Russell and Oakley exchanged glances. Russell took a sip of water, snapping, "It should have been us [getting to the playoffs]." Then he thought of his NBA future, or what future he had left. "I ain't trying to burn no bridges. I gotta play here. Maybe. You never know."

Stackhouse tried to shift the focus to the future. He calmly said that he looked forward to playing without Jordan, a line he repeated so much that it sounded like a sound bite from a politician's stump speech. "I know the other guys in the locker room are looking forward to that challenge, too," he added. "There's no Savior player we're gonna draft."

He softly criticized the Jordan-Collins blueprint for building a team. "We can't keep bringing in eight new players. If you start with a different nucleus every year, then you run the risk of having a situation like this, where things don't come together." The players still didn't truly know one another, he observed. "And here it is game eighty-two." The whole experiment, he concluded, just hadn't worked. And now, with Collins having detonated, everything seemed to have come down around them. Stackhouse shrugged. "I'm just looking forward to getting away and going home, resting up," he concluded. "I'm sure people will be evaluating everybody." He repeated the word with emphasis. "*Everybody*. Something didn't go right here."

Collins talked in the arena hallway, his back against a wall, literally and metaphorically. He said that he was "very very disappointed," disappointed that, as coach, "I never could get our team to play at its highest level; that's my job. . . . We had good players. But we just didn't fit, you know? I thought we would be getting ready for the playoffs. From Michael's standpoint, he desperately wanted to be in the playoffs."

He winced. "There are a lot of people who view us not making the playoffs as Michael failing. And I view it more as us failing him. At forty, he couldn't do all that was necessary to get us into the playoffs. . . . He did his job. I don't think I did mine. And I don't think the team did theirs. I just couldn't get the right fit."

The poor fit meant, among other things, that Jordan never fully developed "trust" in many of his teammates, thought Collins. "It takes a long time to develop that kind of trust. That's why I say you can't be thin-skinned and play with greatness. *You can't.* I think through this year T-Lue has become a guy he really trusts, and Bobby Simmons. And Laettner."

Collins treasured the trustworthy players, the tough ones. He had been that kind of player. He'd had stress fractures in both feet, coming back too soon from rehab and blowing out a knee because he was essentially playing on one leg. He drove the lane on any big man, took a charge from any power forward, and then entered the coaching world to discover there were only a handful of players that tough. He paid homage to the tough in the way ministers talk about saints. Around Philadelphia, he sometimes thought of his old Sixers teammate Steve Mix, a big man of limited skills but ruggedly effective just the same. Mixie, he affectionately called him. "I'd take Mixie *right now*," he said. "Put him down in that old block. I'll tell you one thing: *Mixie would set a fuckin' screen.*"

Mixie was in Collins's mold. He wished he'd had several Mixies to go with a Jordan. But a Mixie was scarce. Instead, you found yourself with young players who, for all their grace and talent, often didn't have the resolve of a Mixie. This he had sought to put in them, cajoling, goading, sometimes berating. He talked of loving them in the beginning, loving Kwame, loving Rip, loving Courtney, loving Stack—his affection real, his devotion total. "You can't have a better friend or a coach who cares more about you than Doug," said his former assistant Alvin Gentry.

It was what all his friends said about him. But he loved as hard as he competed, and that always had carried risks. He was easily wounded, and felt easily betrayed. The love died then. What took its place was too dark for a team's good or his own. His sense of betrayal had overwhelmed him, two nights earlier, and now it seemed unlikely, as he stood before the media in Philly, that he could recover.

Through all his miscalculations and rages, he still wanted to make the players realize how much he cared. Perhaps he would express a little regret about the other night—about the timing of his remarks, if nothing else. I asked him if he had second thoughts about it.

He answered that he had spoken the truth. "We had one game left. Michael was very good with it; he was very fine." Then he shot back: "And what was wrong with the timing?"

I said that I thought people wondered, among other things, whether the criticism of his players was appropriate on the night of Jordan's last game in Washington—whether at the very least it should have been delayed a week or so.

"I wouldn't have been around in another week . . ." he said.

So you had no problem with the timing of your remarks?

His voice quavered. He leaned forward slightly. "I'm a very smart man, Coach. I speak when it's time to speak."

"Thank you," the Wizards p.r. woman called out.

"If you want to play forty-eight minutes and shoot fifty times—it's your night, I don't care what you do," Collins said to him before the game.

"I don't want to play forty-eight minutes," Jordan answered. "And I don't want to shoot fifty times."

"Just tell me what you want to do," Collins requested.

He wasn't quite sure what he wanted. Sixers coach Larry Brown, his old friend and fellow Carolina alumnus, hoped he'd score 100. Jordan came out for the start of the game in his Wizards' blue road uniform and shook hands with Allen Iverson, and the two stood chatting for a moment. In their contrast, you could see much of why an older America, and the mainstream media, had so appreciated Jordan. There was Iverson, with a tattoo on the right side of his neck that said R.A. BOOGIE, just above some Chinese characters in bluish-green and what looked to be a crescent of sorts. Jordan was, in the vernacular of his times, clean. He'd been a guiltless pleasure for America.

Sitting there in Philadelphia, people at press row idly talked about their favorite Jordan game memories. I'd always had a quirky one. He is not making a shot, not even leaping. He is in Utah, grounded and sneaking up behind Karl Malone in Game Six of the 1998 Finals, with the Bulls down by a point, in the final 30 seconds. Malone is clutching the ball, prepared to shoot. The shot never happens. Jordan strips a stunned Malone and then, without calling time-out, begins dribbling upcourt, toward Bryon Russell and history. I love the indomitability of it, the stalking, the seizing, the absolute need in his expression. He made $33 million that year from basketball alone, but he played like his family's well-being hung on making that steal. It said everything about his will and his appetite. The will lifted him; the appetite in time made life hard. It was hard now. It had been hard for a while. He needed to win, and the winning was all gone.

He brushed Iverson's hand, and then they played.

He did not have much. Maybe the golf had taken it out of him. Sixty-four seconds into the game, he missed his first shot, a jumper, and then he had a turnover, on his way to a 6–15 night during which he would score 15 points. He made the final field goal of his career, a jump shot, with 9:41 to play in the third quarter. With Philly leading by 19 and a rout on, he left the game, apparently for good, as the last minutes ticked down.

The crowd chanted for him. When he did not answer their pleas and return to the game, they reverted to being Philadelphians and booed lustily.

He sat on the bench next to Lue, chuckling.

"We want Mike, we want Mike, we want Mike . . ."

Collins pleaded with him to go back in for a short spell. "Michael, I played here," he said to Jordan. "I at least gotta be able to come back to this city. *You gotta go in.* These people want to see you."

Jordan said he was stiff.

Uncharacteristically, Collins pressed him. "Go in for a minute or whatever. Get the ovation. . . . Michael, please. You gotta go out there."

Stiff and smiling, he stepped back on the court with 2:35 left in the game. Fifty seconds later, on orders from Larry Brown, Eric Snow intentionally fouled him, and he scored his last points on two free throws, then exited one second later, with 1:44 left.

Soon he was walking off the floor, shaking hands, a career over. He did not keep the media waiting long, intent on making sure no one had started writing an obituary. He sounded like a club executive: "We did change our team of three years ago, and we will continue to change. We gotta find the right mix to move in the right direction and to get where Philly and a lot of other teams are. . . . There are things on this team that I think we probably need to change or [players who] may need a different atmosphere. . . . I'm trying to get these kids to give up some of that selfishness."

He tried to remain serene. For most athletes, the ends of careers are like rear-end auto crashes: They don't feel the worst of the pain for a few days at least. But Jordan said he had been struck during the game: *It's over.*

"I guess it hits me that I'm not going to be in a uniform anymore, so—" A pause. "That's not a terrible feeling. . . . I got strong enough to say that I need to move away from it. . . ." He steered the discussion back to the future. "Now I have to live through trying to put a basket-ball team on the court that's gonna be a winner for me. I have to live through that."

The p.r. person called out, "Last question."

Has retiring this time been more difficult? someone asked.

Jordan shook his head. *No.* "I don't want to play. It's time for me to move on. It's easier to accept because, physically, I know it's [time]. And I feel it."

"Thank you," said the p.r. person.

But Jordan did not move. He stayed in his chair. He was not quite ready to finish.

Michael, can you walk away happy? someone else shouted.

"Sure. I can walk away happy. I've given everything I could to the game of basketball, physically . . ."

A local reporter concluded by asking him about what it felt like to play his final game in Philadelphia. It seemed like such a disappoint-ingly parochial choice for a final question. But it yielded the most revealing response of the night. Jordan noted that Philadelphia had been in a position to draft him in 1984 until it played too well during the end of a season, moving up in the standings but correspondingly down in its draft position. "Chicago lost a couple games and moved up in the draft," he said, grinning, seizing upon the moment to let

Philadelphia know all that it had lost. "I think [the Sixers' coach at the time] Billy Cunningham had given Coach Smith an [assurance] that if I was there at the third pick, that I would be in Philly. And then Chicago lost games, moved up, and Philly ended up picking this big guy."

The media laughed loudly.

"This big guy from Auburn."

More laughs.

Jordan chuckled. "And that's how things work." He stood.

"Thank you," said the p.r. person, and at last, after 19 years, he was gone.

"See you in Washington sometime," he said to someone on the way out.

He had only three weeks left in the Wizards organization. When it came to Michael Jordan's future, Abe Pollin had left himself room to maneuver. What he said brusquely to me in Wilmington, during pre-season camp in the first Jordan comeback season, conveyed, in retrospect, his uncertainty even then about Jordan ever again being a Wizards executive. Pollin's words were the kind reserved for an applicant whose chances were dicey at best: "We agreed to talk about it."

Once the season ended, Jordan's position unraveled swiftly and orderly. Soon, Abe Pollin's allies within the organization began leaking disparaging information about Jordan to *The New York Times*—including broad criticisms of his stint as the club's president and of his deteriorating relationships with teammates during the comeback.

Nothing about Jordan's executive work habits had changed or could have changed, of course, after he left the club presidency, put on a uniform, drew two seasons' worth of sellout crowds and brought Pollin, by the owner's admission, his first basketball profits in many years. As the money had rolled in, Pollin expressed no disappointment over Jordan's managerial style. At any time during Jordan's executive tenure or playing days, Pollin or his lieutenants could have privately leaked their dismay over how Jordan conducted himself as the team's president or star. That the owners' agents waited until Jordan's playing days ended before criticizing him left no reasonable conclusion other than that Pollin wanted to maximize his profits and his franchise's stature before giving final consideration to cutting Jordan loose.

Nothing cited by the anonymous sources as reasons for Pollin's concerns about Jordan—neither the star's differences with Wizards officials nor his problems with players—had been unknown prior to the second season of the comeback. His differences with Susan O'Malley over marketing matters had become public even before his comeback began. The tensions between Pollin and the Jordan camp over who should hold ultimate power over basketball-related expenditures and player acquisitions had spurred Pollin to vent his frustrations to me in January 2001. The strains between Jordan and his teammates had been much publicized by the end of the first season. By then, I'd already written for *The Washington Post* that he had referred to Kwame Brown as a "flaming faggot," and detailed the tensions between Richard Hamilton and Jordan that augured poorly for any future they might have had together.

The public learned about the Pollin team's long-standing resentments only after Jordan had played his last game, and the gold rush ceased. During the comeback, nothing prompted Pollin, either publicly or privately, to discourage the common assumption in Washington and the professional basketball community that Jordan would be regaining the club presidency. For two profitable seasons, the public Pollin fawned over Jordan: "Michael's great, just great." He left the impression of an owner who felt a lasting bond to the star responsible for transforming his team's profile and financial fortunes.

Virtually overnight, the Pollin camp's posture toward Jordan changed from that of gratitude to contempt and bitterness. The speed with which Pollin jettisoned Jordan from the organization would come at a cost to his reputation among even sectors of Washington and the basketball community critical of Jordan's tenure with the Wizards. In most cases, the scorn for the owner turned not on his axing of Jordan but on the overall perception of his disingenuousness during the previous two years. He looked shamefully devious to a school of observers, a perception costing him a sizable piece of his pristine image as a selfless and kindly do-gooder. To this group, he was now simply one more manipulator who had taken what he could before delivering a shiv. The owner would win the battle for power but, like Jordan, would lose much in reputation.

Still, it was impossible to argue that anyone other than Jordan had precipitated and escalated tensions between the two men. From early in his executive days, during his dismay over the organization's expectations that he would help to market the dreadful Wizards, Jordan had not hesitated to air publicly his differences with Pollin and O'Malley—to put them on notice, in effect—just as he had with his Bulls and later his Wizards teammates. Jordan's designated mouthpieces had criticized

Pollin from the shadows, suggesting that Jordan was being shackled as an executive and that Pollin and O'Malley had their priorities in the wrong places.

Demonstrating a remarkable lack of savvy in human relations for a man approaching midlife, Jordan said things about the boss that a 16-year-old working his first job would understand to be risky to his future chances for advancement and employment. Neither Pollin nor anyone close to him would forget that Jordan, in alluding to his own future in basketball, had discussed the possibility of one day consulting with Ted Leonsis and "Abe, . . . if he's still part of the situation."

For the indefinite future, Pollin would remain very much a part of the situation. Jordan's comment was at once gently obvious—no elderly man endures forever in ownership or in life—and completely tone-deaf to the offense it might cause a superior who had no plans to leave anytime soon.

Pollin was often an afterthought in his discussions about the organization, and the Wizards nothing more or less than one more "option" in his life—the option to be rejected, if his needs were not met. After the season ended, the Jordan camp leaked word to *The Washington Post* that if Pollin tried to cut Jordan's power as president or otherwise angered him, Jordan would leave the organization for good.

It was a public ultimatum, just one more bit of bluster in three years' worth of privately dispensed barbs. Such behavior seldom hurts a superstar player, and never before had it hurt the idol. Those days ended on April 16, 2003. Now all his presumption and the memory of his offhanded comments worked against him: all the references to "Abe" and the suggestions of a future without Pollin; all his public complaints about his marketing duties and his camp's private disdain for Pollin's frugality; all the 11th-hour concessions he had extracted from Pollin during the 2000 negotiations. He had left bad feelings in Chicago and Washington, and now he failed to see the simplest truth in employer-employee relations: that the one who insults the boss often enough will be the one leaving.

The only real surprise was that Jordan could not see what he had wrought, or what was coming. Less than 24 hours after his final game, he was back at MCI as a spectator in a box, watching LeBron James and other high school stars in the Jordan Capital Classic, projecting the confidence and ease of a man poised to reclaim power. He had come to the game wearing a blue football jersey with his number on it, a piece of apparel from the Jordan Brand collection that served as a symbolic reminder that *23 wouldn't* be going away. On the court, LeBron James wore 23, and so the past looked down on the future, though not for terribly long, Jordan turning away to chat and huddle with people. He had returned to MCI, he told people, to "work"— though Pollin had yet to decide upon his future.

Word of player dissatisfaction with Jordan and Collins continued to circulate. That week, the Wizards held what teams commonly refer to as "exit interviews"—discussions involving coaches and individual players in which, among other things, the coaches reveal their hopes and expectations for the following season. Collins and a few other Wizards officials sat down with Stackhouse. The meeting was cordial, with neither Collins nor Stackhouse alluding to their late-season tensions. With Jordan gone, Stackhouse had become the team's unquestionable star, and the coaches seemed to be exhibiting a new deference toward him, Collins especially. But not everyone in the room believed that the peace between the head coach and player was likely to last any longer than Collins's truce with Kwame Brown. Just before the meeting concluded, one official dared to acknowledge the obvious, alluding to the prior difficulties in the Collins-Stackhouse relationship and delivering a recommendation to the coach and star.

"You two should get a divorce," the official said.

Collins sighed, shook his head.

Stackhouse said nothing, recounted one observer at the meeting.

But the statement simply buttressed a growing organizational feeling: *Someone* had to be booted. The coach could not coexist with several of his players. Behind the scenes, some Wizards did their part to hasten the coup, letting Wizards officials know of their frustrations with Collins and Jordan.

Jordan pressed for a meeting with Pollin, who did not immediately respond, triggering anxieties for the first time among Jordan allies. The disclosure of a date for the meeting neatly coincided with the initiation of the Pollin camp's leaks about Jordan's executive work habits and the depth of players' dissension. The owner's mouthpieces did not leak to the Washington papers, as the Wizards organization had become convinced that the Washington media unfairly favored Jordan. Calls were made by anonymous Pollin intermediaries instead to *The New York Times,* which received stories about Jordan's alienating personal style and disappointing managerial performance.

Meanwhile, Jordan turned to one of his friends in the media, Michael Wilbon, issuing his defense in Wilbon's columns and a few other newspaper stories. By publicly wondering who in the Wizards organization was spreading stories about him, Jordan simply hardened the perception of irreconcilable differences between himself and the owner. Jordan never had played this game before, and, in Pollin, he encountered someone with far better instincts for boardroom savagery.

The first signs of Jordan's worry came on Monday, May 5, less than 48 hours before his meeting with Pollin. Amid reports that he had talked about a possible partnership deal with Robert Johnson, the owner of the expansion Charlotte franchise, Jordan insisted he had never spoken to Johnson about joining Charlotte, that such discussions would violate NBA tampering rules and that, more importantly, he wished to be a Wizards executive. No longer did he refer to "options." No longer was he leveraging the possibility of another team against the Wizards.

Chicago was gone. Charlotte was an uncertain proposition at best. Now the possibility of Abe Pollin dismissing him looked greater than ever. Every day brought more focus on his record in Washington: 74–90 as a player, 36–89 as team president, and 110–179 overall. He sensed the precariousness of his position for the first time in his professional life, seeking to exude loyalty to the Wizards organization, insisting he had wanted to be the club president throughout his days in Washington. "I always wanted to resume my responsibilities, always," he said.

Never did he say the one thing, however, that generally gives the wounded a chance at survival; never did he hint that he had made mistakes. Never did he commit himself to rebuilding his relationships with Pollin and other Wizards officials. He had no idea how to rebound and survive.

On the evening before the meeting with Pollin, he dined with friends. His closest associates, including Ted Leonsis, believed he could still regain his old job. Jordan told several friends that he had remarks ready for Pollin, prepared to present a plan to elevate the Wizards. He saw it as a benefit, he told one associate, that the meeting with Pollin would happen at the MCI Center. He believed in the power of home-court advantage, the psychological edge that he thought it gave you, in life as well as in basketball. The owner had built the arena, but only he had filled it. He left the dinner radiating confidence, with one Wizards official later saying, "When has he ever gone into any contest not expecting to win?"

———————

All five people at the meeting the next day had an obvious stake in its outcome, and several of them, if not all, leaked details of the meeting to the press—*The New York Times* and *The Washington Post,* just for starters. Jordan arrived with a longtime advisor, attorney Curtis Polk. Pollin's attorney, David Osnos, sat next to the owner, and Ted Leonsis—on the outs with Pollin—played the role of minority owner, observer and Jordan friend.

Pollin dismissed Jordan at the meeting's start, telling him the organization had decided upon "going in another direction."

Sources said that Jordan reacted by asking, *Why*—and that Pollin wouldn't respond immediately.

Reports seemed in basic agreement about what transpired next.

A heated Jordan asked Pollin if he was a man of his word. Pollin sought to assuage him by saying he would honor his contractual commitment to pay Jordan a severance fee of $10 million.

Jordan angrily responded that he hadn't come to the meeting for money but to become a partner and executive again.

Pollin supposedly said, "I don't want you as a partner, Michael."

Jordan turned to Leonsis and snapped, "Thanks for getting me into this fucking mess."

The meeting ended in five minutes.

He drove off alone in a green convertible, with Illinois plates, its top down, Jordan exposed to the world.

He had a few drinks that night at a couple of his favorite clubs in the area and then got out of town.

Reaction came quickly from an array of basketball executives and commentators, though from few Wizards players. In the immediate aftermath, most Wizards, like Bryon Russell, limited themselves to expressions of surprise. Later, Kwame Brown would voice his relief at the departure of Jordan, but for now he stayed quiet, too. Only a former Wizard immediately dared to offer a veiled public judgment of Jordan's leadership. "He's still considered the greatest player to ever play the game of basketball," Richard Hamilton said to reporters in Detroit. "I don't think anybody can take that away from him. As a team president, I'm not sure."

The media presented the familiar this-was-bound-to-happen story in the days ahead, and the backlash against Jordan became fierce over the next month. It much resembled what happened in another era when an unpopular Soviet leader died or was ousted from power. There was the great purge of anyone or anything associated with the departed ruler. Collins was fired, and all of Jordan's executive underlings gradually shoved out. Pollin stripped the arena bare of any reminders of Jordan—all jerseys, all posters, all trinkets and murals. For a while, the Wizards website had a last vestige of Jordan—an ad for his restaurant—until, finally, the ad too was gone, followed by the restaurant's closing, less than a year later. And he was no more in Washington.

No one anywhere rushed to hire him. In Charlotte, Bob Johnson said he wanted him in an executive role, but Johnson offered neither a share of ownership for free nor final control over basketball decisions—and so Jordan was presented with an offer inferior to that presented, in 2000, by Leonsis and Pollin. He had far less negotiating leverage than three years earlier, and less clout in basketball than at any time since his playing career's beginning.

With a group of investors, he tried to buy the Milwaukee Bucks from its owner, Senator Herb Kohl. The deal looked close to happening, seemingly contingent on the resolution of financing issues and a commitment from the Jordan group to keep the team in Milwaukee for an indefinite period. The deal fell through, with a source close to Kohl saying discussions had been complicated by a lack of personal connection between Jordan and Kohl, with the owner having been slightly put off by Jordan's style in critical moments.

That style had vexed Pollin's people, too. It was never rude in the ordinary sense of that word—aside from that moment, during the 1999 labor negotiations, when Jordan snappishly suggested that Pollin sell his team. But the style reeked of a sense of entitlement. He had viewed it as his mission to run the Wizards one day and to own a large, if not controlling, interest in the team. He had seen it as the role of all others in the organization to defer to his judgment from the moment he arrived. Therefore, no one—not even the owner who built the franchise—could stand in the way of that vision.

If that constitutes delusion or arrogance, I think we are more than a little responsible for it—*we* meaning the culture in general but the media in particular. I don't mean responsible in that dopey way that suggests the athlete is misunderstood or blameless. Only that, from the beginning of that compact between sports teams and the press, we have deified young men, infusing them with a sense of entitlement, helping to create the conditions by the late 20th century under which an idol like Jordan came to believe that virtually anything he did could be justified in pursuit of "winning"—to be broadly defined as the acquisition for himself of championship rings, and endorsement deals, and an ownership share, or whatever competitive urge whetted his appetite at the moment. Other people—teammates, an owner, the rest of the league, an apparel company, the media—were useful as supporting players only so long as they could aid him in the acquisition of things that accompanied or facilitated winning.

Because winning had become the paramount ethic in the sports culture, anything he did—including abusing teammates or running roughshod over business associates—was justified for years as an instrument for fulfilling that ethic. To realize that the ethic derived solely from *games* and the *business* of games is to realize the ethic was manufactured, and that the idolatry bestowed today upon those who personify the ethic has sprung from artifice. The result is a mythology that has coarsened sports and society, which is an enduring lesson of the Jordan comeback saga.

We have a cultural need, in and out of sports, for heroes. When we are without heroes, it is said, we "don't know how far we can go"—a line oft quoted from Bernard Malamud's great baseball novel, *The Natural*. But it is important not to turn sports idols into deities at a cost to what is real. If we ascribe qualities to athletes that don't exist in them, then we are all part of a ruse; *we* become the creators and directors of our own mythmaking machine.

And, ultimately, we see the cost of that machine when the gods get even slightly used up, as Michael Jordan was by the end of his comeback. When he no longer could leap halfway up a backboard, people began struggling to remember what they worshiped about him, while he carried himself as if he had the same clout he enjoyed in his glory days, his presumption unchanged. The resulting fall was long and hard.

Many people saw their fortunes suffer in the wake of the Jordan fiasco and departure. The Wizards watched their season ticket sales drop to about 10,000 seats, with MCI not much more than half-filled on many nights. The team's new general manager, Ernie Grunfeld, and its new coach, Eddie Jordan, found themselves saddled with a team of injured stars and erratic young players who still included Kwame Brown, capable of scoring 25 points against an All-Star one night and delivering a dreadful game against a mediocre rival the next. Brown and new point guard Gilbert Arenas began publicly quarreling at mid-season. Larry Hughes alternately soared and struggled. Christian Laettner became regarded as a malcontent and a headache, suspended by the league for five games after failing three drug tests. The team's new leader, Jerry Stackhouse—who had been charged in the off-season with assaulting a real-estate agent asking him to vacate a rented beach house that he had continued occupying beyond the terms of his lease (the assault charge was dismissed, and all nastiness swept away, following an out-of-court settlement)—continued to struggle after Jordan's departure. In 2003, he had summer surgery on his troubled right knee only after signing a two-year, $18 million contract extension that Abe Pollin approved without having Stackhouse submit to a thorough knee exam. Stackhouse missed the first half of the season, then, after playing for a short stretch in the second half, complained of knee pain, taking a seat on the bench, pronouncing his knee not ready for the rigors of play. The Wizards reclaimed their traditional spot as a league doormat. At the season's end, the Wizards traded away Stackhouse, Laettner, and a draft pick to Dallas for Antawn Jamison.

In Detroit, Richard Hamilton helped to lead his team to the 2003–2004 NBA championship, with the Pistons knocking off the Lakers in the finals, and Hamilton at last victorious over his longtime nemesis, Kobe Bryant. Detroit had gotten the best of the Stackhouse–Hamilton trade, everyone agreed now. Resisting an opportunity to gloat, Hamilton spoke conciliatorily about Jordan, downplaying talk of their differences, saying that he had felt "hurt immediately after" the trade, but that he had come to understand the game was "a business."

Meanwhile, Jordan continued looking for a place to land. He had no involvement in basketball during the 2003–2004 season, doing what actors between movies do, keeping his face out there.

He did a television spot in Chicago for NBC's coverage of the 2003 U.S. Open golf championship, the tournament being staged on a nearby course. His garb was familiar. He wore a black shirt, gray pants, jaunty black cap and a silver earring in his left ear. The camera focused on him staring down at a basketball court, then solemnly lifting his head and, while clutching a ball, staring into the camera. "We built a dynasty in this town," he said and then, alluding to the golfers, added, "Now it's their time to do something great."

The hole in his life forced him out, changed his routines. Everything was different. Following his 1999 retirement, he had stayed away from Bulls games in Chicago. Now he showed up occasionally at the

United Center to watch his old team, a reminder to the public and the barons of the sport that he was still around. He attended the 2004 All-Star Game in Los Angeles. He traveled to Denver to be on hand when the Nuggets clinched an NBA playoff spot for the first time since 1995. His presence was attributable to the ascendancy of the Nuggets' star rookie, Carmelo Anthony, a Jordan Brand endorser whom he had chastised in a phone call, a month earlier, after an irritated Anthony refused his coach's order to reenter a game during the fourth quarter. The story of Jordan's call to Anthony made the rounds, as did the Anthony association with Jordan Brand. *Keeping the face out there.*

He stayed busy with Nike and the Jordan Brand, but his allure and power continued to ebb. In early 2004, *Time* magazine's list of the "World's Most Influential People" included Tiger Woods, Lance Armstrong, soccer star David Beckham, and even a football coach, New England's two-time Super Bowl winner Bill Belichick. Jordan's omission from a roster of the weighty—an unthinkable event only a couple of years earlier—simply evinced a further decline in his commercial clout.

His old aloofness steadily gave way to something needier. His coyness was gone. Increasingly, he signaled he wanted back in the sport. His publicist Estee Portnoy said his interest in acquiring ownership of an NBA franchise remained "very strong." David Stern tried to help, telling the media in a telephone conference call before the start of the 2004 NBA playoffs that he continued to believe that Jordan would someday own a team, predicting that it would happen within the next few years. "I think nothing is as good of an advertisement for the openness of the sport than having its most recognized figure be an owner," he said, framing the matter as an issue about social and economic justice. No other sports commissioner in history was so skilled at making players with fortunes in the hundreds of millions sound like the proletariat. But no other sports commissioner ever had so owed his personal stature and influence to a few transcendent players, with Jordan at the top of the list. Stern would fight for him. The commissioner and others held out the hope that the Phoenix franchise might be a possibility for Jordan in time. The Suns' owner, Jerry Colangelo, indicated that he was interested in selling a minority share of his team to a buyer who would, several years later, have the option of purchasing the team. Nothing happened immediately. Jordan looked elsewhere. During the summer of 2004, reports circulated that he had entered into serious negotiations to become an owner of the Miami Heat, rumors that his publicity team did nothing to discourage, with Estee Portnoy reiterating Jordan's ownership ambitions. The Heat issued a terse statement, saying the team was not for sale. But it seemed increasingly likely that, with Stern's assistance, Jordan would one day acquire a team somewhere.

Meanwhile, Jordan filled his days in the kinds of ways the celebrated, wealthy and underemployed do. In January 2004, he hosted the Michael Jordan Celebrity Invitational Golf Tournament on Paradise Island in the Bahamas, near one of his favorite casinos. He returned home and watched his oldest son, Jeffrey, play junior varsity basketball at his private high school in a Chicago suburb.

Status quo prevailed in his family life. He remained married to Juanita Jordan, though their marriage remained as private as ever and he generally journeyed alone. He became a frequent guest at a variety of sports events, showing up at a Cubs game in a luxury box, smiling as cameras and eyes turned his way during a break in the game. No one rushed him; no throng howled his name. The game resumed and the eyes shifted to the younger men on the field, the stars of the moment.

He has returned to a world much closer to the one Mike Jordan once inhabited, the one with fewer shouts. It is the place where all sports idols must go eventually, leaving open the question as to how well he will cope with it. He is our creation nearly as much as his own, and so the culture is invested in him in a way it seldom feels toward athletes, hoping he finds that serenity often elusive to legends. His friends are confident he will land somewhere, likely sharing in the ownership of a club. But if it happens, they know that another desk awaits him, and that it gets very quiet in an office. Idols don't often face quiet.

I remember him best this way: One afternoon during his executive stint, he stood by his office window and looked out on the street, the parking lot, that pharmacy in the distance. The faint blare of a horn occasionally floated up from the street. As I prepared to leave, he was staring out the window at nothing in particular. He looked at once imperious and trapped, like a magnificent specimen under glass.

"Anything out there?" I asked.

He shrugged. "No, no." He smiled. "Sometimes you see a kid dribbling a ball or something like that," he said.

He could never hear the sound of the dribbled ball, but something always occurred to him: The dribbling kid had a game somewhere. He looked down. Nothing was out there. He turned back, his office soundless. "It gets quiet in here," he said, and moved about his office, picking up things, putting them down, finally exiting, in search of voices and faces. He had half a life yet to lead. It is an idol's burden.

Acknowledgments

In the late summer of 2001, two editors at the newspaper for which I work, *The Washington Post,* invited me to lunch, where they asked whether I would be interested in spending the next year writing a series of feature stories about the comeback of Michael Jordan. The chance to spend an entire season and, as it happened, nearly all of a second observing and writing about Jordan the player and idol proved irresistible.

Much of what happened during the comeback was contentious. From the beginning of the Jordan odyssey, the *Post*'s editors gave me the freedom to chronicle what I saw and, in the process, faithfully depict what effect the comeback had on a team, an industry and on Jordan himself. At some point I came to believe that this was a story not merely about Jordan's appetites but our own, and so what was initially a sports story for me also became a cultural examination. I am grateful that Simon and Schuster provided me with the opportunity to expand on my reporting, granting me the independence to assess what the Jordan comeback revealed about him, us and the place of athletic idols in our epoch.

I swiftly understood that Michael Jordan and his top publicity aides did not want this book written. Consequently, I am indebted to those individuals who, at professional risk to themselves, spoke to me. They provided information on the condition that their identities would not be revealed, and so, unable to thank them by name, I will say simply that this book would not have been possible without their candor. In almost all instances, these sources admired aspects of Jordan, particularly his commitment as a player to winning. But his bouts of heavy-handedness sometimes worried or offended them. In the end, they believed the full story deserved to see light.

During that time, I benefited greatly from my associations with a variety of *Post* colleagues, beginning with the two editors who looked after my stories during the first of the two comeback seasons. Emilio Garcia-Ruiz, now the sports editor of the *Post,* was one of my two luncheon hosts on that first day, and, throughout the project, provided me with unflagging support and valuable advice.

The other editor at lunch that afternoon, Bill Hamilton, the assistant managing editor for enterprise at the *Post,* shepherded my work that first season. Editors do not come any better than Hamilton. He raised vital questions, edited my stories with grace, and buoyed me with his support and humor.

The Washington Post Magazine's articles editor, David Rowell, presided over my two magazine stories about Jordan. He brought his meticulous and elegant craftsmanship to the task.

At Simon and Schuster, Brant Rumble deftly edited this book under a tight deadline. His clear vision and keen sense of style made him a wonderful guardian of the manuscript.

My thanks to John Paul Jones for his painstaking attention to detail during the copyediting and proofreading stages.

There are others whose involvement proved critical. There would not have been any Jordan stories for me at all but for the kind interest of the then-editor of *The Washington Post Magazine,* Glenn Frankel, who asked me, in late 2000, to write a piece about Jordan the basketball executive. Tom Shroder, who succeeded Frankel, generously invited me during Jordan's last season to write a magazine story about the final months of the comeback.

My agent David Black provided me with astute editorial advice and unbridled optimism throughout all stages of the book's gestation.

At the *Post,* several talented colleagues—Tom Jackman, Stephen Fehr, Liz Seymour, David Cho, Victoria Benning and Michael Shear—aided me by offering their perspectives on Jordan and, in some cases, reading passages of my early drafts. I am grateful to a group of *Post* editors closely involved with my work since my arrival at the paper—Marylou Tousignant, Jo-Ann Armao, Bob Barnes and Scott Vance—and for the hearty encouragement of the *Post*'s executive editor Leonard Downie Jr. and managing editor Steve Coll.

I admired the work of three *Post* colleagues—Thomas Heath, Peter Perl and Greg Sandoval—whose stories about everything from Wizards' ownership to the franchise's ticket sales helped to inform my perspective on the business practices of Abe Pollin's organization.

Similarly, I benefited, at the start of the project, by absorbing several Jordan books, including four illuminating works—David Halberstam's

Playing for Keeps, Sam Smith's *The Jordan Rules,* Rick Telander's *In the Year of the Bull* and Melissa Isaacson's *Transition Game.*

Because so much of the job necessarily involved seeing the same comrades at airport terminals, I was lucky to be flying often with two superb basketball beat writers, *The Washington Post*'s Steve Wyche and *The Washington Times*' John Mitchell. And, in Washington, I always enjoyed the observations of Scott Jackson, an insightful radio reporter.

Then there were the familiar basketball figures who generously offered their insights—Dean Smith, Bill Guthridge, Tex Winter, Jack Ramsey, Frank Layden, Red Auerbach, Pat Williams, Alvin Gentry and Bill Cartwright, among them—and a sterling group of journalists who kindly shared their perspectives: Ira Berkow, David Halberstam, Jack McCallum, Sam Smith, Roscoe Nance, Ian Thomsen, Lacy Banks, Mike Wise and the late Mark Kram.

Some individuals deserve a special note. Amid the many sources who understandably spoke only with a guarantee of anonymity, I deeply appreciated the willingness of former Bulls player Brad Sellers to talk on-the-record about his Chicago days and, in particular, the relationship there between Doug Collins and his players, especially Michael Jordan. Tex Winter spoke for several hours over the course of three trips I made to Los Angeles. Before the start of the Jordan comeback (when he could still sit for a formal interview without requiring Jordan's permission), Tim Grover graciously answered my questions at his gymnasium in Chicago.

I'll forever be appreciative of the friends whose support over the years has meant so much to me—especially Steve Gelman, David Sendler, Dr. Russell P. Sherwin, Edward Sierra, Craig and Diann Smith, Marcia Burnam, Bruce Burnam and Griffin Smith, jr.

And, as always, I feel incalculably lucky to live in a home graced by the love and support of my wife, Jane, and our son, Cameron. They are the best parts of my life, through which everything good flows.